Richard Gilbert's
200 CHALLENGING WALKS
IN BRITAIN AND IRELAND

RICHARD GILBERT'S
200 CHALLENGING WALKS
—— IN BRITAIN AND IRELAND ——

A COMPANION FIELD GUIDE TO
'THE BIG WALKS', 'CLASSIC WALKS' AND 'WILD WALKS'

DIADEM BOOKS · LONDON

Looking west along the ridge of Suilven towards the summit of Caisteal Laith (Chapter 21).

Published in 1990 by Diadem Books, London
First published as trade paperback 1992

Trade enquiries to Hodder and Stoughton Ltd,
Mill Road, Dunton Green, Sevenoaks, Kent TN13 2YA

British Library and Cataloguing in Publication Data

Gilbert, Richard, 1937 Nov 17-
    200 challenging walks in Britain
    and Ireland.
    1. Great Britain Recreations: Walking
    I. Title 796.590941

ISBN 0-906371-62-7
ISBN 0-906371-79-1 TPB

Colour separations by J. Film Process, Bangkok

Printed and bound in Great Britain
by Butler and Tanner, Frome and London

ACKNOWLEDGEMENTS The Author and publisher wish to thank the many walkers who have assisted with advice or photographs in the production of this companion guide to the large format books *The Big Walks, Classic Walks* and *Wild Walks*. The maps from the original books, too numerous and expensive to redraw have been adapted into a two colour style by Don Sargeant who worked under considerable pressure to a tight time schedule. Expert advice was provided by Donald Bennet, Dave Matthews, Trevor Jones, Hamish Brown and Joss Lynam, the latter a constant mentor on all aspects of Irish mountaineering and hill walking. The author is indebted to his family and friends who accompanied him, in all weathers, during his 'journeys of discovery' through the uplands of Britain and Ireland. A full list of helpers follows: John Allen, Ken Andrew, Donald Bennett, Hamish Brown, Brian Chugg, Phil Cooper, John Gillham, Andy Hosking, D. Harvey, Peter Horsfall, Phil Iddon, Trevor Jones, Dave Matthews, Jerry Rawson, Tom Rix, Don Sargeant, E. A. Shepherd, Patrick Simms, Maurice and Marion Teal, Peter Wild and Ken Wilson.

* Indicates photographs originally published in monochrome in the earlier books.

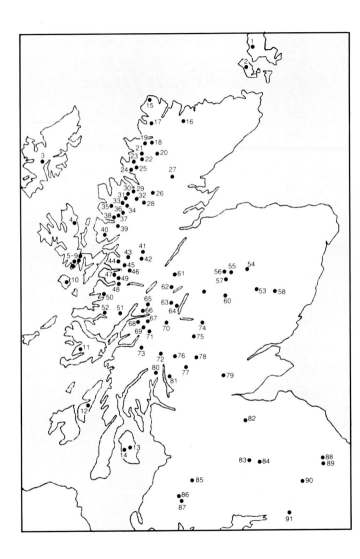

CONTENTS

some titles abbreviated

Original chapters in The Big Walks (BW), Classic Walks (CW) and Wild Walks (WW) indicated after each entry

Preface *page* 12

THE ISLANDS OF SCOTLAND

1	**The Orkney Coastal Walk** Orkney (WW 1)	15
2	**The Hoy Coastal Walk** Orkney (WW 1)	16
3	**The Clisham Ridge** Harris (CW 6)	17
4	**Explorations in Trotternish** Skye (CW 7)	18
5	**Sgurr nan Gillean** Skye (CW 8)	19
6	**Across the Cuillin** Skye (CW 9)	20
7	**The Round of Coire Lagan** Skye (BW 14)	21
8	**The Red Cuillin Traverse** Skye (WW 10)	22
9	**Bla Bheinn – Clach Glas** Skye (WW 11)	23
10	**The Cuillin of Rhum** Rhum (BW 15)	24
11	**Ben More of Mull** Mull (CW 22)	25
12	**The Paps of Jura** Jura (WW 22)	26
13	**Arran's Rocky Ridges** Arran (BW 28)	27
14	**The Pirnmill Hills** Arran (WW 23)	28

SCOTLAND (North of the Great Glen)

15	**Cape Wrath** Sutherland (CW 1)	29
16	**Ben Loyal** Sutherland (CW 2)	30
17	**Foinaven and Arkle** Sutherland (BW 1)	31
18	**The Stack of Glencoul** Sutherland	32
19	**Quinag** Sutherland (CW 4)	33
20	**Ben More Assynt** Sutherland (CW 3)	34
21	**Suilven** Sutherland (BW 2)	35
22	**Cul Mor and Cul Beag** Ross and Cromarty (WW 2)	36
23	**Stac Pollaidh** Ross and Cromarty (CW 5)	37
24	**Ben More Coigach** Ross and Cromarty (WW 3)	38
25	**Beinn an Eoin** Ross and Cromarty (WW 3)	39
26	**Beinn Dearg Forest** Ross and Cromarty (WW 4)	40
27	**Coast to Coast** Ross and Cromarty	41
28	**The Fannichs** Ross and Cromarty (BW 3)	42
29	**An Teallach** Ross and Cromarty (BW 4)	43
30	**Beinn Dearg Mhor** Ross and Cromarty (WW 5)	44
31	**The Great Wilderness** Ross and Cromarty (BW 5)	45
32	**Mullach Coire Mhic Fhearchair** Ross and Cromarty (WW 7)	46
33	**The Loch Maree Traverse** Ross and Cromarty (WW 6)	47
34	**Slioch** Ross and Cromarty (CW 10)	48
35	**The Flowerdale Forest** Ross and Cromarty (WW 8)	49
36	**Beinn Eighe** Ross and Cromarty (BW 7)	50
37	**Liathach** Ross and Cromarty (BW 6)	51
38	**Beinn Alligin** Ross and Cromarty (CW 11)	52
39	**Beinn Damh** Ross and Cromarty (WW 9)	53
40	**The Applecross Hills** Ross and Cromarty	54
41	**The Loch Mullardoch Circuit** Inverness-shire (WW 13)	55
42	**Glen Affric: Mam Sodhail** Inverness-shire (BW 9)	56
43	**The Five Sisters of Kintail** Inverness-shire (BW 8)	57
44	**The Saddle of Glen Shiel** Inverness-shire (CW 13)	58
45	**The South Kintail Ridge** Inverness-shire (BW 10)	59
46	**Spidean Mialach/Gleouraich** Inverness-shire (CW 12)	60
47	**Ladhar Bheinn** Inverness-shire (BW 11)	61
48	**Sgurr na Ciche** Inverness-shire (BW 12)	62
49	**Across Knoydart: Ben Aden** Inverness-shire (WW 12)	63
50	**The Rois Bheinn Ridge** Inverness-shire (BW 13)	64
51	**Garbh Bheinn** Inverness-shire (WW 18)	65
52	**Beinn Resipol** Inverness-shire (WW 17)	66

SCOTLAND (South of the Great Glen)

53	**Balmoral Forest: Lochnagar** Aberdeenshire (BW 19)	67

54	**Beinn a'Bhuird / Ben Avon** Aberdeenshire (BW 21)	68
55	**Ben Macdui and Glen Luibeg** Aberdeenshire (WW 14)	69
56	**Lairig Ghru** Inverness-shire / Banff (CW 14)	70
57	**Cairngorm 4000s** Inverness-shire / Banff (BW 20)	71
58	**Fungle / Clash of Wirren** Aberdeenshire / Angus (WW 15)	72
59	**Minigaig Pass** Perthshire / Inverness (WW 16)	73
60	**Glen Tilt** Perthshire / Aberdeenshire (BW 27)	74
61	**Corrieyairack Pass** Inverness-shire (CW 15)	75
62	**Creag Meagaidh** Inverness-shire (BW 16)	76
63	**Ben Alder Forest** Inverness-shire (BW 22)	77
64	**A Ben Alder Crossing** Inverness / Perth (CW 17)	78
65	**Ben Nevis / Lochaber Traverse** Inverness (BW 18)	79
66	**The Mamores** Inverness-shire (BW 17)	80
67	**Aonach Eagach Ridge** Argyllshire (BW 23)	81
68	**Bidean nam Bian** Argyllshire (CW 18)	82
69	**Buachaille Etive Mor** Argyllshire (CW 19)	83
70	**Rannoch Moor** Argyllshire (WW 19)	84
71	**The Black Mount** Argyllshire (CW 21)	85
72	**Ben Lui Horseshoe** Perthshire (BW 25)	86
73	**Ben Cruachan** Argyllshire (CW 20)	87
74	**Schiehallion** Perthshire (CW 16)	88
75	**Ben Lawers / The Tarmachans** Perthshire (BW 24)	89
76	**The Crianlarich Hills** Perthshire (BW 26)	90
77	**The Loch Lubnaig Hills** Perthshire (WW 21)	91
78	**Ben Vorlich / Stuc a'Chroin** Perthshire (CW 24)	92
79	**The Ochils** Clackmannan (WW 20)	93
80	**A Day on the Cobbler** Argyllshire (CW 23)	94
81	**Ben Lomond** Stirling (CW 25)	95

SOUTHERN SCOTLAND AND THE BORDERS

82	**The Pentlands** Midlothian / Lanarkshire (CW 26)	96
83	**The Southern Uplands** Peebles / Dumfries (BW 31)	97
84	**The Ettrick Hills** Peebles (WW 23)	98
85	**The Cairnsmore** Dumfries and Galloway (WW 25)	99
86	**The Merrick** Kirkcudbright (BW 29)	100

87	**Around Loch Enoch** Kircudbright (CW 27)	101
88	**The Cheviot Hills** Northumberland (BW 30)	102
89	**Hedgehope Hill** Northumberland (WW 26)	103
90	**Kielder Forest** Northumberland (WW 27)	104
91	**Hadrian's Wall** Cumbria / Northumberland (CW 28)	105

ENGLAND: THE LAKE DISTRICT (also The Isle of Man)

92	**The Back o' Skidda'** Cumbria (WW 29)	106
93	**Saddleback by Sharp Edge** Cumbria (CW 30)	107
94	**High Street** Cumbria (WW 29)	108
95	**Helvellyn by Striding Edge** Cumbria (CW 33)	109
96	**Fairfield / Deepdale Horseshoe** Cumbria (WW 28)	110
97	**The Buttermere Circuit** Cumbria (CW 31)	111
98	**Great Gable** Cumbria (CW 32)	112
99	**The Ennerdale Horseshoe** Cumbria (BW 35)	113
100	**Lakeland Three Thousanders** Cumbria (BW 33)	114
101	**Shap to Ravenglass** Cumbria (BW 36)	115
102	**The Great Langdale Horseshoe** Cumbria (BW 34)	116
103	**The Wast Water Circuit** Cumbria (WW 30)	117
104	**The Coniston Fells** Cumbria (CW 34)	118
105	**Harter Fell / Black Combe** Cumbria (WW 31)	119
106	**The Manx Hills** Isle of Man (CW 36)	120

ENGLAND: THE PENNINES

107	**Around Weardale** Durham	121
108	**Teesdale and Crossfell** Cumbria / Durham (BW 32)	122
109	**Around Swaledale** North Yorkshire (WW 32)	123
110	**Wild Boar Fell / The Howgills** Cumbria (BW 37)	124
111	**Ingleboro. / Penyghent / Whernside** N. Yorks (BW 39)	125
112	**Pen Hill / Buckden Pike** N. Yorkshire (WW 33)	126
113	**Great Whernside / Buckden Pike** N. Yorks (CW 37)	127
114	**Malham Cove / Gordale Scar** N. Yorks (CW 38)	128
115	**Wharfedale: The Dales Way** N. Yorks (CW 39)	129
116	**Bowland: Ward's Stone** Lancashire (CW 35)	130

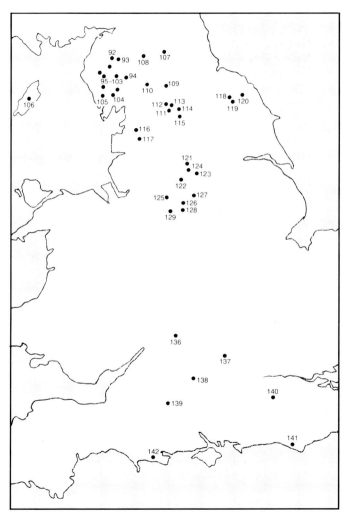

117	**Bowland: Wolf Fell/Fiendsdale** Lancs (WW 35)	131
118	**The Lyke Wake Walk** North Yorkshire (BW 38)	132
119	**Black Hambleton: the Drove Road** N. Yorks (CW 40)	133
120	**Across the North York Moors** N. Yorks (WW 34)	134

ENGLAND: THE PEAK DISTRICT

121	**High Peak: Marsden to Edale** W. Yorks/Derbs (BW 41)	135
122	**The Derwent Watershed** S. Yorks/Derbyshire (BW 40)	136
123	**The Eastern Edges** S. Yorks/Derbyshire (CW 41)	137
124	**Kinder Scout from Edale** Derbyshire (CW 42)	138
125	**The Western Peak** Cheshire/Derbyshire (CW 44)	139
126	**Dovedale** Staffordshire/Derbyshire (CW 43)	140
127	**The White Peak: Eight Dales** Derbyshire (WW 36)	141
128	**The Manifold Valley** Staffordshire (WW 37)	142
129	**The Roaches to Axe Edge** Staffs/Derbys (WW 38)	143

ENGLAND: THE WELSH MARCHES

130	**Long Mynd/Stiperstones** Shropshire (CW 45)	144
131	**Caer Caradoc** Shropshire (WW 39)	145
132	**Brown Clee Hill** Shropshire (WW 39)	146
133	**High Dyke** Shropshire/Powys (CW 46)	147
134	**The Malvern Hills** Hereford/Worcester (CW 47)	148
135	**Forest of Dean** Hereford/Gloucester (CW 48)	149

SOUTHERN ENGLAND: COTSWOLDS/CHEVIOTS/DOWNS

136	**The Cotswolds** Worcester/Gloucester (CW 50)	150
137	**The Chilterns** Bucks/Oxfordshire (CW 49)	151
138	**The Ridgeway** Berkshire (CW 51)	152
139	**The Wiltshire Downs** Wiltshire (CW 52)	153
140	**The North Downs** Surrey (CW 59)	154
141	**The South Downs** East Sussex (CW 60)	155
142	**The Dorset Coast** Dorset (CW 58)	156

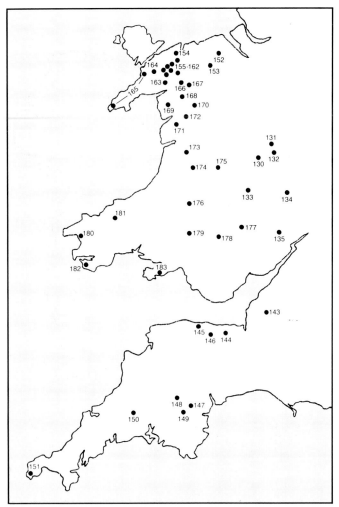

SOUTH WEST ENGLAND

143	**The Mendip Hills** Somerset/Avon (CW 53)	157
144	**The Quantocks** Somerset (CW 55)	158
145	**The Exmoor Coast Path** Somerset/Devon (WW 41)	159
146	**Exmoor: The Dunkery Circuit** Somerset (CW 54)	160
147	**Eastern Dartmoor** Devon (WW 40)	161
148	**North to South Across Dartmoor** Devon (BW 42)	162
149	**Dartmoor: A Visit to Cranmere Pool** Devon (CW 56)	163
150	**The Granite Tors of Bodmin Moor** Cornwall (WW 42)	164
151	**Lamorna Cove to Pendeen Watch** Cornwall (CW 57)	165

WALES

152	**The Clwydian Hills** Clwyd (CW 61)	166
153	**The Denbigh Moors** Clwyd (WW 44)	167
154	**The Northern Carneddau** Gwynedd (WW 45)	168
155	**The Cwm Eigiau Horseshoe** Gwynedd (CW 62)	169
156	**Tryfan and the Bristly Ridge** Gwynedd (BW 44)	170
157	**The Glyders from Pen-y-Gwryd** Gwynedd (CW 63)	171
158	**The Welsh Three Thousanders** Gwynedd (BW 45)	172
159	**The Snowdon Horseshoe** Gwynedd (BW 43)	173
160	**Snowdon by the Miners' Track** Gwynedd (CW 65)	174
161	**Snowdon: Llanberis to Beddgelert** Gwynedd (CW 64)	175
162	**Moel Siabod and Moel Meirch** Gwynedd (WW 47)	176
163	**Cnicht and the Moelwyns** Gwynedd (CW 66)	177
164	**Moel Hebog to Craig Cwm Silyn** Gwynedd (CW 67)	178
165	**The Rivals/Mynydd Mawr** Gwynedd (WW 46)	179
166	**The Migneint and Arenig Fach** Gwynedd (CW 69)	180
167	**Eastern Migneint** Gwynedd (WW 43)	181
168	**Arenig Fawr to Rhobell Fawr** Gwynedd (CW 68)	182
169	**The Rhinog Ridge** Gwynedd (BW 46)	183
170	**The Berwyns/The Arans** Clwyd/Gwynedd (BW 47)	184
171	**Cadair Idris from the South** Gwynedd (CW 70)	185
172	**Across the Dovey Forest** Gwynedd (WW 48)	186

173 **Plynlimon (Pumlumon)** Dyfed (BW 48)   187
174 **Strata Florida/The Teifi Pools** Dyfed (WW 50)   188
175 **Radnor Forest to Llandeilo Hill** Powys (WW 49)   189
176 **The Abergwesyn Common** Powys (WW 51)   190
177 **The Black Mountains** Powys/Gwent (BW 50)   191
178 **The Brecon Beacons** Powys (BW 49)   192
179 **Carmarthen Fan** Dyfed/Powys (WW 52)   193
180 **St David's Head to St Non's Bay** Dyfed (CW 71)   194
181 **The Presely Hills** Dyfed (CW 73)   195
182 **Stackpole Quay to Freshwater West** Dyfed (CW 72)   196
183 **The Gower Peninsula** West Glamorgan (WW 53)   197

IRELAND

184 **The Aghla – Errigal Horseshoe** Donegal (CW 74)   198
185 **The Sperrin Skyway** Tyrone (WW 54)   199
186 **The Donegal Coast: Slieve League** Donegal (WW 55)   200
187 **The Mourne Wall Walk** Co. Down (BW 52)   201
188 **The Benbulbin Group** Sligo/Leitrim (CW 75)   202
189 **The Nephin Ridge Walk** Mayo (WW 56)   203
190 **Mweelrea** Mayo (CW 76)   204
191 **The Glencoaghan Horseshoe** Galway (CW 77)   205
192 **The Maum Turks** Galway (BW 53)   206
193 **The Lug Walk Classic** Wicklow (BW 51)   207
194 **The Galty Ridge** Limerick/Tipperary (CW 78)   208
195 **Knockmealdown** Tipperary/Waterford (WW 58)   209
196 **Brandon Mountain** Kerry (CW 79)   210
197 **Macgillicuddy's Reeks** Kerry (BW 54)   211
198 **The Mangerton Horseshoe** Kerry (WW 59)   212
199 **Knocknagantee/Mullaghanattin** Kerry (WW 57)   213
200 **The Beara Border Walk** Cork (BW 55)   214

     The Traverse of the Black Cuillin Ridge Skye   215

The Walks in Categories   220
Index   224

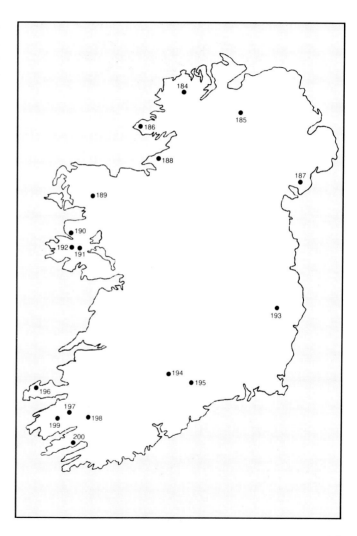

PHOTOGRAPHS IN THE TEXT

between pages 32 and 33

1   Approaching Suilven (Chapter 21). *Photo: Richard Gilbert*
2   Near the summit of Seana Bhraigh (Chapter 26). *Photo: Tom Rix*
3   Traversing An Teallach (Chapter 29). *Photo: Don Sargeant*
4   Beinn Eighe – Coire Mhic Fhearchair (Chapter 26).
    Photo: Don Sergeant
5   Liathach – approaching Mullach an Rathain (Chapter 37).
    Photo: Phil Iddon
6   Ascending Beinn a'Bhuird (Chapter 54). *Photo: Don Sergeant*
7   Heading towards The Sneck and Ben Avon (Chapter 54).
    Photo: Don Sergeant
8   Ben Nevis from Aonach Mor (Chapter 65). *Photo: Phil Iddon*

between pages 96 and 97

9   The Aonach Eagach Ridge (Chapter 67). *Photo: Jerry Rawson*
10   Panorama of the Mamores (Chapter 66).
    Photomontage: E. A. Shepherd
11   Loch Enoch from The Merrick* (Chapter 86). *Photo: Ken Andrew*
12   Crinkle Crags and Bow Fell (Chapter 102). *Photo: Jerry Rawson*
13   High Street (Chapter 94). *Photo: Jerry Rawson*
14   Great Gable and Scafell from above Ennerdale (Chapter 99).
    Photo: Jerry Rawson
15   Scafell Pike from Eskdale (Chapter 101). *Photo: Jerry Rawson*
16   Great Gable from Lingmell (Chapter 98). *Photo: Jerry Rawson*

between pages 160 and 161

17   The Howgills – descending Arant Haw (Chapter 110).
    Photo: John Gillham
18   Penyghent (Chapter 111). *Photo: Phil Iddon*
19   Park House Hill and Dovedale (Chapter 126). *Photo: Ken Wilson*
20   The Malvern Ridge* (Chapter 134). *Photo: Marion Teal*

21   The Dorset Coast Path* (Chapter 142). *Photo: Andy Hosking*
22   The Cornish Coast Path (Chapter 151). *Photo: Marion Teal*
23   The Brecon Beacons (Chapter 178). *Photo: Phil Iddon*
24   The western slopes of Snowdon (Chapter 161).
    Photo: Jerry Rawson

between pages 192 and 193

25   Cadair Idris – Cwm Cau (Chapter 171). *Photo: Jerry Rawson*
26   The Nantlle Ridge (Chapter 164). *Photomontage: Jerry Rawson*
27   The North Ridge of Tryfan (Chapter 156). *Photo: Jerry Rawson*
28   The Glencoaghan Horseshoe* (Chapter 191). *Photo: Phil Cooper*
29   The Galty Ridge from Galtymore* (Chapter 194).
    Photo: Hamish Brown
30   The Cuillin Ridge – Sgurr Alasdair (final chapter).
    Photo: Jerry Rawson
31   Descending the Inaccessible Pinnacle (final chapter).
    Photo: Jerry Rawson
32   A rescue team in the Cairngorms. *Photo: Jerry Rawson*

* Indicates photographs originally published in monochrome in the earlier books.

PREFACE

200 Challenging Walks is a complete collection of the mountain, moorland and coastal expeditions originally described and fully illustrated in the three large-format books: *The Big Walks*, *Classic Walks* and *Wild Walks*.

A wandering spirit is inborn in many of us. Given the chance we would love to roam in wild country where Man has never ventured, and discover for ourselves the hidden secrets of our planet. While this is no longer possible in Britain and Ireland our own mountains, uplands and coastlines can provide magnificent expeditions that are lonely, challenging, beautiful and steeped in history.

In 1980 Ken Wilson and I published *The Big Walks*, a collection of fifty-five of the very best long walks in Britain and Ireland. These expeditions were all extremely tough and required skill, stamina and the utmost determination from the walker. The extensive use of colour and black-and-white photographs, taken for the most part in the heart of the hills and showing walkers active on the ridges and fells and in the corries, surprised many readers. The most frequent reaction was astonishment at so much wild country existing on our doorstep.

The second book in the series, *Classic Walks*, comprised seventy-nine high-quality and popular walks which had withstood the test of time. In general these walks were shorter and less serious than those in *The Big Walks*, yet few could be described as afternoon rambles. The classic walker has more time to enjoy the surroundings and to explore the various historical sites and literary associations connected with the itineraries. Mountains such as Great Gable, Snowdon and Bidean nam Bian, and walks over the Roman Wall and Offa's Dyke are firm favourites with the walking public because their quality has remained undiminished over the years.

The sixty-two routes in *Wild Walks*, published in 1988, attempted to cater for those walkers who seek to explore remote and unfashionable country. My criteria for a walk to be wild included remoteness, untamed landscape and impressive natural features. The length of the walk and the height of the objective were immaterial if it included trackless moorland, lonely corries, silent tarns and broken crags.

Of course, as many readers have pointed out, there is a good deal of overlap in the three books. Many *Big Walks* are both wild and classic, while several *Wild Walks* deserve a place in *The Big Walks* on account of their length and severity. In *200 Challenging Walks* all classification has been dispensed with and the four walks needed to make up the 200 came from previous reserve lists.

The overall selection of routes has been my personal choice, although many friends and acquaintances have influenced me: so has the policy of obtaining an adequate geographical spread in order to cover most areas of high mountain and moorland country in Britain and Ireland. However, I make no excuses for the concentration of expeditions in North-West Scotland. This region is, scenically, the most priceless asset in these islands, and the quality of the landscape is such that I would be depriving the reader by not making considerable use of it.

A few walks, such as Brown Clee Hill (the highest in Shropshire) and the Malverns, gain selection because they are close to major centres of population yet succeed, against all the odds, in retaining an untamed character.

Repeating the twelve coastal walks included in the book gave me intense pleasure. I have always been moved by the surging power of waves spending their energy against rocky cliffs. I liken it to the roaring of the wind and the slow erosion by weathering of mountain peaks. The wonderfully wild and indented coastline of the British Isles and Ireland is one of their most thrilling features.

It is heartening to read of the rapid growth in the numbers of walkers in Britain and Ireland. Our magnificently varied countryside can cater for all tastes, from the rock specialist to the Sunday afternoon rambler. All categories of walker should be able to find real challenge amongst these two-hundred routes.

Challenge means different things to different people. The modest Sunday afternoon rambler or the family with small children will find challenge enough on the Cotswolds or South Downs itineraries, where a surprisingly high degree of commitment is necessary for success. The long-distance walker will be extended by such routes as 'Across Scotland', the 'Derwent Watershed' and the 'Lakeland 3,000s'. The backpacker will find lonely and exquisite overnight campsites on the high ridges overlooking Loch Mullardoch. The coastal walker will thrill to the fearsome cliffs and jagged skerries of Donegal, while the scrambler can rejoice in airy ridges ranging from An Teallach, Rhum and The Saddle to Striding Edge and Bristly Ridge.

At the hardest end of the scale we have the traverse of the Black Cuillin ridge on the Isle of Skye. Without exception, all mountain walkers and climbers in Britain aspire to this route; the greatest challenge of them all. This expedition is, for technical difficulty, head and shoulders above any other mountain traverse in Britain, for it requires the whole spectrum of mountaineering skills: route-finding, stamina, speed over difficult ground, scrambling and rock-climbing ability up to Very Difficult standard. It is, of course, suitable only for the fully trained mountaineer, and I have expanded this theme in the route description, but I hope that many readers will progress in aptitude and confidence and, eventually, complete successfully the Black Cuillin traverse.

Thus, as an extended supplement to the book, I have described this most demanding and serious route. In addition, for the small number of exceptionally fit and experienced mountaineers who buy this book to seek challenge and inspiration, I have extended the Cuillin ridge itinerary over Blaven and Clach Glas, with an optional return to Glen Brittle via Coruisk and the Dubh's ridge.

Likewise, for the growing number of snow and ice climbers, the winter traverse of the Cullin ridge may provide them with the ultimate test of skill and endurance.

In the original three books I invited a number of guest authors to contribute certain essays. These authors were specialists in particular regions and their writing reflected their own enthusiastic response to the scenery. In this book, however, in order to produce a more compact guide, I have rewritten each chapter in a shorter and more standard form. But I have, in every case, included an overall description which captures the atmosphere of the walk as well as providing enough essential detail for the route to be followed on an Ordnance Survey map. The times given are for a fit party, in good conditions, and they do not include stops.

I have continued the practice, begun in *Wild Walks*, of using the old Scottish counties in addition to the new and uninformative regional names, such as 'Highland'. These vast new areas may be easier to administrate, but the distinctive hill groups that are found within them are in danger of losing their old identities and traditions.

Overseas Visitors

I hope this book will appeal to the overseas visitor to Britain and Ireland who wishes to walk, off the beaten track, in some of our most remote and beautiful locations. The two-hundred mountain, moorland and coastal walks are the best which can be found in our islands, and they should provide a host of ideas.

Visitors will find no crudely blazed paths through the mountains and only a minimum of waymarks, even on the popular routes. I suspect they will be surprised and impressed at the rocky ruggedness of many of our hills, and the astonishing diversity to be found in relatively small areas. The white limestone of the Yorkshire Dales, the warm granite of the Cornish cliffs, the eroded peatlands of the Pennines and the rock spires of the Black Cuillin exemplify the myriad features which delight the adventurous walker in Britain and Ireland.

Intending walkers will have no difficulty in obtaining the admirable Ordnance Survey maps (on sale in main newsagents and bookshops) and warm hospitality in whatever locality they decide to explore.

Wildlife

One of the great joys of walking off the beaten track is the variety of wildlife which can be seen. Thus, during my travels in the preparation of this collection of walks I have seen adders, herds of feral goats, a family of badgers, otters, foxes, a pine marten, eagles, peregrine falcons and many hundreds of deer. These have been the highlights for me but, in addition, I have enjoyed a wide selection of bird-life, together with a rich and varied flora. In May or June any walk over the moors and dales of northern England will be accompanied by the continued crying of curlew, the piping of plover and the song of larks.

Oystercatchers turning over shells on lonely beaches, ptarmigan waddling over stony plateaux, the flash of white as a flock of snow buntings wheels across a high corrie; all these are unforgettable experiences for the adventurous walker. Likewise, I treasure the memory of colonies of purple saxifrage, bravely flowering on the Donegal cliffs in April after an unseasonal weekend of blizzards.

Safety Notes

Most of the walks in this books are far from help and many are major mountaineering routes. None are blazed with marking paint, save the odd stretch of footpath in Ireland leading to a shrine. It is therefore important to take adequate safety precautions.

I must point out to readers that I have written this book from a mountaineering point of view, for I am essentially a climber turned mountain walker. Thus some readers may encounter difficulties on sections which I have described only briefly. If this is the case I apologise and I do urge caution. Many of these expeditions are long and should only be attempted when a broad selection of easier routes have been successfully completed. An indication of the seriousness of each walk is given in the preliminary notes.

The major factor in safe mountaineering is experience, and this can only be built up slowly. The inexperienced walker should start with some of the easier, low-level walks and gradually build up to the more demanding expeditions. Even the most experienced mountaineer will revise his plans in the light of the fitness of his party, the conditions underfoot and the weather.

Efficient and accurate map and compass work must become second nature and this can take much practice to perfect, particularly in bad weather. Read carefully the account of your prospective walk before setting out and follow the route on the map. When you are in the hills it is important to refer to the map constantly, for you should know exactly where you are at all times. Situations can change rapidly, requiring bold decisions. In the face of threatening weather, darkness or the tiring of a member of the party it is essential to get off the high ground and into the valley by the quickest possible route. If in doubt, don't forge on hoping for the best, turn about and return to base.

Try not to overload your rucksack but do take certain essential items. The main priorities are warm clothes, efficient waterproofs and, in winter, an ice axe. In addition, crampons should be carried on to the hills in winter and used if necessary, while emergency food, compass, whistle, first-aid kit and exposure bag should be packed as a matter of course.

If you leave your car parked in a mountain area, leave a note behind the windscreen giving your name, route and estimated time of return. If you are staying at a Youth Hostel or hotel, leave details of your proposed itinerary with someone in authority.

If an accident should occur, you must carry out the emergency drill:

(a) The International Distress Call is six blasts on a whistle, or six shouts or flashes of a torch. The answering signal is three blasts.

(b) After first fixing a map reference for the position of the casualty, send a fit member of the party to summon help. He/she should dial 999 and report to the Police, who co-ordinate all mountain rescue services.

Responsibility

Several of the most popular footpaths described in this book are suffering severe erosion from the sheer number of boots that trample them. Much time and effort is being put into footpath repair by the National Parks, the National Trust and other conservation bodies. Please help these organisations by using any waymarked detours or artificially constructed pathways.

Man-made paths can look raw and incongruous at first, but they soon merge into the landscape and many stretches are merely experimental because different methods of dealing with erosion are on trial.

The described walks do not necessarily follow designated rights-of-way, although not once was I stopped during the twelve years preparation of this book. However, I appeal to walkers selecting routes in the Scottish Highlands to check access locally during the deer-stalking season (mid-August – mid-July).

On all the walks it is imperative to conform scrupulously to the Country Code.

I hope that *200 Challenging Walks* will become an indispensable companion for all walkers; a book that can be carried easily in a side pocket of the rucksack, or kept in the glove-box of the car for use when necessary. It is a passport to many days of intense pleasure, exercise and satisfaction in the wild regions of our islands.

RICHARD GILBERT
Crayke, York 1990

THE ORKNEY COASTAL WALK

Map OS Sheet 6 *Start/Finish* Birsay Bay (246280)/Stromness (255092) *Distance/Time* 20 miles/32km, 9 hrs

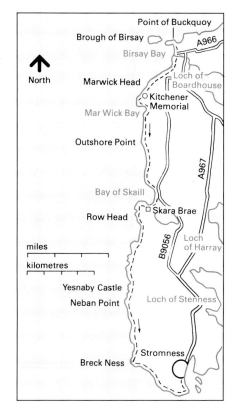

> *Grading* Easy but exposed walking along the top of dramatic and sea-girt cliffs.
> *Escape Routes* The walk may be terminated at Bay of Skaill, where the B9056 road runs along the shore.
> *Transport* Airport at Kirkwall. Ferry services: Scrabster/Stromness; John O'Groats/Burwick (summer only). Bus: Stromness/Brough of Birsay (Mondays only).
> *Accommodation* Hotels/Guest Houses at Stromness. Youth Hostels at Kirkwall and Stromness.

From St John's Head on Hoy you can look north to the distant tidal island of Brough of Birsay off the Orkney Mainland. The rocky coast is rimmed by white surf, sea birds wheel and scream around the stacks and skerries, and the promontories of Breck Ness, Row Head and Marwick Head thrust defiantly into the turbulent Atlantic.

It is a tough expedition of twenty miles from Brough of Birsay to Stromness. For most of the way there is no path and you must battle over the switchback cliffs and across the barren bays, eyes streaming in the tearing wind which constantly batters this northerly outpost of Britain. But the rewards are great: in bright spring sunshine the scene is a kaleidoscope of colour, a restless blue sea with tossing white

horses, creamy surf, red cliffs capped with green turf and an azure sky. A walk to blow away the cobwebs and purge the soul.

At Birsay Bay, as the combers race in over the sand, you strike out south towards Marwick Head. A massive stone tower has been built on the cliff edge as a memorial to Earl Kitchener of Khartoum, who was drowned when the cruiser *Hampshire* went down off the Head in 1916. Marwick Head is now a bird sanctuary, the breeding ground for 35,000 guillemots.

South of Mar Wick Bay the sea has carved the rocks into weird and wonderful shapes; arches, stacks, caves and blow-holes where the waves drive in with a clap of thunder.

On the south side of the Bay of Skaill the ancient village of Skara Brae has been excavated, and is open to the public. It was occupied by stone-age man between 3100 and 2500BC, but was later covered and preserved by wind-blown sand.

Climbing up from Skara Brae to Row Head the cliff top is a mass of sea pinks, but it is also littered with slivers of rock whirled up lethally from below by gale force winds.

Turning east into Hoy Sound the beach is littered with jagged chunks of rusty metal, a

legacy of the more recent history of the Sound and Scapa Flow. These sheltered waters were the assembly point for Atlantic convoys in the last war and, in 1916, for Jellicoe's Grand Fleet before the battle of Jutland. They are also the resting place of the German High Seas Fleet, scuttled in 1919.

THE HOY COASTAL WALK

Map OS Sheet 7   *Start/Finish* Linkness Pier (245050)   *Distance/Time* 13 miles/21km, 7 hrs

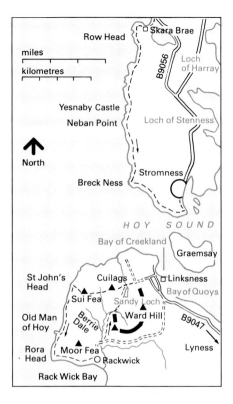

Grading Easy but intoxicating walking above dramatic cliffs and through sheltered glens.
Escape Routes None.
Transport Airport at Kirkwall. Ferry services: Scrabster/Stromness; John O'Groats/Burwick (summer only). Daily ferry: Stromness/Hoy.
Accommodation B & B at Rackwick and Linkness. Hotels/Guest Houses at Stromness. Youth Hostels at Stromness and North Hoy.

The traveller to Orkney who takes the P & O ferry from Scrabster to Stromness, will be captivated by the close-up views of the stupendous cliffs bordering the west side of the island of Hoy.

Proceeding north along the Hoy coastline there is a break in the cliffs at Rack Wick Bay, where the white surf rolls up a wide beach, then the rust coloured cliffs rise to over 300ft on Rora Head. Next comes the Old Man, a top heavy finger of weathered sandstone, standing out from the cliffs and precariously balanced on a plinth of granite. But when looking north, the Old Man is seen against the background of St John's Head where it plays second fiddle to gigantic cliffs, falling sheer or overhanging, fully 1,140ft into the boiling sea.

When a strong westerly wind is driving Atlantic rollers against the cliff-girt coast of Hoy, columns of spray are thrown into the air, the ground trembles and the roar of the waves is awesome. Under such conditions the Hoy coastal walk is an enthralling, unforgettable experience and you feel part of the ceaseless battle between waves and rock which is being waged below your feet.

Although it is possible to stay overnight on Hoy (at Rackwick or Linksness), most walkers will wish to return to Stromness in the evening. However, the schedule of ferries is such that you will have only about seven hours on Hoy. There is no time to dawdle.

From the Linksness pier take the road to Sandy Loch, and then make straight for St John's Head via the summit of Cuilags. Quite suddenly you catch your breath as you arrive above the highest sea cliffs in Britain, whence a muddy path leads south to a wide bay where the Old Man of Hoy commands the stage.

One could sit on the cliff edge for hours, mesmerised by the restless waves pounding the cliffs, the swooping fulmars and black-backed gulls, the rafts of guillemots riding the swell and the lines of shags standing erect or spreading their wings on the offshore skerries.

The path now rounds Rora Head, where the outflowing stream from Loch of Stourdale hurtles down the cliffs into the sea in a spectacular waterfall. Now drop down to the bouldery beach of Rack Wick Bay and take the rough road back through the hills to Sandy Loch and Linksness pier.

THE CLISHAM RIDGE

Map OS Sheet 14   *Start/Finish* Maaruig river bridge (174058)   *Distance/Time* 11 miles/18km, 6-7 hrs

Grading *A rough, rocky and switchback mountain walk. Needs care in misty weather for cliffs abound.*
Escape Routes *Beyond Mulla-fo-dheas easy descents may be made E into Glen Scaladale, thence to Ardvourlie.*
Transport *Caledonian-MacBrayne's car ferries: Uig/ Tarbert and Ullapool/Stornoway. Daily bus: Tarbert/ Stornoway.*
Accommodation *Hotels at Tarbert. B & B locally. Youth Hostels at Ullapool and Stockinish (Harris).*

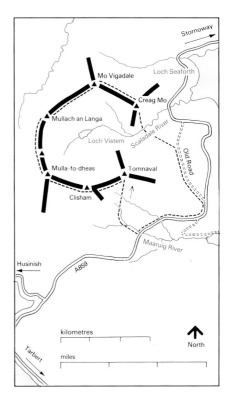

Clisham, 2,622ft/799m, is the highest point on the Long Isle; the largest island of the Outer Hebrides, incorporating Lewis and Harris. Harris, in the south, is wild, mountainous country and although a few isolated communities eke out a precarious existence on the coast, the interior is as rocky and desolate a region as any I know. Atlantic storms batter the hills persistently, few rivers are bridged and only brave and competent walkers should venture into this most hostile of territories.

Clisham, however, rises just north of the Stornoway to Tarbert road and its ascent is simple. A much more worthwhile and demanding expedition is to include Clisham in a circuit of the Glen Scaladale horseshoe. By so doing you will sample much more of the peculiar flavour of the Harris hills, and maybe

understand why they are almost completely neglected by the walking public.

South-east of Clisham the A859 crosses the Maaruig river, and this makes a convenient starting point. Wet and rough slopes of boulders and coarse grass lead up to a bealach and then to Tomnaval, the first nail in the horseshoe. The conical peak of Clisham dominates to the south-west and its ascent is easy. Stay awhile at the cairn for, in clear weather, the views are unparalleled: long fiords penetrate deeply into the hills, lochs fill every indentation while craggy mountains roll away to the west, including Strone Ulladale above Loch Resort which boasts the most sustained overhanging cliff in these islands. South, the entire string of the Outer Hebrides can be seen stretching to Barra Head, east a low grey outline marks the Scottish mainland while, out to the west, you may discern the black teeth of the St Kilda group, the most far flung and enigmatic islands in Britain.

Mulla-fo-dheas is steep and rocky, and perhaps the most interesting peak on the horseshoe with corries eating into the ridge on both sides. As you proceed northwards over Mullach an Langa and Mo Vigadale the ridge broadens

and becomes grassy.

Care is needed on the final peak, Creag Mo, which ends abruptly in a line of crags; skirt it well to the south to reach the Scaladale river.

A path now runs east to Ardvourlie Castle, but the quickest route to Maaruig Bridge is to ford the river and take the old road which crosses the hills west of Clett Arad.

EXPLORATIONS IN TROTTERNISH

Map OS Sheet 23   **Start/Finish** (The Storr and Beinn Edra) Loch Fada (491495)/Staffin (482682)   **Distance/ Time** 16 miles/26km, 7-8 hrs; **Start/Finish** (Quirang) Loch Langaig (463709)   **Distance/Time** 6 miles/10km, 3 hrs

Grading The Storr/Beinn Edra traverse is a long and energetic day over rough ground. The Quirang is easy but it can be confusing in mist.
Escape Routes The Storr/Beinn Edra escarpment can be descended to the E in several places and almost anywhere to the W. Descent from the Quirang area presents no difficulty in clear weather.
Transport Express bus services to Portree and Uig from Glasgow, Edinburgh and Inverness. Weekday bus service: Portree/Staffin/Kilmaluag.
Accommodation Varied accommodation in Portree. Hotels at Duntulm and Flodigarry. B & B at Staffin and Kilmaluag. Youth Hostels at Uig and Broadford.

On a wet day the Cuillin climber may drive to Portree, and perhaps tour the northern peninsula returning via Uig. But he may not realise that a ridge of most unusual peaks runs north from Portree, along the Trotternish peninsula, for nearly twenty miles. These mountains are tertiary basalt, which has weathered in places to give clusters of weird and wonderful pinnacles, particularly on The Storr in the south and the Quirang in the north. To allow time to thoroughly explore these unique hills it is best to make two separate expeditions, as described here.

The Storr rises to 2,360ft/719m, six miles north of Portree, and is notable for a fantastic detached pinnacle rising sheer for 160ft east of a line of cliffs. This pinnacle, the Old Man of Storr, is the most impressive of several rock spires rising from the corrie floor and, being undercut on all sides, it looks extremely precarious. However, in spite of its instability and the crumbly rock it has had several ascents, the first by Whillans and Barber in 1955.

From Loch Fada climb easily to Beinn a'Chearcaill and head north to The Storr. To reach the base of the Old Man find a way through the cliffs half-a-mile south of The Storr, and enter a world of buttresses, pinnacles, hollows and lochans, which contains rich communities of alpine flora.

The cliffs behind the Old Man are too steep to be climbed but, by proceeding north, a way can be found up the north ridge of The Storr, thereby regaining the main spine of Trotternish.

Walk north along the escarpment of the ridge, enjoying expansive views of islands and hills, for seven switchback, but exhilarating, miles to Beinn Edra. Scramble through broken cliffs and strike north-east across the rough moorland to Staffin.

The Quirang

From Loch Langaig a path leads up grassy slopes and then screes to a valley containing crags, knolls and pinnacles, the sharpest of which is called 'The Needle'. This magnificent situation, set between vertical rockwalls, is known as the 'Pillared Stronghold'.

Walk south to circumvent the cliffs and climb up onto Quirang's summit, Meall nan Suireamach, 1,799ft/542m, which is a wonderful viewpoint for the Trotternish hills and the island-dotted sea. Continue northwards and descend into Coire Mhic Eachainn, whence you can swing round the eastern nose of Sron Vourlinn and regain Loch Langaig.

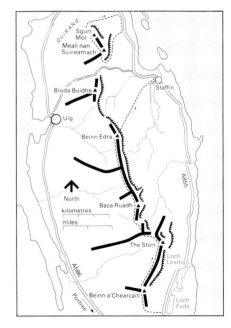

SGURR NAN GILLEAN

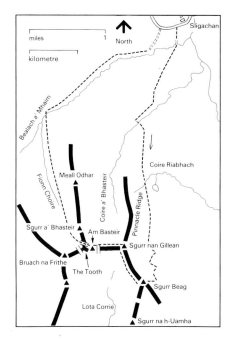

Map OS Sheet 32 (SMT 'Cuillin'/Outdoor Leisure 8)   **Start/Finish** Sligachan Hotel (486298)
Distance/Time 9 miles/14km, 7 hrs

Grading A mild rock-scramble by the Tourist Route.
The descent of the W ridge is more serious and a rope
should be used for safety.
Escape Routes In bad weather it is best to return
down the Tourist Route. From Bealach a'Bhasteir
descend N down Coire a'Bhasteir, there is a path
but beware of loose rock.
Transport Daily bus service: Kyleakin/Portree.
Accommodation Sligachan Hotel. Varied
accommodation in Portree. Youth Hostels at Glen
Brittle, Broadford and Kyle of Lochalsh.

It is strange to realise that, in the second half of
the nineteenth century, British climbers were
actively at work in the alps, yet the Cuillin of
Skye was virtually unknown. Nowadays even
the most ardent alpine climber is amazed by
the stupendous rock spire of Sgurr nan
Gillean which towers above Sligachan and,
together with Gillean's west ridge and the ugly
fang of the Bhasteir Tooth, makes one of
Britain's classic mountain vistas.

The *voie normale* from Sligachan follows
the Tourist Route; but this is a misnomer.
Although the Tourist Route is the easiest way
up Gillean, it involves some exposed rock
scrambling on the summit ridge and it is not
suitable for the novice walker or the faint
hearted.

From the Sligachan Hotel a path runs south,
over rather wet, peaty and heathery moors,
crossing two sizeable burns by wooden
bridges. As the path rounds a shoulder to gain
the upper reaches of Coire Riabhach, above
the lochan, you obtain wonderful views of the
Pinnacle Ridge which provides the climber
with a thrilling route, of only modest grade, to
the summit of Sgurr nan Gillean.

The approach to Sgurr nan Gillean is hard
work, especially in the summer when the
midges can irritate to distraction, but the close
proximity of the serrated Blaven-Clach Glas
ridge (chapter 9) south-east across Glen
Sligachan is inspiring.

The going becomes increasingly rocky and
rough, and the last 1,000ft climb to the south-
east ridge of Sgurr nan Gillean is over
inexorable loose screes and slopes of sharp,
chaotically piled, boulders. It is with great
relief that you reach the ridge and can look
down west into the depths of wild Lota Corrie.
A great sweep of the Cuillin ridge is now
visible from Sgurr nan Gillean to Sgurr
Alasdair, but it is the long limb of Druim nan
Ramh that dominates across Harta Corrie.

Pick the best way up the crest of the ridge to
the tiny, pointed summit of Sgurr nan Gillean,
and enjoy the magnificent view of Skye and the
Inner Hebrides.

The west ridge is sharp and loose and its
descent needs care, particularly near the
bottom where the pinnacle known as the
'Policeman' used to stand. This short section
may need a safety rope.

Traverse under Am Basteir, on the north
side, to reach Fionn Choire whence, below
Bealach a'Mhaim, a good track runs back to
Sligachan.

ACROSS THE CUILLIN BY LOCH CORUISK

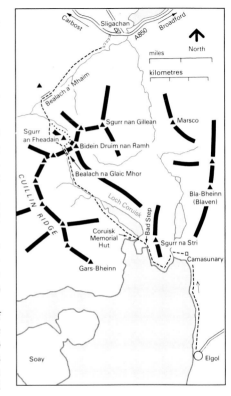

Map OS Sheet 32 (SMT 'Cuillin'/Outdoor Leisure 8) *Start/Finish* Elgol (519140)/Sligachan Hotel (486298)
Distance/Time 17 miles/27km, 9 hrs

> **Grading** *A serious mountaineering expedition which should not be attempted by the inexperienced.*
> **Escape Routes** *None. The climbing hut beside the Scavaig River is private (JMCS). When not in use it is locked.*
> **Transport** *Bus services: Kyleakin/Portree via Sligachan. Post-bus Broadford/Elgol.*
> **Accommodation** *Sligachan Hotel. Varied accommodation Portree, Broadford and Elgol. Youth Hostels at Glen Brittle, Broadford and Kyle of Lochalsh.*

The reputation of the Cuillin as a playground for the rock climber is richly deserved. No other place in Britain or Ireland can offer such a diversity of rock architecture in such a grand setting, and the pulse begins to race as soon as you cross the ferry at Kyle.

But the delights of the Cuillin can be experienced too by the competent hill walker, and here I describe a Cuillin traverse that enters the heart of the mountains at Loch Coruisk, crosses the main ridge and descends to the historic Sligachan Hotel. This magnificent route combines the best of coastal scenery with wild corries and towering crags, pinnacles and buttresses. On all sides misty islands float on the blue ocean, contributing to the romance associated with the Isle of Skye.

From Elgol a path runs above the shore of Loch Scavaig to a sandy bay at Camasunary. It then skirts south of the imposing, isolated mountain of Sgurr na Stri to enter the Coruisk basin. In one place, 'The Bad Step', an angled slab of clean rock drops into the sea; this must be negotiated with care, using a line of generous cracks for holds.

Cross the Scavaig river by stepping stones to the west bank, where there is a (locked) Memorial Hut and a perfect, sheltered anchorage behind Eilean Glas. If the river is in flood keep to the rougher north side of Loch Coruisk.

Don't be overawed by the magnificence of your surroundings, but follow the path to the north end of Loch Coruisk and climb up into the amphitheatre. Black cliffs on all sides appear to block the way ahead, but if you continue northwards, keeping the great wall of Druim nan Ramh on your right, and zig-zag up through boulder-fields and scree, you will arrive at the broad saddle of Bealach na Glaic Mhor. This pass is one of the lowest on the main ridge, 2,492ft/759m, and it divides Bidein Druim nan Ramh and Sgurr a'Mhadaidh.

From the bealach you can descend steeply into Coir'a'Mhadaidh or (preferably) traverse under the north cliffs of Bidein and cross the Sgurr an Fheadain ridge to gain the wider and easier angled Coir'a'Tairneilear.

As you reach the grassy Coire na Creiche look out for a good path running north to Bealach a'Mhaim, on the main Sligachan-Glen Brittle trade-route.

THE ROUND OF COIRE LAGAN

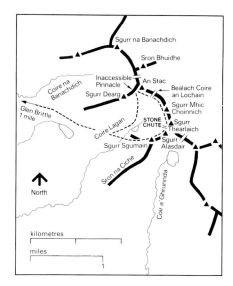

Map OS Sheet 32 (SMT 'Cuillin'/Outdoor Leisure 8) **Start/Finish** Glen Brittle Memorial Hut (411216)
Distance/Time 8 miles/13km, 8 hrs

> **Grading** Very Difficult rock climbing is necessary
> to complete the described route, but this can
> be reduced to Moderate if the difficulties are
> bypassed.
> **Escape Routes** The Alasdair Stone Chute and
> An Stac screes lead into Coire Lagan.
> **Transport** Bus services: Kyleakin/Carbost.
> Infrequent service Carbost/Glen Brittle.
> **Accommodation** Sligachan Hotel. B & B, Youth
> Hostel and BMC Climbing Hut in Glen Brittle.

It is a pity to leave the Cuillin of Skye solely to the rock climber for a competent hill walker, with a head for heights and some scrambling ability, can easily savour the delights of this unique mountain range.

While it is true that certain sections of the ridge do require climbing expertise and the use of a rope, it is quite possible to venture into the heart of the Cuillin, climb to dizzy heights on many of the rock spires and thrill to the exposure of the narrowest ridges in our islands. Nowhere exemplifies better the magnificence of the Cuillin than Coire Lagan, a mountain sanctuary set in an amphitheatre of historic and much-loved rocky peaks.

The round of Coire Lagan will appeal to mountaineers having a variety of aspirations. While the rock climber can follow a purist's route over every pinnacle and buttress, the walker can avoid the difficulties yet still make the ascent of the principal peaks. In misty weather though, this expedition becomes more serious because the Cuillin rocks are magnetic and compasses cannot be relied upon.

From Glen Brittle climb easily up the south flank of Sron na Ciche, peep over the edge at the biggest rock face in the Cuillin, and continue to Sgurr Sgumain. To gain the summit of Sgurr Alasdair, 3,309ft/993m, via the south-west ridge, you must either negotiate the *mauvais pas* (rock climbers) or turn this rock step on the right (walkers).

Beyond Alasdair you descend to the top of the Great Stone Chute, and here walkers should continue on down to upper Coire Lagan and regain the ridge at Bealach Coire Lagan via the An Stac screes.

Rock climbers will climb Sgurr Thearlaich and then Sgurr Mhic Choinnich, via King's Chimney or Collie's Ledge, to arrive at the same point.

A short descent, followed by a very loose scramble up scree slopes running between two crags, now leads to the Inaccessible Pinnacle of Sgurr Dearg, perhaps the most famous climbers' peak in all Scotland. The east ridge is graded moderate.

In clear weather the west ridge of Sgurr Dearg, over Sgurr Dearg Beag and Sron Dearg, makes an interesting descent to Glen Brittle. However, the way onto the ridge is complex, and in mist it is advisable to retreat down the screes to Coire Lagan and the well-beaten track, past Loch an Fhir-bhallaich, to the glen.

[21]

THE RED CUILLIN

Map OS Sheet 32 (Outdoor Leisure 8)   **Start/Finish** Sligachan Hotel (486298)   **Distance/Time** 10 miles/16km, 8-9 hrs

> **Grading** Easy going over mainly rounded and scree-covered hills, apart from a steep scramble down the N ridge of Marsco.
> **Escape Routes** Easy descents into Glen Sligachan from any of the low bealachs.
> **Transport** Bus service: Kyleakin/Portree through Sligachan.
> **Accommodation** Sligachan Hotel. Varied accommodation Portree and Broadford. Youth Hostels at Glen Brittle, Broadford and Kyle of Lochalsh.

It is extraordinary that the bulky, scree-covered hills of the Red Cuillin, and the jagged precipitous peaks of the Black Cuillin, should sit side by side on the island of Skye, when their appearance and character are as different as chalk and cheese.

In Tertiary times gabbro welled up through the earth's crust, and arched the surface layer of basaltic lava to form the Black Cuillin. Subsequent intrusions of dolerite, followed by weathering, produced the serrated ridges we see today. In the same era an intrusion of granite formed the Red Cuillin which, in the absence of dykes and sills, have eroded into more rounded hills.

The Red Cuillin traverse is easy, thus you have a wonderful opportunity to appreciate the unique surroundings, perhaps better than on a day of concentration on the main ridge itself. A traverse from Glamaig over Beinn Dearg to Marsco leads you into the heart of the Cuillin, giving unsurpassed and ever-changing views of Bla Bheinn and the entire main ridge from Sgurr nan Gillean to Gars-bheinn.

From Sligachan a stubby ridge of heather, scree and boulders leads straight to Sgurr Mhairi, the 2,537ft/775m summit of Glamaig. A more interesting approach is from Sconser where easier angled slopes rise to An Coileach, whence a fine ridge runs south to Sgurr Mhairi.

It is worth spending a few minutes on the summit of Glamaig to look around. As you gaze north across Portree and the Storr to the distant hills of Harris, and then turn clockwise, Dun Caan on Raasay, the Applecross Hills, the Five Sisters of Kintail, Bla Bheinn, neighbouring Beinn Dearg, the Pinnacle Ridge of Sgurr nan Gillean, the thrusting ridge of Druim nan Ramh and McLeod's Tables all come into view.

Walking south over the scree-covered whale-backs of the Red Cuillin, it is Marsco that wins respect as the dominant peak of the range. With steeper shoulders and a sharper summit it is altogether haughtier than its more mundane neighbours.

A scramble up the east side of Coire nan Laogh leads to the summit ridge of Marsco. The ridge is a revelation; it snakes up to a tiny cairn, while plunging slopes on either side provide a degree of exposure reminiscent of the Mamores' ridges.

Continue north along the ridge, carefully picking your way through broken cliffs, until the heather and grass of Glen Sligachan are reached, 1,000ft below.

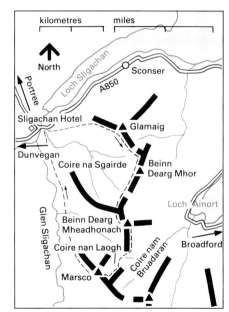

THE BLA BHEINN – CLACH GLAS RIDGE

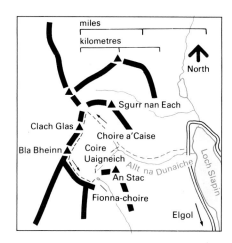

Map OS Sheet 32 (Outdoor Leisure 8)   **Start/Finish** N end of Loch Slapin (561216)
Distance/Time 6 miles/10km, 7 hrs

Grading An exposed traverse of a rocky arête. A rope is necessary to safeguard certain sections. In bad conditions and in winter the ridge should be left to experts.
Escape Routes Descend E into Choire a' Caise from the Clach Glas/Bla Bheinn bealach.
Transport Bus services: Kyleakin/Portree via Sligachan. Post-bus Broadford/Elgol.
Accommodation Sligachan Hotel. Varied accommodation Portree, Broadford and Elgol. Youth Hostels at Glen Brittle, Broadford and Kyle of Lochalsh.

Technically the Bla Bheinn-Clach Glas ridge is a rock climb, although in good conditions a competent mountaineer would romp over the exposed sections without recourse to a safety rope. It is one of the most 'difficult' expeditions in this book, but I have included it for the sake of the increasing numbers of hill walkers who have enough climbing expertise to enjoy mixed routes. And enjoyable it most certainly is; John Mackenzie, writing in *Wild Walks*, reckons it cannot be surpassed by any other mountain group in Britain.

The expedition requires all-round mountaineering skills, for the route is complex and difficult to define. Any party must have considerable experience and the ability to seek out viable paths through a plethora of walls, slabs, buttresses and gullies.

The great wedge of gabbro, making the Bla Bheinn-Clach Glas massif, rises east of Strath na Creitheach and is thus isolated from the main Black Cuillin. Its serrated ridge is prominent from most of the peaks on the main ridge, as well as from the Elgol road as it rounds the head of Loch Slapin.

Park beside Loch Slapin and follow the boggy path which runs up beside the Allt na Dunaiche into Choire a'Caise. Screes lead to the bealach under the north ridge of Clach Glas where the climbing starts.

An initial wall of rock is turned by a left traverse, but thereafter the best plan is to keep to the crest of the ridge, by-passing insurmountable obstacles as they arrive.

Many wonderfully exposed positions are encountered which can be fully enjoyed from the security of excellent holds.

From the wafer-thin summit of Clach Glas the way down descends a crack in a very exposed slab, which then leads to an arête. This arête looks particularly impressive from below, but it is not hard and was christened 'Pilkington's Imposter' by the early pioneers.

A flat, grassy platform on the bealach under Bla Bheinn is a haven of peace and security; it is known as the 'Putting Green'.

Ahead lies a jumble of walls and pinnacles threaded by loose gullies. Weave your way upwards to gain a stone chute which leads to the easy east ridge of Bla Bheinn.

From the southern of the twin summits it is an easy descent into Fionna-choire, where you meet the return path running through Coire Uaigneich to Loch Slapin.

THE CUILLIN OF RHUM

Map OS Sheet 39   **Start/Finish** Kinloch (403995)   **Distance/Time** 19 miles/31km, 10-11 hrs

> *Grading* A long and arduous mountain traverse involving some rock scrambling. A safety rope should be carried.
> *Escape Routes* Bealach an Oir S down Glen Dibidil. W from Bealach an Fhuarain to Glen Harris.
> *Transport* Small Isles ferry Mallaig to Rhum several times a week. Rail services to Mallaig from Fort William and Glasgow.
> *Accommodation* Camping with permission from NCC. Hotel Kinloch Castle. Bothy at Dibidil.

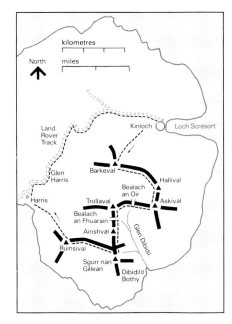

The island of Rhum is only small, measuring seven miles by nine, but it contains perhaps a greater variety of scenery than any other similar area of land in Britain, and it is rightly known as the jewel of the Inner Hebrides.

Caledonian MacBraynes run a 'small isles' ferry several times a week from Mallaig, but if you wish to stay overnight you must write first for permission from the Nature Conservancy Warden.

For many years Rhum was run as a sporting estate by the Bullough family, but it was bought by the Nature Conservancy Council in 1957 and has since become a National Nature Reserve. Many important research programmes are undertaken on Rhum: a major study of red deer has been in progress since 1972 and Rhum was the site of the successful experiment to reintroduce the white-tailed sea eagle to Britain.

Accommodation may be obtained in the splendid Kinloch Castle where you will be entertained in style and luxury. Several estate cottages offer bed and breakfast, a primitive bothy is available at Dibidil on the south coast and camping is allowed at Kinloch.

The complete traverse of the Cuillin of Rhum is one of Britain's great mountain expeditions. It bears no comparison with Skye but it does involve some mild scrambling over sharp ridges of volcanic rock, sandstone and gneiss. In addition walkers must remember that, apart from Kinloch, Rhum is uninhabited and help is far away.

From Kinloch follow the track west for a mile and then strike across the very rough hillside to Barkeval. The summit gives a good view of the peaks to come as well as the island spread out below and its neighbours: Eigg, Muck and Canna.

Continue over Hallival, Askival and Trollaval; these names are of Norse origin and were landmarks for passing ships. Hallival's ridge is a breeding ground for Manx shearwaters and it is honeycombed with burrows. The notorious Askival pinnacle is in fact an easy slab which can be turned on the east if necessary.

From Bealach an Oir scramble up the rocks to Trollaval, descend to Bealach an Fhuarain and then pick your way through broken crags onto Ainshval and Sgurr nan Gillean.

Continue west to Ruinsival and descend steeply to the Greek temple (actually the Bullough's mausoleum) at Harris. The difficulties are now over and you can enjoy the easy track leading, in six miles, to Kinloch.

BEN MORE OF MULL

Map OS Sheet 48   **Start/Finish** On B8035 beside Loch na Keal (507368)   **Distance/Time** 6 miles/10km, 4 hrs

Grading A splendid airy ridge walk with many interesting steep, but easy, sections.
Escape Routes Alternative descent due S from the summit to the A849.
Transport MacBrayne's ferry: Oban/Craignure. Bus service Craignure/Salen.
Accommodation Hotels and B & B in Tobermory, Craignure and Salen. Youth Hostels in Tobermory and Oban.

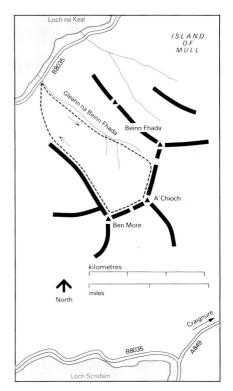

Apart from Skye the only other Scottish island that requires a visit from the Munro-bagger is Mull. Ben More, 3,169ft/966m, was certainly one of the highlights of my Munro round.

I shall never forget that brilliant January morning as we disembarked from the Craignure bus and walked south from Salen alongside Loch na Keal. Birds were singing on the shore, snowdrops were out and fresh powder snow was pluming off Ben More in the stiff wind. Our schedule was desperately tight, but we climbed Ben More and made it back to Craignure for the 4.30 p.m. Oban ferry, in the last flicker of daylight.

Any mountain which rises straight from sea-level has added stature and attractiveness. Mull lies in the heart of the Hebrides, and an ascent of Ben More can give ever-widening views over islets and skerries around the coast and beyond to far distant lands.

The well-known landmarks of Mull, the Dutchman's Cap in the Treshnish Islands and Fingal's Cave on Staffa, are due to the underlying Tertiary basalt. Ben More's summit is the highest point reached by the Tertiary basalt in Scotland. Extensive weathering has eroded the cone of Ben More exposing the layered beds of this lava.

Ben More, and its splendid outlier A'Chioch, are conical hills whose upper slopes consist of rough, angular boulders strewn chaotically in all directions. A long glen, Gleann na Beinn Fhada, runs from the shore of Loch na Keal, at a point opposite the island of Eorsa, to the north ridge of A'Chioch.

The ascent of this grassy glen, keeping beside the lively burn, makes the best approach to the hills. Once you have gained the north ridge you can clamber up the rocks and ledges, enjoying the freedom and spaciousness of the situation, to A'Chioch's summit.

More of the same exhilarating scrambling follows as you descend to a col and then tackle the north-east ridge of Ben More.

On a clear day the summit will give you views from the Cuillin of Skye to Barra, Coll and Tiree. Below, in the mouth of the loch, lies the island of Inch Kenneth where the Kings of Scotland were said to be buried when the sea was too rough for a journey to be made to Iona.

Descend, easily, the stony north-west ridge over the shoulder of An Gearna to the road alongside Loch na Keal.

[25]

THE PAPS OF JURA

Map OS Sheet 61   **Start/Finish** Craighouse (527672)   **Distance/Time** 18 miles/29km, 9 hrs

Grading A tough walk over exposed and stony hills with no recognised tracks.
Escape Routes Easy descents to the glen from either of the bealachs separating the three peaks.
Transport MacBrayne's ferry: Kennacraig/Port Askaig (Islay). Daily ferry: Port Askaig/Feolin (Jura). Charlie's bus Feolin/Craighouse.
Accommodation Hotel and B & B at Craighouse.

Jura, or Deer Island from the Norse *Dyr Oe*, is a long and mountainous island lying in the Hebrides north of Islay. Its wild hills and rugged coastline inspired George Orwell to write *Nineteen Eighty Four*; he bought a cottage on Jura with the proceeds from *Animal Farm* hoping that the sea air would cure his tuberculosis.

Three superb individual mountains called the Paps dominate Jura making full use of their height as they rise straight from sea level. During the last ice-age Jura spawned nineteen glaciers, their legacy being evident in the inexorably steep slopes of quartzite boulders which characterise the Paps, particularly the principal peak Beinn an Oir, 2,571ft/784m (Hill of Gold). This was the highest peak reached by Thomas Pennant on his historic tour of Scotland in 1769.

For a single day's expedition to Jura from Islay it is not necessary to take a car, because the short ferry is met by a bus which takes you to Craighouse, the main village on Jura.

Walk north along the coast road which overlooks the Sound of Jura until you reach the bridge over the Corran river. Take the path alongside the river to Loch an t-Siob, then climb steeply up the east ridge of Beinn Shiantaidh, the first Pap, passing a group of lochans on the shoulder. Now descend scree slopes to a lochan on the bealach, and negotiate

some crags to gain the rocky main east ridge of Beinn an Oir.

Just before you reach the summit of Beinn an Oir you pass some ruins and a man-made causeway. This may have been built by surveyors during the Great Triangulation of the UK in 1852, for Beinn an Oir was one of the principal sighting points. As with all island peaks the views are enthralling: Loch Tarbet, the sandy bays of Islay, waves breaking on the uninhabited west coast of Jura and the whirlpools of Corryvreckan.

The south face of Beinn an Oir is split from top to bottom by a scree shoot and this makes a quick route of descent to Na Garbh-Lochanan. Beinn a'Chaolais is a boulder-strewn cone of no great difficulty and then, from Gleann Astaile, a direct climb brings you to the summit of Aonach-bheinn. From here you can head east over Glas Bheinn to the tiny, settlement of Keils, and thence to Craighouse.

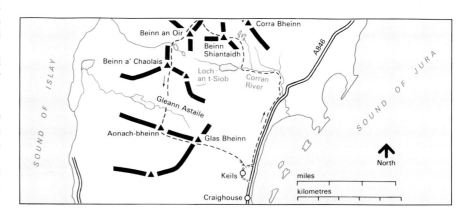

ARRAN'S ROCKY RIDGES

Map *OS Sheet 91*   **Start/Finish** *Brodick (022360)*   **Distance/Time** *21 miles/33km, 12-13 hrs*

Grading A long walk over rocky and switchback ridges involving some exposed scrambling. A safety rope should be carried.
Escape Routes Descend to Glen Rosa from Bealach an Fhir-bhogha or the A' Chir/Cir Mhor bealach.
Transport Steamer service: Ardrossan/Brodick and (summer) Claonaig/Lochranza. Bus service: Brodick/Sannox/Lochranza.
Accommodation Hotels and B & B in Brodick, Corrie and Sannox. Youth Hostel at Lochranza.

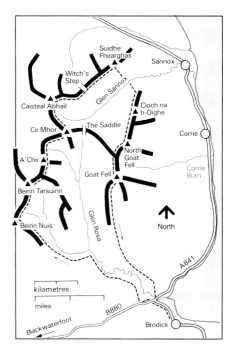

Arran, the holiday isle set in the Clyde and overlooking Kintyre, provides ridge-walking of a standard second only to the Cuillin of Skye.

The rock is coarse-grained, weathered granite which is exceptionally rough on the hands. The weathering process, combined with intrusions of basaltic dykes, has carved the rock into crazy pinnacles and deep gullies. Slopes of fine granite sand fall away from the ridges and chunks of rotten rock can be pulled away by hand. Two long and beautiful glens, Glen Sannox from the north and Glen Rosa from the south, split the hills into two distinct ridges.

Either of these two ridges would make a fine excursion, but this expedition combines them both to give a long and arduous day involving some airy scrambling although, in the absence of snow and ice, a rope should not be necessary.

Beinn Nuis, the day's first objective, is easily reached from Glen Rosa via an iron water pipe running down the lower slopes. The ridge is easy until Beinn Tarsuinn, when it narrows and some scrambling may be enjoyed over castles of grey sandstone. Interest is maintained on the rocky ridge of A'Chir which involves the ascent of some exposed slabs. Difficulties are not great, however, for the angle is gentle, the adhesion excellent and the route well scratched.

At the notorious *mauvais pas* an arrow marks the place where you must descend a twelve-foot wall on the east side and then traverse to meet a lower path.

Cir Mhor is Arran's shapeliest peak, rising to 2,618ft/798m. Cliffs abound and as you climb the south-west ridge you can admire the stupendous rock prow, the Rosa Pinnacle.

Beyond Caisteal Abhail you meet an extraordinary gash in the ridge. This is the famous 'Witch's Step', or Ceum na Caillich, and its negotiation involves an awkward move up a steep slab.

The main ridge now broadens out to Suidhe Fhearghas whence you descend into Glen Sannox, ford the river and climb steeply to the north ridge of Cioch na h-Oighe, an unrelenting plod of nearly 2,000ft.

As you head south to Mullach Buidhe and Goat Fell you meet several more exposed and crumbling sections of ridge, but most can be avoided.

Goat Fell is a tourist's mountain and its summit blocks have been defaced by graffiti; a disappointing end to such a thrilling circuit.

[27]

THE PIRNMILL HILLS OF ARRAN

Map OS Sheet 69   **Start/Finish** Pirnmill (872442)   **Distance/Time** 12 miles/19km, 6-7 hrs

Grading A straightforward mountain traverse over a fine granite ridge with superb sea and coastal views.
Escape Routes Easy descents from many of the bealachs to the A841 on the W side.
Transport Steamer service: Ardrossan/Brodick and (summer) Claonaig/Lochranza. Bus service: Brodick/Lochranza/Pirnmill.
Accommodation Hotels in Lochranza. B & B in Pirnmill. Youth Hostel at Lochranza.

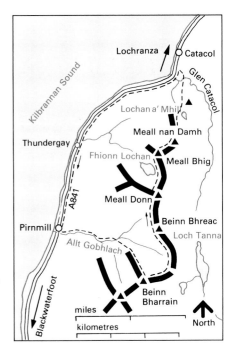

Few hill walkers to the Isle of Arran venture further afield than the main range of peaks: Goat Fell, Cir Mhor and Caisteal Abhail. They can choose either to make the magnificent, but extremely arduous, complete traverse of the ridges as described in Chapter 13, or they can spend several days climbing the ridges piecemeal, allowing time to linger on the summits and savour the views. Almost certainly they will gaze west from Beinn Tarsuinn or the A'Chir ridge, across Glen Iorsa to the Pirnmill Hills.

While Arran's main peaks and ridges are sharp and shattered, requiring some scrambling ability and a head for heights, the Pirnmill Hills allow carefree walking. They rise abruptly from the A841 island ring-road and look straight down to Kilbrannan Sound and

across to Kintyre; they are mainly rounded hills with broad, though distinct, ridges, their corries are shallow and several contain lochans in the most picturesque and tranquil of settings.

Except in the peak holiday season you are unlikely to meet other walkers in the Pirnmill Hills, and you can enjoy utmost peace amongst the deer, divers and golden eagles.

From the village of Pirnmill a path runs up beside the Allt Gobhlach, a short but spectacular burn which foams down from Glas Choirein in a series of falls and cascades. Head for the prominent ridge which runs north-west from the highest of Beinn Bharrain's twin peaks and divides Glas Choirein from Coire Roinn. This ridge is quite narrow and rocky and provides a most interesting route of ascent; it so absorbs one's attention that the effort of such a direct climb to the day's highest peak is scarcely noticed. Note that the exposed sections can easily be avoided on the west side.

Apart from the north-west ridge Beinn Bharrain is smooth and rounded with cropped grass and heather interspersed with loose granite boulders. From its summit 2,368ft/721m, you can look across to Ben More on Mull, Islay,

the Paps of Jura and the distant Antrim coast of Ireland.

Easy walking leads north over the whale-back hump of Beinn Bhreac to Meall Donn, where you gaze down in wonder at the exquisite oval Fhionn Lochan ringed with sandy beaches.

Descend the spur east of Coirein Lochain, climb the isolated top of Meall nan Damh, and drop down to Lochan a'Mhill, thence through bracken and birch woods to Catacol Bay.

THE CAPE WRATH COASTAL WALK

Map OS Sheet 9   *Start/Finish* Oldshoremore (202585)/Cape Wrath lighthouse (259748)
Distance/Time 16 miles/26km, 8 hrs

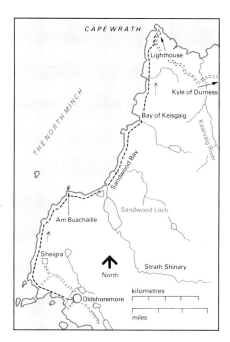

Grading *A long and rough walk over trackless hills and cliff-tops. In wet weather river crossings could be troublesome.*
Escape Routes *From Sandwood Bay a track runs inland to Blairmore.*
Transport *Minibus service (summer): Cape Wrath/ Kyle of Durness. Railway station at Lairg. Bus services: Durness/Kinlochbervie/Lairg and Kinlochbervie/Oldshoremore.*
Accommodation *Hotels and B & B at Kinlochbervie and Durness. Youth Hostels at Durness and Tongue.*

Gale lashed, pounded remorselessly by Atlantic rollers, and virtually uninhabited, the coastline south of Cape Wrath offers the walker an exhilarating and memorable experience. Here are found sheer cliffs of grey gneiss, skerries and islets sending the waves into columns of spray with a clap of thunder, wheeling, screaming sea-birds and wide sandy bays.

Before setting out on this expedition be sure to phone Durness 244, to check the times of the minibus and ferry that will take you from the lighthouse to the Cape Wrath Hotel at Kyle of Durness. The alternative is an extra sixteen miles of walking, at the end of an already very arduous day.

As you proceed northwards from Oldshoremore, hug the coastline wherever possible, at times descending to hidden coves where you will startle the oyster catchers, and at other times traversing round cairned hillocks on heather moorland and eroded peat.

At Port Mor a stack of rock thrusts skyward, topped by an extraordinary ovoid stone, covered with yellow lichen, like the egg of a prehistoric bird. Further on, as you draw level with the island group of Am Balg, the cliffs rise to 400ft and, if you peer over the edge, you will see the famous pinnacle of Am Buachaille (the herdsman) rising 220ft above the waves. It was first climbed by Tom Patey in 1967.

Barely have you regained your composure after Am Buachaille than, rounding the cliff, one of the most glorious sights in Britain unfolds. Below your feet lies Sandwood Bay, a mile-long sweep of golden sand bounded by rolling dunes and crashing breakers that make you want to shout for joy.

Spend a few minutes watching the gannets diving for fish, and then climb to the cliff-top on the north side of the bay. Look back at lonely Sandwood Loch, the haunted cottage beyond the dunes and the tidal islands where legends tell us mermaids play.

The last six miles to Cape Wrath are exceptionally tough as you switchback from cliff-top to bouldery beach, but the scenery becomes even more dramatic. Waves boom through caves and blowholes, spray leaps from the shattered rocks and a natural arch runs through the headland at Bay of Keisgaig. Watch out for great skuas (bonxies) which divebomb unwelcome visitors.

Cape Wrath lighthouse and the accompanying cottages come as an anti-climax; man-made structures are incongruous in a natural environment of such grandeur.

BEN LOYAL

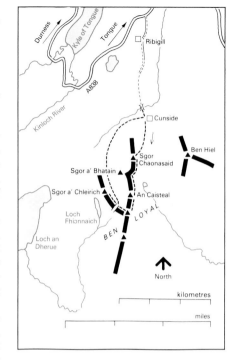

Map *OS Sheet 10* **Start/Finish** *Ribigill (582542)* **Distance/Time** *9 miles/14km, 5-6 hrs*

Grading *A fine, but remote, mountain walk. Some exposed scrambling on the summit of Sgor a' Bhatain.*
Escape Routes *None.*
Transport *Railway station at Lairg. Bus services: Lairg/Altnaharra/Tongue and Tongue/Durness.*
Accommodation *Hotels and B & B at Durness, Tongue and Altnaharra. Youth Hostels at Durness and Tongue.*

Ben Loyal, 2,504ft/764m, makes Corbett's list of 2,500-footers by just four feet. Yet it has no need of any arbitrary statistic to enhance its stature, for it possesses such inherent quality that it could be considered the perfect Scottish mountain.

Ben Loyal divides the rough, harsh, quartzite mountains of the Reay Forest from the flat, saturated moorlands of the Flow Country of eastern Sutherland. Its combination of shapely summits, narrow but rounded ridges, bold crags, smoothly sculptured corries, lochans, gorges and wooded slopes not only gladdens the eye of the visitor to the far north-west but provides the hill walker with a day of extravagant pleasures.

From the village of Tongue, an unfenced road runs south off the A838 to Kinloch Lodge at the head of the Kyle of Tongue. Park near Ribigill Farm and follow the path south to the shieling of Cunside. Throughout this two-mile approach march you are presented with magnificent views of the craggy north face of Sgor Chaonasaid.

Skirt the steepest section of the face to the east and scramble up rather ledgy, broken ground to the sharp summit. Descend a short distance to a bealach and then climb up to the rocky twin summits of Sgor a'Bhatain; this involves the traverse of a narrow granite crest, but it can be avoided on the east side if necessary.

An Caisteal, further south, is the true summit of Ben Loyal and it carries a trig. point perched on a granite tor. The view south and west includes many of Britain's most enigmatic mountains, and emphasises the diversity of hill country we can enjoy. From South Wales to the Yorkshire Dales, on through the Southern Uplands to the Central Highlands and finally to Ben Loyal we can discover untold treasures.

Ben Loyal looks to Ben Hope, Ben More Assynt, the folded hill of Meallan Liath Coire Mhic Dhughaill and the mountains of the Reay Forest. Below stretches the watery wastes of the Flow Country, Loch Loyal, Loch Eriboll, the Pentland Firth and the distant cliffs of St John's Head on Hoy.

Keep to the broad summits surrounding the shallow, unnamed north-facing corrie and make for the prominent rock nose of Sgor a'Chleirich above Loch Fhionnaich. Retrace your footsteps south to the bealach, and scramble down into the corrie, whence the burn guides you down through the woods of Coille na Cuile to the bare moorland.

FOINAVEN AND ARKLE

Map *OS Sheet 9* **Start/Finish** *Gualin House (305565)/Laxford Bridge (237468)*
Distance/Time *20 miles/32km, 10 hrs*

> **Grading** *A tough walk over two of Sutherland's most spectacular peaks. Very rough ground including narrow quartzite ridges.*
> **Escape Routes** *From the Foinaven/Arkle bealach descend SW to Loch Stack. From Foinaven ridge E down screes to Strath Dionard.*
> **Transport** *Railway station at Lairg. Bus service: Lairg/Laxford Bridge/Rhiconich/Durness.*
> **Accommodation** *Hotels and B & B at Rhiconich and Durness. Youth Hostels at Durness and Tongue.*

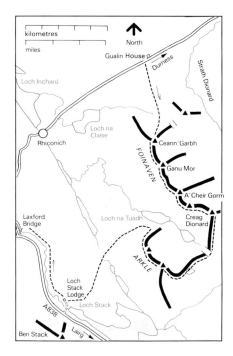

Visitors to north-west Scotland are inspired by the peaks of Torridon, An Teallach, Coigach and Assynt, but few venture across the Kylesku bridge to the barren hills of the Reay Forest.

The layman associates the names of Foinaven and Arkle with the brilliant racehorses owned by the Duchess of Westminster, but these thoroughbreds were christened after the equally magnificent peaks which dominate the far north-west, rising high above the scarred bedrock of gneiss. Foinaven throws down excessively steep scree slopes from an airy ridge which connects with Arkle by a low bealach.

Four miles along the desolate A838 north of Rhiconich stands the isolated Gualin House, and this makes a convenient starting point for the walk. Weave through the myriad shallow lochans and make for the bealach between Cnoc a'Mhadaidh and Ceann Garbh. There is no path across the undrained moor, where the purple moor grass grows at its thickest and the sphagnum is deepest.

As you climb through the bluffs of rock and boulder fields on the east ridge of Ceann Garbh a watery landscape unfolds; lochans fill every trough and hollow, the long fingers of Lochs Inchard and Laxford penetrate far inland while breakers can be seen on the golden strand of Balnakeil Bay on the north coast.

Foinaven's highest peak, Ganu Mor 2,980ft/908m, can be seen at the end of a ridge which sweeps round with mathematical precision forming a perfect parabola. On a still summer's day a climber sitting on Ganu Mor can hear the constant shifting of quartzite screes – an eerie sound.

Follow the main ridge of shattered quartzite south to Creag Dionard, then drop steeply to the cushion of moss on the bealach (1,200ft) under Arkle.

The summit ridge of Arkle is mainly broad and stony, except in one place where it narrows dramatically to a razor edge. Many of the massive blocks are fissured like limestone pavements in the Yorkshire Dales.

Half-a-mile beyond Arkle's northern summit leave the ridge and pick your way down the screes towards Loch na Tuadh. On lower ground you meet a track leading to Loch Stack Lodge.

Follow the path along the bank of the river to Laxford Bridge. The Laxford is a salmon river (*Lax fjord* – salmon fjord). In season you can watch the salmon at rest lying head to tail in the clear pools or flashing like silver as they leap the rapids.

NORTH WEST WILDERNESS – THE STACK OF GLENCOUL

Map *OS Sheet 15*   **Start/Finish** *Unapool (238328)*   **Distance/Time** *18 miles/29km, 9-10 hrs*

Grading A long expedition through desolate, uninhabited and rugged mountain country.
Escape Routes None. The shoulder of Beinn Aird da Loch is the point of no return.
Transport Bus service (not Sun): Ullapool/Skiag Bridge.
Accommodation Hotels and B & B at Kylesku, Scourie and Lochinver. Youth Hostels at Achmelvich and Durness.

Many drivers heading north from Ullapool to Durness stop at the Kylesku bridge to watch the seals and herons, and to marvel at the mighty north face of Quinag's Sail Gharbh, every seam highlighted by the slanting rays of sunshine. Looking east, down Loch Glencoul, they will be equally impressed by a region of bare rock faces, deep gorges and chunky peaks of ancient Lewisian gneiss. Particularly prominent is the grey castle, the Stack of Glencoul, which rears over Loch Beag at the head of Loch Glencoul.

A long and arduous expedition is needed to explore this barren and uninhabited area, but connoisseurs of wild mountain country will find ample reward.

From the hamlet of Unapool, near Kylesku, you must tackle the trackless, tussocky and boggy ground on the south shore of Loch Glencoul. But in summer you can delight in the seals sunning themselves on the rocks, and the dragonflies, foxgloves, cotton-grass, bog asphodel, buttercups and bog myrtle.

Near the headland overlooking Eilean an Tuim, a cliff must be traversed by a narrow and exposed path that twists and turns across its steep face above the loch.

Half-a-mile south of Loch Beag, ford the river and weave your way up through rocky outcrops to the Stack of Glencoul. Here, in a cool, shady gully bright with yellow saxifrage, I disturbed a ring ouzel.

The glen of the Abhainn an Loch Bhig is an exceptionally steep, rocky defile and, on the south side, the famous waterfall, Eas a'Chual Aluinn, roars down from the lip for 650ft in a streak of foam. Extraordinarily, this fall is complemented by another cascade of white water falling from a similar height on the north side.

The Stack, 1,621ft/494m, is the blunt end of a ridge, holding many lochans, which divides the massifs of Beinn Leoid and Ben More Assynt.

Scramble down between cliffs to Glen Coul,

walk under some enormous bare rock walls to Glencoul House, and cross rough hillside to Loch Glendhu. The head of Gleann Dubh is another fascinating area of woods and crags.

Cross the river by a footbridge and begin the long walk back to Kylesku. This is a lovely, peaceful walk at the end of such a rugged day; the path runs above the loch where the water is so clear you can see down to the rocks on the sea-bed, entwined with fronds of seaweed and dotted with sea urchins.

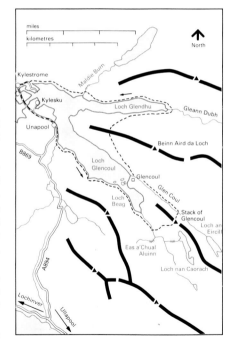

1 Approaching Suilven from the east (Chapter 21). Photo: Richard Gilbert

2   Near the summit of Seana Bhraigh looking east to Creag an Duine (Chapter 26). Photo: Tom Rix

3   (right) Traversing the Corrag Bhuidhe pinnacles of An Teallach (Chapter 29). Photo: Don Sargeant

4 *On the ascent Beinn Eighe – pausing to absorb the splendours of Coire Mhic Fhearchair (Chapter 26). Photo: Don Sargeant*

5 Approaching Mullach an Rathain during the traverse of Liathach (Chapter 37). Photo: Phil Iddon

6 7 *Ascending Beinn a' Bhuird (above) and traversing above the rim of Garbh Choire (right) heading towards Cnap a Chleirich, The Sneck and Ben Avon. Crossing this remote Cairngorm massif in winter is one of the most serious mountain traverses in Britain (Chapter 54). Photos: Don Sargeant*

8   Ben Nevis and Carn Mor Dearg seen from the slopes
of Aonach Mor (Chapter 65). Photo: Phil Iddon

A TRAVERSE OF QUINAG

Map OS Sheet 15   **Start/Finish** 2 miles N of Skiag Bridge (232273)   **Distance/Time** 8 miles/13km, 6-7 hrs

> **Grading** A fine mountain walk that should present no difficulties in good conditions.
> **Escape Routes** Easy descents from bealachs on the main ridge into the two eastern corries.
> **Transport** Bus service (not Sun): Ullapool/Skiag Bridge.
> **Accommodation** Hotels and B & B at Lochinver, Inchnadamph and Kylesku. Youth Hostels at Achmelvich and Ullapool.

The opening of the Kylesku bridge in 1985 marked the demise of the old car ferry and the end of an era. Generations of drivers had queued happily on the slip-way, watching the seals and the herons, and marvelling at the towering buttresses of Quinag's Sail Gharbh and Sail Gorm. Although the new bridge curves skillfully across the narrows of Loch a'Chairn Bhain, drivers cannot afford more than a fleeting glance at regal Quinag, one of the few mountains in the north-west having a stature to match Suilven, Cul Mor and Ben More Coigach.

From the south it is the flat cut-off summit of Spidean Coinich which is easily identifiable, rising prominently above Loch Assynt.

In conditions of mist, high wind or snow and ice Quinag should only be attempted by an experienced and well-equipped party. Unrelentingly steep slopes, sheer in many places, fall from the Y-shaped ridges, and even in summer the mountain demands respect. Nevertheless, situated as it is between the mountains of Coigach and the Reay Forest, and overlooking the foam-flecked islands of Eddrachillis Bay, it provides a walk of utmost exhilaration.

The A894 crosses Quinag's south-east ridge at a height of about 250m, and this is a welcome bonus. From a lay-by easy grassy slopes, dotted with boulders, lead up to the subsidiary summit of Spidean Coinich. Here you meet vast slabs of fissured and glacier-scoured sandstone, which make for very easy going. If you keep to the north side of the ridge, the cliffs falling away towards Lochan Bealach Cornaidh provide a taste of exposure.

Scramble over the rock nose of Spidean Coinich, continue to the northern outlier, Point 713m, and descend loose rock to the Bealach a'Chornaidh. Hereafter the ridges become more rounded, but their convex shapes belie the cliffs below and discretion is needed.

From the northernmost summit of Sail Gorm feast your eyes on the most spectacular hill and coastal scenery in Britain, and then retrace your steps south. Most walkers will want to make the short diversion to the highest point on Quinag, the 2,653ft/808m trig. point on Sail Gharbh.

Return to the bealach between Sail Gharbh and Point 745m, then scramble down loose south-facing slopes towards Lochan Bealach Cornaidh. A stalkers' path surprisingly appears through the rough tussocky grass, boulders and heather and leads you rapidly back to the road.

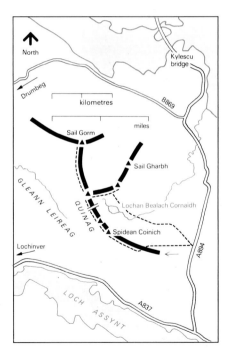

CONIVAL AND BEN MORE ASSYNT

Map OS Sheet 15   *Start/Finish* Inchnadamph Hotel (252217)   *Distance/Time* 11 miles/8km, 6-7 hrs

Grading A rough mountain walk involving steep slopes of sharp quartzite boulders and an exposed rocky ridge.
Escape Routes None to the N, S or E of the range. Descend from the Conival/Beinn an Fhuarain or Conival/Ben More Assynt bealachs by the described routes.
Transport Bus services: Lairg/Lochinver and (summer) Ullapool/Lochinver.
Accommodation Inchnadamph Hotel. Varied accommodation in Lochinver and Ullapool. Youth Hostels at Achmelvich, Durness and Ullapool.

Most climbers who attain the remote summits of Quinag, Canisp, Suilven and Cul Mor are content to gaze dreamily over the bays and islands of the magnificent indented coast of north-west Scotland. But, when they turn eastwards, they will revel in the considerable mountain massif comprising Conival and Ben More Assynt, which sends down fans of white quartzite scree to green glens. When the sun glistens on the wet rock the scene is reminiscent of Foinaven or the eastern slopes of Beinn Eighe.

Inchnadamph is the best centre for exploring these mountains. The hotel is popular with walkers, fishermen, and student geologists for the rock structure of the area is exceedingly complex. The approach route to Conival is up Gleann Dubh, with the path following the Traligill river. Limestone outcropping occurs in the glen, and the associated lush grass and varied flora is a relief after the bogs which characterise so many northern hills.

In one place the Traligill river emerges from under a limestone cliff and, further up the glen, a number of caves can be seen. If you bring a torch you can amuse yourself exploring some of these underground chambers.

The main bulk of Conival fills the head of the glen, and it is tempting to make straight for the summit. However, a ring of crags guards this direct approach and it is best to head north-east, still following the burn, to reach the bouldery bealach between Conival and Beinn an Fhuarain.

The north ridge of Conival is broad but rough, and it gives wonderful views northwards across the desolate rocky hills of upper Glen Coul to the Reay Forest.

From Conival's summit, 3,234ft/987m, the ridge to Ben More Assynt can be seen snaking away to the east. A short scramble is needed to reach the bealach, before beginning the long ascent to the rock castles on the summit of Ben More Assynt, 3,272ft/998m.

If transport could be arranged the south-east ridge could be descended to Loch Dubh Beag, whence a long walk-out takes you past Benmore Lodge to the A837. But to return to Inchnadamph, retrace your footsteps to the col east of Conival and descend the grand Garbh Choire until you can traverse westwards, underneath cliffs, to reach the Conival – Breabag bealach.

Follow the Allt a'Bhealaich down into Gleann Dubh, meeting the path near the caves just two miles from Inchnadamph.

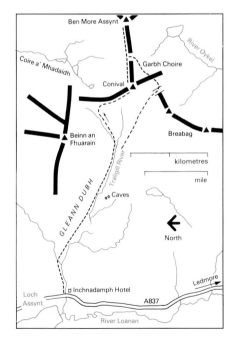

SUILVEN

Map *OS Sheet 15*   **Start/Finish** *Ledbeg (243133)/Lochinver (093225)*   **Distance/Time** *16 miles/26km, 8 hrs*

Grading *A stiff walk over remote and rough country. Some scrambling on Suilven's E ridge.*
Escape Routes *None. The easiest descent from Suilven is N from the bealach under Caisteal Liath.*
Transport *Bus services: Lairg/Lochinver and (summer) Ullapool/Lochinver.*
Accommodation *Hotels at Lochinver and Inchnadamph. B & B locally. Youth Hostels at Achmelvich and Ullapool.*

In the far north-west of Scotland, between Ullapool and the Kylesku bridge, lies the remarkable mountain scenery of Coigach and Assynt. The base rock is ancient Lewisian gneiss which provides a plinth for the spectacular peaks of Torridonian sandstone that rise separately as great monoliths of rock, many of them capped by white Cambrian quartzite.

Viewed from the A835 road Suilven appears as a serrated whale-back, but from the fishing village of Lochinver it is dramatic. The west end of Suilven rears over the village and completely dominates the view inland; this western summit is called Caisteal Liath, the Grey Castle. There is no other mountain in Scotland that makes more of its modest height, for it is only 2,399ft/731m.

Suilven is remote and difficult of access from any direction. The impervious gneiss holds many shallow lochs which interconnect and guard the steep flanks of the mountain.

Although the usual ways of ascent climb steep gullies to a low bealach on the main ridge, the best route traverses the entire ridge from east to west finishing at Lochinver. At the end of the day you should arrange transport back to the starting point at Ledbeg because the bus service is infrequent.

From Ledbeg it is a rough, tough, six-mile walk to the eastern rock pinnacle of Suilven. There is no path, but once over the low hill of Cnoc an Leathaid Bhig you have an uninterrupted view of your objective and this, together with the close proximity of Canisp, Stac Pollaidh and Cul Mor, will spur you on.

The ascent to the main ridge of Suilven is a simple scramble up a succession of ledges but, as you walk west, you arrive at a curious cleft in the sandstone strata which can easily be stepped across, and then at an abrupt drop where cliffs fall away for 100ft. The way down to the bealach involves an airy move down the north side of the ridge, followed by a traverse west to gain easier ground.

Pause amongst the scattered boulders on Suilven's summit and enjoy unsurpassed views of the mountains and the western seaboard, with waves breaking on scattered islands and rocks in Enard Bay.

From the low bealach east of Caisteal Liath descend the loose gully towards Loch na Gainimh to meet a stalkers' path. This runs westwards through the grounds of Glencanisp Lodge to the white-fish port of Lochinver.

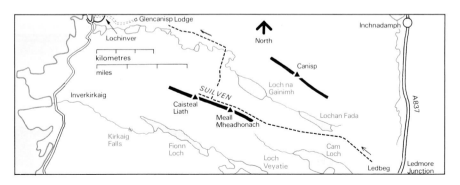

THE FORTRESSES OF CUL MOR AND CUL BEAG

Map OS Sheet 15   *Start/Finish* Loch Lurgainn (127089)   *Distance/Time* 11 miles/18km, 8 hrs

> **Grading** A serious expedition requiring precise navigation and some rock scrambling. Hazardous river crossings in wet weather.
> **Escape Routes** From Cul Mor descend the broad E ridge to the A835.
> **Transport** Bus services: Inverness/Ullapool; Ullapool/Achiltibuie; Ullapool/Inverkirkaig/Lochinver.
> **Accommodation** Hotels, B & B and Youth Hostels at Ullapool and Achiltibuie.

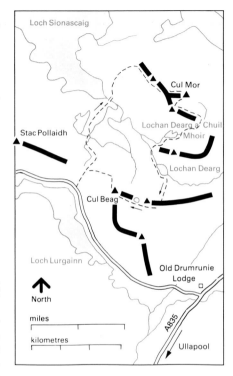

Between the bristles of Stac Pollaidh and the sublime outline of Suilven there lies a magnificently wild and lonely region of lochs, islands, tumbling rivers and ancient woodlands. Access from the east is guarded by Cul Mor and Cul Beag, two complex peaks which tend to be neglected by the walker.

From the south or west, Cul Mor is revealed as a formidable mountain. It rises abruptly from the base rock, the approach is protected by broken ground and a linked network of lochs and rivers, while great sweeps of bare rock fall from the summit plateau.

My recommended walk enters the heart of the mountains from the south, climbs the steep west nose of Cul Mor, descends to the secret Lochan Dearg a'Chuil Mhoir and then traverses Cul Beag. Steep scrambling, some

tricky route-finding and two potentially hazardous river crossings are involved.

A mile east of the Stac Pollaidh car-park a stalkers' track winds its way north to a sandy bay at the west end of Loch an Doire Dhuibh. Ford the exit stream of Lochan Gainmheich with care, and scramble up the blocks of Torridonian sandstone and loose gullies of the stubby west nose of Cul Mor.

A broad plateau rises gently to the true summit of Cul Mor, where the weathered sandstone gives way to angular boulders of grey quartzite.

Cul Mor provides expansive views: the classic silhouette of Suilven across Loch Veyatie, the peaks and pinnacles of Quinag, the primeval landscape below and, out in the west, the waves breaking white on the rugged coastline and islands of Enard Bay.

From the subsidiary summit of Creag nan Calman descend east to meet the burn which rushes through a ravine on its way to Lochan Dearg a'Chuil Mhoir. This is a lonely and beautiful loch with sandy bays, overlooked by ferocious 500ft cliffs on the north side. The loch's exit stream plunges 600ft into Gleann Laoigh in a series of cascades and you should

descend carefully, keeping to the left bank and avoiding rocky bluffs where necessary.

Once in Glenn Laoigh cross the stream and walk up to Lochan Dearg, above which is the first point of weakness in the Cul Beag cliffs.

The most satisfactory way off Cul Beag is straight down the steep north slopes to the bealach under Cioch a'Chuil Bhig, thence to the stalkers' path at Lochan Fhionnlaidh.

STAC POLLAIDH –
THE PERFECT MINIATURE

Map *OS Sheet 15*   **Start/Finish** *The Inverpolly Nature Reserve car-park (108095)*
Distance/Time *3 miles/5km, 3-4 hrs*

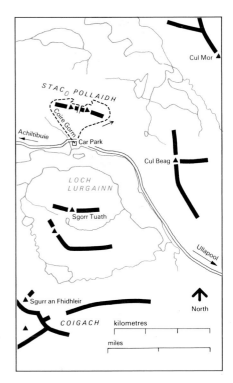

> **Grading** *A short walk involving steep slopes of loose rock and some exposed scrambling.*
> **Escape Routes** *Easy descents S or N from the bealach at the lowest point on the ridge.*
> **Transport** *Bus services: Inverness/Ullapool; Ullapool/Achiltibuie; Ullapool/Inverkirkaig/Lochinver.*
> **Accommodation** *Hotels, B & B and Youth Hostels at Ullapool and Achiltibuie.*

I always feel like laughing when, driving north from Ullapool, Stac Pollaidh bursts into view behind the tree-ringed loch at Drumrunie. It is impudent and mischievous in the way that it dispenses with preliminaries and rises straight out of the moorland, thrusting jagged, rocky spikes into the air like a fossilised stegosaurus.

Stac Pollaidh is a sandstone mountain, its heavy erosion being the result of successive ice ages and weathering for, unlike the neighbouring peaks of Cul Mor and Quinag, it has no protective cap of white quartzite.

North of the Inverpolly Nature Reserve car-park Stac Pollaidh rises in three giant steps, with the angle of the face ever increasing. Although it is possible to follow the worn path straight up the peat-hags and screes to the summit ridge, a much more rewarding route approaches from the north side.

Take the cairned path which makes a rising traverse, passing under the buttresses of the east summit and then zig-zagging up the loose northern slopes to meet the summit ridge at its lowest point.

The highest point of Stac Pollaidh lies at the extreme western end of the ridge, and it can be reached by a twenty-minute scramble. The confident climber will keep mainly to the exposed arête, but the walker may prefer to take the sandy path which winds along the south side of the mountain, under the sandstone tiers, until a narrow bealach is reached.

The walk is a delight, as the path meanders through gigantic bluffs and pinnacles of rounded, weathered sandstone, crosses the tops of steep gullies, and occasionally holds the airy crest of the ridge itself.

The western tower of Stac Pollaidh, on which is built the summit cairn, can only be reached by negotiating the celebrated *mauvais pas*. This takes the form of an exposed rock step, fifteen feet high, on which there are excellent holds, but it needs respect and a cool head. The inexperienced mountain walker should leave this step alone, since a slip could have disastrous consequences.

From the summit you can look over Enard Bay, the Summer Isles and Suilven, whose primeval shape dominates the landscape north across Loch Sionascaig.

Retrace your footsteps until the path traverses the top of a sandy scree run. Descend this to a lower path, which by-passes a lochan under the western end of Stac Pollaidh and leads down to the car-park.

BEN MORE COIGACH AND THE FIDDLER

Map OS Sheet 15   *Start/Finish* Culnacraig (064039)/Drumrunie Old Lodge (166053)
Distance/Time 10 miles/16km, 6 hrs

Grading *A fine mountain walk offering unsurpassed views over the NW seaboard. Some easy scrambling on the crest of the ridge.*
Escape Routes *From Ben More Coigach's summit descend the Allt nan Coisiche glen to Culnacraig.*
Transport *Bus services: Inverness/Ullapool; Ullapool/Achiltibuie; Ullapool/Inverkirkaig/Lochinver.*
Accommodation *Hotels, B & B and Youth Hostels at Ullapool and Achiltibuie.*

One of the best-loved views in north-west Scotland is that of the great wall of Ben More Coigach seen across Ardmair Bay, particularly when it is outlined against a fiery red sky.

The ancient, weathered sandstone gives the mile-long summit ridge of Ben More Coigach a saw-like appearance, and on the south side the slopes fall away extremely steeply. Behind the great ridge, on the west side, rise numerous satellite peaks, amongst which hidden glens, corries, lochans and cliffs abound. Much of this area is not visible from the narrow road which runs through the Inverpolly Nature Reserve, although it is possible to steal a glimpse of the plunging precipices of the Fiddler.

For the traverse of the main ridges of Ben More Coigach start from the road-end at

Culnacraig, just beyond Achiltibuie. Ford the Allt nan Coisiche at 1,000ft and make straight for the abrupt end of the ridge where you can savour the firm, rough sandstone and the ever-increasing views. This is peerless scrambling in an open situation, free of difficulty yet sufficiently exposed to heighten the senses.

The ridge rises in sandstone steps so steeply from the water's edge that a bird's-eye view is enjoyed of the islands, the skerries and the fishing boats. One could imagine tossing a stone straight into the sea.

If you can tear your eyes away from the Summer Isles and the white cottages dotted

around Badentarbat Bay, you can see right across the Minch to the low outline of the Harris hills.

A succession of rock towers and sandy paths make up the ridge leading east to the principal summit, 2,438ft/743m. The towers can easily be climbed direct, although sheep tracks provide alternatives for the timid.

The finest peak in Coigach is Sgurr an Fhidhleir (Fiddler's Rock), 2,285ft/703m, which rises to a sharp point one mile along the north-west ridge from the main top. This is a detour well worth making to see sheer cliffs on three sides, the home of ravens and golden eagles, and to enjoy unsurpassed views north over Suilven and Quinag to the Reay Forest peaks of Foinaven and Arkle.

Returning to the main massif, a steep descent leads to the whale-back ridge of Beinn Tarsuinn which, in turn, descends gradually to Lochanan Dubha. The junction by Old Drumrunie Lodge makes a convenient rendezvous for your transport.

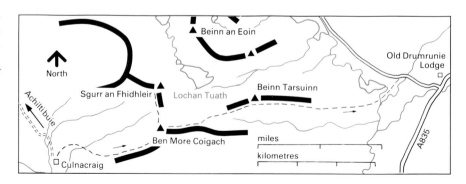

BEINN AN EOIN

Map OS Sheet 15   **Start/Finish** Loch Lurgainn (138066)   **Distance/Time** 4 miles/6km, 4 hrs

Grading A delightful half-day's walk over rarely visited sandstone hills in the heart of Coigach.
Escape Routes E from the lochan under Sgorr Tuath to the shore of Loch Lurgainn.
Transport Bus services: Inverness/Ullapool; Ullapool/Achiltibuie; Ullapool/Inverkirkaig/Lochinver.
Accommodation Hotels, B & B and Youth Hostels at Ullapool and Achiltibuie.

Just north of Ben More Coigach rise the delightful outliers of the Beinn an Eoin group. These compact hills can be walked in half the time necessary for the Ben More Coigach traverse. Choose an afternoon following a morning's rain, when the clouds are racing away leaving the air washed and sparkling, or a long summer evening: then Beinn an Eoin will provide an unforgettable walk.

From the south end of Loch Lurgainn it is a wet slog across saturated moorland to the base of Cioch Beinn an Eoin. Then, quite abruptly, the layered sandstone rears up, your hands come out of your pockets, and you are scrambling up over the ledges and through the gullies, picking whichever route takes your fancy. The occasional rowan or holly tree grows out of a fissure in the rock where it has been protected from grazing.

Easy walking across smooth glacier-scoured slabs of sandstone leads from the Cioch, along a broad ridge, to the 2,027ft/618m summit of Sgorr Deas. The ridge is littered with round boulders, scattered at random and unmoved since the retreat of the ice 10,000 years ago. Just below the summit, in a secluded hollow of the ridge, nestles a tiny lochan, its dark waters seemingly fathomless.

Across the glen the stupendous rock prow, the Fiddler, rises 1,000ft sheer above Lochan Tuath. Facing north and spending most of its time in shadow, the Fiddler makes a Very Severe, exposed and intimidating rock climb.

Another lonely loch is passed on the bealach under Sgorr Tuath. It is perfectly set in an amphitheatre of rock buttresses and, on my last visit, a pair of red-breasted mergansers were peacefully swimming on its wind-ruffled surface.

From the loch a scramble up through more gullies and rock towers leads to the ridge of Sgorr Tuath. The summit block is split by a gash, twenty foot deep, which could be a serious hazard under snow or white-out conditions.

The rock pinnacles of Sgorr Tuath have been sculptured into weird and fantastic shapes, providing the ideal foreground for views north to Quinag, Canisp, Suilven, Stac Pollaidh, Cul Mor, Stoer Point and, on a clear day, to Foinaven and the western cliffs of Handa Island.

Under a dark sky this is Norse-God country. It engenders a sense of wonder and awe, but it draws me back year after year.

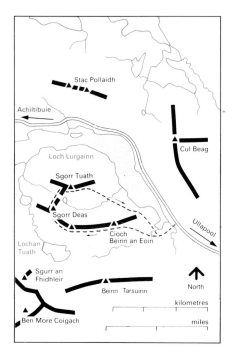

ACROSS THE BEINN DEARG FOREST: INVERLAEL TO OYKEL BRIDGE

Map OS Sheets 20 and 16   **Start/Finish** Inverlael (182853)/Oykel Bridge Hotel (8385009)
Distance/Time 23 miles/37km, 10-11 hrs

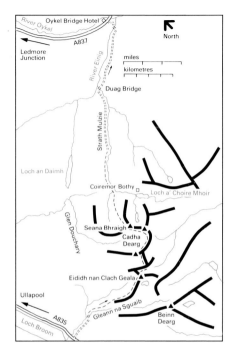

Grading A long and serious walk involving the traverse of one of Scotland's remotest mountains.
Escape Routes None. Emergency shelter could be found at Coiremor bothy.
Transport Bus services: Inverness/Ullapool passes through Inverlael; Lairg/Lochinver passes through Oykel Bridge.
Accommodation Oykel Bridge Hotel. Varied accommodation in Ullapool and Lairg. Youth Hostels at Ullapool and Carbisdale Castle.

Although the main cluster of peaks making up the Beinn Dearg Forest is reasonably accessible from the south, the northern outlier, Seana Bhraigh, is distinctly remote. It lies in a desolate and craggy region of the Northern Highlands, amongst steeply convoluted mountains and unspoilt glens, which can be visited on a demanding, yet delightful, expedition from Loch Broom to Oykel Bridge.

Take the track through Inverlael Forest into Gleann na Sguaib and, at Eas Fionn waterfall, strike straight up the rough heathery slopes to Eididh nan Clach Geala. From here you look across three miles of desolate wasteland to the west-facing crags of Seana Bhraigh. The going is tough through a maze of bogs, burns, peat hags, lochans, hillocks and crags.

On the north side of the plateau the ground falls away precipitously to Cadha Dearg, the corrie of upper Glen Douchary, and the most interesting route follows the lip of the cliffs. To the south, rough boggy ground, interspersed with rock outcrops, gradually descends to Gleann Beag which drains into the Dornoch Firth at Bonar Bridge. Since the Douchary river runs into the Atlantic, the plateau is a true watershed of Scotland.

Seana Bhraigh throws down wet, mossy cliffs into Cadha Dearg. Streams cascade down these cliffs which are of seamed and shattered schists producing terraces, chasms and fissures. The summit bears a stumpy OS pillar surrounded by a low circular wall of stones. Only feet away a wall of black rock plunges down over a thousand feet towards Loch Luchd Choire. This loch is enclosed by a cirque of vegetated cliffs rising to An Sgurr, a subsidiary summit of spiky rock on the northern end of Creag an Duine which commands the northeast side of the great amphitheatre.

Head north down the ridge with the full extent of Strath Mulzie running away into the distance, eight miles to the forestry plantation below Duag Bridge.

Strath Mulzie is wide and desolate, only narrowing at the upper end where Loch a'Choire Mhoir is enclosed between crags. The north ridge of Seana Bhraigh allows an enticing peep into the upper corrie where the lonely greystone cottage of Coiremor sits beside the Loch.

The walk-out, past Corriemulzie Lodge to Oykel Bridge is pleasant enough with the lively river your constant companion. In wet weather, though, the fording of the tributary, Allt a'Choire Bhuidhe, could pose a problem.

COAST TO COAST IN A DAY

Map OS Sheets 20 and 21   *Start/Finish* Inverlael (180861)/Ardgay (590892)   *Distance/Time* 33 miles/53km, 12 hrs

---

Grading A very long walk through lonely and uninhabited glens. River crossings could be difficult.
Escape Routes None. Emergency shelter could be found at Glenbeg bothy (313835).
Transport To return to starting point: train service Ardgay/Dingwall then bus service Dingwall/Inverlael.
Accommodation Hotels and B & B in Ullapool and Bonar Bridge. Youth Hostels at Ullapool and Carbisdale Castle.

Measurement and classification provide the framework for several challenging walks described in this book: Welsh 3,000s, Cairngorm 4,000s, Lakeland 3,000s and so on. From studying maps it became clear to me that Scotland is very thin in places, and the use of a pair of dividers confirmed that the country between Loch Broom and the Dornoch Firth is the thinnest of all.

Thus, early one summer's day, I set out from the seaweedy shores of Loch Broom and by evening had dipped my toes into the muddy waters of the Dornoch Firth. The crossing was not too arduous, the route very diverse, the scenery entrancing and the completion immensely satisfying.

From Inverlael you walk through the forest to emerge into Gleann na Sguaib, a superb glen in the best Scottish tradition. A lively river tumbles down in a series of cascades, running in places through deep, dark gorges, while the south side of the glen is bounded by broken cliffs overgrown with birch and rowan.

A narrow path winds up through a group of tiny lochans to the bealach at 2,750ft/838m, under the vast bulk of Beinn Dearg.

Pick your way down moraines to Loch Tuath, a remote and shallow loch decorated with reeds and water lilies. The loch is enclosed by great slabs of grey rock rising to the summit of Cnap Coire Loch Tuath on the north side, while Cona Mheall seals it off from the south.

Continue past Loch Prille, cross a tiresome area of black peat, and drop down to the broad strath of Gleann Beag, with the rocky turrets of Seana Bhraigh just appearing over the ridge.

Make for the open bothy of Glenbeg Cottage and then pass under the rugged, splintered cliffs of Carn Loch Sruban Mora. Soon afterwards the merry burn is channelled off into pipes, and a Land Rover track leads down the glen to the prosperous, whitewashed Deanich Lodge.

A long six-mile stretch of track through Gleann Mor lies ahead but, near Alladale Lodge, the bare hillsides sprout birch and willow, the river enters a gorge and the path twists through bracken, foxgloves and Caledonian pines.

You pick up a tarmaced road at Glencalvie Lodge and this runs north to a magnificent stand of pine, spruce, beech, oak and Wellingtonia trees in the grounds of Amat Lodge. The road follows the turbulent river Carron for ten miles, until it meets the Dornoch Firth at Ardgay.

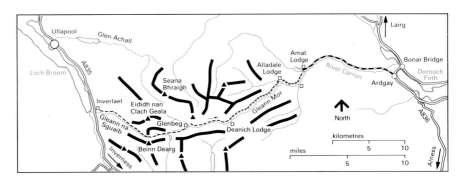

THE FANNICHS

Map OS Sheets 19 and 20   **Start/Finish** Loch Glascarnoch (278742)/Braemore Junction (209777)
Distance/Time 26 miles/42km, 12 hrs

Grading A long walk with considerable up and down work. Mainly good going underfoot.
Escape Routes From Sgurr Mor descend NE to the Mhadaidh Glen and A835. From Sgurr nan Clach Geala descend W to Loch a' Bhraoin.
Transport Railway station at Garve (13 miles). Bus service: Inverness/Ullapool passes the start and finish.
Accommodation Aultguish Inn. Dundonnell Hotel. Hotels, B & B and Youth Hostel in Ullapool.

The Fannichs are a compact group of mountains containing nine separate Munros, lying south of Braemore on the Garve–Ullapool road. The mountains are mainly rounded and grassy, although the highest peak, Sgurr Mor 3,637ft/1,110m, rises to a beautifully sharp and pointed summit which is prominent when looking back east from Loch Broom.

Except for two outlying peaks the entire range can be traversed in a single day, providing one of the most rewarding expeditions in the Highlands. The Beinn Dearg Forest hills and An Teallach are close neighbours of the Fannichs, while in clear weather Torridon, the Summer Isles and even the Outer Hebrides can all be seen.

At the western end of Loch Glascarnoch the road crosses the sizeable Torrain Duibh burn by a bridge. This is where you should leave the road and walk up beside the burn into the hills. The path soon peters out and you struggle through deep heather and hags and over hidden boulders and hummocky moraines.

After two miles strike up the heathery slopes of Meallan Buidhe, and then make for the summit of An Coileachan. The going becomes easier the higher you climb and, having won your first summit, at 3,015ft/923m, you can look forward to a high level walk of ten miles to A'Chailleach, the last peak of the day.

The ridge leading to the spire of Sgurr Mor is covered with moss and flat stones and it steepens considerably on the final slopes but, except in winter, it presents no difficulty.

Across Coire Mhoir to the west you will see, under Sgurr nan Clach Geala, a triangular face of bare rock. This is the largest rock face in the Fannichs and it provides many severe summer and winter climbs.

Descend to the small summit of Carn na Criche and then swing round to the north-east ridge of Sgurr nan Clach Geala. Continue to Sgurr nan Each and then drop steeply down to the watershed under the craggy eastern ridge of Sgurr Breac at 1,900ft.

Find a way through the rock outcrops to the ridge and walk easily across to A'Chailleach. The north ridge of A'Chailleach leads down to Loch a'Bhraoin, through stands of decaying Caledonian pines. Beside the loch you will meet a path which crosses the outflow by a bridge and eventually leads to the main road, three miles south of Braemore Junction.

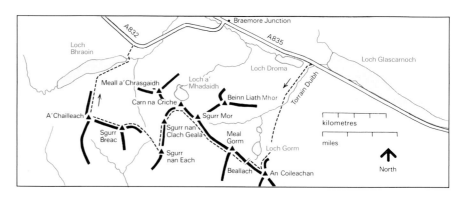

AN TEALLACH

Map *OS Sheet 19* **Start/Finish** *Dundonnell Hotel (089880)* **Distance/Time** *12 miles/19km, 9-10 hrs*

Grading A high and rugged mountain traverse. Some difficult rock climbing is involved if all the pinnacles are traversed but these may be avoided. Escape Routes S down Cadha Ghoblach between Corrag Bhuidhe and Sail Liath. Steep descent to Loch Toll an Lochain from bealach between Sgurr Fiona and Bidein a' Ghlas Thuill. Transport Bus service: Inverness/Braemore Junction/Ullapool. Infrequent service: Braemore Junction/Dundonnell. Accommodation Hotel and B & B in Dundonnell. Climbing Hut, The Smiddy, Dundonnell (JMCS). Youth Hostels Ullapool and Carn Dearg.

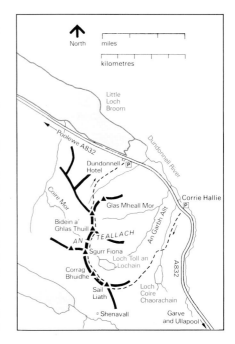

An Teallach (the Forge) engenders more awe and mystery than any other peak in Wester Ross. Glimpses of its saw-toothed summit ridge can be had from the Ullapool–Garve road near Loch Droma and on the steep descent to Dundonnell from Braemore, and these reinforce its legendary impregnability.

In the eighteenth century Thomas Pennant described the range as 'horrible and awful with summits broken, sharp and serrated and springing into all terrific forms'.

Although the complete traverse of the mountain, which includes two Munros, is a long and serious expedition, the rock-scrambling sections can easily be avoided. Thus I recommend An Teallach to all experienced hill walkers and

scramblers; it has few equals on the mainland of Britain.

Park at the lay-by near Corrie Hallie and take the Achneigie track south towards the Great Wilderness. The path crosses the Allt Gleann Chaorachain and zig-zags up to the plateau under Sail Liath. At the top of the path, marked by a cairn, the Shenavall track comes in from the west; follow this for a mile and then strike straight up the rough and bouldery slopes to the summit of Sail Liath.

The most interesting views are east to Beinn Dearg and the Fannichs, and south to the delightful rocky peak of Beinn Dearg Mhor – a miniature replica of An Teallach itself.

After a short, switchback section you arrive under the bristling pinnacles of Corrag Bhuidhe. On the north side the ground falls away sheer to the grey waters of Loch Toll an Lochain, lending a touch of exposure to the traverse. It is quite possible to keep entirely to the airy crest of the sandstone pinnacles, for the rock is sound and the holds ample, but the less confident can take a winding, sandy path that contours the rocks on the south side. A massive block, overhanging the abyss and known as Lord Berkeley's Seat, is passed

before the splendidly pointed summit of Sgurr Fiona is won.

The ridge now broadens and the main top, Bidein a' Ghlas Thuill (3,484ft/1,062m) comes as something of an anticlimax.

A well-marked path now descends to the bealach south of Glas Mheall Mor and thence to the burn running north-east under black boilerplate slabs. Here the enjoyment ends for the so-called 'Tourist Path' is boggy and badly drained and the Dundonnell Hotel comes as something of a relief.

[43]

BEINN DEARG MHOR
FROM SHENAVALL

Map OS Sheet 19　**Start/Finish** Corrie Hallie (114852)/Gruinard Bay (962912)
Distance/Time 18 miles/29km, 10-11 hrs

Grading A long expedition over remote and rugged mountains. Some rock scrambling involved and river crossings which could prove troublesome.
Escape Routes None. Emergency shelter at Shenavall bothy and boat house at W of Loch na Sealga.
Transport Infrequent bus services: Gairloch/Inverness and Ullapool/Gairloch.
Accommodation Dundonnell Hotel. Varied accommodation in Ullapool, Poolewe, Gairloch and Aultbea. Youth Hostels in Ullapool and Carn Dearg.

The stalkers' path from Corrie Hallie, leading south into the heart of the Fisherfield Forest, is the start of many of Scotland's greatest walks. It climbs up through Gleann Chaorachain to a loch-studded plateau and contours below the rough eastern slopes of An Teallach, where deep heather and slabs of red sandstone lead up to the pinnacles and buttresses of Coire an Lochain.

Opposite Loch Coire Chaorachain a narrow, cairned path branches off to the right, crosses the shoulder of Sail Liath and gradually descends to Shenavall bothy in Strath na Sealga.

Beinn Dearg Mhor, at only 2,974ft/908m, holds the centre of the stage. Its summit forms the apex of a semi-circle of cliffs ringing a high corrie. The symmetry is perfect and is reminiscent of the north corrie of Ben Lui, except that the scene is grander with deep gullies, split buttresses and rock towers.

Two unbridged rivers guard the base of Beinn Dearg Mhor and great care is needed in fording them; a rope should be carried as a safeguard.

A shallow green depression rises from the rough slopes behind Larachantivore cottage, leading to a band of rocks high up on Beinn Dearg Mhor. This is the direct route to the summit although an easier, but longer, alternative is to strike north from Gleann na Muice Beag into a wide corrie which leads straight to the summit ridge.

A great fang of rock overhangs the top of the north-facing corrie and the cairn is built just beyond, at the end of a short spur. Whatever the conditions it is a thrilling summit: in good weather the view extends south right across the wilderness of the Fisherfield Forest with rank after rank of rugged mountains, north to the jagged ridge of An Teallach, and when cloudy the mists swirl between black, dripping cliffs of bare rock, the abyss below your feet seemingly fathomless and like the gateway to hell.

Beinn Dearg Bheag, too, is a revelation adding an unexpected bonus to the day. Its long summit ridge is knife-edged, and it includes four rock turrets. Broken cliffs, blocks and towers of sandstone must be scrambled over in a manner worthy of the Torridonian giants to the south.

Descend the rocky west end of the mountain to reach Loch na Sealga, and the Land Rover track running beside the Gruinard River which roars a tempestuous course for six miles into Gruinard Bay.

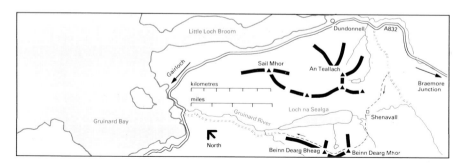

ACROSS THE GREAT WILDERNESS: DUNDONNELL TO POOLEWE

Map OS Sheet 19   **Start/Finish** Corrie Hallie (114852)/Poolewe (857808)   **Distance/Time** 29 miles/47km, 12 hrs

Grading An exceptionally long and arduous walk across a remote and mountainous wilderness.
Escape Routes None. Emergency shelter at Shenavall and Carnmore.
Transport Bus service: Inverness/Braemore Junction/Ullapool. Infrequent services: Inverness/ Poolewe; Braemore Junction/Dundonnell and Dundonnell/Poolewe.
Accommodation Dundonnell Hotel. Varied accommodation in Poolewe. Climbing Hut, The Smiddy, Dundonnell (JMCS). Youth Hostels in Ullapool and Carn Dearg.

Perhaps the most dramatic area of mountain wilderness in Britain lies in Ross-shire, between Loch Maree and Little Loch Broom. Certainly Munro baggers regard A'Mhaighdean, situated in the heart of this wilderness, as being their toughest proposition.

A traverse of the wilderness from Dundonnell to Poolewe, taking in the summits of Ruadh Stac Mor and A'Mhaighdean and skirting the mighty An Teallach and the elusive Beinn Dearg Mhor, is one of the finest expeditions in Britain. But, be warned, this is a major undertaking; bad weather can spring up unannounced and help is far away. Walkers must take full equipment and be prepared for any eventuality.

From Corrie Hallie take the Achneigie track which runs through woods of birch and hazel with wild roses, primroses and violets. At the cottage turn right to Shenavall bothy and cross the two rivers, which run through the Strath into Loch na Sealga, to pick up the path again at the estate cottage of Larachantivore. These are dangerous rivers and in wet weather a safety rope must be used.

The path now proceeds south up Glenn na Muice and then, at the impressive crag of Junction Buttress, turns right and ascends Glenn na Muice Beag. At Lochan Feith Mhic'il-lean leave the path and head straight for the rocky summit of Ruadh Stac Mor.

A'Mhaighdean rises south across a bealach and it is worth spending a few minutes on the summit of this prized Munro to appreciate the wildest of mountain scenes. Straight down below is the small Gorm Loch and beyond stretches Lochan Fada, with Slioch rising behind. Ahead is the long precipice of Beinn Lair and to the west the Dubh Loch nestles under dark cliffs, while the Fionn Loch runs north-west for six miles. Smaller lochs, each in their rock basins, abound.

Descend to the east end of Fuar Loch Mor and thence to Fuar Loch Beag and the Dubh Loch, where you meet the path from Carnmore, a remote house supplied in summer by boat across the Fionn Loch.

A very long and, in places, boggy path runs north-west to Kernsary and Poolewe, passing under the north face of Beinn Airigh Charr with its sweeping walls of clean grey rock.

Finally you meet a metalled road at Loch Kernsary which, together with the surrounding estate, was owned by Osgood MacKenzie who built the world famous gardens at Inverewe.

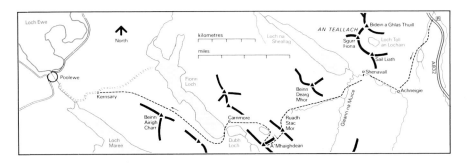

MULLACH COIRE MHIC FHEARCHAIR'S EAST RIDGE

Map OS Sheet 19 and 20   **Start/Finish** Loch a'Bhraoin roadhead (162760)/Corrie Hallie (114852)
Distance/Time 22 miles/35km, 10-11 hrs

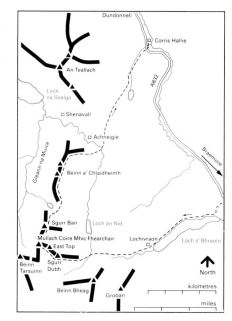

Grading A long and serious expedition over rough mountainous country, involving some rock scrambling and a difficult river crossing towards the end of the day.
Escape Routes Head S from Sgurr Dubh towards Kinlochewe. Emergency shelter at Shenavall bothy and Lochivraon cottage.
Transport Bus service: Inverness/Braemore Junction/Ullapool. Infrequent services: Braemore Junction/Dundonnell and Ullapool/Gairloch.
Accommodation Dundonnell Hotel. Varied accommodation in Ullapool, Aultbea and Poolewe. Climbing Hut, The Smiddy, Dundonnell (JMCS). Youth Hostels in Carn Dearg and Ullapool.

As you drive west from Garve along the A835 towards Ullapool, firstly the massive hump of Beinn Dearg, secondly the shapely peaks and high interconnecting ridges of the Fannichs and finally the splintered outline of An Teallach dominate the view. But if you turn off south at Braemore Junction and head for Dundonnell, another range of attractive peaks fills the horizon; these are the eastern outliers of the Great Wilderness, crowned by Mullach Coire Mhic Fhearchair at 3,326ft/1,019m.

Although the ascent of these remote peaks is usually accomplished from Shenavall bothy, often on a horseshoe round including A'Mhaighdean, a highly original and rewarding approach may be made from the east. Thus a seldom-used stalkers' path provides access from this direction, while a high-level traverse north from the Mullach leads over two Munros to the upper reaches of Strath na Sealga and the splendid Achneigie to Corrie Hallie path, described in several other chapters in this book.

Leave the A832 at a locked gate near the east end of Loch a'Bhraoin, follow the rough path to a boathouse beside the loch and continue along the water's edge to the decayed stalkers' cottage of Lochivraon. A mile or two further up the glen you pass the ruined bothy of Feinasheen, and then you are confronted by steep cliffs and enormous sheets of slabby rock falling from both Sgurr Ban and the east ridge of Mullach Coire Mhic Fhearchair.

To attain the East Ridge it is necessary to scramble up a grassy break or an easy gully. The higher you climb up the ridge the rockier and narrower it becomes until, beyond Sgurr Dubh, some quite airy sections are enjoyed. However, the short section linking the East Top to the main summit is quite straightforward.

A long and switchback ridge continues north over Sgurr Ban and Beinn a'Chlaidheimh, passing the lonely lochan of Loch a'Bhrisidh on the bealach. Spectacular views down to Gleann na Muice and up to Beinn Dearg Mhor and An Teallach are your constant companions as you negotiate the bruising quartzite boulders underfoot.

Easy grassy slopes run down in a north-easterly direction into upper Strath na Sealga where the river crossing can be exceedingly troublesome in wet weather. A safety rope should be carried and used without hesitation if the need arises.

Once over the river a broad track leads north to Loch Coire Chaorachain, the wooded Gleann Chaorachain and the car-park at Corrie Hallie.

BEINN LAIR AND
THE LOCH MAREE TRAVERSE

Map OS Sheet 15   *Start/Finish* Poolewe (857808)/Kinlochewe (028619)   *Distance/Time* 26 miles/42km, 10-11 hrs

Grading A long, tough walk across a remote and inhospitable region. In winter this itinerary should only be attempted by an experienced party.
Escape Routes None. Emergency shelter at Carnmore and Letterewe.
Transport Railway station at Achnasheen. Bus services: Gairloch/Kinlochewe/Achnasheen and (infrequently) Poolewe/Inverness.
Accommodation Hotels and B & B at Poolewe and Kinlochewe. Youth Hostels at Torridon and Carn Dearg.

Slioch, Beinn Lair, Meall Mheinnidh and Beinn Airigh Charr form a high wall of mountains running along the north side of Loch Maree from Kinlochewe to Poolewe. They delineate the southern boundary of the 'Great Wilderness' containing the Strathnasheallag and Fisherfield Forests. Not until An Teallach is passed and Dundonnell is reached is there a permanent dwelling: 19 miles as the crow flies.

From the south, Slioch, rising like a fortress above Loch Maree, provides one of the classic mountain views in Britain. However, when seen from the remote peaks north of Lochan Fada, Mullach Coire Mhic Fhearchair, Beinn Tarsuinn and A'Mhaighdean, it is the line of plunging cliffs on Beinn Lair that draws the eye. An early guidebook reported: 'Beinn Lair

possesses, for a distance of two-and-a-half miles, what is possibly the grandest inland line of cliffs to be found in Scotland.

The route into the mountains from Poolewe takes the private road along the north bank of the River Ewe to Inveran, and then to the cottage at Kernsary.

Although the Carnmore path is narrow, boggy and indistinct it is vastly preferable to ploughing through coarse grass, heather and hags. A large burn rushes through Strathan Buidhe, but it is bridged high up and an excellent stalkers' path continues over the pass to Letterewe.

Turn off the Letterewe path at the Allt Folais and climb back up to the Bealach Mheinnidh under the west ridge of Beinn Lair. Hug the edge of the great north-facing cliffs for a mile and then head south-west to the huge quartzite cairn on the summit of Beinn Lair. Continue eastwards over the outlier of Sgurr Dubh and then descend to meet a path at Loch Garbhaig.

The Abhainn na Fuirneis foams down to Loch Maree in a series of spectacular waterfalls, the path following the burn to the lochside. In the early eighteenth century, iron ore was smelted with charcoal at Furnace for the manufacture of cannons, and much of the old oak forest was felled. Nevertheless, the oak woods that remain on the north side of Loch Maree are some of the finest in the Highlands.

A delightful switchback path runs through the woods to Kinlochewe. Loch Maree, looking its most majestic, stretches away to the west, waves lap the shores of tiny bays while cascades of water streak down from the upper slopes of Slioch.

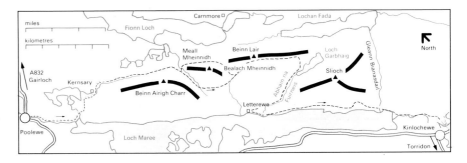

SLIOCH

Map *OS Sheet 19 (Outdoor Leisure 8)*   **Start/Finish** *Kinlochewe Hotel (028620)*   **Distance/Time** *18 miles/29km, 8 hrs*

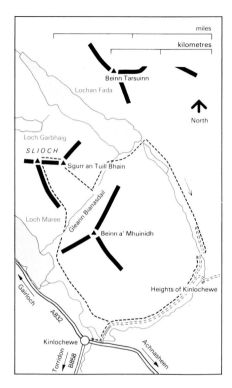

> **Grading** *A classic Highland mountain walk. Most of the route follows a path, but some rough terrain must be negotiated on Slioch itself.*
> **Escape Routes** *None. The nearest shelter and available help is at Kinlochewe.*
> **Transport** *Railway station at Achnasheen. Bus services: Inverness/Achnasheen/Kinlochewe.*
> **Accommodation** *Hotels at Kinlochewe and Loch Maree. Ling Hut in Glen Torridon (SMC). Youth Hostel at Torridon.*

If there is one view which sums up the beauty of the West Highland scene, it is that of snow-capped Slioch seen across the blue waters of Loch Maree. Gnarled Scots pines on the south bank of the loch make the perfect foreground, while the proud oaks of Letterewe clothe the lower slopes of Slioch, under the buttresses of rich Torridonian sandstone.

Nowadays it is not usually possible to secure a boat to take you across Loch Maree, to make a direct assault on Slioch, but the alternative approach from Kiniocnewe is equally delightful.

From the Land Rover track leading to Heights of Kinlochewe, a path branches off to the west and runs along the north bank of the Kinlochewe river. You pass through decayed woods of oak, alder and birch while waves lap the pebbly shoreline of Loch Maree. Above the

path precipitous slopes fall from Mealan Ghobar, and the rock is streaked with foam after a night's rain.

Beinn a'Mhuinidh throws down glistening buttresses into the remarkable rift of Gleann Bianasdail, while the burn roars down a deep ravine which is bridged a short way up from the loch.

Take the path which winds up into Gleann Bianasdail on the west side of the burn, and look out for the herd of wild goats which frequents this rugged and desolate region.

Leave the path at some waterfalls and climb the grassy, ledgy southern slopes of Meall Each to reach a lochan on the bealach under Sgurr Dubh.

The long south-east ridge of Slioch makes a fascinating ascent; two lochans are passed on the shoulder and then steep, bouldery slopes lead to the broad summit at 3,217ft/980m. To the south you can look to Flowerdale and the northern corries of Beinn Eighe, to the north the complex hills and corries of Fisherfield can be seen extending from Beinn Lair to An Teallach while below Loch Maree and its tree-covered islands runs west for twelve miles. The eastern slopes of Slioch fall into a green,

grassy corrie in which deer can often be seen grazing.

The stony ridge curves round to Sgurr an Tuill Bhain and an easy descent into upper Gleann Bianasdail. Cross the burn as it flows into Lochan Fada and walk past several delectable sandy bays at the eastern end of the loch to meet a broad track running back to Kinlochewe.

THE PEAKS OF THE FLOWERDALE FOREST

Map OS Sheet 19 (Outdoor Leisure 8) *Start/Finish* Am Feur Loch on the Kinlochewe–Gairloch road (856720)
Distance/Time 24 miles/39km, 10-11 hrs

Grading A long mountain walk in a very remote area. Some airy scrambling on the ridge of Beinn Dearg.
Escape Routes From the E summit of Beinn Dearg descend S to Coire Dubh or Coire Mhic Nobuil. Emergency shelter at Poca Buidhe bothy or Loch na h-Oidhche boat house.
Transport Railway station at Achnasheen. Bus services: Gairloch/Achnasheen and Gairloch/Inverness.
Accommodation Hotels at Kinlochewe, Loch Maree and Gairloch. B & B locally. Youth Hostels at Torridon, Carn Dearg and Craig.

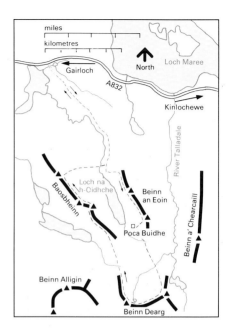

Flowerdale Forest: the name alone should be sufficiently emotive to entice walkers to this remote region of Ross-shire. Yet few visitors venture west of the Torridon giants.

When viewed from the lofty heights of Liathach's Spidean a'Choire Leith or Beinn Eighe's Ruadh-stac Mor, much of the Flowerdale Forest appears flat and boggy, a desolate area criss-crossed by rivulets and patterned with a mosaic of tiny lochans. A bleak and watery world, not unlike Coigach to the north. But the quality of the landscape is transformed by three superb individual peaks which rear up from the sandstone bedrock to a height of nearly 3,000ft. Baosbheinn, Beinn an Eoin and Beinn Dearg have fine ridges linking their principal summits which throw down steep, gully-seamed shoulders enclosing wild corries and dark lochans.

The Flowerdale Forest peaks are not easily won. A stalkers' path runs in for six miles, from the Gairloch–Loch Maree road to a boat house at the northern end of Loch na h-Oidhche, but from there onwards the going is trackless. You must pick your own way up the steep, rough slopes of heather and boulders and negotiate your own route through the crags and along the ridges which, on Beinn Dearg, are exposed and require some scrambling ability.

It is a steep pull up from Loch na h-Oidhche to the ridge of Beinn an Eoin, which gives glorious views of the islets and bays of Loch Maree, the oak woodlands of Letterewe and the stupendous massif of Slioch.

Broken slopes west of the summit lead to the cottage of Poca Buidhe and to the barren wilderness of glacier-scoured sandstone, shallow pools and rock debris under Beinn Dearg.

A green gully provides a simple route to Carn na Feola, the eastern summit of Beinn Dearg, but to attain the main top, at 2,995ft/914m, some exposed scrambling is required, reminiscent of the Corrag Bhuidhe buttresses of An Teallach. Beinn Dearg provides a thrilling insight into the jaws of Liathach: the plunging cliffs of Coire na Caime, the northern pinnacles and the Am Fasarinen pinnacles.

As you wind your way up through the sandstone formations on Ceann Beag, Beinn Alligin and the Horns thrust purposefully into the sky across Loch a'Bhealaich. The Baosbheinn ridge continues north in a series of rocky turrets before descending to a broad shoulder. The approach path is regained below An Reidh-choire.

BEINN EIGHE, A TORRIDON GIANT

Map *OS Sheet 25 (Outdoor Leisure 8)*   **Start/Finish** *Glen Torridon (958568)/Kinlochewe Hotel (028620)*
Distance/Time *13 miles/21km, 8-9 hrs*

> **Grading** *A long traverse over one of Scotland's grandest mountains. Some rock scrambling is involved and a safety rope should be carried.*
> **Escape Routes** *Steep quartzite screes can be descended to the Torridon road from many places on the main ridge.*
> **Transport** *Bus services: Inverness/Kinlochewe and Kinlochewe/Torridon.*
> **Accommodation** *Hotels at Kinlochewe and Torridon. Ling Hut in Glen Torridon (SMC). Youth Hostel at Torridon.*

As you drive down Glen Torridon from the north Beinn Eighe presents unrelenting slopes of white quartzite screes, and then Liathach bursts into view and takes the prize with its terraced walls and pinnacles of sandstone. I am reminded of Ruskin's lines:

> 'These great cathedrals of the earth,
> with their gates of rock, pavements
> of cloud, choirs of stream and stone,
> altars of snow, and vaults of purple
> traversed by the continual stars!'

From the west, however, it is Beinn Eighe which wins the day because its principal peak, Ruadh-stac Mor, 3,309ft/1,010m, falls away in the stupendous Coire Mhic Fhearchair. The summit ridge of Beinn Eighe is as narrow and

airy as Liathach's and, it too, provides a serious mountaineering expedition, particularly in winter.

From the Coire Dubh car-park take the path that keeps to the west side of the burn. You pass under the eastern prow of Liathach and then cross the burn to make a rising traverse of the rough shoulder of Sail Mhor.

As you work round to the north side of Sail Mhor you pass under towering buttresses of red sandstone and then, quite suddenly, you are in Coire Mhic Fhearchair, confronted by one of the most dramatic sights in all Scotland. A dark lochan spills out over the lip of the corrie in a cascade of waterfalls, while above

the lochan rise three giant buttresses of white quartzite standing on a plinth of sandstone. The cliffs are fully 1,300ft high and provide excellent rock climbing on clean, sound quartzite.

The view looking west out of the corrie mouth is equally delightful, but in complete contrast to the triple buttresses. The hills of the Flowerdale Forest rise abruptly from the flat, boggy floor, Beinn an Eoin and Baosbheinn being particularly prominent.

On the east side of the corrie easy but exasperating scree slopes run up to the summit cairn of Ruadh-stac Mor.

The main ridge runs east from Coinneach Mhor over the subsidiary summits of Spidean Coire nan Clach, Sgurr Ban, Sgurr an Fhir Duibhe and Creag Dubh. Care is needed in places, particularly on the rock teeth known as the Black Men of Sgurr an Fhir Duibhe. There is no easy way round these obstacles.

From the last summit, Creag Dubh, follow the eastern ridge down towards the Allt a'Chuirn which meets the road one mile south of Kinlochewe.

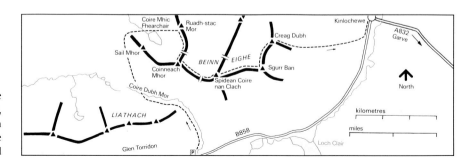

LIATHACH

Map OS Sheet 25 (Outdoor Leisure 8)   **Start/Finish** Glen Torridon car-park (958568)/Torridon House (869576)
Distance/Time 9 miles/14km, 7 hrs

Grading A magnificent high mountain traverse which can become serious in bad conditions. A safety rope should be carried.
Escape Routes Once the traverse has been started there are no easy descents from the ridge until W of Mullach an Rathain.
Transport Bus services: Inverness/Kinlochewe and Kinlochewe/Torridon.
Accommodation Hotels at Kinlochewe and Torridon. Ling Hut in Glen Torridon (SMC). Youth Hostel at Torridon.

Liathach towers above Glen Torridon as a stupendous monolith of bare rock, and when it is clothed in fresh snow and viewed across Loch Clair (one of the classic mountain views in Britain) it looks impregnable. In winter the traverse of Liathach is a major mountaineering expedition, but in good conditions it can be safely accomplished by experienced hill walkers with a good head for heights and some scrambling ability.

However, once a party has embarked upon the traverse of the three-mile summit ridge, they are committed to finish it or to return by the route of ascent, for the ridge is poised over rock buttresses and towers and few escape routes can be found.

Start the walk from the Coire Dubh car-park in Glen Torridon. Since the eastern top of Liathach, Stuc a'Choire Dhuibh Bhig, is precipitous on the Coire Dubh side it is best to ascend Coire Liath Mhor on the south side to gain access to the ridge proper.

Walk down the road for a mile and then strike up the steep hillside beside the Allt an Doire Ghairbh. For a few hundred feet there is a rough path, but after that you must pick your own way through the rock outcrops until you arrive at the bealach on the ridge. The bealach is mid-way between the eastern top and the impressive triangular-shaped face of Spidean a'Choire Leith, 3,456ft/1,054m.

The traverse ahead over Spidean a'Choire Leith to the western summit of Mullach an Rathain is sheer delight. Although the going is always interesting and demanding you have time to appreciate the dramatic rock scenery on both sides and the tantalising glimpses of the remote Flowerdale Forest peaks beyond Beinn Dearg.

Having descended from Spidean a'Choire Leith you arrive at the famous Pinnacles of Am Fasarinen, where the ridge narrows to a razor edge. The drop on the north side is sheer and the exposure is high, but the difficulties are short-lived and can be avoided altogether by a detour path 100ft below.

After the Pinnacles the ridge broadens out and becomes grassy for a stretch before climbing again to the bouldery summit of Mullach an Rathain. Descend the quartzite slopes west for half-a-mile and then, on the south side, you will find a scree shoot which can be run right down to the heather just above Torridon Village.

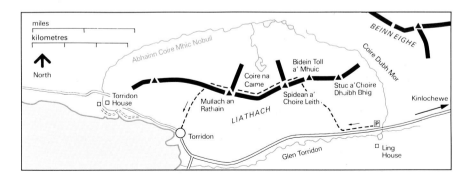

BEINN ALLIGIN,
THE JEWEL OF TORRIDON

Map *OS Sheet 24 (Outdoor Leisure 8)*   **Start/Finish** *Car-park near the Coire Mhic Nobuil road bridge (867577)*
Distance/Time *9 miles/14km, 7 hrs*

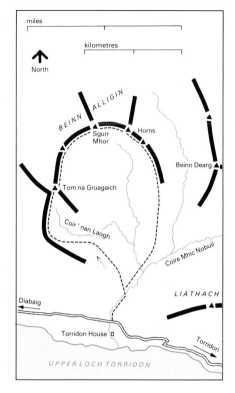

Grading *A fine traverse of a lofty mountain ridge, involving some mild scrambling. Much more serious under full winter conditions.*
Escape Routes *From Tom na Gruagaich descend SW. The Horns may be bypassed on the S side.*
Transport *Bus services: Inverness/Kinlochewe; Kinlochewe/Torridon and Torridon/Inver Alligin.*
Accommodation *Hotel, B & B and Youth Hostel in Torridon village. Ling Hut in Glen Torridon (SMC).*

Of the giants of Torridon, Liathach and Beinn Eighe engender awe, with their uncompromisingly steep shoulders, deep corries and towering buttresses of striated sandstone. Beinn Alligin, which rises above Loch Torridon a few miles west of Liathach, is altogether more modest. It too throws down sandstone cliffs from narrow ridges, but it presents a friendlier face to the world. When Beinn Alligin is seen from across the blue water of Loch Torridon, bathed in spring sunshine and capped with snow, it fully justifies its nickname of the Jewel of Torridon. The mountain is owned by the National Trust for Scotland and access is unrestricted at all times of the year.

From the car-park beside the bridge over the Amhainn Coire Mhic Nobuil, take the stalkers' path on the east side of the burn and walk through woods of Scots pine, birch, alder and rhododendron. Cross the burn by a wooden bridge and make your way up the rough and boggy lower slopes of Coir' nan Laogh.

South of the corrie the nose of Na Fasreidhnean rears up in steps of broken crags and grassy ledges. Tackle the nose direct, it gives easy scrambling in some airy situations and you hardly notice you are gaining height, until suddenly you reach the south ridge of Tom na Gruagaich. An alternative (easier) route follows the corrie burn to the plateau of Tom na Gruagaich.

Tom na Gruagaich has a line of crags overlooking the fearsome corrie of Toll a'Mhadaidh, which falls sheer from Alligin's main summit, Sgurr Mhor, 3,232ft/985m. The face of Sgurr Mhor is rent by a deep cleft, where a sizeable slice of rock fell away in a previous era. A wide fan of scree and a chaos of boulders on the corrie floor is evidence of this remarkable rock fall.

Carefully descend the rocks north of Tom na Gruagaich and follow the corrie rim round onto Sgurr Mhor. A magnificent vista opens out: west across the Sound of Raasay to the Quirang, south to Beinn Damh and Applecross, and north to the remote Flowerdale Forest.

The east ridge extension of Alligin takes you over three Rathains, or Horns. This involves an exciting traverse of sandstone pinnacles and can be the highlight of the day. The descent from the third Horn is simple: a cairned path leads down to the Allt a'Bhealaich burn and Coire Mhic Nobuil.

BEINN DAMH

Map OS Sheets 24 and 25   **Start/Finish** Loch Torridon Hotel (887542)   **Distance/Time** 9 miles/14km, 6-7 hrs

> **Grading** An exhilarating mountain walk along a broad ridge giving fine views of the Torridon peaks. A steep, scrambly descent is involved.
> **Escape Routes** Descend easily into Coire Roill from the bealach between Beinn Damh and Sgurr na Bana Mhoraire.
> **Transport** Railway stations at Lochcarron and Achnasheen. Bus service: Lochcarron station/ Torridon.
> **Accommodation** Hotels at Torridon, Shieldaig and Lochcarron. B & B locally. Youth Hostel at Torridon.

Beinn Damh misses Munro status by just forty-three feet and is thus left mostly undisturbed. Yet, from its northern outlier, Sgurr na Bana Mhoraire, a lofty and stony ridge runs over two miles south to its principal summit at 2,957ft/902m. This ridge provides an inspiring mountain walk, worthy of Beinn Damh's position amongst the giants of Torridon.

In its heyday the Ben-Damph estate was thriving deer forest, and the adjacent craggy mountains, giving way to well-wooded lower slopes, ravines and waterfalls combined to make a romantic Highland scene. Fortunately the great days of the estate have left a legacy of beautifully constructed stalkers' paths, which make for easy walking into the heart of the mountains.

Beside the road bridge over the Allt Coire Roill, a gate gives access to a path running up through woods towards Beinn Damh. Gaps in the trees allow views down to some magnificent cascades and falls, as the burn thunders through a ravine.

Once clear of the trees the path zig-zags up to the saddle under the north-west ridge of Beinn Damh. It is well worth deviating north along the bouldery ridge to gain the turret-like summit of Sgurr na Bana Mhoraire, which commands a panoramic view of the Sound of Raasay, the Cuillin, the corries of Applecross, Beinn Alligin and Liathach.

Having regained the saddle, proceed south along the whale-back ridge which becomes rugged underfoot as the rounded sandstone gives way to angular blocks of quartzite. Height may be saved by following a cairned path which contours two subsidiary summits on the west side.

Beinn Damh's cairn is perched above awesome cliffs, a craggy spur runs out to the north, while on the southern slopes light-coloured rocks form a strange stirrup-shaped mark which is clearly visible from the Kishorn road and the Applecross hills. The cliff-girt massif of Maol Chean-dearg rises above Glen a'Bhathaich as an immense sugar loaf.

Scramble down the sharp south-east ridge until you reach a gap, from here it is possible to descend steeply into a wide corrie. Climb back over the Drochaid Coire Roill to meet a stalkers' path running back to Loch Torridon. This path provides a close view of Beinn Damh's east-facing cliffs. Towering up in tiers of black rock and seamed with fissures they look very fierce in the shadow of a late afternoon.

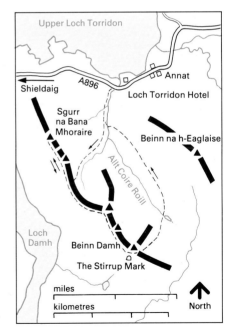

THE APPLECROSS HILLS

Map OS Sheet 24   *Start/Finish* Tornapress, E of Loch Kishorn (838422)   *Distance/Time* 13 miles/21km, 7-8 hrs

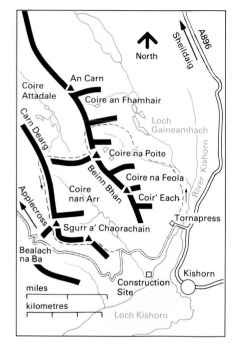

Grading A long day amongst rugged and rocky mountains. Difficult route finding in mist.
Escape Routes Descend S into Coire nan Arr from Bealach nan Arr.
Transport Railway stations at Lochcarron and Achnasheen. Bus service: Lochcarron station/ Torridon passes through Kishorn.
Accommodation Hotels at Lochcarron, Shieldaig and Torridon. B & B at Kishorn. Youth Hostels at Torridon and Kyle of Lochalsh.

Like freshly baked loaves, removed from the oven and set out in a line to cool, the Applecross Hills sit squatly on the barren moors west of Glen Shieldaig.

Even by Torridon standards the corries and buttresses of the Applecross Hills are impressive, with miles of cliffs and acres of steep, bare rock. On the north side Beinn Bhan sends down four great corries ringed by cliffs. Proceeding south, the wide Coire nan Arr penetrates deeply into the hills dividing Beinn Bhan from Sgurr a'Chaorachain, whose mighty eastern peak towers above the Howard Doris construction yard on the shores of Loch Kishorn.

Fascinating and awe-inspiring, this walk runs under the corries of Beinn Bhan, climbs the rocky ridge to the northern summit of the mountain, traverses round the cliff-edge of Coire nan Arr to Sgurr a'Chaorachain, and then descends the terraced nose to the road. There is no path, and it calls for some scrambling and route-finding ability and a good head for heights.

From the bridge at Tornapress, take the Loch Gaineamhach path for a mile and then make a rising traverse to Lochan Coire na Poite. This is a lonely lochan in a wild amphitheatre. A buttress of rock rises dizzily for 1,000ft into the main corrie, while a natural rock dam forms an inner corrie enclosing two more lochans.

The north side of the corrie is enclosed by a broad ridge of broken sandstone outcrops, and this provides an entertaining route of ascent to the summit plateau of Beinn Bhan.

Surprisingly, you meet a shallow lochan surrounded by lush grass on Beinn Bhan. Hug the edge of the cliffs to give yourself sensational views down plunging precipices into the heart of Coire na Poite, as well as west to Dun Caan on Raasay and the Quirang on Skye.

From the 2,936ft/896m summit, it is a long and rough descent over shattered boulders to Bealach nan Arr and subsequent ascent to the radio mast on Sgurr a'Chaorachain. Quickly pass this hideous intrusion and scramble along the narrow east ridge to the principal summit. You gain a close view of the prodigious Cioch buttress which juts out into Coire nan Arr like the prow of an ocean liner.

Experienced mountaineers can negotiate the very steep, terraced abutment of Sgurr a'Chaorachain to descend directly towards Tornapress. Others must return to the radio mast and descend easy slopes to Bealach na Ba.

THE LOCH MULLARDOCH CIRCUIT

Map OS Sheet 25   *Start/Finish* Mullardoch dam (220317)   *Distance/Time* 38 miles/61km, 3-4 days

Grading A long and serious backpacking expedition over some of the largest and loneliest mountains in the Highlands. A major undertaking in winter.
Escape Routes From Carnach to Killilan and Dornie. From bealach E of Sgurr nan Ceathreamhnan S to Alltbeithe Youth Hostel.
Transport Bus services: Inverness/Beauly and Beauly/Cannich.
Accommodation Hotels and B & B at Cannich. Youth Hostels at Cannich, Ratagan and Alltbeithe (Glen Affric).

The vast tract of wild mountainous country running north from Kintail to Achnasheen is almost uninhabited. It is the abode of arctic hares, deer, foxes, ptarmigan and eagles, and the high ridges are only visited by the occasional stalker and a few intrepid hill walkers.

Twelve Munros overlook the pencil-thin Loch Mullardoch, and most can be reached only by hours of arduous walking, thus the circuit is particularly suited to a backpacking expedition of several days.

In winter or early spring this major expedition can provide a test of mountaineering ability and commitment unrivalled in Britain. High mountain camping in snow always demands expertise, first-class equipment and a cool head. But the Mullardoch hills are exceptionally isolated and exposed; help is far away and in the face of a fierce blizzard, survival rather than progress may be paramount.

From the Mullardoch dam, eight miles west of Cannich, easy grassy slopes run up to Carn nan Gobhar which is linked to Sgurr na Lapaich by a narrow ridge. But, continuing west, it is necessary to descend steep boulder slopes, in a southerly direction for 600ft, before working round to the bealach under the long east ridge of An Riabhachan.

For three miles, en route to An Socach, this ridge twists and turns and rises and falls, imparting a feeling of freedom and spaciousness. Descend An Socach to Loch Mhoicean, where you meet the Land Rover track to Iron Lodge and Carnach.

It is worth detouring to visit the impressive Falls of Glomach, before climbing the north-west ridge to the summit of Sgurr nan Ceathreamhnan, that most celebrated of West Highland peaks. The way ahead can now be seen clearly: steeply down the curved east ridge to another An Socach, and then up and across the massive head and shoulders of Mam Sodhail and Carn Eige.

To walk slowly along this magnificent ridge, savouring the corries, the lochans and the views down to the exquisite woods of Affric, while surrounded by the silhouettes of familiar and much-loved hills, is all we can ask of life. When carrying a tent and provisions the pressure is off, it is easy to drop down a short way from the ridge and find a sheltered nook for the night.

Tom a'Choinich gives a sporting scramble over rock gendarmes, but Toll Creagach presents no difficulty and grassy slopes run down gently to Mullardoch dam.

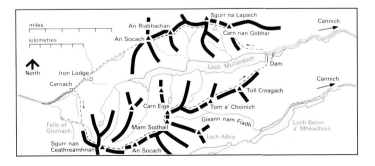

GLEN AFFRIC AND MAM SODHAIL

Map OS Sheets 25 and 33   **Start/Finish** Loch Beinn a'Mheadhoin (215242)/Cluanie Inn (075117)
Distance/Time 26 miles/42km, 13-14 hrs

Grading An exceptionally long and arduous mountain traverse. The few stretches of rock scrambling can be avoided.
Escape Routes From Bealach Coire Ghaidheil descend S to Glen Affric. Alltbeithe Y.H. is left unlocked even in winter.
Transport Bus services: Beauly/Cannich and Glasgow/Portree which passes Cluanie Inn.
Accommodation Hotels and B & B at Cannich. Cluanie Inn. Youth Hostels at Cannich, Ratagan and Alltbeithe (Glen Affric).

This magnificent and demanding walk takes you across the main watershed of Scotland and traverses the highest range of mountains north of the Great Glen. It is Scotland at its most wild, remote and beautiful. The mountains attract a great deal of snow and a sunny spring day spent on this traverse, when the snow is crisp and frozen, is quite peerless.

Make sure your party is fit and competent, and arrange for accommodation or a car at the finish, which is at the Cluanie Inn in Kintail.

Start the walk from the bridge at the entrance to Glen Fiadh, two miles short of Affric Lodge. A good path runs up beside the burn but, after a mile-and-a-half strike northwards up steep grass to Toll Creagach. Ahead lies a ridge walk of eleven miles, much of it high above the thin,

grey Loch Mullardoch to the north, and the Loch Affric/Beinn a'Mheadhoin system to the south. The latter lochs are exquisitely set amongst stands of Caledonian pines and birch.

Proceeding west you cross Tom a'Choinich, which has several narrow sections guarded by rock pinnacles, and then climb the rounded shoulders of the massive peaks of Carn Eige and Mam Sodhail. There is no higher ground in Scotland north of Carn Eige, 3,877ft/1,183m, but Mam Soul is the best viewpoint, considered by many to be unsurpassed in Britain. It was one of the principal sighting stations during an

early survey of Scotland, and the ruins of a stone shelter used by the surveyors can be seen near the summit cairn.

The next major objective, Sgurr nan Ceathreamhnan, can be seen rising high above its neighbours, five miles away as the crow flies. But the intervening ridge is broad and undulating and the twin summits of Ceathreamhnan beckon you on. With five grand corries, bounded by five major ridges, Ceathreamhnan can match any peak in Scotland for sheer beauty. It is a mountain for the serious walker and mountaineer, not for the tourist – its remoteness sees to that.

The grassy south ridge can be descended to the swift River Affric; don't risk a dangerous crossing but detour three-quarters of a mile to the bridge near Alltbeithe Youth Hostel.

After such an invigorating high-level traverse it is inevitable that the boggy path over the 1,370ft bealach to the An Caorunn Mor and Cluanie comes as rather an anticlimax..

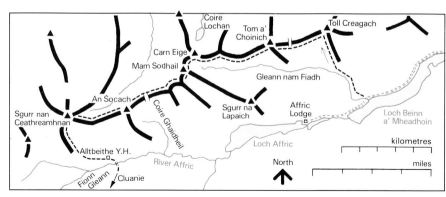

KINTAIL: THE FIVE SISTERS RIDGE

Map *OS Sheet 33*   **Start/Finish** *Cluanie Inn (075117)/Shiel Bridge(935190)*   **Distance/Time** *14 miles/23km, 9-10 hrs*

Grading *A high level mountain walk over an undulating and, at times, rocky ridge.*
Escape Routes *The low bealach W of Saileag provides a simple descent to Glenshiel.*
Transport *Bus services: Glasgow/Portree and Inverness/Portree which pass through Glenshiel.*
Accommodation *Hotels at Cluanie and Shiel Bridge. Youth Hostels at Ratagan and Kyle of Lochalsh.*

Perhaps Scotland's most classic romantic view is that of Eilean Donan Castle, with the Five Sisters of Kintail in the background rising above the blue waters of Loch Duich. However, the much-loved Five Sisters are only the most westerly group of a long ridge of mountains, running north of Glen Shiel from Cluanie to the head of Loch Duich.

The highest of the Sisters is Sgurr Fhuaran, which throws out massive grassy shoulders to the west; these slopes, 3,500ft high, are possibly the longest in all Scotland.

The complete traverse of these eight mountains makes a long and arduous, but very rewarding, day and in order to enjoy the best of the magnificent coastal views it should be tackled east to west.

From Cluanie Inn strike straight up the steep, grassy slopes, well to the west of the Allt a'Chaoruinn. At 1,800ft you reach a well-formed ridge running to the summit of Sgurr an Fhuarail, which gives panoramic views north to Ciste Dhubh, and beyond to Sgurr nan Ceathreamhnan and the Glen Affric giants.

Proceeding west you descend to a low bealach before climbing to Sgurr a'Bhealaich Dheirg, whose true summit is poised at the end of a short subsidiary ridge. It is an airy scramble to gain the cairn but should only give difficulty in winter conditions.

The main ridge now broadens and after Saileag you descend to a grassy saddle, at 2,400ft the lowest point of the entire ridge.

With the first section of the ridge completed you now start on the Five Sisters proper. The going becomes increasingly rough as you snake over Sgurr na Ciste Duibhe and Sgurr na Carnach to the splendid, isolated peak of Sgurr Fhuaran, which stands haughtily above its neighbours. From its large cairn Skye and the Inner Hebrides look very close, and the Outer Hebrides have been seen stretching from Harris to Barra Head. On the mainland you can see peaks ranging from Assynt to Ben Alder and Ben Cruachan.

Descend the steep north ridge to the bealach under Sgurr nan Saighead; care is needed because the northern slopes fall away in considerable, though broken, cliffs.

Easy walking now leads over Sgurr nan Saighead to the huge, flattish mass of Sgurr na Moraich, the last of the Five Sisters. Grassy slopes now run down to the road one mile north of Shiel Bridge.

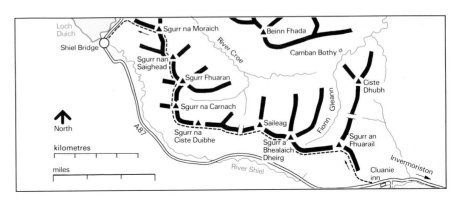

THE SADDLE OF GLEN SHIEL

Map OS Sheet 33   *Start/Finish* Shiel Bridge (935190)   *Distance/Time* 12 miles/19km, 7 hrs

---

Grading A fine mountain walk, but sections of the
ridge are rocky and exposed and the route is not
recommended for the inexperienced.
Escape Routes Descend E from the lower part of the
Forcan Ridge to Bealach Coire Mhalagain, thence
into Glen Shiel.
Transport Bus services: Glasgow/Portree and
Inverness/Portree pass through Shiel Bridge.
Accommodation Hotels at Cluanie and Shiel Bridge.
B & B locally., Youth Hostels at Ratagan and Kyle of
Lochalsh.

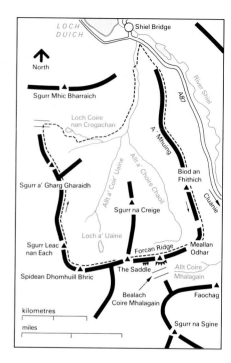

The Saddle of Glen Shiel typifies the proud
giants of the Western Highlands. Heavy rainfall
has encouraged green, vegetatious growth on
the lower slopes, while the summit ridges are
weathered and eroded into sharp rocky crests.
Soaring straight up from the shore of Loch
Duich, the Saddle makes full use of its 3,317ft/
1,010m, and its stature matches that of its
loftier neighbour, Sgurr Fhuaran, north across
Glen Shiel. In fact the Saddle presents its finest
profile to the north: a pointed summit
supported by keen, knife-edged shoulders of
rock, curving away to the east and west with
mathematical precision.

Two fine corries have been scoured from
the north face of the Saddle, divided by a long
ridge which runs out to Sgurr na Creige. These
corries merge on lower ground and their
burns form a considerable river, Allt Undalain,
which runs into Loch Duich at Shiel Bridge.

From Shiel Bridge a circular walk can en-
compass both corries, as well as enjoying the
traverse of the sensational Forcan Ridge which
can pose severe problems in full winter
conditions.

The eastern arm of the circuit comprises the
knobbly ridge of A'Mhuing, which leads easily
to Biod an Fhithich. Next comes the individual
peak of Meallan Odhar which gives a preview
of the Forcan Ridge ahead.

Grass soon gives way to boulder-fields and
rocky outcrops, the angle increases, the ridge
narrows and the Forcan Ridge has arrived.
Slabs of schist fall away from the edge and
castles of shattered rock can be climbed direct,
or circumvented if desired. Ledges abound
and the rock crest is not sustained; in summer
you should find few difficulties and will be
able to enjoy Scottish mountaineering at its
classic best.

Beyond Sgurr nan Forcan the ridge broadens,
but remains craggy and tortuous. The Saddle
itself commands views extending from Liathach
and the Cuillin of Skye, to Knoydart and Ben
Nevis. Nearer at hand Coir' Uaine drops sheer
to a tiny lochan ringed with broken crags.

The ridge continues west, following some
iron stakes, to the second main peak, Spidean
Dhomhuill Bhric. Although still rocky, the
difficulties gradually diminish as you traverse
above the lip of Coir' Uaine, over Sgurr Leac
nan Each and Sgurr a'Gharg Gharaidh to the
bealach under Sgurr Mhic Bharraich. A path
runs east from here into the lower corrie,
leading to the Allt Undalain and Shield Bridge.

SEVEN MUNROS:
THE SOUTH KINTAIL RIDGE

Map *OS Sheet 33*   **Start/Finish** *Cluanie Inn (075117)/Glenshiel Battle Site (990132)*
Distance/Time *13 miles/21km, 7-8 hrs*

---

*Grading In good conditions this is an exhilarating
and fairly straightforward mountain traverse.
Escape Routes Easy descents N into Glen Shiel from
many of the bealachs on the ridge.
Transport Bus services: Glasgow/Portree and
Inverness/Portree pass through Cluanie and
Glenshiel.
Accommodation Hotels at Cluanie and Shiel Bridge.
B & B locally., Youth Hostels at Ratagan and Kyle of
Lochalsh.*

To the south of Glen Shiel, and roughly
between Cluanie Inn and the Glen Shiel battle
site, where the Redcoats fought the Jacobites
in 1719, lies a high ridge eight miles long and
containing no less than seven Munros. If you
are interested in Munro-bagging, there is no
pleasanter or more productive day in all
Scotland. The walk is most enjoyable when
done from east to west, for then you will get
the best of the views down Loch Duich, Loch
Hourn and across to Skye. Northwards lie the
three great glens of Affric, Cannich and Strath-
farrar, with their accompanying mighty peaks,
while to the south rise the peaks surrounding
Loch Quoich, Loch Arkaig and Glenfinnan.

In summer the going is easy and, with
several simple escape routes down to Glen
Shiel, you should have a carefree day. In

winter or spring the walk is equally delightful,
but the condition of the snow will determine
the length of your day. I have known powder
snow on the ridge to be plumed and honed to
a razor edge after a spell of bad weather.

From Cluanie Inn an old road crosses the
western end of Loch Cluanie by a causeway,
and continues over the shoulder of Creag
a'Mhaim to Loch Loyne. This road, which
meets the broad north ridge of Creag a'Mhaim
near the Allt Giubhais bridge, provides an easy
route of ascent up the day's first objective.

Beyond the flat and rather featureless summit of Druim Shionnach the ridge narrows
and steepens to the highest point of the day,
Aonach air Chrith at 3,342ft/1,019m. The north
face of Aonach air Chrith is precipitous and
huge rock buttresses are thrown out into the
amphitheatre below.

The ridge continues westwards with few
changes of direction, and it undulates gently
without descending to low bealachs. Sgurr an
Lochain is named after the tiny lochan in the
high corrie below the summit; it is a fine
conical peak with steep slopes on all sides.

If you have time in hand, stay on the final
summit of Creag nan Damh for a few minutes
and admire the view. The dominating peak to
the west is the Saddle while, across Glen Shiel,
Sgurr Fhuaran tops the neighbouring peaks
and the Five Sisters of Kintail. The sharp
pointed peak to the south is the very
inaccessible Sgurr na Ciche above Loch Nevis.

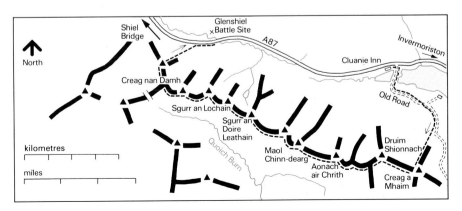

SPIDEAN MIALACH AND GLEOURAICH

Map OS Sheet 33   **Start/Finish** Loch Quoich side, 1½ miles E of Quoich Bridge (033026)
Distance/Time 9 miles/14km, 5-6 hrs

Grading A rough walk over two splendid West Highland peaks. The north sides of the ridges are precipitous and care should be taken in bad weather.
Escape Routes Head S to Loch Quoich from the low bealach between the two peaks.
Transport Bus services: Fort William/Invergarry/Inverness. Infrequent service: Invergarry/Kinlochhourn.
Accommodation Hotels at Invergarry and Tomdoun. Youth Hostel at Loch Lochay.

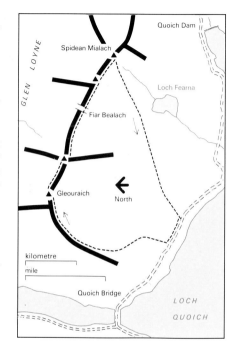

Not even the constant stimulus provided by the seven Munros on the South Kintail ridge (chapter 45), can totally absorb the attention of the mountain walker. He must gaze south with approval at the splendid twin peaks of Spidean Mialach and Gleouraich, which rise steeply beyond the desolate Glen Loyne and present bold, craggy fronts to the north.

Access to these fine mountains is easy, for the new road which runs west from Tomdoun, along the north shore of the raised Loch Quoich, passes under their gentle southern slopes.

Before the rain-gauge at Kinlochquoich was drowned by the rising water it recorded many astonishing readings. Devotees of the Western Highlands will know well how wet this area is, but the ten inches of rain that fell in a single December's day in 1954 is frightening. It is not surprising that the loch was dammed for hydro-electricity; the present level is 100ft higher than the old and the rock-fill dam is the largest of its kind in the country.

A mile before the road reaches Quoich Bridge it passes a luxuriant patch of rhododendrons. This is all that remains from Glenquoich Lodge which is now submerged.

However, on striking up the hillside west of the Allt Coire Peitireach in the general direction of Gleouraich, you will be delighted to meet an ancient stalkers' path which makes for very easy going up the broad ridge. Originally the path was so beautifully constructed, with such attention paid to drainage, that it is still in perfect condition. Tiny burns are skilfully bridged with natural stones and, when contouring steep ground, the path is expertly shored up with dry-stone abutments.

The path takes you to a subsidiary top on the south-west ridge, leaving you to ascend some quite rough, bouldery slopes above north-facing cliffs to the summit of Gleouraich.

Proceed west, keeping to the edge of the broken escarpment for two-thirds of a mile, and then descend south-eastwards to the bealach at 2,400ft, above Coire na Fiar Bhealaich.

Spidean Mialach presents a magnificent buttress of rock to the north-west, but otherwise is less precipitous than Gleouraich. It has twin summits, the eastern being the highest at 3,268ft/996m.

You can descend the rough, heathery, boulder-strewn southern slopes in any direction to meet the road, but the wide corrie of the Allt a'Mheil makes as convenient a route as any.

LADHAR BHEINN AND THE ROUGH BOUNDS OF KNOYDART

Map OS Sheet 33 *Start/Finish* Kinlochhourn (950067)/Inverie (766001) *Distance/Time* 22 miles/35km, 11 hrs

Grading A long and rough walk through a remote and mountainous area. Some mild scrambling along an exposed ridge.
Escape Routes None. If time is short the ascent of Ladhar Bheinn can be omitted and the Mam Barrisdale pass descended to Inverie.
Transport Bus service: Invergarry/Kinlochhourn (infrequent). Ferry: Mallaig/Inverie thrice weekly or private hire from the Knoydart Estate.
Accommodation Hotels at Tomdoun. Bothy at Inverie. Varied accommodation at Mallaig. Youth Hostel at Garramore.

When I am asked to name my favourite mountain in Scotland I answer without any hesitation, 'Ladhar Bheinn in Knoydart'. I cannot be alone in this choice because Ladhar Bheinn offers the perfect combination of grandeur and remoteness, together with the close presence of the sea.

The walk I recommend involves not only the ascent of Ladhar Bheinn, but also a traverse of the aptly named Rough Bounds of Knoydart.

Kinlochhourn is the start of the walk, but before you stride away into the wilderness you must check the times of the infrequent ferry service across Loch Nevis from Inverie to Mallaig. A large party might find it worthwhile to organise their own private ferry.

The crossing takes about forty-five minutes and provides an ideal, though unusual, end to a magnificent day's walking. As the sun disappears behind the Cuillin of Skye, and the western horizon is alight with a greenish glow, you can enjoy perfect peace and contentment as you chug back to civilisation.

From Kinlochhourn a six-mile switchback path runs along the side of Loch Hourn to Barrisdale Bay; a hauntingly beautiful and lonesome spot. Ben Sgriol rises gently behind the fishing village of Arnisdale across Loch Hourn while, to the west, Ladhar Bheinn towers dramatically above Coire Dhorrcail.

An old stalkers' path snakes across the hillside into the sanctuary of Coire Dhorrcail. Cross the corrie burn and climb the steep, grassy slopes of Druim a'Choire Odhair, whence a narrow ridge leads to the summit of Ladhar Bheinn, 3,343ft/1,019m. With cliffs falling away on the north and east sides it is an airy perch, and it offers distant views across the Sound of Sleat to the Cuillin of Skye.

Follow the summit ridge south-east for half-a-mile until it descends to a low bealach at 2,300ft, and climb again to the subsidiary peak of Aonach Sgoilte. A rough descent eastwards now takes you to the Land Rover track running through Gleann an Dubh Lochain to Inverie. Half-way down the track you pass an imposing monument to the family of Lord Brocket.

Inverie nestles peacefully amongst woods and banks of rhododendrons and, on one occasion, I was lucky to see a golden eagle being harried by a pair of peregrine falcons. You should find plenty of interest while you wait for the boat to Mallaig.

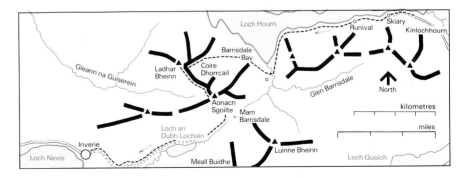

GLEN DESSARRY AND SGURR NA CICHE

Map OS Sheet 33 **Start/Finish** Strathan (978915)/Kinlochhourn road (998030)
Distance/Time 17 miles/27km, 10 hrs

Grading A long and serious walk over uninhabited and mountainous country.
Escape Routes Refuges at A' Chuil bothy (Glen Dessarry) and Sourlies (Loch Nevis). From bealach between Garbh Chioch Mhor and Sgurr na Ciche descend SW towards Loch Nevis.
Transport Infrequent bus services: Invergarry/ Kinlochhourn and Fort William/Achnacarry.
Accommodation Hotels at Tomdoun and Gairlochy Youth Hostel at Glen Nevis.

This walk, running from the west end of Loch Arkaig to the Kinlochhourn road near Quoich Bridge, involves a crossing of one of the most untamed areas of Scotland.

The expedition is serious, for there are no escape routes and help is a long way off. Although the terrain is rough, it is not too severe and any hazards are likely to be caused by natural occurrences.

The weather is unpredictable and is often extremely bad; there are no bridges and the rivers and burns rise quickly to flood level and become unfordable. The northern section of this walk is particularly vulnerable, and you should bear in mind the possibility of having to make long detours late in the day, or even being benighted.

However, don't be discouraged by this intro-

duction for the walk includes the ascent of Sgurr na Ciche, a remote and superbly dramatic peak, and the traverse of perhaps the most rugged area to be found in Britain today.

The walk starts with a long approach march through the wide and rather dreary Glen Dessarry, which has suffered recently at the hands of the foresters. It is a relief to strike up to the bealach under Sgurr nan Coireachan and begin the high traverse westwards.

Garbh Chioch Mhor is a chunky mountain with bluffs of rock and tiny lochans abounding on its broad ridge. A line of old fence posts is useful in mist but in clear weather your eyes will feast on Sgurr na Ciche, which rises symmetrically on all sides to 3,410ft/1,040m. It is one of the most spectacular mountains on the Scottish mainland, eclipsing even Sgurr Mor Fannich for dramatic sharpness of form.

A way through the rocks can be found by traversing to the south side before scrambling up the final 500ft. The actual summit is needle sharp and there is barely room for the trig. point.

Descend north-eastwards, taking care to avoid several lines of broken crags, until you reach a bealach under Meall a'Choire Dhuibh. Now drop another 1,000ft to the floor of Coire nan Gall.

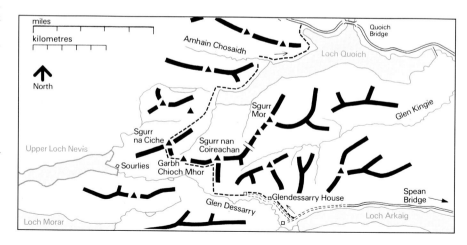

A path runs to the regulating dam at the western end of Loch Quoich where it meets an old road. But this road keeps disappearing into the loch leaving you to fight your way east, towards Quoich Bridge, along the rough shoreline.

As a final warning, do not take chances with the swift Amhain Chosaidh.

Chapter 49

Grading *A serious expedition over rugged and remote mountains where help is far away.*
Escape Routes *From Bealach na h-Eangair descend W to Glen Carnach.*
Transport *Bus service: Fort William Station/ Achnacarry at E end of Loch Arkaig on school days only.*
Accommodation *Varied accommodation at Fort William, Spean Bridge and Gairlochy. Youth Hostel at Glen Nevis.*

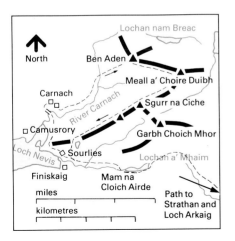

ACROSS KNOYDART TO BEN ADEN

Map *OS Sheet 33* **Start/Finish** *Sourlies bothy at the head of Loch Nevis (869950)*
Distance/Time *10 miles/16km, 8-9 hrs*

Knoydart: the wettest, roughest, remotest and wildest peninsula in these islands. Any expedition to Knoydart is an adventure, and in this chapter I describe the ascent of Ben Aden which rises to 2,905ft/887m at the upper end of Glen Carnach. Ben Aden, in the heart of Knoydart, represents, with Ladhar Bheinn, the close communion between sea and wild mountains that makes up the unique West Highland experience.

Even in the wilds of Knoydart it is possible to find shelter, for Sourlies bothy, a primitive but dry cottage on the shore of Loch Nevis, is open to allcomers and is kept in first class order by the Mountain Bothies Association.

Sourlies makes a convenient base for the ascent of Ben Aden, the only disadvantage being the rather dreary four-hour approach march from Loch Arkaig through Glen Dessarry and over the Mam na Cloich Airde, where you are apt to be pounded remorselessly by westerly gales.

As soon as you round the shoulder behind Sourlies and enter Glen Carnach, Ben Aden can be seen dominating the head of the glen. It presents a rocky face to the south which is split by a conspicuous gully. A scrambling route can

be found beside this gully which leads directly to the summit of Ben Aden, although more gentle slopes can be ascended on the west side if required.

An astonishing view unfolds from the summit cairn: the long arms of Lochs Hourn and Nevis, Ladhar Bheinn, Ben Sgriol, Skye, Rhum, Eigg and the line of the Outer Hebrides. Inland almost every peak in the Northern and Western Highlands can be seen, ranging from An Teallach and Ben Wyvis, through Sgurr nan Ceathreamhnan, Mam Soul and Kintail to Sgurr Thuilm, Beinn Resipol and Ben More on Mull.

Pick your way down the rocky east ridge of Ben Aden towards the Bealach na h-Eangair, contour the head of the desolate glen running west from Meall a'Choire Dhuibh, and scramble up the north-east ridge of Sgurr na Ciche.

It is a relief to escape the shadowy and rather grim north face of Sgurr na Ciche and emerge into the sunshine on the pointed summit of one of Scotland's greatest peaks.

Drink your fill from this magical perch and then, with prawners rippling the waters below, amble your way down the delightful long south-west ridge back to the haven of Sourlies.

THE ROIS BHEINN RIDGE OF MOIDART

Map *OS Sheet 40*   **Start/Finish** *Glenfinnan (897810)/Lochailort (767824)*   **Distance/Time** *18 miles/29km, 9 hrs*

Grading *A mountain traverse in a rarely visited region of Scotland. The ridge is mainly broad and grassy but becomes rocky in the later stages.*
Escape Routes *The low bealach W of Beinn Odhar Bheag provides an easy descent N, before the main massif is reached.*
Transport *Rail service: Fort William/Mallaig runs through Glenfinnan and Lochailort.*
Accommodation *Hotels and B & B in Glenfinnan and Lochailort. Youth Hostels at Glen Nevis and Garramore near Arisaig.*

Moidart is unfashionable country for the climber and hill walker. It is out on a limb, wet and rough, and it boasts no Munros. Knoydart, too, is rough and remote but as such it is famous and Ladhar Bheinn attracts the ambitious walker.

South of the railway line between Glenfinnan and Lochailort lie two ranges of mountains. On the west side there is the Rois Bheinn/Druim Fiaclach group, which is linked to the Beinn Odhar Mhor and Bheag group, overlooking Loch Shiel, by a bealach at 1,250ft.

A traverse of both ridges involves a long day's walk over trackless hills, but the location gives superb views of the western seaboard and the Inner Hebrides, while the railway provides speedy transport back to the start.

This is not an expedition for the timid walker, the area is a true wilderness and, with the absence of paths, experience and judgment are required to select the best lines of attack.

The subsidiary top of An-t-Sleubhaich is the first objective when you leave Glenfinnan, and this marks the beginning of a broad ridge, dotted with perched boulders, which leads to the summit of Beinn Odhar Mhor. One mile further south rises Beinn Odhar Bheag, at 2,895ft/882m, the highest point of the day's walk. Both mountains are characterised by vast slabs of bare rock, evidence of the extensive

glacier system which carved out Loch Shiel.

The sinuous ridge which runs west from Bealach a'Choire Bhuidhe to Rois Bheinn is hard work; shapely summits rise above low bealachs and you are for ever negotiating rocky outcrops and boulder fields. Beinn Mhic Cedidh is a graceful spire, Druim Fiaclach has a sharp ridge giving a touch of exposure and Sgurr na Ba Glaise commands several wild corries falling away steeply on the north side.

Rois Bheinn has twin summits and, although the trig. point is built on the east summit, it is the west that provides the best view.

Prominent out to the west is the Sgurr of Eigg, with the Cuillin of Rhum beyond. Nearer at hand are the Glenfinnan hills and Knoydart, with the dark waters of Loch Eilt and its pine-covered islands far below. Loch Sunart glints ten miles away to the south.

An easy, grassy descent leads to the Alisary burn and the road beside Loch Ailort, just two miles from the railway station.

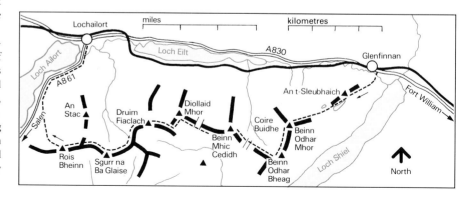

GARBH BHEINN OF ARDGOUR

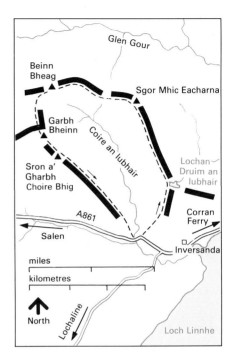

Map *OS Sheets 40 and 49 (Tourist Map)*   **Start/Finish** *The road junction at Inversanda (933593)*
Distance/Time *9 miles/14km, 7-8 hrs*

Grading *A superb mountain circuit including the traverse of one of Scotland's finest and rockiest peaks. Care needed with route finding in mist.*
Escape Routes *Descend E from Bealach Feith 'n Amean into Coire an Iubhair.*
Transport *Corran ferry. Bus service: Ardgour/ Inversanda/Kilchoan.*
Accommodation *Hotel at Corran. B & B locally. Youth Hostels at Glencoe and Fort William.*

In the 1950s aspiring Scottish mountaineers could obtain only meagre fare from the libraries and bookshops. However, two exceptions were W. H. Murray's *Mountaineering in Scotland* and *Undiscovered Scotland* which I knew almost by heart and certainly inspired me to spend my school holidays hitching up the A1 to explore the Highlands.

Garbh Bheinn of Ardgour is one of Murray's most stimulating chapters and I thrilled to the distinctive outline of this giant of the west when spied from the hills of Glen Coe, Ben Nevis and Lochaber.

Ardgour is tiresomely inaccessible; you must either take the Corran Ferry across Loch Linnhe, or undertake a 75 mile drive via Glenfinnan, Lochailort and Loch Sunart. But the effort is handsomely rewarded when you explore Garbh Bheinn's ridges, corries, glens and cliffs, for few other mainland mountains display so much scoured rock.

From Inversanda the long Coire an Iubhair penetrates deeply into the mountains, as far as the low Bealach Feith'n Amean dividing the northern slopes of Garbh Bheinn from Beinn Bheag. A horseshoe walk round the hills encompassing Coire an Iubhair makes a highly satisfactory expedition. For the first half of the day you can marvel at the cliffs falling sheer from Garbh Bheinn's summit ridge and then, during the second half, you can get to grips with the mountain itself.

Walk up the easy, grassy slopes of Druim an Iubhair, passing a lonely lochan on the shoulder, and then climb more steeply to Sgor Mhic Eacharna. Now drop down to a bealach at 1,575ft and ascend Beinn Bheag which is a truly magnificent viewpoint for the classic features on the east face of Garbh Bheinn: the Great Ridge rising from the corrie floor straight to the summit cairn, the Pinnacle Ridge further to the right and the North-East Buttress.

A steep and rather loose descent leads to Lochan Coire an Iubhair on the Bealach Feith'n Amean, some old fence posts emerge in places which would aid navigation in mist.

Imposing rock buttresses on the north flank of Garbh Bheinn seem to block the way ahead, but it is quite easy to weave a way through these outcrops and so gain the summit ridge 1,000ft above.

Keeping to the cliff-edge walk to the summit cairn at 2,903ft/867m, continue over a subsidiary top and enjoy the long, easy descent over Sron a'Gharbh Choire Bhig to the road.

BEINN RESIPOL

Map OS Sheet 40   **Start/Finish** The highest point on the Strontian to Polloch road (838666)/Resipole Farm (722640)
Distance/Time 10 miles/16km, 6-7 hrs

> **Grading** A straightforward walk, although some
> steep ground and broken cliffs must be avoided on
> the N and E sides of the mountain.
> **Escape Routes** Descents from almost anywhere S to
> the road on Loch Sunart-side.
> **Transport** Corran ferry. Bus service: Ardgour/
> Strontian/Resipole/Kilchoan.
> **Accommodation** Hotel at Strontian. B & B locally.
> Youth Hostels at Glencoe and Fort William.

How often have we gazed west from the principal summits of the Western Highlands to a primitive world of lochs, hills and islands. Far beyond Loch Linnhe and the dominating peak of Garbh Bheinn in Ardgour, tucked between lochs Shiel and Sunart, the perfect cone of Beinn Resipol rises proudly above this watery wilderness.

Beinn Resipol, at 2,774ft/845m, stands supreme on the rugged peninsula of Ardnamurchan, which runs west for 26 miles until sheer cliffs plunge into the stormy seas of the Atlantic Ocean.

Ardnamurchan is rough, wild, windy and wet but on a rare still day in spring or early summer, you may find Beinn Resipol in a benign mood. With primroses decorating the banks of the burns, birch buds bursting into leaf and rivulets of melt-water coursing down from snow patches in the high corries, then Beinn Resipol will provide a memorable day.

The summit of the road running north from Strontian, at 1,100ft, is a convenient and energy-saving start for the Beinn Resipol traverse. Trackless and boggy slopes lead west, passing relics of the lead mining industry which flourished here in the eighteenth century. The lead from these mines was used in the bullets fired by the English at the Battle of Waterloo. Historians will appreciate too that a new element, strontium, was discovered in this region in 1764.

Before launching onto Resipol's chunky east ridge you must pass a dam at the end of Lochan Dubh, and then descend to a bealach above Coire an t-Suidhe. Here, a line of cairns marks an ancient coffin trail leading across the hills from Ardnastang to Polloch.

As you approach the summit of Resipol the going gets rougher and rockier, with loose crags abounding on the broad ridge. However, the exposed rocks add interest to the ascent and the view from the summit is one of the finest on the western seaboard. Westwards you look to the small isles, Skye, Mull and the Outer Hebrides, while inland many of the old favourites of the Western Highlands can be appreciated from an unusual direction. Beinn Resipol reinforces the adage that it is not always the highest peaks that make the best viewpoints.

Drop steeply down from the west ridge to the delightful Lochan Bac an Lochain, whence you can follow the banks of the Allt Mhic Chiarain to the roadside near Resipole Farm.

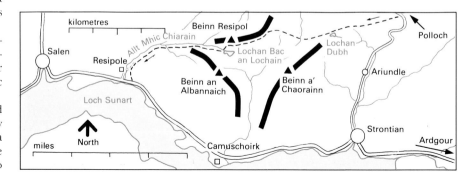

BALMORAL FOREST
AND LOCHNAGAR

Map OS Sheets 43 and 44 (Tourist Map)   *Start/Finish* Spittal of Glenmuick (310851)/Braemar (310851)
Distance/Time 17 miles/27km, 9 hrs

Grading A high and exposed walk over one of Scotland's best loved and most historic mountains.
Escape Routes Emergency shelter at Lochcallater Lodge. Descend to Dubh Loch Glen from bealach E of Carn an t-Sagairt Mor.
Transport Bus services: Ballater/Aberdeen and Ballater/Braemar.
Accommodation Varied accommodation at Braemar and Ballater. Aberdeen University hut at Allt na-giubhsaich. Youth Hostels at Ballater, Braemar and Inverey.

This walk traverses the Royal Balmoral Deer Forest, an area steeped in tradition and romance which was much loved by Queen Victoria and Prince Albert.

Byron wrote:

'England! Thy beauties are tame and domestic to one who has roved o'er the mountains afar: Oh for the crags that are wild and majestic! The steep frowning glories of dark Lochnagar!'

Start from the car-park at Spittal of Glenmuick, and take the rough road across the glen to the cottage of Allt-na-guibhsaich. The entire upper region of Glen Muick is a Wild Life Sanctuary, but this has not prevented a Land Rover track being bulldozed over the open hillside to form a link with Deeside.

Leave this track below the watershed and follow the cairned path which slants up through the heather to the bealach under Meikle Pap. Suddenly you are confronted by one of Scotland's finest prospects: the corrie of Lochnagar where a mile-long cirque of cliffs rises 1,200ft above a corrie loch. In winter Lochnagar's cliffs provide a number of classic gully climbs: Raeburn's, Parallel A and B, Polyphemus, Douglas-Gibson's and Black Spout.

Walk round the cliff-edge to the northern-most end where the cairn of Cac Carn Mor is built just above the top of Black Spout gully. The true summit of Lochnagar, Cac Carn Beag, 3,789ft/1,155m, lies a quarter-of-a-mile back from the cliffs.

The view is extensive, particularly to the south where there is no higher mountain massif. Arthur's Seat in Edinburgh and even the Cheviots have been sighted.

Skirt the edge of another great north-west-facing corrie, Coire Lochan an Eoin, to reach the top of a prominent rocky spur called the Stuic Buttress. Keep well north of the high, barren wasteland known as the White Mount. In summer the Mount is a carpet of rich moss which attracts enormous herds of deer.

Continue west above a third corrie which contains two lochans, and then climb the broad north-east ridge of Carn an t-Sagairt Mor, 3,430ft/1,047m. The mountainside hereabouts is strewn with the wreckage of a crashed plane.

Make your way down boulders and heather towards Loch Callater, and pick up an excellent stalkers' path leading to Callater Lodge. A private road runs down Glen Callater to meet the A93, a comfortable two-mile walk from Braemar.

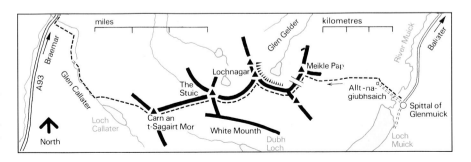

BEINN A' BHUIRD AND BEN AVON

Map OS Sheet 36 (Tourist Map) **Start/Finish** Linn of Dee (062896)/Cock Bridge (257092)
Distance/Time 29 miles/47km, 13-14 hrs

Grading An exceptionally long and tough walk over high and remote mountains.
Escape Routes None. A tiring party should not continue beyond Beinn a' Bhuird to Ben Avon but should retreat from The Sneck to Glen Quoich.
Transport Bus service: Aberdeen/Braemar; Grantown/Elgin and Grantown/Aviemore.
Accommodation Cock Bridge Inn. Hotels and B & B at Tomintoul and Braemar. Youth Hostels at Inverey, Braemar and Tomintoul.

The influx of visitors to the Cairngorms, following the development of Aviemore as a major tourist and skiing centre, means that only in the more remote hills and glens can one still experience the solitude and excitement of this unique range.

West of Glen Derry lie two huge mountains, Beinn a'Bhuird and Ben Avon, which are rarely visited. The corries of Beinn a'Bhuird rival the best that Braeriach can offer, while the glens surpass in beauty even Glen Derry and Rothiemurchus.

Only fit and experienced parties should attempt this walk, for the mountains are remote and unforgiving and help is far away. A winter crossing of these hills is one of the toughest and most serious mountain expeditions in Britain.

The walk starts along the well-beaten track running north through Glen Lui from Linn of Dee. Half-a-mile beyond the bridge turn

sharply right, along a narrow path which leads through a defile into Glen Quoich.

A wonderful scene lies before you. The combination of Beinn a'Bhuird and Ben Avon, rising high above the Old Caledonian forests, and fast rivers sparkling over their rocky beds, cannot be bettered.

Before you can start to climb up through the trees on the south shoulder of Beinn a'Bhuird, you must wade the Dubh Ghleann tributary of Quoich Water. Take care, for this burn rises very quickly in wet weather.

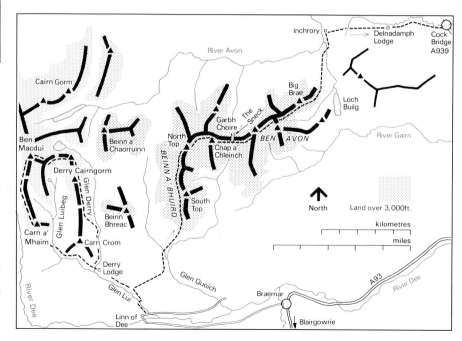

Beyond the south top of Beinn a'Bhuird you skirt the precipitous edge of the great Coire an Dubh Loch, where cornices last well into the summer. Continuing north across the plateau you pass another magnificent east-facing corrie, Coire nan Clach, before reaching the highest point of Beinn a'Bhuird at 3,924ft/1,196m.

One mile north-east lies Cnap a'Chleirich, a cluster of granite rocks overlooking the stupendous Garbh Choire, one of the great sights of the Cairngorms. The corrie is deep and wide and is pierced by a prow of clean rock, called the Mitre Ridge.

Cross the low bealach, the Sneck, and climb to the granite tor on the summit of Ben Avon at 3,843ft/1,171m. The plateau stretches away with other tors dotted about at regular intervals.

From Big Brae, on the north side, descend into Glen Builg. Here you meet a path leading to Inchrory Lodge and, in another six miles, to Cock Bridge on the Braemar to Tomintoul road.

Chapter 55.

BEN MACDUI AND THE GLEN LUIBEG CIRCUIT

Map OS Sheets 43 and 36 (Tourist Map)   *Start/Finish* Linn of Dee (062896)   *Distance/Time* 20 miles/32km, 10-11 hrs

To venture on to the Cairngorm plateau in winter, with a Siberian wind whipping up snow devils and nipping your ears and nose, is an exhilarating experience for the hardened hill walker. But in early summer the snow patches recede, families of ptarmigan emerge from the boulder fields, snow bunting skim over the screes, the least willow, three-fingered rush and woolly hair moss creep across the beds of decayed granite; then the desolate plateau takes on a fragile beauty.

Ugly ski developments preclude an approach to the mountains from the north, but the long glens running south to the Dee are majestic. Live rivers rush through gorges and along twisting beds, while the hillsides carry sizeable remnants of the old Caledonian pine forest. A wide variety of contrasts can be enjoyed by a day's walk over the hills enclosing the Luibeg Burn: Derry Cairngorm, Ben Macdui and Carn a'Mhaim.

From Linn of Dee walk up Glen Lui to historic Derry Lodge, cross the river by a footbridge and continue up Glen Derry. At any time the lower stretch of the glen is paradise. In the summer the aroma of pine needles pervades the air, ants scurry underfoot and

birds chatter in the branches; you may see a crossbill, crested tit, siskin or goldcrest. In winter all is silent and even the river may be stilled. Deer stand in small herds, seeking the shelter of the trees and nuzzling for moss under the snow.

After a mile leave the path and strike west to the bealach under Carn Crom, then continue north over rough ground to the summit of Derry Cairngorm. Even in June the cliffs of Coire Sputan Dearg, across the glen, may be rimmed with cornices and Lochan Uaine, in the hollow below, criss-crossed with ice. This lochan, at 3,142ft, is one of the highest in Scotland.

Easy walking round the head of Glen Luibeg and the edge of Coire Sputan Dearg leads to Ben Macdui, 4,296ft/1,309m, Britain's second highest mountain.

Carefully descend the wide boulder field of upper Coire Clach nan Taillear to the bealach under Carn a'Mhaim. The north ridge of Carn a'Mhaim is nearly two miles long and it snakes up stepwise to the summit providing an airy route of ascent.

Descend directly to Glen Luibeg where an iron bridge crosses the burn.

THE LAIRIG GHRU

Map OS Sheets 36 and 43 (Tourist Map/Outdoor Leisure 3)   **Start/Finish** Coylumbridge (915106)/E of the Linn of Dee (068898)   **Distance/Time** 19 miles/31km, 8-9 hrs

Grading A long and rough walk through a remote mountain range. The pass is 2,733ft/833m high and the crossing can be dangerous in deep snow.
Escape Routes None. Emergency shelters at the Sinclair Hut and Corrour Bothy.
Transport Railway stations at Aviemore and Aberdeen. Bus services: Aviemore/Coylumbridge and Aberdeen/Braemar.
Accommodation Varied accommodation in Aviemore, Coylumbridge and Braemar. Youth Hostels at Aviemore, Loch Morlich, Inverey and Braemar.

The Lairig Ghru is the most famous hill pass in Britain. This deep defile splits the Cairngorms like a knife, producing two distinct mountain groups: Cairn Gorm and Ben Macdui to the east and Braeriach and Cairn Toul to the west.

What could offer a more natural challenge than the Lairig Ghru, linking Speyside with Deeside? For many years this route has been accepted as a test-piece for aspiring hill walkers. The full 27 mile route between Aviemore and Braemar is a considerable undertaking, there are no escape routes and fitness and commitment are prerequisites.

The Pools of Dee at the Lairig Ghru's summit, 2,733ft/833m, is a lonely and desolate spot, many miles from help, and the weather can be severe at any time of the year.

With tourist developments spreading further into the hills each year, most Lairig Ghru walkers prefer to start from Coylumbridge and finish at Linn of Dee, thereby lopping eight miles off the purists' route.

From Coylumbridge walk up the narrow road to Whitewell and take the waymarked path through the sweet-smelling pines of Rothiemurchus Forest. The Druie river is crossed by the 'Cairngorm Club Footbridge', and then the path winds slowly through the trees emerging at about 1,500ft. Your feet are cushioned by pine needles and the gnarled old trees induce a feeling of utter contentment.

However, at the Sinclair Hut, 2,000ft, the scene changes dramatically. Now you can look over the Spey valley to the backdrop of the Monadhliath mountains, while ahead Sron na Lairig and Creag an Leth-choin (Lurcher's Crag) close in menacingly.

The Pools of Dee mark the summit of the pass and provide more open views of the cliffs of Braeriach and the great Garbh Choire, Cairn Toul and the Devil's Point.

The rather boggy path descends the lower slopes of Ben Macdui, which sweep up unrelentingly on the east side. Opposite Coire

Odhar a footbridge crosses the Dee, leading to Corrour Bothy. This open bothy is a life-saver in an emergency, although it has no facilities bar a roof and four walls.

Continue round Carn a'Mhaim to historic Derry Lodge, where there is a public telephone. This old lodge is set amongst pines in the most tranquil of settings. Deer congregate here in winter, fed by the keeper from Luibeg, across the river.

A Land Rover track leads pleasantly through Glen Lui to the Braemar road at Linn of Dee.

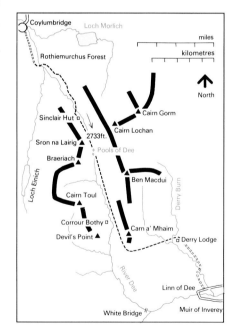

THE CAIRNGORM FOUR THOUSANDERS

Map OS Sheet 36 (Tourist Map/Outdoor Leisure 3)   *Start/Finish* Whitewell (917085)
Distance/Time 29 miles/47km, 15 hrs

Grading An exceptionally long and arduous walk over a high and extensive plateau. It is very vulnerable and exposed to bad weather.
Escape Routes From Cairn Gorm down Fiacaill a' Choire Chais. From Ben Macdui to Loch Etchachan. From Cairn Toul to Glen Geusachan. From Braeriach to Gleann Einich.
Transport Railway station at Aviemore. Bus service: Aviemore/Inverdruie/Cairn Gorm chairlift.
Accommodation Varied accommodation in Aviemore, Sinclair Hut, Corrour Bothy. Youth Hostels at Aviemore, Loch Morlich, Inverey and Braemar.

The ancient, granite mountains of the Cairngorms have weathered into rounded humps and broad ridges, while glacier-scoured corries have eaten into their extensive plateaux.

Nowhere else in these islands resembles more closely an arctic environment than the high Cairngorms, and many species of arctic flora, mosses and lichens have been discovered. When you stand on Ben Macdui or Braeriach during a winter anticyclone, well wrapped up against the piercing cold yet enjoying brilliant sunshine, it is not hard to realise that your latitude of 57° places you north of Moscow and Labrador.

For high, open walking across featureless plateaux the Cairngorms have no rival in these islands, and no walk exemplifies this better than the tour of the four 4,000ft tops: Ben Macdui, Cairn Gorm, Braeriach and Cairn Toul.

To complete this expedition in a single day is a tough challenge for the fit and ambitious hill walker, but the ordinary mortal can enjoy these glorious surroundings equally well by allowing more time.

Either way, the Cairngorms must be taken seriously, particularly under winter conditions when a number of tragic accidents have befallen even experienced parties.

Take the Lairig Ghru path from Whitewell, and walk up through the sweet-smelling pines of Rothiemurchus. Just before the Sinclair Hut strike up to the rocky summit of Creag an Leth-choin (Lurcher's Crag). Now you have gained height it is pleasant and easy walking round the head of Coire an Lochain and Coire an t-Sneachda to Cairn Gorm.

Retrace your footsteps to Cairn Lochan and follow the well-beaten track south to Ben Macdui.

Descend easy but rough slopes to the bealach under Carn a'Mhaim, thence to Glen Dee and the bridge over the river near Corrour Bothy.

A zig-zag path leads up Coire Odhar to the bouldery ridge of Cairn Toul and on to Sgor an Lochain Uaine (the Angel's Peak). This is a superb stretch of airy walking with steep and rocky slopes plunging down towards the Lairig Ghru.

The quality continues as you round the vast amphitheatre of Garbh Choire to reach the summit of Braeriach. On the way you pass a spring bubbling up from a green oasis, this is the Well of Dee, the true source of the river Dee.

The rounded north-west ridge of Sron na Lairig leads easily down into the entrancing Gleann Einich and the Whitewell path.

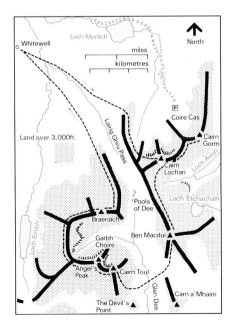

THE FUNGLE AND THE CLASH OF WIRREN

Map OS Sheet 44   **Start/Finish** Aboyne (523980)/Bridgend (536684)   **Distance/Time** 23 miles/37km, 8-9 hrs

> **Grading** The walk follows an ancient path over rolling, heather-clad hills.
> **Escape Routes** Motor roads are crossed at Birse Castle and Tarfside.
> **Transport** Bus services: Aberdeen/Aboyne; Aberdeen/Ballater; Edzell/Brechin/Aberdeen.
> **Accommodation** Hotels and B & B at Aboyne and Edzell. Youth Hostels at Ballater and Glendoll.

The vast range of mountains extending southwest from Aberdeenshire is known loosely as the Grampians. But the ancient name was Mounth, from the Gaelic *Monadh* meaning mountain. Nowadays, Mounth is used to describe old rights-of-way across these mountains, for there were no roads as such in the Highlands before the arrival of General Wade in 1726. The Mounth paths were chosen for their drainage and firmness and, because they are now only used by shepherds and occasional walkers, they provide wonderfully wild walks over lonely hills and moors, linking villages and glens in the Grampians.

Here I describe a Mounth walk (The Fungle) running south from Aboyne on Deeside to Glen Esk, and I extend it over the Clash of Wirren, by the Whisky Road, to Bridgend.

The path from the Dee ascends the valley of the Allt Dinnie, passing through woods of sweet chestnut, birch, sycamore, hazel and maple. Higher up it winds through stands of Caledonian pines, deep heather and bilberry shrubs bearing fruit the size and sweetness of cherries.

Beyond Birse Castle the path becomes indistinct, petering out altogether on the hag-ridden bealach between Tampie and Mudlee Bracks. But the walking is majestic and the sense of space and freedom profound. As far as the eye can see the purple heather-clad hills of the Grampians sweep on to distant horizons. These are rounded, folded hills where rushing burns have carved seams and gorges out of the bedrock; only here can flourish ribbons of scrub trees and shrubs where the sheep are unable to graze.

At Tarfside you cross the river North Esk by a footbridge, climb to the bealach between Garlet and Cowie Hill and cross the Burn of Berryhill before descending through the Clash of Wirren to Tillybardine. The Clash of Wirren is one of the secret hollows of the Grampians; a spring rises in an area of lush green grass below a craggy outlier of West Wirren Hill.

This path, which runs south from Glen Esk to the West Water valley and Glen Lethnot, is known as the Whisky Road. It was used by smugglers, with ponies laden with illicit spirits, bound for lucrative markets in the city of Brechin.

It is three miles from Tillybardine to Bridgend but the West Water valley is a haven of serenity, an appropriate finale to this most beautiful walk through the foothills of the Grampians.

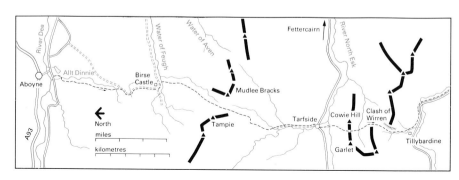

THE MINIGAIG PASS

Map OS Sheets 35 and 43   **Start/Finish** Blair Atholl (870652)/Kingussie (757005)
Distance/Time 27 miles/43km, 11-12 hrs

Grading A long expedition through remote hills. A serious undertaking in winter or early spring when the snow lies deep.
Escape Routes From Bruar Lodge to Calvine. Emergency shelters at Bruar Lodge and Allt Sheicheachan bothy.
Transport Railway stations at Kingussie and Blair Atholl. Bus services: Glasgow/Inverness and Edinburgh/Inverness will stop on demand.
Accommodation Hotels and B & B at Blair Atholl and Kingussie. Youth Hostels at Perth, Pitlochry and Kingussie.

The A9 trunk road between Blair Atholl and Kingussie follows the line of the military road built by General Wade in 1728. Before General Wade's arrival the only route north was the Minigaig Pass, which is shown on maps made in 1725 and 1689. Other archives indicate that the Minigaig replaced an earlier pass constructed in the thirteenth century by the Comyns of Ruthven castle near Kingussie.

General Wade's road over Drumochter, linking Blair Atholl and Kingussie, is 36 miles in length, 10 miles longer than the Minigaig. But, whereas the Minigaig rises to 2,750ft/838m, Wade's road only tops 1,485ft/452m.

In several places the line of the Minigaig can be discerned through the heather, culverts,

walls and paving stones that have survived over 250 years of neglect. Today the Minigaig offers a long walk through extremely beautiful glens and across a high, exposed plateau. Snow lies deep until late spring, navigation would be very difficult in mist and there are no satisfactory escape routes.

Start from Blair Atholl and walk through imposing wrought iron gates into the grounds of Blair Castle. The path winds through exotic fir trees and then breaks out into Glen Banvie.

In Glen Bruar you pass the Allt Sheicheachan bothy, and follow cart tracks, to arrive at Bruar Lodge, one of Scotland's most prestigious shooting lodges.

For three miles a Land Rover track runs beyond Bruar Lodge, passing a loch and the cliffs of Creag na-h-Iolair, while the burn rushes headlong from the hills producing cascades and deep, clear trout pools overhung by birch, rowan and alder.

At the head of the glen climb up gently undulating heathery hills to a broad plateau. Cross the Caochan Lub, a swift stream of pure water which was a popular grazing area with cattle drovers.

A quartzite cairn at 2,750ft/838m, just south of Leathad an Taobhain, marks the high point of the Minigaig. The Allt Coire Bhran falls away into a wide glen which merges into Glen Tromie.

Glen Tromie provides a welcome contrast to the bare corrie of the Allt Bhran. The river sparkles between banks of alder, Caledonian pines, gorse, broom and juniper while remnants of ancient birch forest grow on the hillsides.

At Glentromie Lodge cut across the slopes of Beinn Bhuidhe to Ruthven barracks near Kingussie: a gaunt ruin since Prince Charlie's Highlanders fired it in 1746.

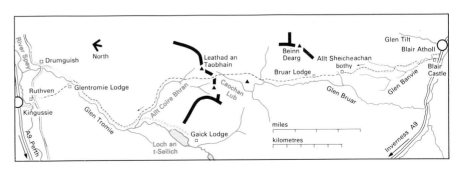

THROUGH THE GRAMPIANS BY GLEN TILT

Map OS Sheet 43   **Start/Finish** Blair Atholl (870652)/Braemar (152915)   **Distance/Time** 31 miles/50km, 11-12 hrs

Grading A long but easy walk through a remote Highland glen.
Escape Routes None. But emergency shelter might be found at Fealar Lodge (2 miles W of Falls of Tarf) and Bynack Lodge.
Transport Railway station at Blair Atholl. Bus service: Aberdeen/Ballater/Braemar.
Accommodation Varied accommodation at Blair Atholl and Braemar. Youth Hostels at Inverey, Braemar, Kingussie and Pitlochry.

There are three great Cairngorm passes: the Lairig Ghru which has a fearsome reputation but remains a popular tourist route, Glen Feshie which is wide and featureless, and plans for a road through it linking Speyside with Deeside have often been mooted, and Glen Tilt which combines remoteness with dramatic and beautiful scenery.

To enter Glen Tilt from Blair Atholl take the road towards Old Blair, cross the river by a fine stone bridge and turn right down a rough estate road. The road runs at first through banks of rhododendrons but, as the glen opens out, the river becomes the main feature, thundering through ravines or sparkling merrily in its bouldery bed.

Marble Lodge is a low, grey stone cottage, but Forest Lodge is a sizeable edifice con-structed of stone and sheltered by a belt of trees. The area is thriving deer forest and huge herds roam the hills. Many deer do not survive a hard winter and, one March day, I passed six dead animals lying on the banks of the river.

Four miles beyond Forest Lodge the Land Rover track peters out and the path passes through a defile, clinging to steep slopes above the river. On the south side of the glen the massive bulk of Beinn a'Ghlo completely dominates the view.

As you round a corner a roar of water announces the Falls of Tarf. The River Tarf leaps down a rocky amphitheatre in three giant steps before joining the Tilt. This is romantic Scotland at its best. Below the falls the Tarf is spanned by a suspension bridge, built in 1886 as a memorial to Francis Bedford, drowned in the Tarf at the age of eighteen.

Soon after the Falls the river turns east and disappears up a ravine. The path to Deeside continues north along the Allt Garbh Buidhe for another two miles to the watershed. Here the ruin of Bynack Lodge stands gaunt among a stand of decayed pines, while the rounded hump of Ben Macdui rises impressively to the north.

Downhill now to the Geldie Burn and White Bridge which spans the Dee, a considerable river despite a mere ten miles' flow from its source.

Before tackling the last six miles to Braemar it is worth a brief stop to marvel at the Linn of Dee, and the feat of Menlove Edwards who swam through that boiling cauldron in 1931.

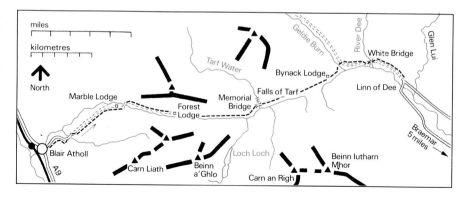

THE CORRIEYAIRACK PASS

Map OS Sheets 34 and 35   **Start/Finish** Garvamore (523947)/Fort Augustus (378092)
Distance/Time 17 miles/27km, 6 hrs

Grading An easy hill pass but can be exposed at the 2,507ft/764m summit.
Escape Routes None.
Transport Railway station at Dalwhinnie. Bus services: Dalwhinnie/Laggan Bridge/Garvamore and Fort William/Fort Augustus/Inverness.
Accommodation Hotels and B & B at Laggan Bridge, Dalwhinnie and Fort Augustus. Youth Hostels at Loch Lochy, Loch Ness, Kingussie and Pitlochry.

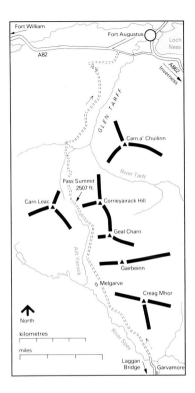

The Corrieyairack is one of the most famous hill passes in all Scotland. It is steeped in history at every step, it passes through glorious hill and glen country, and it follows an excellent broad track the whole way, making route-finding easy.

In the eighteenth century General Wade was despatched north in an attempt to subdue the Jacobites. He soon realised that good communications were the key to success, and he set about building roads linking the garrisons at Inversnaid, Ruthven, Fort Augustus and Inverness. Thus we have the superb military road over the Drumochter Pass, the line followed today by the A9, rendering obsolete the old Minigaig Pass which took a direct line over the hills between Blair Atholl and Kingussie (chapter 59).

In 1731 General Wade constructed a new road, branching west from Dalwhinnie and leading to Fort Augustus over the Corrieyairack Pass. The road was fifteen feet wide and was built by 500 soldiers, although Wade did not need to break virgin ground for the pass had been a droving road for centuries, and it had also been used by Montrose during the Covenanting Wars of the seventeenth century.

From Laggan drive to the old stone bridge over the river Spey at Garvamore; this is St George's Bridge built by General Wade in 1732. It is 150ft long with two arches, and it blends perfectly with the surroundings.

Walk along the road to Melgarve and then take the track on the north bank of the Allt Yairack burn. You pass a number of small bridges which Wade built over the minor burns; all are now tumbled down although the Corrieyairack was regularly crossed by tourists in carriages until the middle of the last century. Now begins a series of twelve huge zig-zags which take you to the top of the pass at 2,507ft/764m.

As you gradually descend the stony track on the north side of the pass to Glen Tarff, you can look ahead to the hills of Kintail and Affric. On the lower slopes the glen becomes more wooded and you can catch glimpses of Loch Ness.

The fort at Fort Augustus was built by General Wade in 1729, but it was fired by the Jacobites in 1746. Dr Johnson stayed there in 1773. It was subsequently restored and given by Lord Lovat to Benedictine monks to be used as a boys' school.

CREAG MEAGAIDH

Map OS Sheet 34   **Start/Finish** Aberarder Farm (480870)/Glen Spean (390817)
Distance/Time 16 miles/26km, 9 hrs

> **Grading** A moderate mountain walk over broad, boulder-strewn ridges.
> **Escape Routes** From the Window down to Coire Ardair and from Bealach a' Bharnish down Glen na h'Uamha to Loch Laggan-side.
> **Transport** Railway station at Tulloch. Infrequent bus service: Fort William/Loch Laggan/Aviemore.
> **Accommodation** Hotels at Roy Bridge and Loch Laggan. B & B at Newtonmore. Youth Hostels at Glen Nevis and Kingussie.

A traverse of the Creag Meagaidh range encompasses all that is best in Scottish hill walking. It involves the ascent of four separate Munros (adequate motivation in itself), broad and level ridges, steep faces and extensive plateaux.

The highest point of the walk is the summit of Creag Meagaidh, 3,700ft/1,130m, which is sufficiently elevated to provide views ranging from the Cairngorms to Knoydart, and from Torridon to Ben Nevis.

Standing in the northern part of the Central Highlands, Creag Meagaidh carries a great deal of snow which lasts well into the summer; and in Coire Ardair it boasts one of the most magnificent winter corries in Scotland, both scenically and from a climbing point of view. Thus, as is so often the case in Scotland, the walk is best done in spring when the cliffs of Coire Ardair are still plastered white. On an east-west traverse Coire Ardair and Coire na h'Uamha can be seen to their best advantage.

From Aberarder Farm, midway along Loch Laggan, a track runs beside the Allt Coire Ardair. Leave this after a mile and head straight up the southern slopes of Carn Liath to its bouldery summit.

A broad ridge now stretches westwards, finally curving south to enclose the superb Coire Ardair. From the subsidiary top of Poite Coire Ardair you can look down to the corrie lochan nestling under 1,500ft buttresses which are seamed by gullies or 'posts', providing severe winter climbs.

The only break in the corrie's defences is on the north side, where an abrupt break in the cliffs forms a window. This escape route was used by Bonnie Prince Charlie in 1746 after his defeat at Culloden.

Under winter conditions an ice-axe and crampons will be necessary to ascend the 500ft slopes leading from the window to the summit plateau of Creag Meagaidh. The OS pillar lies half-a-mile back from the cliffs, but in a white-out the Meagaidh plateau is confusing and potentially dangerous.

Continuing westwards you drop down 1,000ft to Bealach a'Bharnish, and then make a gradually ascending circumnavigation of the wide Coire na h'Uamha of Beinn a'Chaoruinn. This grand corrie is much more broken than Coire Ardair, but it looks extremely fine in winter.

It is but a simple descent of the south ridge of Beinn a'Chaoruinn to reach the main road near Craigbeg, eight miles from Aberarder.

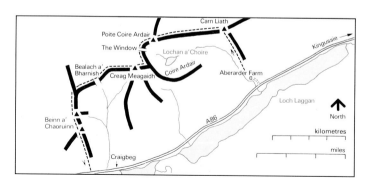

THE BEN ALDER FOREST

Map *OS Sheets 41 and 42* **Start/Finish** *Corrour Station (356665)/Dalwhinnie (634849)*
Distance/Time *28 miles/45km, 11-12 hrs*

Grading *An exceptionally long and serious walk over remote mountainous country.*
Escape Routes *From the Beinn Eibhinn–Aonach Beag ridge descend S to Bealach Dubh and seek shelter at Corrour Lodge or Culra Lodge Bothy.*
Transport *Railway stations at Corrour and Dallwhinnie. Bus services: Edinburgh or Glasgow/Dalwhinnie/ Inverness.*
Accommodation *Hotel and B & B at Dalwhinnie. Youth Hostels at Loch Ossian and Kingussie.*

The Ben Alder Forest is a large and remote area of the Highlands, bounded by Rannoch Moor, Loch Laggan and Loch Ericht. To enter the heart of the region entails a long approach march, for there is no public road within ten miles of Ben Alder itself.

This walk starts from the isolated station of Corrour Siding on Rannoch Moor, traverses the high peaks north of Ben Alder and finishes at Dalwhinnie. Only a strong, fit and well-equipped party should attempt this twenty-eight-mile expedition, for the memory of the horrific accident at New Year 1951, when four experienced climbers died in a blizzard near Corrour Lodge, still haunts the area.

Although there is no escape route, Culra Lodge bothy near the north end of the main ridge could be used as an emergency shelter.

The West Highland Railway provides a particularly satisfying way of reaching the start of the walk, and the early morning train from Glasgow to Fort William arrives at Corrour soon after 9.00 a.m.

Walk along the track on the north side of lovely Loch Ossian, passing through sweetly smelling woods of larch, and look out for herons and many varieties of wader feeding on the shore.

Cross the footbridge beyond Corrour Lodge and take the narrow path up Glen Labhair for two miles, then turn off north and climb heathery slopes to the summit of Beinn

Eibhinn, 3,611ft/1,100m. The massive bulk of Ben Alder dominates the view east, while to the west, across Loch Treig, rise Stob Coire Easain and Stob a'Coire Mheadhoin. Outlined to the north is the long ridge of the Creag Meagaidh range.

The ridge ahead is easy, and as you cross Aonach Beag and Geal Charn you can savour the rough, but fast, walking country at high altitude with panoramic views. Head north-east from Geal Charn, through a break in the cliffs, to a narrow spur leading to a bealach between two lochans under Carn Dearg.

From Carn Dearg it is downhill all the way to Dalwhinnie, first to Culra Lodge bothy, which is dry and comfortable, although rat-infested, and then to meet a stalkers' track to Loch Pattack. Look back to the important east-facing corries of Ben Alder which are often ringed with snow throughout the summer months, before heading for Dalwhinnie along the seven-mile Land Rover track running beside Loch Ericht.

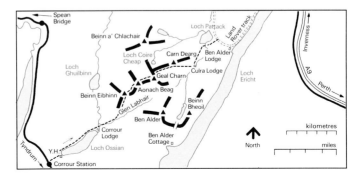

A BEN ALDER CROSSING

Map *OS Sheet 42*   **Start/Finish** *Rannoch Station (422578)/Corrour Station (356664)*   **Distance/Time** *from Rannoch Station 28 miles/45km, from Bridge of Gaur 22 miles/35km, 2 days*

> **Grading** *A two-day expedition over remote mountainous terrain. For the experienced walker only.*
> **Escape Routes** *None. Emergency shelter at Culra Lodge Bothy, Corrour Lodge and Ben Alder Cottage.*
> **Transport** *Railway stations at Corrour and Rannoch. Bus service: Rannoch Station/Kinloch Rannoch.*
> **Accommodation** *Hotels at Rannoch and Bridge of Orchy. Youth Hostel at Loch Ossian (summer only).*

Ben Alder, 3,757ft/1,148m, stands supreme north-east of Rannoch Moor. It vies with A'Mhaighdean for the privilege of being the most inaccessible Munro. The motorist on the A9 might glimpse this white-coated monster, glinting in winter sunshine above Loch Ericht, and the rail traveller, rattling across Rannoch Moor on a bed of brushwood, might glance east at its massive bulk. But the hill walker is drawn to Ben Alder by its size, remoteness and grandeur.

Two days should be allowed for this expedition, with an overnight halt at Benalder Cottage and the use of the West Highland Railway for the return leg.

The morning train to Rannoch Station is met by a post-bus which will whisk you six miles to Bridge of Gaur. From Rannoch Lodge the path to Benalder Cottage winds north, through new forestry and across open moorland, to the Alder Burn; this river is not bridged and in wet weather a safety rope must be used.

Benalder Cottage sits squatly under the southern slopes of Ben Alder, it is a comfortable bothy and wood is available from the shore of Loch Ericht or the plantation across the burn.

Before supper explore the rocky slopes above the cottage for Cluny's Cage, the underground hideout where Bonnie Prince Charlie took refuge from Cumberland's troops after Culloden.

Rise early on the second day, for you have far to go and a train to catch. Climb easily beside the burn to Bealach Breabag, and then head north across boulder fields to the Ben Alder plateau. Quite suddenly the full glory of the Garbh Choire bursts into view: a mile-long curve of broken cliffs falling 1,000ft to the dark Loch a'Bhealaich Bheithe, while rock buttresses rise from the corrie floor.

The summit plateau is bleak and exposed, in winter allow a wide margin for cornices, and it can be a relief to lose height down the broad and easy-angled north-west ridge into the glen. When you reach the Uisge Labhair, spare a thought for the four walkers who perished at this spot in a ferocious blizzard at New Year 1951.

At Corrour Lodge you meet Land Rover tracks which run pleasantly north and south of Loch Ossian to Corrour Station. If you have time before your train is due, you can chat to the warden of the Loch Ossian Youth Hostel at the western end of the loch.

BEN NEVIS AND THE LOCHABER TRAVERSE

Map OS Sheet 41 (Tourist Map)   **Start/Finish** Youth Hostel in Glen Nevis (127718)/Spean Bridge (221816)
Distance/Time 25 miles/40km, 13 hrs

Grading An exceptionally arduous walk over the highest hills in the British Isles. In winter conditions it is a major mountaineering expedition.
Escape Routes From Carn Mor Dearg down NW ridge to Allt a' Mhuilinn. From Aonach Mor down N ridge to Leanachan Forest. From Stob Coire Easain down N ridge to the Cour Glen.
Transport Railway stations at Fort William and Spean Bridge. Bus service: Fort William/Glen Nevis (summer only).
Accommodation Varied accommodation in Fort William and Spean Bridge. Youth Hostel at Glen Nevis.

This most arduous mountain walk takes in not only the highest mountain in Britain, but also two other 4,000ft peaks and a long ridge walk across the heart of Lochaber.

During the winter months the complete walk from Glen Nevis to Spean Bridge should not be attempted in a single day. Even during April you can expect delays through step-cutting or cramponing and benightment is always a risk. However, if you start from Glen Nevis, you can find a number of places on the Grey Corries ridge from which you can escape to Glen Spean. Grey Corries is the name given to the range comprising Sgurr Choinnich Mor, Stob Coire Easain and Stob Choire Clauraigh, whose slopes fall away in grey screes.

May or June are the ideal months for this walk. The days are long and, because these hills carry an immense amount of snow, you can expect an exhilarating day, with the ridges clear yet the corries still ringed with snow, and the huge cornices on the Aonachs still in place.

From the Glen Nevis Youth Hostel put your head down, grit your teeth, and follow the nightmarish pony-track to the summit of Ben Nevis.

Don't delay on the Ben, you still have far to go and there are more rewarding and remote summits ahead.

Descend the loose slopes in a south-easterly direction for 900ft, taking extreme care in winter conditions (this is one of the principal accident black-spots in the Highlands), to the perfect curve of the Carn Mor Dearg arête. This narrow, rocky ridge leads to the north side of Coire Leis and provides unsurpassed views of Britain's largest cliff, the north face of Ben Nevis.

A well-defined, but steep, ridge leads east from Carn Mor Dearg to a low bealach whence, with no respite, you must climb directly to the saddle between Aonach Mor and Beag. Detour briefly to bag the rounded summit of Aonach Mor.

The Aonach Beag ridge soon narrows and becomes rocky while, beyond the 4,060ft/1,236m summmit, the descent to the col under Sgurr Choinnich Beag can be tricky in snow.

Once on the Grey Corries ridge though the pressure is off and you can enjoy the very best of Scottish ridge walking. The Sgurr Choinnich Mor to Stob Coire Easain section is quite airy but the ridge broadens before Stob Choire Clauraigh, at 3,853ft/1,177m, the last peak of the day.

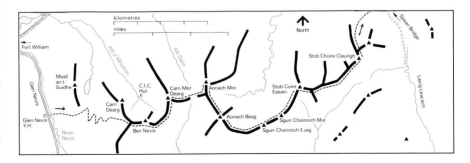

THE MAMORES

Map OS Sheet 41 (Tourist Map)   **Start/Finish** Youth Hostel in Glen Nevis (127718)
Distance/Time 22 miles/35km, 10-11 hrs

Grading A long and undulating walk, mainly above the 3,000ft level.
Escape Routes N down Coire Mhusgain from the bealach between Stob Ban and Sgor an Iubhair. S down Coire na Ba from the bealach between Am Bodach and Stob Coire a' Chairn.
Transport Railway station at Fort William. Bus service: Fort William/Glen Nevis (summer only).
Accommodation Varied accommodation in Fort William. Youth Hostel at Glen Nevis.

Glen Nevis runs between two high and complex ridge systems: the Aonachs–Grey Corries ridge to the north and the Mamores to the south. Both ridges provide considerable challenges for the hill walker.

The Mamores walk I recommend here involves the traverse of a continuous ridge, eight miles long, lying above 2,750ft, and including seven separate Munros. It does not detour to several other peaks lying off the spine of the main ridge, although these could be included by an exceptionally determined party.

Leave the Glen Nevis road one mile beyond the Youth Hostel and walk up a fire break through the forestry plantation to gain the north ridge of Sgorr Chalum. This subsidiary top of 1,823ft/557m marks the end of the two-mile-long northern spur of Mullach nan

Coirean. The angle is gentle and the ascent of the Mullach is delightful, with an ever-widening vista of hills opening out to the north and east as you gain height. Mullach nan Coirean is flat-topped with good corries on all sides, and you should follow the lip of the huge eastern corrie for one-and-a-half miles until you reach the abrupt north ridge of Stob Ban.

The Mamore ridge now winds its way westwards to Na Gruagaichean before turning north to Binnein Mor. In mist route-finding can be a problem because off-shoot spurs and

ridges abound; it is all too easy to stray north onto Sgurr a'Mhaim or An Garbhanach. In clear weather the walk is most exhilarating with views down to the climbers' cottage at Steall in Upper Glen Nevis and across the glen to the great waterslide of the Allt Coire Eoghainn. The north-east buttress of Ben Nevis is outlined against the sky as it plunges down from the summit plateau, while the Carn Mor Dearg arête curves away to the right.

Throughout the day's walk the twin summits of Binnein Mor beckon you on, for this fine mountain, at 3,700ft/1,128m, commands the entire Mamore range and neighbouring peaks extending from Ben Alder to Ben Cruachan.

Descend the broken, bouldery north ridge and traverse the pointed little peak of Binnein Beag to regain the path in Upper Glen Nevis.

It is a rewarding seven-mile walk back to the Youth Hostel, passing the old ruin at Steall and the climbers' cottage beside the waterfall, before descending the magnificent Nevis gorge.

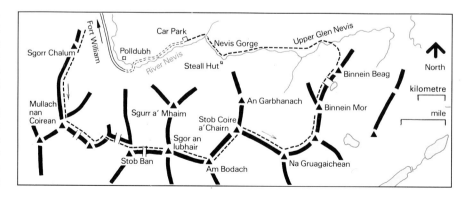

THE AONACH EAGACH RIDGE

Map OS Sheet 41 (Tourist Map) *Start/Finish* Meeting of Three Waters, Glen Coe (175566)/Glencoe village (105590) *Distance/Time* 6 miles/10km, 4-5 hrs (summer) 8-10 hrs (winter)

Grading A moderate scramble in summer; it may be much harder in winter. A rope should be carried.
Escape Routes It is inadvisable to try to descend from the ridge except at its ends. This is particularly true in bad visibility or darkness.
Transport Bus service: Glasgow/Glencoe/Fort William.
Accommodation Hotels and B & B in Glencoe. Bunk house at Leacantuim. Climbing huts at Onich (MC of S) and Lagangarbh (SMC). Youth Hostel at Glencoe village.

Many hill walkers who aspire to become climbers cut their teeth on the Aonach Eagach. In summer this exposed ridge, which bounds the north side of the Pass of Glencoe, is not too daunting although, unlike several similar knife-edges in Scotland, the difficulties cannot be bypassed.

Yet the Aonach Eagach should never be, taken lightly; it requires the use of hands as well as feet, walkers need a head for heights, and there is no simple escape route. From the half-way point it is as easy to continue to the end of the ridge as it is to return. For these reasons the Aonach Eagach has become something of a test-piece; it is a route for mountaineers and, when successfully completed, it opens the way to the Cuillin ridge,

the Torridon ridges, the Corrag Bhuidhe Buttresses of An Teallach and, perhaps, to the Bla Bheinn–Clach Glas ridge on Skye.

In winter the Aonach Eagach is a much more serious undertaking. Parties should be fully equipped and prepared for any eventuality; even experienced winter climbers have been benighted through under-estimating the task.

Start from the cottage at Allt-na-reigh, at 700ft; a traverse from this direction (east) means that the principal problems are tackled early on in the day, in addition you gain a height bonus.

A beaten track winds up the south-east ridge of Am Bodach, which is rocky in its upper sections. Straightaway, from the summit cairn, your hands come out of your pockets as you clamber down slabby rocks to reach the narrow summit ridge of Meall Dearg, 3,126ft/ 953m.

The crux of the Aonach Eagach is the section between Meall Dearg and Stob Coire Leith where a series of pinnacles must be surmounted. Although holds are plentiful, when taken direct they cause the heart to flutter for the exposure is considerable.

Beyond the pinnacles the ridge rises more

easily to Stob Coire Leith and then broadens to Sgor nam Fiannaidh; a line of fence posts can be useful markers here in mist.

A steep and stony descent can be made from the western summit of this mountain to Clachaig Hotel, the path following the west side of Clachaig Gully. However, it is more satisfactory to continue in a north-westerly direction to Sgor na Ciche, the Pap of Glencoe, a magnificent viewpoint for Loch Leven, the Mamores and Beinn a'Bheithir.

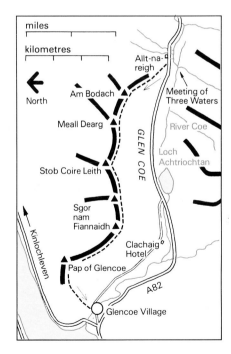

A TRAVERSE OF BIDEAN NAM BIAN

Map *OS Sheet 41 (Tourist Map)*   **Start/Finish** *Loch Achtriochtan (139567)*   **Distance/Time** *9 miles/14km, 6-7 hrs*

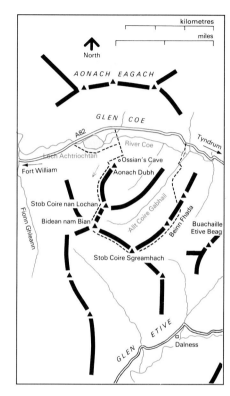

Grading A serious mountaineering expedition involving some rock scrambling. Route finding could be difficult in bad weather. A rope should be carried.
Escape Routes From the bealach between Bidean nam Bian and Stob Coire nan Lochan descend NW into Coire nam Beith or E into Coire Gabhail.
Transport Bus service: Glasgow/Glencoe/Fort William.
Accommodation Hotels and B & B in Glencoe. Bunk house at Leacantuim. Climbing huts at Onich (MC of S) and Lagangarbh (SMC). Youth Hostel at Glencoe village.

As you drive down Glen Coe towards Loch Leven, the rock walls of the Aonach Eagach and The Three Sisters so oppressively confine you that it is easy to miss the occasional fleeting view of Bidean nam Bian.

Bidean stands back from the glen, the rock buttresses of The Three Sisters forming a plinth above which this proud and pointed peak thrusts skyward. At 3,772ft/1,150m, it is the highest mountain in Argyll and it extends an array of rocky ridges to the north and east.

With towering cliffs, gullies, loose rocky slopes and craggy spurs an expedition to Bidean is always a serious undertaking; the mountain takes no prisoners. In winter Bidean is best left to experienced parties.

For confident walkers, who relish a little scrambling, an exciting approach to Bidean is via the face of Aonach Dubh. From the east end of Loch Achtriochtan, climb the grassy buttress to the side of the deep gully which runs up the face east of Ossian's Cave. Traverse west below the cave and scramble up the upper slopes of Aonach Dubh, choosing the easiest line. Continue along the broad ridge to Stob Coire nan Lochan, enjoying the spectacular cliffs falling to the lochans at the head of Coire Gabhail.

A much easier route leaves the Glen Coe road west of Loch Achtriochtan and climbs into Coire nam Beith. The path divides in the upper corrie, and the left-hand branch should be followed to gain the bealach between Stob Coire nan Lochan and Bidean nam Bian.

A short, rough climb leads past several buttresses of clean rock to the summit of Bidean. The view from such a dominating peak is stupendous, particularly north over the Aonach Eagach to the Mamores, Ben Nevis and the Grey Corries, and east to the Black Mount.

Turn south-east from the summit, skirt the head of Coire Gabhail and climb to Stob Coire Sgreamhach. Now head north along the crest of Beinn Fhada, which gives unparalleled

views of the cliffs of Stob Coire nan Lochan. Before the final top, drop down easily from the bealach to the extraordinary, green, fertile, hanging glen known as the Lost Valley.

Pick your way over the chaos of fallen boulders at the jaws of the valley, and cross the River Coe by a footbridge to reach the road at Meeting of Three Waters.

BUACHAILLE ETIVE MOR

Map OS Sheet 41 (Tourist Map)   *Start/Finish* Glen Etive (220520)   *Distance/Time* 7 miles/11km, 5 hrs

Grading A straightforward mountain walk although
some rough and steep slopes must be negotiated.
Escape Routes From the bealach E of Stob Coire
Altruim descend N to the Lairig Gartain or S to Glen
Etive.
Transport Railway station at Bridge of Orchy. Bus
service: Glasgow/Glencoe/Fort William.
Accommodation Hotels at Kingshouse, Clachaig
and Glencoe. B & B in Glencoe. Bunk house at
Leacantuim. Climbing hut at Lagangarbh (SMC).
Youth Hostels at Glencoe village and Crianlarich.

Many of Scotland's greatest peaks hide away
their features in remote corries and glens, to
be appreciated only by the adventurous walker.
The north face of Ben Nevis is a prime
example, as is Coire Mhic Fhearchair of Beinn
Eighe (chapter 36) and the long line of cliffs on
Beinn Lair (chapter 33). But for accessibility
Buachaille Etive Mor is unrivalled and it
flamboyantly displays its wares for all to see:
towering rock walls, buttresses and gullies. Its
stupendous north-facing pyramid makes it the
perfect sentinel for Glen Coe, setting the scene
for the subsequent descent into its grim depths.

The irresistible challenge of the Buachaille,
when seen from the A82 over Rannoch Moor,
has been influential in shaping the careers of
many climbers. W. H. Murray admits that it is

his favourite mountain, and the first impression
that it made has endured.

The Buachaille's acres of bare rock look for-
bidding, but walkers should realise that the
rock cone of Stob Dearg is only the end of a
three-mile ridge, running south above Glen
Etive and barely dropping below 3,000ft. The
summit of Stob Dearg can be reached easily
from either the north or the south sides of this
ridge.

Although the Buachaille traverse can be
linked to Buachaille Etive Beag, or a low-level
return route through the Lairig Gartain, to
make a long mountain circuit, I shall describe
here the shortest, simplest route. Walkers to
this part of Argyll may welcome a less arduous
day after their exertions on Bidean, the
Aonach Eagach, Rannoch Moor, the Black
Mount and the Mamores.

From a point two miles south of the Glen
Etive road junction a steep, but simple, ascent
may be made of the grassy Coire Cloiche
Finne. This leads to the main top of Stob
Dearg, 3,345ft/1,022m, via a bealach on the
south-west side. From this eyrie, poised above
awesome cliffs, you can survey the vast
expanse of Rannoch Moor with its countless

lochans scattering the light like jewels.

The main spine of the Buachaille consists of
four principal tops: south-west of Stob Dearg
is Stob na Doire followed by the much craggier
Stob Coire Altruim. The last peak, Stob na
Broige, is noted for the 1,200ft ravine, known
as Dalness Chasm, which splits the face above
Alltchaorunn. Continue descending the pronounced ridge, until grassy slopes can be seen
to run down to the Glen Etive road near
Alltchaorunn.

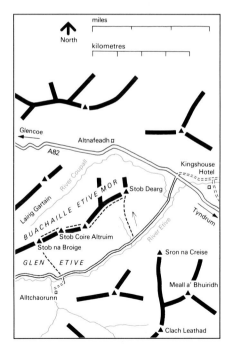

ACROSS RANNOCH MOOR

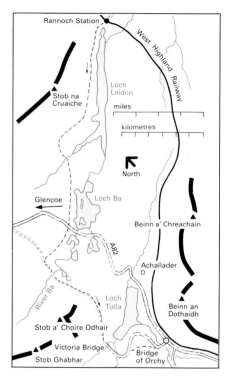

Map *OS Sheets 41, 50 and 51*   **Start/Finish** *Bridge of Orchy (298397) with train to Rannoch to commence walking*
Distance/Time *22 miles/35km, 9-10 hrs*

Grading *A long and strenuous walk with additional hazards in bad weather.*
Escape Routes *From Loch Laidon via Black Corries to Kingshouse.*
Transport *Railway stations at Bridge of Orchy and Rannoch. Bus service: Glasgow/Bridge of Orchy/Fort William.*
Accommodation *Hotels at Bridge of Orchy, Rannoch and Kingshouse. Youth Hostels at Glencoe, Loch Ossian and Crianlarich.*

An aura of dread and foreboding, amounting almost to hysteria, surrounds Rannoch Moor. Maybe the source is tales of whitened skeletons being discovered in the peat (the remains of Irish navvies who worked on the Blackwater Reservoir in 1904), vivid scenes from R. L. Stevenson's *Kidnapped*, or the sheer size and desolation of the wasteland of peat hags, lochans, boulders and blasted trees when seen from the comfort of Kingshouse Hotel, the Fort William train or your car as you speed north along the A82 towards Glen Coe.

There is no disputing the extent of Rannoch Moor, its 300 square miles assure it of Britain's crown, but it is a fascinating area yielding up many treasures to the adventurous walker.

The Moor is not just a treacherous morasse of saturated peat interspersed with stagnant pools, it is a complex association of hillocks, lochans and granite boulders and is the home of a diverse selection of wild life. In summer the Moor is a colourful world of heather, green moss, yellow grass, brown peat, harebells, butterflies and dragonflies. Whitened tree roots emerge from the bogs, many of them thousands of years old, a legacy of the ancient Caledonian Forest. Crannach Wood, above Achallader Farm, is a living remnant of this old forest.

The historic West Highland Railway, which runs up the east side of the Moor, can be used to great advantage for this expedition. From Bridge of Orchy take the morning train to Rannoch Station, shoulder your rucksack and take the path which follows the northern shore of Loch Laiden. Watch out for waders on the sandy shores of the bays.

At the ruin of Tigh na Cruaiche you must detour round the western arm of the loch, and then head south to the western banks of Loch Ba which can be followed to the A82 road. In dry weather you can ford the Abhainn Ba and reach the A82 via the eastern edge of the loch. Either way Eilean Molach, with its thicket of trees and shrubs, shows how Rannoch Moor could have looked today without the ravages of man and beast.

From the road a path runs due west to join the Old Military Road (now the track of the West Highland Way) at ruined Ba Cottage. The last eight miles of the day involve pleasant easy walking through the woods at Forest Lodge, and then across the shoulder of Mam Carraigh to Bridge of Orchy.

THE PEAKS OF THE BLACK MOUNT

Map *OS Sheet 100 (Tourist Map)* **Start/Finish** *Kingshouse Hotel (260547)/Bridge of Orchy Hotel (299397)*
Distance/Time *16 miles/26km, 8 hrs*

> **Grading** *A long mountain traverse involving some mild rock scrambling. Route finding difficult in poor visibility.*
> **Escape Routes** *From Bealach Fuar-chathaidh descend SE into Coire Ba or W into Coire Ghiubhasan.*
> **Transport** *Railway station at Bridge of Orchy. Bus service: Glasgow/Bridge of Orchy/Kingshouse/ Fort William.*
> **Accommodation** *Hotels at Bridge of Orchy and Kingshouse. B & B in Tyndrum and Glencoe. Youth Hostels at Glencoe and Crianlarich.*

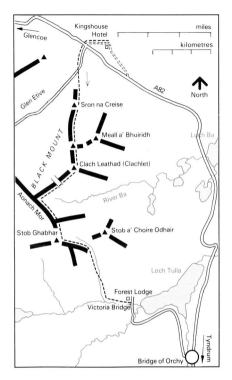

This high mountain traverse across the Black Mount links the hotels of Kingshouse and Bridge of Orchy. It provides an adventurous alternative to the West Highland Way, which follows the Old Military Road along the rim of Rannoch Moor.

Starting from Kingshouse the first objective is Sron na Creise, the shapely peak dominating the southern aspect between Meall a'Bhuiridh and the gash of Glen Etive. Sron na Creise points twin summits to the sky, which are linked by a ridge, curved as the crescent moon.

Strike across the rough moor towards the north ridge of Sron na Creise. It looks imposing but there are easy steps, ledges, ramps and scree gullies which present few difficulties. Near the top, a nose of rock forces

a detour right before you regain the ridge. A short wall requires the use of hands, and then you are beside the summit cairn with Scotland at your feet.

This north summit of Sron na Creise marks the end of a broad and undulating ridge which wanders south towards Clachlet. The steep corries on the east hold large patches of snow, while to the west gentler slopes descend to delectable hidden glens. Just short of Clachlet's main top a narrow ridge runs in from Meall a'Bhuiridh on the east.

South of Clachlet the ground falls away into the vast Coireach a'Ba, and beyond rises the prominent turret-like summit of Stob Ghabhar.

Firstly, a steep descent must be made to Bealach Fuar-chathaidh which can be hard to find in mist. If in doubt descend the easy east ridge of Clachlet to the Military Road.

From the bealach ascend the long north-west ridge, the Aonach Mor, to the huge cairn on Stob Ghabhar. The Central Gully falls away beneath you, a classic winter climb where many an epic battle has been fought.

Follow the smooth curve of the east ridge until a cairn marks the point where the ridge divides. The east ridge, the Aonach Eagach,

provides a short and spicy scramble along its exposed crest. Further down the ridge head off south towards the burn to avoid some cliffs. You meet a stalkers' path beside the Allt Toaig which leads to Loch Tulla and Victoria Bridge, where you may have transport waiting. If not, walk a further three miles, through the remnants of the old forest and finally beside the river, to Bridge of Orchy.

[85]

THE BEN LUI HORSESHOE

Map OS Sheet 50   *Start/Finish* Tyndrum (330302)/Dalmally (161272)   *Distance/Time* 17 miles/27km, 9-10 hrs

---

Grading *A moderate walk over a shapely and compact group of mountains. Several steep and rocky sections are included.*
Escape Routes *From the Ben Oss–Ben Lui bealach descend N down Coire Laoigh to Cononish. From the Ben Lui–Beinn a' Chleibh bealach descend NW to the A85.*
Transport *Railway stations at Tyndrum and Dalmally. Bus services: Glasgow/Tyndrum/Fort William and Glasgow/Dalmally/Oban.*
Accommodation *Hotels and B & B at Tyndrum and Dalmally. Youth Hostels at Crianlarich and Oban.*

Ben Lui rises gracefully to a conical summit, 3,708ft/1,130m high, which is clearly visible from the A82 between Crianlarich and Tyndrum. It has been described as the most beautiful peak in Scotland and, when it is seen dazzling white in the winter sunshine, it is hard to disagree. The high north-east corrie of Ben Lui collects much snow and provides a classic winter climb.

Ben Lui and its three satellite peaks can be traversed in a day from Tyndrum to Dalmally, where accommodation can be obtained. Since the mountains are easily accessible from three sides, long approach marches are not necessary.

Take the path from Tyndrum South station to Cononish Farm, cross the river and fight your way up the rough north ridge of Beinn Dubhchraig. High on the ridge, near a false summit, you pass a group of lochans that mark the way down to the Ben Oss bealach.

Ben Oss is a splendid viewpoint for the east corrie of Ben Lui, the Arrochar hills, Ben More and Stob Binnein and the Mamlorn group.

Descend again to another bealach and climb the ever-steepening south-east ridge of Ben Lui. Keep to the edge of the ridge where you can enjoy the feeling of space and, higher up where the main east ridge joins your path, you will be able to look into the dramatic north-east corrie.

I have climbed this ridge in arctic conditions, when the tearing wind had covered the rocks with luminous green ice, and snow devils were swirling below on the bealach. However, on the sharp summit of Ben Lui there was dead calm and I sat beside the large cairn in peace and solitude, and admired the cornices ringing the north face. It was March and the sun warmed my face reminding me that spring was not far away. The air was clear as crystal and I could easily see beyond Ben Cruachan to Ben More on Mull, while to the north Ben Nevis rose above the Mamores into a blue sky.

Steep and stony slopes lead south-west to the base of the east ridge of Beinn a'Chleibh, whence half an hour's walking and a little rock scrambling give you the fourth Munro.

The broad north-west ridge presents no difficulty on the descent and you soon reach Succoth Lodge beside the railway line.

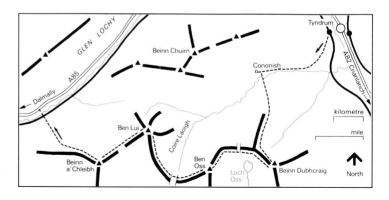

BEN CRUACHAN

Map OS Sheet 50 (Tourist Map)   **Start/Finish** Cruachan Dam access road (115267)
Distance/Time 11 miles/18km, 7 hrs

> **Grading** A fine mountaineering route including the
> traverse of a high and rocky ridge. Can be a serious
> proposition in winter.
> **Escape Routes** In good conditions the S slopes of
> the ridge can be descended to the reservoir.
> **Transport** Railway stations at Dalmally and Taynuilt.
> Bus service: Glasgow/Dalmally/Oban.
> **Accommodation** Varied accommodation at Dalmally.
> Youth Hostel at Oban.

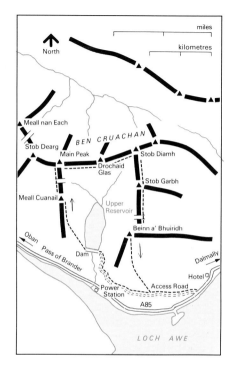

Ben Cruachan, towering to 3,689ft/1,126m, dominates the rich and spectacular country of Lorn, in mid-Argyll, and the hill walker who traverses the narrow summit ridge of the mountain can enjoy divers pleasures. Although the Hydro-Electric Board's pumped storage scheme has ravished the high, south-facing corrie of the Allt Cruachan, and strewn high-tension cables across the lower slopes of the mountain, the intrusion is offset by the extraordinary, romantic scene laid out below.

As you walk up the access road to the Cruachan dam, the view unfolds. The islands of Loch Awe are thickly wooded with deciduous trees, and on my last visit, at the end of October, the leaves were a riot of colour. I could just make out, through the trees, the ruined nunnery on Inishail, and the thirteenth-century castle on Fraoch Eilean. A little further to the east, the imposing, grey castle of Kilchurn stood out against the vivid yellow of the oaks.

However, on rounding the shoulder of Beinn a'Bhuiridh, Cruachan's upper corrie comes into view with its hideous concrete dam. Being invisible from below, no attempt has been made at landscaping.

Cross the dam and climb the grassy slopes of Meall Cuanail; a fence is a useful guide in mist. A cairned path then zig-zags up the granite screes to Main Peak, which gives outstanding views south-west, beyond the mouth of Loch Etive, to the Firth of Lorne, Mull, Colonsay and the Paps of Jura.

A quick detour may be made to the outlier of Stob Dearg (the Taynuilt Peak), before heading east over Drochaid Glas to Stob Diamh.

The ridge is predominantly rocky, and you pick your way across steeply-angled slabs and giant boulders. Friction on the coarse-grained granite is excellent and the traverse, although exposed in places, is not difficult in good conditions. In winter though the ridge can give an exacting climb, and the appropriate equipment, including ropes, must be used.

A word of warning, Drochaid Glas throws out a rocky spur to the north-east. Don't stray along this spur but drop down steeply, south, before turning east along the main ridge.

Once on Stob Diamh the going is easy over grassy slopes which give way to boulders near the top. Descend the broad south ridge over Stob Garbh and Beinn a'Bhuiridh, to meet the Cruachan dam access road near to your starting point.

SCHIEHALLION

Map OS Sheet 42   **Start/Finish** Tempar Farm, 2 miles E of Kinloch Rannoch (687575)/Braes of Foss (757560)
Distance/Time 6 miles/10km, 4-5 hrs

Grading A rough but easy mountain walk.
Escape Routes Schiehallion may be descended almost anywhere.
Transport Bus service: Pitlochry/Tummel Bridge/ Kinloch Rannoch.
Accommodation Hotels at Kinloch Rannoch and Strathtummel. B & B locally. Youth Hostels at Pitlochry and Killin.

Perthshire, with its rich deciduous woodlands, deep glens and peaceful lochs is sheltered from the worst of the westerly gales by the mountain barriers of Argyllshire. Its flavour is reminiscent of the English Lake District.

Perhaps Perthshire's most elegant hill is Schiehallion which, when seen from the north or west, rises in a perfect cone to a height of 3,547ft/1,083m. The name Sidh Chaillean means the Fairy Hill.

Apart from its grace and beauty, Schiehallion is famous for the part it played in a classic scientific experiment in 1774. The experiment was suggested by Nevil Maskelyne, the Astronomer Royal, who reckoned that a large mass (Schiehallion) would attract a small mass hanging from a plumb-line. From the deflection, and the estimated mass of Schiehallion, he was able to work out the gravitational constant and the approximate mass of the earth.

Schiehallion's conspicuous cone is the shapely end of a three-mile ridge which extends north-west from General Wade's Military Road, between Loch Tummel and Keltneyburn. This summit ridge is prominent from the Queen's View, above the east end of Loch Tummel, so named by the impression it made on Queen Victoria when she visited it in 1866.

It is not a demanding expedition to traverse this ridge, particularly if you start from 1,078ft at Braes of Foss on the minor road which cuts across the northern slopes of Schiehallion.

There is a car-park at Braes of Foss farm, whence a waymarked path runs through fields, and then beside forestry, towards Schiehallion's east ridge. The track, which is cairned, climbs through the heather and then over stony ground to meet the ridge at a height of about 2,000ft. Although the going becomes rockier it is always easy and, having passed several false summits, you soon arrive at the top which is marked by a pile of quartzite blocks and a toposcope.

The panorama from Schiehallion extends southwards to Arthur's Seat in Edinburgh, westwards across Rannoch Moor to the Glen-coe Peaks, and beyond to Ben Nevis and the Cairngorms. Below lies long Loch Rannoch with the ancient Black Wood on its south side. This priceless relic of the ancient Caledonian Forest is now managed by the Forestry Commission.

The descent of the north-west ridge to Tempar is much rougher than the east ridge. Quartzite outcrops are exposed in many places and the path traverses beds of loose scree.

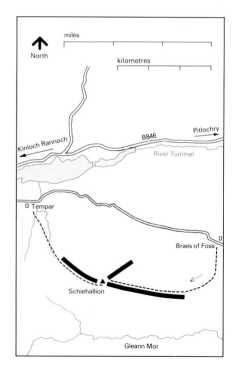

BEN LAWERS AND
THE TARMACHANS

Map OS Sheet 51 *Start/Finish* Lawers village (680399)/Killin (572326) *Distance/Time* 20 miles/32km, 11 hrs

Grading A long and switchback walk over mainly easy ground, although the Tarmachans are rough and bouldery.
Escape Routes Descents from bealachs on the main ridge, S down grassy slopes, are feasible in many places.
Transport Railway station at Crianlarich. Bus service: Killin/Aberfeldy/Callander/Stirling.
Accommodation Hotels, B & B and Youth Hostel at Killin.

Ben Lawers rises to 3,984ft/1,214m in central Perthshire; it is actually the highest mountain in Britain south of Ben Nevis but, because of its huge bulk, it does not always win due respect.

The underlying rock is a lime-rich schist which makes the mountain a botanist's paradise in spring when the slopes are bright with orchids and mountain pansies, while the extremely rare snow gentian, alpine speedwell and alpine forget-me-not can be found in the high corries. For this reason the mountain has been declared a National Nature Reserve.

My recommended itinerary crosses the entire Lawers range and continues over the adjacent and rockier Meall nan Tarmachan. This walk is bliss on a fine summer's day when you can wander lazily along the ridges, picking bilberries and enjoying the flowers and the view. Ben Lawers commands the beautiful county of Perthshire, which has the greatest variety of scenery in all Scotland.

From Lawers village a path runs up the east side of the burn. Follow this for a mile and then ascend the broad south ridge of Meall Greigh and continue easily to Meall Garbh. The ridge now twists and turns as it climbs to the sharply pointed peak of An Stuc which has steep and broken sides. Below lies a deep corrie holding a curious lochan, shaped like a sitting cat, called Lochan nan Cat. Beyond, set in woods, stretches beautiful Loch Tay; fifteen miles long from Killin to Kenmore and never more than a mile across.

The summit of Ben Lawers is so nearly 4,000ft that an enormous cairn was built in 1878, having a height of 12ft and a circumference of 50ft. A man standing on this cairn would thus have his head above 4,000ft. Unfortunately this cairn collapsed years ago.

Descend in a south-westerly direction to the bealach under Beinn Ghlas, another shapely peak, and then swing north-west to the flat-topped Meall Corranaich. An easy ridge now runs down to the road at the south end of Lochan na Lairige.

Meall nan Tarmachan is altogether much rockier than the Ben Lawers massif, and you must weave your way through a complex of outcrops to reach the summit. The rocks continue for a further two miles, as you head west over Beinn nan Eachan and Creag na Caillich, before you can find a way down grassy slopes towards Killin.

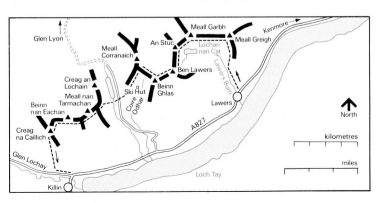

RIDGE WANDERING IN PERTHSHIRE: THE CRIANLARICH HILLS

Map OS Sheets 51 and 56   *Start/Finish* Benmore Farm (414258)/Inveraran Hotel (318185)
Distance/Time 19 miles/31km, 12-13 hrs

Grading A long walk over rocky, mountainous terrain. Much ascent and descent is involved.
Escape Routes From Stob Binnein N down Benmore Glen. From bealachs between Stob Glas and Beinn a' Chroin and between An Caisteal and Beinn Chabhair descend N down easy glens.
Transport Railway station at Crianlarich. Bus services: Glasgow/Crianlarich/Oban and Glasgow/Crianlarich/Fort William.
Accommodation Hotels at Crianlarich and Inverarnan. B & B and Youth Hostel at Crianlarich.

This very long and arduous expedition links Ben More with Beinn Chabhair, crossing the range of individual and shapely hills east of Glen Falloch.

Although these hills are quite easily accessible from main roads, they can be tough propositions in winter, when the use of ice-axe and crampons is imperative on their steep ridges and slopes which rise abruptly from low bealachs and deep glens. In summer though the bands of broken rock are easily negotiated and the walking is easy. In spring the glens are carpeted with bluebells and primroses, growing under the birch, alder and sycamore trees.

Start from Benmore Farm, two miles east of Crianlarich. A path ascends directly to the summit trig. point, 3,843ft/1,174m, of Ben More; the climb is fully 3,300ft and it can be an awful grind on a hot summer's day. In winter Ben More carries a great deal of snow and the slopes just below the cairn have been known to avalanche.

The nearby peak of Stob Binnein is beautifully proportioned, a regular cone with its top cut off, and it is reached via the low bealach Eadar-dha Beinn. Another huge drop, to 1,650ft, is necessary before you can scramble up the rocky east side of Stob Garbh and thence to the twin summits of Cruach Ardrain, 3,428ft/1,046m.

Cruach Ardrain is a most impressive wedge with a steep east face and a pointed summit. Although it is lower than Ben More it is the best viewpoint of the day, particularly for the Crianlarich hills.

The switchback nature of this itinerary shows no sign of abating as you cross to the subsidiary summit of Stob Glas on the south-west spur of Cruach Ardrain, and then descend to 1,700ft under the east top of Beinn a'Chroin. Both An Caisteal (the Castle) and Beinn Chabhair require the same treatment, the latter mountain being particularly rocky. The direct route up Beinn Chabhair is barred by a line of cliffs, which can be avoided by working round to the right to reach grassy slopes.

The north-west ridge provides a gentle descent to Glen Falloch. On the shoulder of Ben Glas, 1,000ft down the ridge, you pass a delightful lochan, called Lochan a'Chaisteil, surrounded by extraordinary pinnacles and castles of rock.

Follow the burn through bracken and trees to the bridge over the Falloch river, just 200m from the Inveranan Hotel.

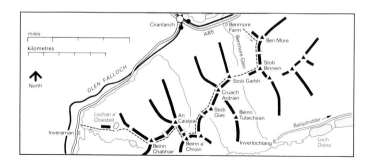

THE LOCH LUBNAIG HILLS: BEN LEDI AND BENVANE

Map OS Sheet 57 (Tourist Map)   *Start/Finish* Ben Ledi car-park (587092)   *Distance/Time* 14 miles/23km, 7 hrs

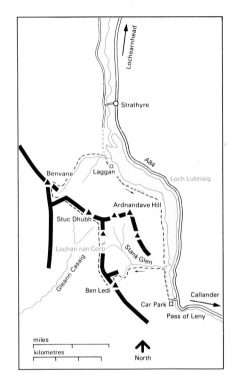

Grading An easy walk over mainly grassy hills.
Escape Routes From Lochan nan Corp a waymarked path descends the Stank Glen to Loch Lubnaig.
Transport Railway station at Stirling. Bus services: Stirling/Callander; Edinburgh/Stirling and Glasgow/ Stirling.
Accommodation Varied accommodation at Callander. Youth Hostels at Stirling, Trossachs, Loch Ard and Killin.

As you drive north along the winding road through Callander towards Crianlarich and Glen Coe, Ben Ledi is the first real mountain that you see. It towers above Loch Lubnaig to a height of 2,873ft/879m, presenting a high, wild corrie and a craggy face to the east. The fact that it does not win Munro status has caused many hearts to flutter with dismay at the thought of the monsters that must lie ahead.

It is particularly satisfying to spend a day on the lonely hills west of Loch Lubnaig, far above the tourist high-spots of the Trossachs, the Falls of Leny and Callander. This hill country was the setting for Sir Walter Scott's epic poem *The Lady of the Lake* and it was where Rob Roy outwitted the Duke of Montrose in the eighteenth century. More recently the TV series *Dr Finlay's Casebook* was based on the town of Callander.

The many visitors that are attracted here can enjoy romantic Scotland at its best: lochs, islands, woods, crags, corries, ravines, tumbling burns and purple heather.

From the car-park at the south end of Loch Lubnaig walk along the track above the loch and turn up into Stank Glen. Climb the open, grassy slopes beside a small burn passing, high up on the hillside, an extraordinary collection of chaotic, splintered boulders set at crazy angles as if cast down by a giant.

The stream drains a small corrie high under the summit ridge of Ben Ledi, and a narrow spur on the north side provides an airy route of ascent.

Ben Ledi commands views extending to Ben Cruachan, Beinn Laoigh, Ben More, Stob Binnein, Ben Lawers and Ben Vorlich. Nearer at hand it looks over Loch Venacher, Loch Katrine, Ben Venue and the beautiful country of the Trossachs, visited by William and Dorothy Wordsworth and Samuel Taylor Coleridge in 1803.

It is an easy two-hour walk round the head of Gleann Casaig to Benvane, for much of the way the route follows a line of old stakes. The tiny Lochan nan Corp, passed on the shoulder, gets

its name from the legend of the funeral party, making for St Bride's chapel in the Pass of Leny, that fell through the ice and were drowned.

From Benvane descend through the forestry to Loch Lubnaig-side, and return to the car-park along the delightfully rural and over-grown track of the old Callander–Strathyre railway.

[91]

BEN VORLICH AND STUC A'CHROIN

Map OS Sheets 51 and 57 (Tourist Map)   *Start/Finish* (recommended route) Ardvorlich (632230)
(alternative route) Braeleny (637111))   *Distance/Time* 12 miles/19km, 6-7 hrs

---

Grading A fairly simple mountain walk in summer but much more serious in winter conditions.
Escape Routes From Bealach an Dubh Choirein descend NW into Choire Fhuadaraich and Glen Ample, or SE into Gleann an Dubh Choirein.
Transport Railway stations at Stirling and Crianlarich. Bus service: Stirling/Callander/Lochearnhead/Killin.
Accommodation Hotels and B & B at Callender and Lochearnhead. Youth Hostels at Stirling, Trossachs, Loch Ard and Killin.

These two rather isolated mountains south of Loch Earn are particular favourites with hill walkers in the Southern Highlands. Being within easy reach of Glasgow and Edinburgh they can make enjoyable one-day excursions, and routes can be planned to suit all tastes and conditions. When driving north a sprinkling of snow on Ben Vorlich gives an idea of what to expect in Glen Coe or Lochaber.

From Ben More or the Crianlarich hills Ben Vorlich is seen to rise majestically, tapering to a point above the dark forests of Strathyre, while Stuc a'Chroin's north-east buttress falls away abruptly to a low bealach.

Circuits of the hills may be undertaken from either Ardvorlich on Loch Earn-side, or from Braeleny near Callander. The northern route is somewhat shorter.

From Ardvorlich House take the track that runs up Glen Vorlich, heading for the north ridge of the mountain. A path leads all the way up the ridge which becomes rocky and quite exposed near the top. When iced this section needs care.

Ben Vorlich's summit, 3,231ft/985m, looks across the Bealach an Dubh Choirein to the craggy and rather intimidating face of Stuc a'Chroin, 3,189ft/975m.

A line of fence posts, which bear left below the summit, lead down to the bealach, whence you can zig-zag up loose, bouldery slopes, weaving your way through the crags, to gain the top of the north-east buttress. Walk towards Stuc a'Chroin's summit, above a line of east-facing crags which have provided some worthwhile winter climbs.

Return to Ardvorlich via the broad north-west shoulder of Stuc a'Chroin, which rounds the head of Choire Fhuadaraich, and the gentle, grassy outlier of Ben Our.

When approaching from the south drive to Braeleny farm, three miles north of Callander, and walk along the Land Rover track to Arivurichardich. This gives access to the south-east ridge of Stuc a'Chroin just beyond the subsidiary summit of Meall na h-Iolaire.

From Stuc a'Chroin scramble down the north-east buttress to Bealach an Dubh Choirein (a cairn marks the start of the descent) and thence gain the summit of Ben Vorlich.

The south-east ridge, which runs above east-facing cliffs, descends gradually to Gleann an Dubh Choirein. Climb back up to the south-east ridge to regain the Arivurichardich path under Meall na h-Iolaire.

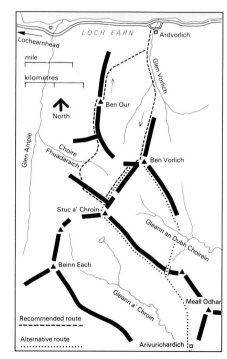

THE OCHILS: ROUND-OF-THE-NINE

Map OS Sheets 57 and 58 *Start/Finish* Dollar Glen (964985)/Menstrie (849971)
Distance/Time 19 miles/31km, 10-11 hrs

Grading A long walk over easy terrain: mainly undulating hills with grass and some heather.
Escape Routes It is easy to turn down any of the glens running S to Dollar, Tillicoultry or Alva.
Transport Railway stations at Stirling and Dunblane. Bus services: Stirling or Alloa to Dollar and Menstrie.
Accommodation Varied accommodation in Dollar, Alva, Stirling and Alloa. Youth Hostels at Stirling and Glendevon.

The Ochils are a range of swelling hills, mainly smooth and grassy and ideal for walking, which rise north of the A91 Stirling to Perth road. Ben Cleuch, 2,363ft/721m, is the highest hill and, from the discovery of mica-schist erratics on the summit, it is surmised that 10,000 years ago a great ice-sheet blanketed the entire range.

Silver, copper and lead have been mined in the Ochils over the ages, and villages grew under the southern slopes: Menstrie, Alva, Tillicoultry and Dollar. Water wheels, powered by the rushing streams, ground corn and spun wool from the sheep grazing the hills above.

The Ochils boast nine hills that exceed 2,000ft, and these provide a framework for a thoroughly enjoyable day's exploration of this gentle range, the 'Round-of-the-Nine'.

From Dollar a path, maintained by the National Trust for Scotland, runs up the picturesque Dollar Glen to Castle Campbell. The castle, which stands on a knoll overlooking the glen, dates from the fifteenth century and was once the stronghold of the Argylls.

Beyond the castle the path runs through a defile following the east side of the burn, passes a plantation and leads to Glenquey Reservoir.

By walking steeply up the grassy slopes on the west side of the reservoir you can gain the broad ridge linking Innerdownie and Whitewisp. Turn south to Whitewisp, so named because it holds snow late into the spring, and

enjoy the open space and expansive views over the plain of Forth. With the wind in your hair and firm turf underfoot this is magnificent walking.

Now swing west to the small cairn on Tarmangie Hill (difficult to locate in mist) and skirt the head of the glen of the Burn of Sorrow. Easy walking continues over King's Seat, but then you must head north-west and descend to the bealach at Maddy Moss, 1,850ft, at the source of the Gannel Burn where the ancient Tillicoultry to Blackford path crosses the hills.

Another slight deviation south is necessary to visit The Law before you attain Ben Cleuch, where you can use the indicator to identify the distant hills: the Cairngorms, Ben Nevis and Galloway.

More idyllic ridge wandering over gentle, undulating hills takes you to Ben Ever and Blairdenon Hill, but one last effort is needed if you are to climb Dumyat from the Menstrie Burn before returning to civilisation.

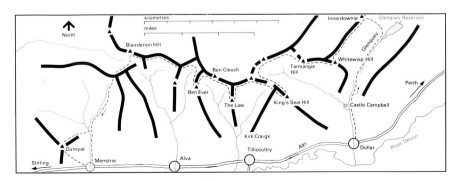

A DAY ON THE COBBLER

Map OS Sheet 56 (Tourist Map)   **Start/Finish** Beside Loch Long (287040)   **Distance/Time** 5 miles/8km, 5 hrs

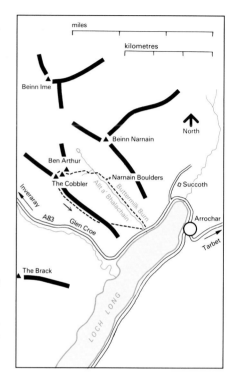

Grading A fine mountain walk in dramatic rock scenery. The walker should attempt only the North Peak since the Centre and South Peaks require some rock climbing.
Escape Routes Down into the E corrie from the bealachs between the peaks.
Transport Railway station at Arrochar. Bus service: Glasgow/Arrochar/Inveraray.
Accommodation Varied accommodation in Arrochar. Youth Hostels at Inverbeg, Ardgartan and Inveraray.

The Cobbler has always been a great favourite with Glaswegians. Its craggy features make it a notable landmark north of Loch Long, and its ready accessibility from Arrochar has made it a popular playground for rock climbers.

In the harsh economic climate of the 1930s many climbers who had neither the time nor the means to travel far afield, found challenge and excitement on Ben Arthur's three chunky peaks. The 1930s climbing scene in the Arrochar Alps is amusingly described in Alastair Borthwick's classic book *Always A Little Further*.

One mile south of the head of Loch Long a bridge crosses the Allt a'Bhalachain (Buttermilk Burn), opposite a pier. Take the path beside the burn, which runs adjacent to a block of forestry into the upper glen, where the crags of

Beinn Narnain dominate the view.

Continue up the glen until you come to a collection of gigantic boulders, the famous Narnain boulders which are sufficiently overhanging to provide shelter for a large party on a wet day. These boulders, like the Shelter Stone of Loch Avon, are among Scotland's most celebrated howffs.

Cross the burn and start ascending the wide east-facing corrie of Ben Arthur, with its three enticing peaks of mica schist. The highest is the Cobbler 'itself, in the centre, at 2,891ft/884m. To the south rises Jean, or the Cobbler's wife, while the North Peak is a fearsome tooth of bare rock, leaning menacingly towards the Cobbler like a panther about to spring on its prey.

In spite of its intimidating appearance, the North Peak is the easiest to climb. To make this ascent keep beside the Buttermilk Burn to the lochan on the shoulder, and ascend Ben Arthur's rough north ridge.

The ascents of the Central and South Peaks require elementary rock-climbing ability. Some exposed positions are encountered, particularly on the South Peak, and a rope should be used for protection. To surmount the Central Peak you need to pass through a

fissure in the rocks to an arête leading to the summit block. A second fissure must then be entered to reach the true summit.

Several routes may be taken up the South Peak, none of them easy, that from the south-west corner being the most popular.

The southern arm of the corrie, and the long south-east ridge, can be descended pleasantly to the plantation beside the Buttermilk Burn.

BEN LOMOND

Map OS Sheet 56 (Tourist Map)   *Start/Finish* Rowardennan (360982)/Inversnaid Hotel (338090)
Distance/Time 9 miles/14km, 5-6 hrs

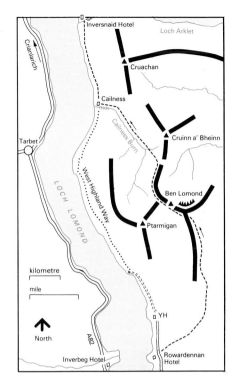

Grading An easy mountain walk under good conditions.
Escape Routes From the N ridge descend easily E to Comer in Gleann Dubh.
Transport Ferry: Inverbeg to Rowardennan.
Bus services: Balloch/Balmaha and Inversnaid/Aberfoyle.
Accommodation Hotels at Rowardennan and Inversnaid. B & B locally. Youth Hostels at Inverbeg, Rowardennan, Loch Lomond and Loch Ard.

Ben Lomond is the most southerly Munro, but well before Sir Hugh's list was published it had become one of the best-loved Scottish mountains. In the eighteenth century adventurous tourists would climb Ben Lomond and write extravagantly about their experiences. Thus John Stodd described 'a stupendous precipice of 2,000ft, exciting a degree of surprise arising almost to terror'. Few people were put off by these fearsome descriptions and it was noted in 1813, 'ladies very commonly go up, and sometimes take with them a piper and other apparatus for dancing'.

Ben Lomond remains an enormously popular mountain; there is an excellent path all the way to the top and it gives wonderfully romantic views of the Southern Highlands.

Most walkers make a 'there and back' ascent from Rowardennan on the east shore of Loch Lomond. This ascent of the long south ridge has much to recommend it but, if transport can be arranged, it is preferable to traverse the mountain, descending north beside the Cailness Burn. This route, which brings you to the Inversnaid Hotel, is described here.

From Rowardennan the path heads northeast reaching the broad ridge of Sron Aonaich at a spring called the Half-Way Well. It then zigzags up steep slopes towards the summit ridge, where you can peer over the crest into the precipitous east-facing corrie.

It is worth spending some time on the summit, 3,192ft/974m, to identify Ailsa Craig, Arran, the Paps of Jura, Ben More on Mull, Ben Cruachan and Ben Nevis. In the eighteenth century Colonel Thornton celebrated his ascent with a sumptuous luncheon, consisting of ptarmigan, moor-cock, smoked ham and reindeer tongue, washed down with champagne, sherbet and cordials which had been specially cooled in the snow.

As soon as you begin the descent of the north ridge you are likely to leave most other people behind. A path runs down to the bealach under Cruinn a'Bheinn and then branches north-west alongside the Cailness Burn.

On the lower slopes the burn rushes over rocks into a wild amphitheatre with dripping, vegetated walls; it then thunders down to the loch through a wooded gorge.

You meet the West Highland Way path on the shore of Loch Lomond, and this takes you very pleasantly north for two miles to Inversnaid.

AROUND GLEN CORSE IN THE PENTLANDS

Map OS Sheet 66   **Start/Finish** The A702 S of Edinburgh at Flotterstone (235630)
Distance/Time 13 miles/21km, 6 hrs

Grading A straightforward walk over mainly grassy hills. When firing occurs on the Dreghorn range a diversion is necessary.
Escape Routes Easy descents can be made from the hills to the reservoir access road running through Glen Corse.
Transport Bus service: Edinburgh/Dumfries passes through Flotterstone.
Accommodation Varied accommodation in Penicuik, Loanhead and Edinburgh. Youth Hostels at Edinburgh (Eglinton Crescent and Bruntsfield).

For hundreds of years the citizens of Edinburgh have taken brisk walks over the Pentland Hills, and filled their lungs with pure air, to escape from the stifling odours of Auld Reekie. This nickname was earned in the days of smoky, peaty fires and references go back well into the eighteenth century.

Nowadays, Edinburgh is clean and bright but the Pentlands, which stretch south-west from the outer suburbs for fifteen miles, serve the city in other ways. Hillend carries one of the longest dry ski-slopes in Britain, reservoirs fill several of the upland valleys and Lothian Council have plans for a Pentlands Park.

Being on the dry, eastern side of Scotland the Pentland Hills have not degenerated into saturated moorlands and eroded peat hags; heather thrives and grazing is widespread. Thankfully, the region has not suffered badly from afforestation.

It is no surprise that the character of the Pentlands closely resembles that of the Ochils, across the Firth of Forth, for both ranges were formed from Old Red Sandstone.

The flavour of the Pentlands can best be enjoyed by a circular walk around Glen Corse. The Logan Burn rises on the high plateau of Kitchen Moss and runs north-east down Glen Corse for five miles. It is dammed in two places, producing the Loganlea and the Glen Corse reservoirs. A thirteen-mile circuit of the hills overlooking the Logan Burn, and its reservoirs, involves an ascent of the principal summits of the Pentlands. You can swing effortlessly along the ridges, enjoying the wide landscapes and the rippling grass, in a manner reminiscent of other Southern Upland walks described in chapters 83, 84 and 85.

From Flotterstone walk up Glen Corse and then take the path beside a wood to the upper slopes of Castlelaw Hill; continue on to Allermuir Hill where there is a direction-finding indicator. Watch out for red flags, for there is an army presence on these hills.

The hills to the north of the glen are rather featureless and on Black Hill the going through deep heather can be quite taxing.

As you round the head of the Logan Burn the sharp peak of West Kip is prominent. This heralds a superb, switchback section over Scald Law, 1,899ft/579m, and Carnethy Hill with views east to the Bass Rock and north to the Ochils and Ben Ledi.

Easy slopes run down from Turnhouse Hill to the entrance of the glen.

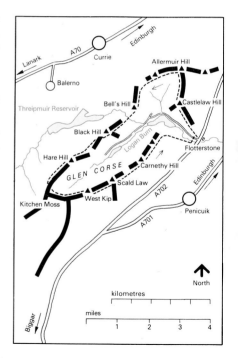

9   The Aonach Eagach Ridge in winter (Chapter 67). Photo: Jerry Rawson

10   The view south from Carn Mor Dearg to the peaks of the Mamores (Chapter 66). Photomontage: E. A. Shepherd

11 Dawn mists clear from Loch Enoch in the view looking east from The Merrick (Chapter 86). Photo: Ken Andrew

12 *The principal peaks of the Langdale Horseshoe – Crinkle Crags and Bow Fell seen from near Red Tarn (Chapter 102). Photo: Jerry Rawson*

13 (left) Looking north along the High Street ridge (Chapter 94

14 Great Gable and the Scafell group seen from Red Pike on the northern ridge of Ennerdale (Chapter 99). Photos: Jerry Rawso

15   *Scafell Pike, Broad Crag and Esk Hause in a view from Upper Eskdale (Chapter 101). Photo: Jerry Rawson*

ACROSS THE SOUTHERN UPLANDS: PEEBLES TO MOFFAT

Map OS Sheets 72, 73, 78 and 79   **Start/Finish** Peebles (240402)/Moffat (083055)
Distance/Time 35 miles/56km, 14-15 hrs

Grading An exceptionally long walk over remote and undulating hills.
Escape Routes St. Mary's Loch road at the Megget Stone. Loch Skeen to Grey Mare's Tail car park. SW to Ericstane from Hart Fell.
Transport Railway station at Lockerbie. Bus services: Lockerbie/Moffat/Peebles; Peebles/Edinburgh and Peebles/Glasgow.
Accommodation Varied accommodation at Peebles and Moffat. Youth Hostels at Melrose and Broadmeadows (Selkirk).

The Southern Uplands sweep north from the Scottish Border to the Pentland Hills. They form a region of exquisite beauty, with wooded valleys, tumbling rivers, rolling fells, ruined abbeys and severe, solid towns of grey stone.

In appearance the Southern Uplands resemble the Cheviots, but they are wilder, the grass is rougher, the heather deeper and the tops lonelier. It is easy to understand how the Border region inspired Wordsworth and Sir Walter Scott to write their romantic poetry, and it has been the source of many legends and ballads.

For this walk I have selected the isolated range of hills between Peebles and Moffat, because they are mainly untouched by forestry. Their valleys, draining north to the River Tweed,

are particularly fine and the two towns provide first-class accommodation and communications.

From Peebles' town centre take the road south over Tweed Bridge into Glen Sax. Almost immediately you start climbing the folded, heather-covered hills to Preston Law, and the start of a thirty-mile high-level walk over wild, rolling moorlands, before dropping below 1,400ft again at Moffat.

Throughout the day old boundary fences or dry-stone walls guide you over the broad ridges. Occasionally sheep tracks ease the way through the deep heather and tussocks, but generally you must contend with rough going underfoot, including saturated bogs and peat hags. Nevertheless, this is little penance for such an expedition, with the breeze ruffling the moor grass, idyllic views down to hidden valleys, waterfalls and cascades, and glimpses of the blue waters of St Mary's Loch. Above all the solitude is memorable. On my crossing I saw not a soul; curlews and plovers were my only companions.

Throughout the northern half of the walk the intrusive radio beacon on Broad Law is your guiding light. Then, from Cairn Law, you drop down to the Megget Stone beside the only

tarmaced road crossing these hills, and pause for breath before tackling the second leg.

From Lochcraig Head you overlook magical Loch Skeen whose outflow, the Tail Burn, plunges over 200ft cliffs in a cascade of white water. This is the NTS-owned Grey Mare's Tail and is well worth the short detour to visit.

Continuing south, the huge massifs of White Coomb and Hart Fell both have loose cliffs and escarpments, while the razor-sharp edge of the outlying Saddle Yoke is an exceptional feature for these hills.

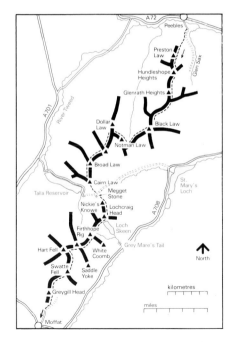

THE ETTRICK HILLS

Map OS Sheet 79   **Start/Finish** Ettrick Church (260144)   **Distance/Time** 22 miles/35km, 10 hrs

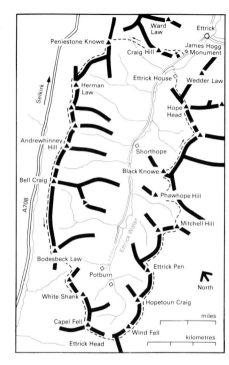

Grading A long switchback walk over trackless hills of coarse grass, heather and peat.
Escape Routes From the low col S of Bodesbeck Law to Potburn. From most points on the walk easy slopes lead down to the Ettrick valley.
Transport None to Ettrick. The nearest towns are Hawick , Selkirk, Moffat, Langholm and Lockerbie.
Accommodation Hotels at Tushielaw and Buccleuch. B & B at Ettrick. Youth Hostels at Snoot (Roberton) and Broadmeadows (Selkirk).

Ettrick typifies the grand walking country of the Southern Uplands. The hills are rounded and bald, bracken is creeping up from the valley, while moor-grass and heather on the upper slopes provide a meagre bite for a scant population of sheep. In places broken crags and grey, lichen-encrusted boulders emerge from the turf, while eroded gullies carry tumbling burns down to the valley.

A few patches of deciduous woodland remain in the valley bottom and on the banks of Ettrick Water, but extensive planting of conifers on the south side is rapidly altering the landscape. Nevertheless, most of the principal summits, including the rounded dome of Ettrick Pen, the highest hill in the region at 2,270ft/692m, rise well above the trees. A Tibetan settlement, complete with pagoda, has been established at neighbouring Eskdalemuir, and the inhabitants must feel very much at home amongst these hills.

In the early part of the nineteenth century James Hogg, the Ettrick Shepherd, brought fame to the area. Hogg was born in Ettrick and worked as a shepherd at Yarrow near St Mary's Loch. He spent his spare time writing poetry, was discovered and taken under the wing of Sir Walter Scott and introduced to Edinburgh society. His best known poem, *The Queen's Wake*, was published in 1813.

The unbroken horseshoe of hills which encloses Ettrick Valley can be traversed in a single day's walk of twenty-two miles. This is an energetic, switchback course over rough, trackless and at times boggy hills, but the spaciousness, freedom, solitude and lack of a single road or dwelling, will prove irresistible to the wild walker.

Little route description is necessary because, once you have left the valley at Ettrick Church and climbed over Craig Hill to Peniestone Knowe, you just follow the smooth undulating hills south-west to Capel Fell, beyond Potburn at the headwaters of Ettrick Water.

Enticing views are obtained to the west, of the rolling hills on the Peebles to Moffat itinerary, White Coomb, Firthhope Rig and Saddle Yoke while, in the valley, light sparkles on Loch of the Lowes, St Mary's Loch, Loch Skeen in its secret hollow and the silver thread of the Grey Mare's Tail.

At the black bog at Ettrick Head turn northeast and head for home, via the massive cairn on Ettrick Pen which provides views of almost the whole of the southern lowlands of Scotland.

CAIRNSMORE OF CARSPHAIRN

Map OS Sheet 77   **Start/Finish** *Green Well of Scotland near Carsphairn (557945)*
Distance/Time *16 miles/26km, 8-9 hrs*

Grading A tough walk over remote, trackless hills. In misty weather care must be taken to avoid crags on Beninner, Moorbrock Hill, Windy Standard and Cairnsmore.
Escape Routes Few. From Windy Standard descend N to Afton reservoir access road. Emergency shelter at Clennoch byre.
Transport Bus service: New Galloway/Carsphairn/ Ayr.
Accommodation Hotels at Carsphairn, Dalmellington and St. John's Town. B & B locally. Youth Hostel at Kendoon.

'There's Cairnsmore of Fleet,
   And Cairnsmore of Dee,
   And Cairnsmore of Carsphairn:
   The biggest of the three.'

Galloway's hills are smoothly contoured, rounded and folded and they rise from unspoilt valleys containing blue lochs, salmon rivers and grey stone villages.

The open landscape is ideal for walking, the hills are high but gentle and difficulties are few. Attractive outcrops of weathered granite occur high up on some of the hills. Steep escarpments of loose vegetated rock are found on Cairnsmore, Beninner, Moorbrock and Windy Standard but these are easily avoided. As on the Northumberland fells you are always conscious

of the great vault of sky overhead, and on a windy day, with clouds racing in from the west, there cannot be a more exhilarating experience than a long walk over the roof of Galloway.

Outside Merrick and the Rhinns of Kells, the wildest hill area is Cairnsmore of Carsphairn. East of Loch Doon, Cairnsmore rises to 2,614ft/ 797m and magnificent rolling hills continue north, round the watershed of Water of Deugh, and on for many miles.

Forestry, the blight of Galloway, has made few inroads into the Cairnsmore hills and the high tops, ridges and plateaux continue to provide superlative walking country.

From the bridge over the Water of Deugh climb the conical hill, Craig of Knockgray, which is a wonderful viewpoint for the Cairnsmore group. Behind you runs the long backcloth of the Cairnsgarroch – Corserine – Rhinns of Kells ridge described in chapter 86.

Galloway grass is brutally tough and it is a relief to reach the high ridges where short heather and moss take over.

Continue north over Knockwhirn to Beninner and then descend slopes of loose scree to the marshy watershed under Moorbrock Hill. Easy going takes you on to Windy Standard,

which just escapes the cloak of forestry, and then you must swing south over Dugland and head for home.

Two rivers must be forded at Clennoch before you tackle the 1,440ft pull up to Cairnsmore. The views back to Windy Standard are lovely, especially when the hills are patterned by shifting cloud shadows.

The summit of Cairnsmore is boulder-strewn and carries a large cairn; views extend from Arran to Criffel and Cairnsmore of Fleet.

An easy descent of the broad south ridge takes you past a tiny lochan under Black Shoulder, over Dunool and Willieanna and down to a Land Rover track beside Water of Deugh.

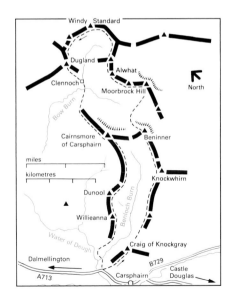

MERRICK AND THE RHINNS OF KELLS

Map OS Sheet 77 *Start/Finish* Glen Trool car-park (415803) *Distance/Time* 24 miles/39km, 9-10 hrs

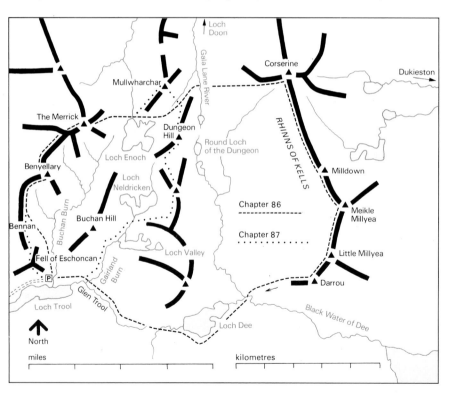

The hills of Galloway rise to 2,764ft/843m at the Merrick, and there are a dozen more in excess of 2,000ft. It is an area of high moorland, outcrops of granite, lochs and forests. Much of Galloway has been declared a Forest Park and the landowners allow free access on to the hills. However, the attractive open hillsides are gradually being planted with conifers and the work of the Forestry Commission is evident everywhere. Only on the high tops and ridges will you be free from fencing and drainage ditches, but apart from this the Galloway Forest is sheer delight and a paradise for hill walkers.

Galloway is rich in tradition, legend and history and many of the place names have a magical sound. Where else would you find 'Rig of the Jarkness', 'Curleywee', 'Long Loch of the Dungeon' or 'Clatteringshaw's Loch'?

This walk starts from Glen Trool, ascends the Merrick and Corserine, the two highest mountains in Galloway, and then traverses the high ridge known as the Rhinns of Kells.

From the Glen Trool car-park the Merrick path follows the Buchan Burn, passes Culsharg cottage, and climbs to the broad shoulder of Benyellary. A wall now runs up to Merrick's sum-

---

Grading A long walk over rough and tussocky ground. In wet weather river crossings could be hazardous.
Escape Routes From Gala Lane N to Loch Doon. From Corserine descend SE ridge to Dukieston.
Transport Railway stations at Dumfries and Stranraer. Bus services: Dumfries/Newton Stewart and Ayr/Newton Stewart.
Accommodation Hotels at Newton Stewart. B & B locally. Youth Hostels at Minnigaff and Kendoon.

mit cairn, built on the edge of an escarpment.

The Merrick is the highest of a group of mountains connected by ridges which together make the shape of a hand. The range is known as the Merrick-Shalloch Rhinns, or 'Range of the Awful Hand'.

North-east of the summit a steep spur descends to Loch Enoch, a delightful loch of inlets, sandy bays and islets.

Make for the defile between Mullwharchar and Dungeon Hill; there is no vestige of a path and it is arduous going across thick tussocky grass and knobbles of clean granite. Running away northwards, into the far distance, can be seen Loch Doon, immortalised by Robert Burns in his poem, *Ye Banks and Braes*.

Cross the Gala Lane river (very difficult in wet weather) and fight through deep heather and moor grass up the west ridge of Corserine.

Glorious walking now follows as you traverse the Rhinns of Kells, passing tiny lochans and acres of waving cotton-grass and harebells. Darrou marks the end of the ridge, after which it is an easy descent to the valley of the Black Water of Dee, thence to the beautiful woods of Glen Trool.

Chapter 87

Grading *A tough walk over remote and rugged hills. In wet weather river crossings could be hazardous.*
Escape Routes *None, but the ascent of Merrick may be omitted and a return to Glen Trool made via the Buchan Burn.*
Transport *Railway stations at Dumfries and Stranraer. Bus services: Dumfries/Newton Stewart and Ayr/ Newton Stewart.*
Accommodation *Hotels at Newton Stewart. B & B locally. Youth Hostels at Minnigaff and Kendoon.*

THE ROUND OF LOCH ENOCH

Map *OS Sheet 77* **Start/Finish** *Glen Trool car-park (415803)* **Distance/Time** *14 miles/23km, 7 hrs*

In the previous chapter I described a sweeping walk over the principal ridges of the Galloway Forest Park. Here we explore the rough, granite hills and the lonely lochs of the very heart of Galloway. Hills that are so remote, and have such stable underlying rock, that they were seriously considered by the Atomic Energy Authority as a site for the disposal of radioactive waste.

Once again Glen Trool car-park makes a convenient starting point. Cross the Buchan Burn by the Earl of Galloway's bridge built in 1851, and take the waymarked path that contours round Buchan Hill and leads to the Gairland Burn. Keep west of Loch Valley and make for the short, but tempestuous, stretch of river linking this loch with Loch Neldricken. At a sheepfold a line of stepping stones helps you cross the water to gain the south-west ridge of Craignaw.

Craignaw is typical of the central Galloway hills; slabs of granite, loose boulders and outcrops abound, lochans fill every scoop and hollow and skill is needed to pick the best way through the broken crags. A few years ago an aircraft crashed into the west-facing cliffs of Black Gairy and wreckage is strewn around.

Scramble down through the line of cliffs at the northern end of Craignaw to reach the Devil's Bowling Green, an area of granite slabs where boulders are scattered at random.

Continue north to the cairn on the bealach below Dungeon Hill, another crag-ringed castle of weathered granite known locally as the Lion's Head. As you climb through the rocks, look east to the notorious Silver Flow, a floating bog which is now a Nature Reserve.

Mullwharchar, 2,270ft/692m, rises north-east of Loch Enoch, only a short distance north of Dungeon Hill. A long line of sheer cliffs, known as the Tauchers, falls away on the north side, and care is needed in mist.

Descend the easy south-west ridge of Mullwharchar to the sandy shore of Loch Enoch and ford the Eglin Lane, which could be troublesome in wet weather. Make for the broad east ridge of Merrick which gives a straightforward, but steep and rather loose, ascent to the summit cairn.

The tourist path, via Benyellary and Culsharg, can be descended to Glen Trool, but a slight detour to include the summits of Bennan and Fell of Eschoncan is recommended.

BORDERLAND: CHEVIOT HILLS

Map *OS Sheets 75 and 80*   **Start/Finish** *Wooler (993280)/Carter Bar (698068)*
Distance/Time *32 miles/52km, 11-12 hrs*

---

*Grading A long walk over remote but grassy hills.
Can be boggy in wet weather.*
*Escape Routes From Auchope Cairn N along
Pennine Way to Kirk Yetholm. From Mazie Law
descend Heatherhope Valley to Hownam. From
Chew Green S to Byrness.*
*Transport Railway station at Berwick. Bus services:
Berwick/Wooler; Newcastle/Wooler; Newcastle/
Carter Bar/Edinburgh.*
*Accommodation Hotels and B & B at Wooler and
Byrness. Youth Hostels at Wooler, Byrness and Kirk
Yetholm.*

From Carter Bar on the west and Wooler on the east the view of countless miles of rolling hills, making up the Cheviots, is irresistible to the walker.

The Cheviots were thrown up by volcanic action millions of years ago, but now they are worn to rounded summits with steep sides and deep valleys. They are mostly smooth and grassy and, since to date the Forestry Commission have not planted extensively, they provide hill walking *par excellence*. To the south the streams drain into the Coquet and to the north into the Tweed, both famous salmon rivers.

This walk is from the ancient Northumbrian market town of Wooler to Carter Bar, where the A68 crosses the Scottish border. Much of the route follows the border fence.

Where the Wooler to Langleeford road crosses the Carey burn, strike up the heathery slopes towards Cold Law, whose white-painted trig. point can easily be seen against the sky.

On Scald Hill you meet a fence and a dreadfully eroded path to The Cheviot. The actual cairn is built on a plinth of turf, completely surrounded by quagmire, but it provides superb views east to the Farne Islands.

At Auchope Cairn a marker post informs you that you have met the line of the Pennine Way, which swings north on its last lap to Kirk Yetholm.

The switchback path over the high backbone of the Cheviots is always delightful, and in places the ground is carpeted with cloudberries. The area is steeped in history and the path passes Bronze Age burial mounds, standing stones and ancient drove roads, and looks down on the sites of Roman forts. Occasional glimpses of remote farmsteads set at the head of deep, grassy valleys are your only contact with civilisation on the Scottish side. On the English side many of the outlying hills are in a firing range and, when red flags are flying, the booming of guns echoes round the valleys.

Soon after Black Halls the path becomes wide and well-constructed. This is the Roman road, Dere Street, which runs from York to Trimontium. The path now descends to Chew Green, once a Roman camp, later a medieval settlement and, in the eighteenth century, a meeting point for cattle drovers.

With the border fence as your guide, cross Hungry Law, Catcleugh and Arks Edge to reach your destination at Carter Bar.

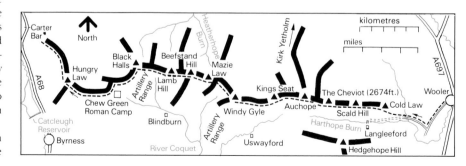

LINHOPE SPOUT AND HEDGEHOPE HILL

Map OS Sheets 81 and 80 *Start/Finish* Hartside (975162) *Distance/Time* 12 miles/19km, 6 hrs

Grading A rough walk over lonely and trackless fells.
Escape Routes Comb Fell and Hedgehope can be descended easily N to the sheltered Harthope valley near Langleeford.
Transport Bus service: Newcastle/Morpeth/Powburn/Wooler.
Accommodation Hotels, B & B and Youth Hostel at Wooler.

Many walkers striding out along the marked trail of the Pennine Way, or struggling through the deep, black bog of Cheviot's plateau, gaze longingly at the wild, rolling hills to the south: Hedgehope, Comb Fell, Bloodybush Edge and Cushat Law.

While access to the main Cheviot hills is restricted from the south by extensive artillery ranges at Otterburn and Redesdale, lovely river valleys penetrate deep into the hills from the east: College valley from Kirknewton, the valley of the Harthope burn from Wooler and the Breamish valley running west from Ingram.

The Breamish is a considerable river, fed by tributary burns which rise in the hills south of the Cheviots. Although the Forestry Commission have planted wide areas of hillside on the south of the Breamish, near Alwinton, the hills to the north are wild, lonely and rarely visited except by shepherds. The river rises in typical Cheviot country; the hills are rounded and smooth and they roll away irresistibly into the distance. Walking is excellent over close cropped grass and heather, but bracken is rapidly encroaching on the lower slopes. Curlews, plovers and larks abound and, on my last visit, I saw wheatears and, high on the fells, two young badgers scampering over the heather back into their set.

From Hartside, a farm set in the delectable Breamish valley and surrounded by gorse and broom, a good track leads to Linhope Manor, which is hidden by exotic trees and rhododendrons, and continues to the waterfall of Linhope Spout. The Linhope Burn plunges, in a cascade of white water, over a forty-foot rock step into a deep, black pool overhung by trees and moss-covered rocks. The Spout, set amidst barren hills, yet enclosed in a leafy glade, is one of the most romantic waterfalls in England. The Linhope Burn rises exceptionally quickly after rain, when the falls become ferocious.

Climb the fell west of Ritto Hill and walk over High Cantle which looks over High Bleakhope, one of the remotest farms in England. Continue north, passing some pink granite outcrops on Coldlaw Cairn, to the massive bulks of Comb Fell and Hedgehope Hill. The going is easy through heather and cloudberries, while the views from Hedgehope, 2,343ft/714m, are expansive.

Descend in an easterly direction over Dunmoor Hill to the rocks of Cunyan Crags. Hartside farm is tucked away behind some fir trees, a mile away across the bracken and heather.

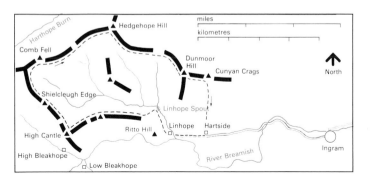

KIELDER FOREST AND THE BORDER FELLS

Map *OS Sheet 81*   **Start/Finish** *Carter Bar (698068)*   **Distance/Time** *27 miles/43km, 12 hrs*

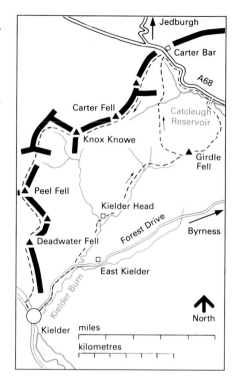

Grading *A rough, tough walk over England's remotest fells. In bad weather an overnight stop in Kielder village is advisable.*
Escape Routes *Kielder village is reached at the half-way point.*
Transport *Bus service: Newcastle/Carter Bar/ Edinburgh.*
Accommodation *B & B at Kielder and Byrness. Youth Hostels at Byrness and Bellingham.*

Much of the 32-mile crossing of the Cheviots, described in chapter 88, follows the Scottish border, and the fells continue to run untamed westwards to Kielder. I recommend here a circular walk from Carter Bar, crossing the highest fells to Kielder and returning via the forest, the valley of the White Kielder Burn, Chattlehope Spout and Catcleugh Reservoir.

This is an energy-sapping, rough, tough walk of 27 miles over England's remotest fells where, in emergency, help is far away. Allow at least twelve hours to complete the walk and in winter, when deep snow could be a major problem, it would be wise to arrange accommodation in Kielder village, which is the half-way point.

From Carter Bar the climb up to Catcleugh Shin and Carter Fell is easy, yet they offer far-ranging views of the Cheviots, Redesdale, the Wauchope Forest and the broad valley of the Tweed.

Old mine workings are passed on Carter Fell, along with a small tarn, and then you follow a line of boundary stones to Knox Knowe. The stones are marked N for the Duke of Northumberland and ⊓ (a back-to-front D) for the Douglas estate; the work of an illiterate stone-mason. Watch out too for the Cheviot herd of wild goats which frequents this desolate area; the leader is a massive and magnificent billy with a beard trailing to his knees and long curved horns.

Just before Peel Fell you pass the Kielder Stone, a colossal chunk of gritstone estimated to weigh 1,500 tons, which perches incongruously on the open fellside. Legend has it that the stone served as a *post office* in the dark days when messengers from Scotland and England dared not venture into enemy territory.

Peel Fell, 1,975ft/602m, is the highest point on the walk and on a clear day you can see both the Solway Firth and the North Sea.

From Deadwater Fell marvel at Kielder Water, the largest man-made reservoir in Britain, and Kielder Forest, the largest forest, before descending to Kielder village.

The homeward route follows the broad valley of the White Kielder Burn to the watershed on Girdle Fell. You must then scramble down beside the 75ft waterfall, Chattlehope Spout, to reach Catcleugh Reservoir, or continue over high ground, passing White Crags and the head of Bateinghope Burn, to reach Carter Bar.

HADRIAN'S WALL

Map *OS Sheet 86 (Historical Map of the Roman Wall)* **Start/Finish** *Sewing Shields (810702)/Lanercost Priory (555638)*
Distance/Time *19 miles/31km, 8-9 hrs*

> **Grading** *Easy, except for a river crossing at Willowford which, in bad conditions, could mean a 3-mile detour.*
> **Escape Routes** *The route can be cut short almost anywhere.*
> **Transport** *Railway station at Hexham. Bus services: Hexham/Haltwhistle via Roman Wall (summer only); Brampton/Carlisle.*
> **Accommodation** *Hotels at Chollerford, Wall, Twice Brewed and Lanercost. B & B locally. Youth Hostels at Greenhead, Once Brewed and Acomb.*

We are extremely fortunate that Hadrian's Wall, an exceptional historical monument, should also provide a high-level walk over some of northern England's wildest country.

In AD122 Emperor Hadrian visited Britain and, to define the northern frontier, ordered a wall to be built from the Tyne to the Solway. The wall was to be 10ft thick and supported by forts, milecastles and turrets. As additional protection on the north side a deep ditch was dug, while on the south side a wider ditch, or *Vallum*, was excavated to provide a demarcation zone.

The Wall, which was 15ft high, repelled invaders until AD196, when it was overrun by barbarians who devastated northern England as far south as York. It was left to Emperor Severus to re-establish control and rebuild the Wall. Finally, towards the end of the fourth century, it was abandoned by the Romans.

Over the years many of the faced stones have been removed from the Wall for building and road making but, especially over the wilder sections, it is still in a fair state of preservation.

From Sewing Shields farm, west of Choller-ford, follow the stub of Wall along the whin sill escarpment to Housesteads Fort and Crag Lough, a 100ft crag first explored by George and Charles Trevelyan and Geoffrey Winthrop Young in the last century. With wooded slopes overlooking a reedy lake, this is the most picturesque and famous stretch of the entire Roman Wall.

Broken cliffs continue to Steel Rigg, beyond which the Wall runs over open, undulating moorlands leading to Winshields, 1,230ft/ 345m, the highest point on the Wall. The next fort is Great Chesters, its mossy and grass-covered walls in pleasant contrast to House-steads' orderliness. An elevated stretch between Cockmount Hill and Walltown Crags commands a panoramic view north, with moors and forests extending to the Scottish border. South can be seen the brooding, flat-topped bulk of Cross Fell.

At Walltown Turret the Wall disappears for a spell, and is not regained until Poltross Burn Milecastle near Gilsland Station. Thereafter you descend to the river Irthing at Willowford. Cross the river with care and climb up to Harrow's Scar Milecastle, whence a clean stretch of Wall, carrying several inscriptions, runs west to Birdoswald Fort.

At Banks leave the Wall and descend back into the Irthing valley at Lanercost where it is pleasant to await your transport under the sycamore trees beside the glorious twelfth-century Augustinian Priory.

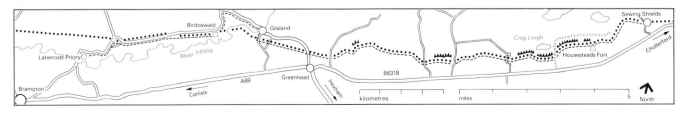

THE BACK O' SKIDDA

Map OS Sheet 90 (Tourist Map)   **Start/Finish** Mosedale (356322)/Bassenthwaite (230323)
Distance/Time 12 miles/19km, 5-6 hrs

Grading An easy traverse of rounded and mainly heather-clad hills.
Escape Routes N from High Pike to Nether Row and Caldbeck. S from Great Lingy Hill to Grainsgill and the Caldew valley.
Transport Railway stations at Penrith and Carlisle. Bus services: Keswick/Penrith and Keswick/Carlisle.
Accommodation Varied accommodation in Keswick. B & B locally. Youth Hostels at Keswick, Cockermouth, Derwent Water, Thirlmere and Carrock Fell.

From the wind-scoured summits of Skiddaw and Blencathra the fells Back o'Skidda', Great Calva, Knott, High Pike and Carrock Fell, look rounded, grassy and rather ordinary, particularly when compared with the much-loved and shapely peaks south of the Vale of St John.

The Back o'Skidda' hills are more in tune with the Northern Pennines, and devotees of Cross Fell, the Howgills and Swaledale, will relish their loneliness, their lack of paths and enclosures, the coarse moor grass and, in places, the evil peat hags.

A crossing of the fells from Mosedale to Bassenthwaite is an easy day, there are no difficulties and escape routes abound, yet the hills are as wild as any in Lakeland and a haven of peace and solitude even on the busiest holiday weekend.

Carrock Fell rises steeply north of the cluster of stone-built cottages at Mosedale. A gabbro intrusion has produced crags and the lower slopes are a tangle of heather, gorse and juniper and are strewn with boulders. An Iron Age hill fort was built on the summit and the remains of the walls can be clearly seen.

High Pike sprouts an extraordinary array of accessories: a stone bench, wind shelter, OS trig. point, ruined buildings and various cairns and stakes. It is easily climbed from the north and has been used throughout the ages as a beacon, being clearly visible from Carlisle.

Rounding the head of Grainsgill, where wolfram mines were operated early this century, you must negotiate the peat bogs and ooze of Miller Moss before climbing the grass slopes of Knott, 2,329ft/710m, the highest point of the day. This is a wonderful viewpoint for the west coast, from the Solway to the Irish Sea extending to the Isle of Man.

Great Calva is at the end of a broad subsidiary ridge, and this central hill gives an unusual prospect south of the sweeping north slopes of Skiddaw and Bowscale Fell, as well as through the Glenderaterra valley to distant Thirlmere and Helvellyn.

Make your way down the south ridge to the track near Skiddaw House and its protective belt of trees. The path skirts a strange craggy coomb known as Dead Crags, and then passes beside Whitewater Dash which plunges down the dale through a wooded ravine. Coleridge visited the falls and described them as 'the finest water furies I ever beheld'.

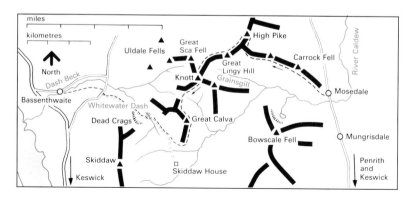

SADDLEBACK BY SHARP EDGE

Map OS Sheet 90 (Tourist Map/Outdoor Leisure 5)   **Start/Finish** Mungrisdale (364305)
Distance/Time 8 miles/13km, 6 hrs

Grading *Easy, except for Sharp Edge which commands respect, particularly in wet weather. In winter conditions the Edge should be left to experienced mountaineers.*
Escape Routes *From Blencathra summit descend either Scales Fell or continue SW along the ridge to Blease Fell.*
Transport *Railway station at Penrith. Bus service: Penrith/Threlkeld/Keswick.*
Accommodation *Hotels at Mungrisdale, Scales, Troutbeck and Threlkeld. B & B locally. Youth Hostels at Keswick and Carrock Fell.*

One of the best views of Saddleback (Blencathra) is obtained as you approach Lakeland along the main road from Penrith. As the road dips towards the River Glenderamackin the narrow spur, called Sharp Edge, delineates the northern extent of the mountain, and as you pass under the southern slopes a succession of pronounced ribs can be seen emanating from the summit: Scales Fell, Doddick Fell, Hallsfell, Gategill Fell and Blease Fell. All those fine ridges make direct, steep routes of ascent, but here I describe an unusual circuit from the east which includes the ascent of the problematic Sharp Edge.

From Mungrisdale a track runs south of The Tongue, reaching the broad plateau under Bowscale Fell. Walk round the rim of the broken escarpment of Bannerdale Crags and then descend to the Glenderamackin col just north of Saddleback. Contour beneath the decayed rocks of Foule Crag to meet the lower, grassy section of the Sharp Edge ridge. At this point you get your first view of the secret hollow holding Scales Tarn, which is a rather gloomy and forlorn little lake, receiving the minimum of sunlight.

The introduction to Sharp Edge is gradual. The grassy ridge slowly becomes rockier but, as the ground falls away on either side with ever-increasing concavity, your pulse quickens.

Suddenly, beyond a narrow gangway, the ridge steepens dramatically and you must clamber up some rather polished slabs and grooves. This section requires care; there are plenty of holds but they are not always obvious. The rocks tend to become greasy in the wet and, in winter, they can pose severe problems.

The angle soon eases and the rocks give way to gentle, grassy slopes running up to Saddleback, 2,847ft/868m.

Enjoy the magnificent view south across the Vale of St John to the misty hills of Central Lakeland, and then descend the grassy slopes of Scales Fell into the upper reaches of Mousthwaite Comb. Climb the whale-back outlier of Souther Fell, which provides a most unusual prospect of Saddleback, and thence return to Mungrisdale.

Those walkers who wish to sample the heady delights of Sharp Edge in a much shorter day should start from the inn at Scales. A well-beaten track ascends Mousthwaite Comb and reaches Sharp Edge via the outflow of Scales Tarn.

The whole length of Saddleback's summit ridge may be traversed, followed by a simple descent of the rounded, heathery Blease Fell to Threlkeld.

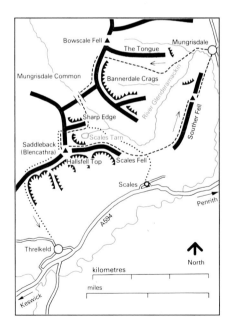

HIGH STREET

Map OS Sheet 90 (Tourist Map/Outdoor Leisure 5, 7)   **Start/Finish** Patterdale (398158)/Troutbeck (413028)
Distance/Time 12 miles/19km, 6 hrs

Grading A fine mountain walk. No difficulties should be encountered in good conditions.
Escape Routes From The Knott descend W to Hayeswater. From the Froswick–Ill Bell–Yoke ridge descend W to the Hagg Gill Valley.
Transport Railway stations at Penrith and Windermere. Bus services: Penrith/Patterdale and Windermere/Ambleside/Keswick.
Accommodation Varied accommodation in Patterdale, Glenridding and Troutbeck. Youth Hostels at Patterdale, Ambleside and Windermere.

The long, high, broad ridge which runs right down the eastern side of the Lake District, and which is so conspicuous from the Howgills, has been used as a road since prehistoric times. It was adopted by the Romans to link their fort of Brocavum in the Eden Valley with Ravenglass, and was called Brethestrete.

The main ridge extends from Loadpot Hill to Garburn Pass and the central section, which rises to 2,719ft/828m, is known as High Street. In this chapter we approach High Street from Patterdale and walk south to Troutbeck; this gives an easy, yet diverse, walk along a distinct ridge overlooking numerous coves and tarns. Being on the outermost fringe of Lakeland, High Street is not too popular and solitude can often be enjoyed.

From Patterdale take the path which makes an ascending traverse of the southern slopes of Place Fell towards Boardale Hause. Just before attaining the hause it winds up the grass to the rock turrets of Angletarn Pikes and descends to Angle Tarn, situated most attractively under Buck Crag.

Skirt under Saturna Crag and climb the screes to the imposing conical summit of The Knott, which at once provides an unexpected view east to Haweswater Reservoir. In mist a wall will now guide you south to High Street.

The Roman Road is met at the Straits of Riggindale on the north side of High Street and it provides charming views down into the depths of Riggindale, to Hayeswater and (later) east to Blea Water. Thought by some to sit in the crater of an extinct volcano, Blea Water is a deep, dark tarn ringed by craggy slopes.

In the early nineteenth century shepherds held a fair on the summit plateau of High Street, and it is still called Racecourse Hill on some maps.

Bear south-east to the gigantic 14ft-high cairn on the subsidiary summit of Thornthwaite Crag; this beacon gives extensive views south over Windermere.

Continuing south along the Roman Road you switchback over the shapely summits of Froswick and Ill Bell; both hills fall away sheer to the east above Kentmere Reservoir. Next comes the more rounded hill of Yoke which, too, presents a 1,000ft face (Rainsborrow Crags) to the east.

The fells now become broad, peaty and rather uninteresting. A stone wall leads down to Garburn Pass, whence a good track takes you into Troutbeck.

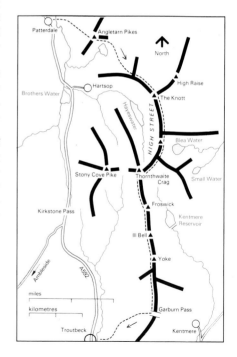

HELVELLYN BY STRIDING EDGE

Map *OS Sheet 90 (Tourist Map/Outdoor Leisure 5)*   **Start/Finish** *Patterdale (390161)*
Distance/Time *8 miles/13km, 5-6 hrs*

Grading A tough mountain walk involving some airy
ridge scrambling. A serious route in winter conditions.
Escape Routes From Helvellyn summit proceed N
towards Raise, where easy slopes lead down towards
Glenridding.
Transport Railway stations at Penrith and Windermere.
Bus services: Penrith/Patterdale and Glenridding/
Ambleside/Windermere.
Accommodation Varied accommodation at
Patterdale, Hartsop and Glenridding. Youth Hostels
at Patterdale, Grasmere, Greenside and Windermere.

Helvellyn thoroughly deserves its reputation
as the most popular mountain in England. Its
broad whale-back makes for a simple ascent
by the tourist, it exceeds the magic 3,000ft, it
has many historical and literary associations
and it commands breathtaking views over
central and western Lakeland and eastwards to
the High Street range.

Although mainly grassy slopes fall away to
the west, the eastern flanks are precipitous.
Broken crags descend to a succession of wild
and lonely coves: Cock Cove, Ruthwaite Cove,
Nethermost Cove, Brown Cove and Keppel
Cove. But Helvellyn's most famous feature is
the sharp ridge of Striding Edge, which thrusts
boldly eastwards from the summit plateau. From
the rocky arête of Striding Edge you look south

into the upper recesses of Nethermost Cove
and north to the ruffled waters of Red Tarn.

Over the years Striding Edge has won marked
respect. In summer it provides spice to the
ascent of Helvellyn although, with good
balance, you need hardly remove your hands
from your pockets. Narrow paths traverse
below the rocky crest, but most mountain
walkers will accept the challenge and relish
the exposure. It is a less formidable arête
than Crib-goch, and it offers no problem
comparable to the greasy slabs of Sharp Edge.

In winter the final few hundred feet of steep,
loose rocks below the plateau will provide the
crux. Most accidents occur here or on the
descent to the broader Swirral Edge, which
this expedition recommends as a return route
to Patterdale.

Park in Glenridding, walk down the road to
Patterdale and enter Grisedale. A gate gives
access to a green pasture, grazed by Herdwicks,
and a path runs across the slopes of Birkhouse
Moor to meet the eastern extremity of Striding
Edge at a stone wall.

Striding Edge starts easily enough, but narrows as it approaches the main body of
Helvellyn. Finally you clamber down a rock

step and zig-zag up the tiresome screes to
Helvellyn's summit, 3,118ft/950m.

The correct descent-line to Swirral Edge is
marked by a cairn on the cliff-edge just north of
the OS pillar. In icy conditions ice-axes, crampons and a rope for protection may have to be
used before you reach the safety of the rocks.

Continue across the col to the marvellous
viewpoint of Catstycam, descend to Red Tarn
and return to Patterdale over Birkhouse Moor,
enjoying the view of Ullswater snaking north
for seven miles.

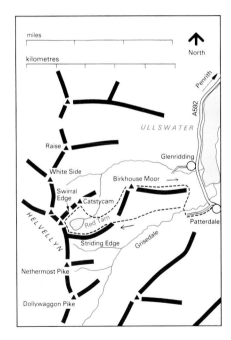

FAIRFIELD AND THE DEEPDALE HORSESHOE

Map OS Sheet 90 (Tourist Map/Outdoor Leisure 5)   **Start/Finish** Patterdale (390161)
Distance/Time 10 miles/16km, 5-6 hrs

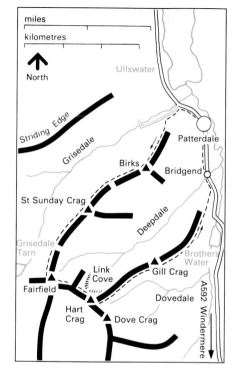

Grading A fine mountain traverse in the heart of Lakeland. Some scrambling on the approach to Fairfield and careful route finding necessary on the descent from Hart Crag.
Escape Routes From Deepdale Hause into Grisedale or Deepdale.
Transport Railway stations at Penrith and Windermere. Bus services: Penrith/Patterdale and Glenridding/Ambleside/Windermere.
Accommodation Varied accommodation at Patterdale, Hartsop and Glenridding. Youth Hostels at Patterdale, Grasmere, Greenside and Windermere.

From Lakeland's western fells Fairfield appears as a flat grassy hump, and walkers looking for an exciting day's expedition would not give it a further glance. However, to the east and north, Fairfield presents a steep face, broken by cliffs and rocky spurs while three delectable green valleys, Grisedale, Deepdale and Dovedale, run down to Patterdale and Brothers Water.

The upper reaches of Deepdale run right up to the seamed rock face of Fairfield. Deepdale is bounded by the ridges of St Sunday Crag and Hartsop Above How, and they are linked to the main massif of Fairfield by two prominent rocky bluffs: Cofa Pike and Hart Crag. This horseshoe provides a day's walk of startling contrasts: lush green lower slopes, airy ridges,

steep scrambles and bird's-eye views of hidden coves, deep gills and mossy crags with lakes and hills stretching away to far horizons.

Walk into Grisedale, cross a stile and zig-zag up through birch trees towards Black Crag. In spring the ground is thick with primroses and, with every foot gained, more of Ullswater comes into sight in its exquisite setting of rolling fells, crags and woods.

You can now climb to the top of Birks, or take a lower traverse path, to reach St Sunday Crag which has a line of cliffs overlooking Grisedale.

Beyond St Sunday Crag you descend a fine ridge to Deepdale Hause, and can enjoy the jagged silhouette of Striding Edge rearing up across the top of Nethermost Cove. Ahead lies Cofa Pike, its broken buttresses and pinnacles appearing quite daunting from below but, in reality, it is just an easy scramble in all but the severest winter conditions.

On the west side steep slopes run down to Grisedale Tarn while, on the east, you can look into Sleet Cove with its dripping, precipitous walls, more popular with ravens than rock climbers.

Fairfield's summit is flat and contains a profusion of cairns; a compass may be necessary

to locate Hart Crag and the ridge running north-east over Gill Crag. This ridge is broad and rocky and it provides thrilling views into the recesses of Link Cove, one of Lakeland's most secret corners. The 300ft face of Dove Crag lies to the south, up which runs Hangover, one of Lakeland's classic VS climbs.

Easy walking down the lower sections of the ridge leads you back to the woods in Patterdale.

THE BUTTERMERE CIRCUIT

Map *OS Sheets 90 and 89 (Tourist Map/Outdoor Leisure 4)* **Start/Finish** *Buttermere (176170)*
Distance/Time *13 miles/21km, 7 hrs*

Grading A straightforward but long mountain walk over some of the finest of the Lakeland fells.
Escape Routes Easy descents to civilisation from either the summit of Honister Pass or Scarth Gap.
Transport Railway stations at Penrith and Whitehaven. Bus services: Keswick/Cockermouth/Buttermere and Mountain Goat services over Honister and Newlands.
Accommodation Hotels in Buttermere village. B & B locally. Youth Hostels at Buttermere, Honister Hause and Longthwaite.

There is no more idyllic sight in Lakeland than Buttermere when first glimpsed from the twisting roads descending from Honister or Newlands passes. In the same way that Loch Maree is the epitome of the romantic Scottish scene so Buttermere's blue water, surrounded by peaceful, wooded fells and rocky combes, engenders an air of timelessness and tranquillity that is the mark of the English Lake District.

Although Fleetwith Pike thrusts a craggy spur menacingly over the head of Buttermere, the fells to the north and south are mostly friendly and ideal for walking.

Leaving aside Fleetwith Pike we can make a generous circuit of Buttermere, over many of Lakeland's best-loved and most comfortable fells which provide views into countless hidden valleys and combes.

From Buttermere village take the Newlands road for a short distance, until you see the path running up grassy slopes towards Robinson. A tempting ridge projects north from Robinson, leading to High Snab and Newlands, but you should turn south and follow a fence which contours round the head of Little Dale to the northern outlier of Hindscarth.

Returning south to the main ridge you swing east along a quite narrow and rocky ridge to Dale Head. This attractive peak is scarred by mine workings and ancient tracks, cliffs fall away into Newlands valley and the upper slopes are dotted with tiny tarns. It is a magnificent viewpoint for northern Lakeland, particularly Skiddaw.

From Dale Head's large summit cairn a fence post marks the path of descent, south beside Yew Crag quarries to Honister Pass.

South of Honister follow the path up the line of an old rope-way, and then traverse the western slopes of Grey Knotts to Hay Stacks. A variety of paths wind through the chunky rock outcrops and tarns of Hay Stacks, and then you descend to Scarth Gap.

The ridge of High Crag, High Stile and Red Pike gives superlative walking over diverse terrain. Burtness Combe falls away in sheets of rock from High Stile, the highest point of the day at 2,644ft/806m, and broken crags characterise the entire length of the north-facing slopes. Magnificent views of Pillar and Gable, two of Lakeland's greatest stalwarts, are enjoyed from all points along the ridge.

The rock on Red Pike is volcanic and crumbly and easy descents are available, via either Bleaberry Tarn or Scale Force.

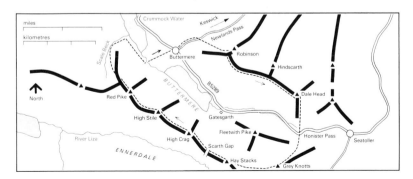

GREAT GABLE BY THE CLIMBERS' PATH

Map OS Sheet 90 (Tourist Map/Outdoor Leisure 4)   **Start/Finish** Seathwaite (235122)
Distance/Time 6 miles/10km, 4-5 hrs

Grading *This walk is not for the inexperienced. It involves a considerable amount of rock scrambling and a rope should be carried.*
Escape Routes *From the S side of Great Gable easy slopes lead down to Lingmell Beck and Wasdale Head.*
Transport *Railway stations at Penrith, Carlisle and Workington. Bus services: Penrith/Keswick; Carlisle/Keswick and Keswick/Seatoller.*
Accommodation *Varied accommodation in Borrowdale. Youth Hostels at Derwentwater, Longthwaite and Honister Hause.*

Great Gable stands aloof at the very hub of the Lake District. Although it has weathered down to a mere stump, its ring of crags on three sides gives it a stature that belies its 2,949ft/899m. The Ennerdale Horseshoe (chapter 99) includes a traverse of Great Gable, but the mountain features so prominently in the annals of Lakeland climbing that I consider it justifies a chapter to itself.

I describe, here, an ascent of Gable by the climbers' path from Sty Head, a path which winds in and out of the south face crags. We gain an insight into the historic routes first explored by Haskett Smith, Robinson, Slingsby, Solly, the Abraham brothers, Herford, Sansom and many others.

From Seathwaite walk up one of the well-beaten tracks to Styhead Tarn. You can either follow the stream to Stockley Bridge and then branch west, or cross the stream at Seathwaite and ascend via Taylorgill Force.

Head up grassy slopes west of Styhead Tarn. As the ground becomes rougher a narrow cairned path snakes across screes to an obvious rock face, Kern Knotts, split by two prominent cracks.

Walk round the base of Kern Knotts and cross the great fan of scree called Great Hell Gate. Next comes Tophet Wall, another huge slab of vertical rock, and then Napes Ridge running up towards Gable's summit several hundred feet above.

Walkers must descend here and skirt round the Napes Ridge to gain Little Hell Gate. A tiresome climb over loose scree will then lead to Gable's summit. But those who relish exciting scrambling can climb up beside Napes Ridge and 'thread the Needle'. This exercise involves passing through the narrow gap between the north side of the Needle and the Napes Ridge. Scrambling down the far side you have a spectacular view of the Sphinx Rock, silhouetted against the meadows of Wasdale.

Looking back at the Needle from the west you can appreciate its unique shape. Its ascent by Haskett Smith in 1886 marks the beginning of English rock climbing.

Clamber up the short ridge behind the Sphinx Rock to meet Little Hell Gate near Gable's summit.

Descend the trade-route to Windy Gap, climb Green Gable and take the path down to Base Brown. The crags above Gillercomb should be by-passed on the right. If in doubt descend Gillercomb itself and return to Seathwaite via the Sour Milk Gill path.

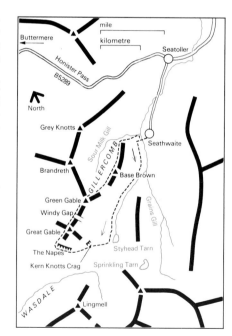

GREAT GABLE AND THE ENNERDALE HORSESHOE

Map *OS Sheet 90 (Tourist Map/Outdoor Leisure 4)*   **Start/Finish** *Ennerdale Scout Centre (087152)*
Distance/Time *21 miles/34km, 12-13 hrs*

Grading. A tough mountain walk over some of the best Lakeland fells.
Escape Routes Scarth Gap to Buttermere or Black Sail. Windy Gap to Sty Head and Borrowdale. Black Sail Pass to Ennerdale or Mosedale.
Transport Railway station at Whitehaven. Bus service: Whitehaven to Ennerdale Bridge (infrequent).
Accommodation Hotels in Buttermere. B & B locally. Youth Hostels at Ennerdale, Black Sail and Buttermere.

It is strange that two Lake District horseshoe walks, the Langdale and the Ennerdale, which are only divided by the Scafells, should be so different. Both walks are of roughly equal length and severity, and the head of each is dominated by a mountain of undisputed stature, Bow Fell and Great Gable respectively, but perhaps the Langdale walk is more contrived? Devotees of the Ennerdale walk will point to its purity and its simplicity; just one sizeable lake and one unbranched dale. But there are many other subtle differences of atmosphere between the two, which will be felt immediately by the discerning hill walker.

From the car-park at the west end of Ennerdale Water skirt the lake and climb to Great Borne, the first nail in the horseshoe. A line of fence posts now leads over Starling and Little Dodd to Red Pike and the start of the Buttermere Fells.

The high ridge over Red Pike, High Stile and High Crag epitomises Lakeland walking at its best. You are surrounded by familiar and well-loved features: Buttermere and Crummock Water, Robinson, Hindscarth, Great Gable and Pillar. Below your feet the light sparkles on Bleaberry Tarn, set in a combe as rough and rocky as a Scottish corrie.

Beyond Scarth Gap, Hay Stacks provides a pleasant diversion with its crags, tarns, hollows and nooks before Brandreth heralds a wide and open section of the walk, which continues

over Green Gable to Windy Gap. Up loose rocks and scree now to the summit of Great Gable, its central position making it one of Lakeland's outstanding viewpoints.

The second half of the walk begins with a descent of screes to Beck Head and a traverse of the slumbering giant of Kirk Fell, which gives wonderful views south to Wasdale and the Scafells. Rather a steep and loose scramble is involved on the descent from Kirk Fell to Black Sail Pass.

The historic mountain of Pillar can be ascended easily from Black Sail via Looking Stead, or by a more sporting route via Robinson's Cairn to the north, which gives an impressive view of Pillar Rock.

From Haycock onwards you can stride out over the rounded, grassy hills of Caw Fell and Iron Crag to Crag Fell. This, the last climb of the day, is craggy on the north with pinnacles and towers.

An easy descent alongside Ben Gill leads to the River Lisa and the car-park.

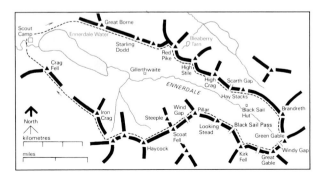

THE LAKELAND THREE THOUSANDERS

Map OS Sheet 90 (Tourist Map/Outdoor Leisure 4, 5, 6)   **Start/Finish** Keswick Market Place (265235)
Distance/Time 46 miles/74km, 16-20 hrs

Grading An exceptionally long and arduous walk.
Many different types of terrain from roads and grassy
fells to loose scree and rough boulders.
Escape Routes From Styhead, Lingmell Col and
Mickledore descend to Wasdale Head. From Esk
Hause descend Grains Gill to Seathwaite.
Transport Railway station at Penrith. Bus services:
Keswick to Ambleside, Carlisle, Whitehaven,
Lancaster and Kendal.
Accommodation Various accommodation in Keswick.
Youth Hostels at Keswick, Derwentwater and
Longthwaite.

Marathon walks in the English Lake District
have provided a popular challenge ever since
1911, when Dr Arthur Wakefield first completed the circuit of the four 3,000ft peaks in
24 hours. Since then, extra peaks have been
added and the best-known marathon of all is
the Bob Graham round of over forty peaks.

The framework for these marathons is still
the ascent of Skiddaw, Scafell, Scafell Pike and
Helvellyn, all within 24 hours, starting and
finishing in Keswick market place.

Of course any strategy and any route is
permitted, but perhaps it is best to make
Skiddaw the first of the four mountains and to
leave before dawn; the ascent is so easy that it
can be accomplished by torchlight.

The path up Skiddaw is wide, simple to
follow and is gently graded, although high up
it is covered with flat, slatey stones. Note that
the OS pillar is on the northern summit.

Descend to Keswick by the same route and
walk the nine miles through Borrowdale to
Seathwaite. Climb up to Styhead Tarn and take
the Corridor Route, which winds across the
slopes under Broad Crag and passes above
Piers Gill. At this point leave the Scafell Pike
path on your left and make for the col under
Lingmell.

A tricky piece of route-finding enables you
to traverse boulder fields and screes, to reach
the sheer cliff of Scafell Crag. Scramble up the
loose scree chute, called Lord's Rake, to the
summit plateau of Scafell.

The direct descent to Mickeldore, by the
series of rocky steps known as Broad Stand, is
suitable only for rock climbers. It is particularly treacherous in wet or icy conditions.
Thus my strong advice is to return down Lord's
Rake (with care), or descend via Fox Tarn, to
reach Mickeldore.

A well-worn path leads to Scafell Pike and
beyond as you switchback over the boulder
fields of Broad Crag and Great End to Esk

Hause. Continue to Angle Tarn and make a
rising traverse to High Raise, whence you can
descend the Wyth Burn valley to Steel End
under Helvellyn.

Take the tourist path up Helvellyn from
Wythburn Church, and descend by the wide
path leading from Lower Man to the King's
Head Inn at Thirlspot.

This mountain marathon is a considerable
achievement and, with your goal nearly completed, the six miles to Keswick will slip by
easily.

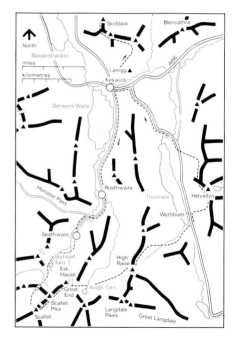

ACROSS LAKELAND: SHAP TO RAVENGLASS

Map *OS Sheets 90 and 96 (Tourist Map/Outdoor Leisure 5, 6)*   **Start/Finish** *Shap Village (563155)/ Ravenglass (085963)*   **Distance/Time** *42 miles/68km, 18 hrs*

> **Grading** *An exceptionally long walk crossing the Lake District from E to W.*
> **Escape Routes** *Numerous.*
> **Transport** *Railway stations at Penrith, Kendal and Ravenglass. Bus service: Kendal/Shap/Penrith. Miniature railway: Eskdale/Boot/Ravenglass.*
> **Accommodation** *Hotels and B & B at Shap and Ravenglass. Youth Hostels at Eskdale and Kendal.*

It is fortunate that the Lakeland 3,000ft peaks' circuit includes such a wide diversity of hill country, for the qualifying height is arbitrary. The purist might be happier with a more natural route such as the traverse of the Lake District range at its broadest part.

Tom Price's original route starts from Shap on the A6 trunk road to the east, and finishes at Ravenglass Estuary on the west coast. It is particularly satisfying to finish a walk at the sea, for the end is defined and one can go no further. Likewise, the extremely popular Lyke Wake Walk, another marathon test-piece described in this book, finishes on the east coast of Yorkshire.

Take the path into Swindale and walk up the Old Corpse Road to Mardale Common, descending to the head of Mardale. It is not difficult to imagine the village submerged as the valley was flooded in 1936.

Climb up steeply to the splendidly narrow ridge of Rough Crag and Long Stile, which gives wonderful views down into Riggindale and to Blea Water. At High Street summit you leave the main north-south axis of the ridge and head north-west to Saturna Crag, Angle Tarn and Patterdale.

Walk through the rather gloomy Grisedale to Grisedale Tarn and enjoy the stirring views up to the crest of Striding Edge and into the depths of Nethermost Cove. The path continues west, to meet the A591 at Dunmail Raise.

Cross the road directly and ascend Steel Fell, whence a rather indistinct path runs west to High White Stones on the bare plateau of High Raise. You have now reached the heart of Lakeland and should keep up the momentum by descending to Stake Pass and contouring round Rossett Pike to Angle Tarn. Up the screes now to Ore Gap and you are through the final mountain massif of this marathon expedition.

There are many delightful routes of descent beside Lingcove Beck and through the rocky bluffs and hillocks of Eskdale. Tom Price keeps well to the west of the river and meets the road near Wha House.

From the Woolpack you can take a pleasant riverside path running through woods to Forge Bridge. The private road under Hooker Crag will be the most popular choice for the final four-mile stretch into Ravenglass, but the energetic can traverse Muncaster Fell and the lazy or exhausted ride the Ratti.

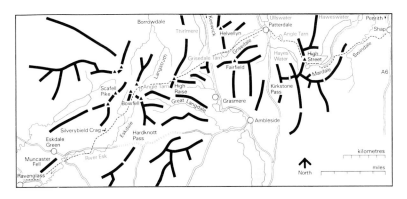

GREAT LANGDALE: THE HORSESHOE WALK

Map *OS Sheet 90 (Tourist Map/Outdoor Leisure 6)*   **Start/Finish** *Elterwater (328047)*
Distance/Time *18 miles/29km, 9-10 hrs*

> **Grading** *A long walk around the head of a fine dale.*
> **Escape Routes** *Descend easily into Langdale from Red Tarn, Three Tarns, Angle Tarn (via Rossett Ghyll), Stake Pass and Stickle Tarn.*
> **Transport** *Railway station at Windermere. Bus service: Windermere/Ambleside/Langdale.*
> **Accommodation** *Varied accommodation in Langdale. Youth Hostels at High Close and Elterwater.*

Langdale is deservedly one of Lakeland's most popular dales, and the paths to Stickle Tarn and up Rossett Ghyll are badly eroded. But, an eighteen-mile circuit around the Langdale skyline from Elterwater, includes many un-spoilt and rarely visited hills, crags, combes and tarns. Walkers like the challenge of the highest hills, irrespective of their quality, but the associated aesthetic rewards are diminish-ing year by year. Nowadays the traditional peace and beauty of the English Lake District is more often found amongst the lowlier and less fashionable hills, of which many are to be found on the Langdale Horseshoe Walk.

The road south from Elterwater to Little Langdale provides an easy way to Lingmoor Fell, which gives extensive views of the myriad peaks to come. Now head north-west to Side Pike before descending to the road near Blea Tarn. Next comes a hugely enjoyable climb up the rough and rocky Pike o'Blisco, before a cairned path leads down to Red Tarn in a more tranquil setting.

You now begin one of Lakeland's classic and most enjoyable hill traverses. The path over Crinkle Crags twists and turns through a maze of minor cliffs, gullies and tarns, with views into the wild upper reaches of Eskdale, Oxendale and Mickleden.

Three Tarns marks the junction of several paths and the way ahead can be confusing; you should climb the scree slopes and then traverse left above the cliffs of Bow Fell Links to reach Bow Fell's rocky summit.

The terrain eases as you descend northwards to the broad and grassy col of Ore Gap and then, more steeply to Angle Tarn, one of Lake-land's best loved landmarks. Continue easily over Rossett Pike to the Stake Pass where you change direction and head south-east to Martcrag Moor and Pike o'Stickle. You can look back across Mickleden to the serrated outline of Bow Fell and Crinkle Crags, more reminiscent of Torridon than the Lake District.

Like Bow Fell the Langdale Pikes have a big mountain feel about them; the area abounds in cliffs and rock castles and, as you descend Harrison Stickle, you have a splendid view of Pavey Ark, the rock climbers' playground overlooking Stickle Tarn.

From the tarn inflow a path runs up to Blea Rigg, and easy walking follows over Castle How, Raw Pike, Silver Howe and Red Bank, all hills with great charm, thence down to Elterwater.

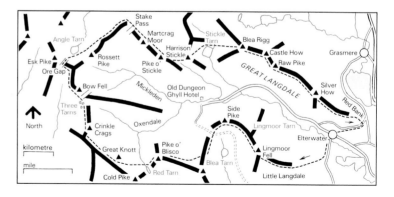

THE WAST WATER CIRCUIT

Map *OS Sheet 89 (Tourist Map/Outdoor Leisure 6)* **Start/Finish** *Strands (125040)*
Distance/Time *17 miles/27km, 10 hrs*

Grading A long hill traverse with plenty of steep, rough ground. Yewbarrow needs care under winter conditions.
Escape Routes The route may be terminated at Wasdale Head or Overbeck Bridge.
Transport Railway stations at Whitehaven and Ravenglass. Bus service: Whitehaven/Millom/ Gosforth. Miniature railway: Ravenglass/Eskdale.
Accommodation Hotels at Strands and Wasdale Head. B & B locally. Youth Hostels at Wastwater and Eskdale.

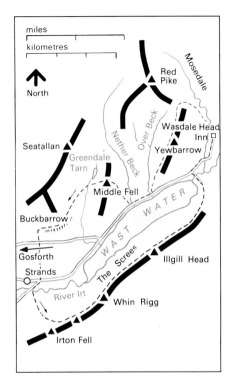

Wast Water lies amidst the grandest mountain scenery in Lakeland. Perhaps it is the great depth of the lake (the deepest in England) and the unrelenting screes falling straight into the dark waters under Whin Rigg that give it an aura of gloom and foreboding.

In only a few miles Wasdale runs from the pastoral coastal strip of West Cumbria right into the heart of the mountains. The stupendous rock peak of Great Gable fills the head of the dale, while the rock buttresses of Yewbarrow, Middle Fell and Buckbarrow rise steeply on the west side. This rugged scene is more akin to Snowdonia or Scotland than the gentle fells of Lakeland.

From Nether Wasdale take the footpath which climbs steeply to Irton Fell, runs beside a block of forestry and continues gradually to Whin Rigg. For nearly two miles cliffs fall away abruptly, ending in the great screes which fan down into Wast Water itself. At Illgill Head, the highest point on the ridge at 1,998ft/609m, you begin the easy descent of the long north-east ridge to Bracken-close, the bridge over Lingmell Beck and the Wasdale Head Inn, centre of much of the early Lake District climbing and still regarded as a shrine.

The return route over the western fells is demanding and it starts with an ascent of Yewbarrow, one of Lakeland's shapeliest peaks for its imposing wedge is guarded by rocky spurs.

From Mosedale zig-zag up the stony hillside on the north side of Dore Head screes, once one of Lakeland's finest scree runs but now run-out down to bedrock. But from Dore Head an exhilaratingly steep and rocky scramble up Stirrup Crag takes you to the narrow crest of Yewbarrow at 2,058ft/627m. You can look north-east straight into the amphitheatre bounded by the rock walls of Great Gable, Lingmell and the Scafells.

Descend the south ridge to the remarkable cleft of Great Door and then detour to the north side to reach Wast Water at Overbeck.

Pick your way through the tangle of bracken, bilberries and crags on the eastern slopes of Middle Fell while the charming Nether Beck tumbles below, down its rocky bed overhung with oak, alder, hazel and birch.

Easy slopes lead down to Greendale Tarn, where you should traverse across to Buckbarrow, skirt the top of the crags and drop down to the Wasdale road near Gill farm.

[117]

THE CONISTON FELLS

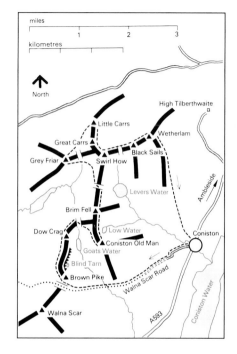

Map OS Sheet 97 (Tourist Map/Outdoor Leisure 6) **Start/Finish** Coniston (302975)
Distance/Time 14 miles/23km, 7 hrs

Grading A fine mountain walk that should give no difficulty in good conditions. Care is needed in mist.
Escape Routes Easy descents to Coniston from Goat's Hause, Lever's Hause and Swirl Hause. Tracked route from Wetherlam to Tilberthwaite.
Transport Railway station at Windermere. Bus services: Windermere/Ambleside/Coniston and Ulverston/Coniston.
Accommodation Varied accommodation in Coniston. Two Youth Hostels at Coniston: Holly How and Coppermines House.

As you approach the Coniston fells from Ambleside you may be shocked by the plethora of mine workings which scar the base of the hills. Extraction of copper ore was carried out between the sixteenth and the nineteenth centuries, while slate quarries too have bitten deeply into the hills. Spoil heaps, shafts, levels, access roads, railways, engine houses and ruined miners' cottages abound. However, as you climb up into the hills these ancient industrial relics provide a fascinating insight into past eras; you could spend days exploring them.

Coniston Water, which stretches away straight as an arrow for five miles, has more recent historical significance: Sir Donald Campbell was killed here in January 1967 in an attempt on the world water-speed record.

The Coniston fells are characterised by a complex series of ridges, deep combes, valleys, tarns and crags. Situated in the south of Lakeland they give wonderful views north to the Scafell range and south-east to the Pennines. This fourteen-mile expedition provides a Cook's Tour of the principal hills and ridges of the Coniston fells.

Take the Walna Scar Road to the ridge under Brown Pike, turn north and scramble up the rough ridge which overlooks Blind Tarn, and leads to the top of Dow Crag. In the 1920s Dow Crag became the testing ground for rock tigers, and it soon joined the ranks of Gable, Scafell, Pillar and Gimmer Crag.

Goats Water sits darkly below in the great, wild combe and you follow the edge of the cliffs round to Goats Hause and Coniston Old Man, 2,633ft/801m. Look out south-westwards over the Duddon estuary to locate the Isle of Man, and then head north over the broad ridge of Brim Fell to Swirl How. This fine ridge overlooks Levers Water and Seathwaite Reservoir, and it becomes rocky on Great How Crags.

If time allows visit the attractive outliers of Grey Friar, Great Carrs and Little Carrs before descending the rocky Prison Band (awkward in winter conditions) to the col under Black Sails. The wreckage of a plane can be seen on Broad Slack, the crags overlooking Greenburn.

A re-ascent takes you to the rounded summit of Wetherlam, which looks down to the tarns and woods of Little Langdale.

The long south ridge of Wetherlam is called Ladstones, and it provides a simple way down to the mine workings beside Church Beck, on the outskirts of Coniston.

HARTER FELL AND BLACK COMBE

Map *OS Sheets 89 and 96 (Tourist Map/Outdoor Leisure 6)* **Start/Finish** *Hard Knott Pass (203009)/Whicham (132825)*
Distance/Time *20 miles/32km, 9 hrs*

> **Grading** *A rough, tough walk over mainly trackless fells.*
> **Escape Routes** *Minor roads cross the route at Brown Rigg and one mile S of Buck Barrow.*
> **Transport** *Railway stations at Silecroft and Ravenglass. Miniature railway: Ravenglass to Eskdale.*
> **Accommodation** *Hotels and B & B in Eskdale, Millom and the Duddon valley. Youth Hostel at Eskdale.*

Harter Fell can be said to be the last real bastion on the south-west side of the Lake District. It rises as a perfect cone to a height of 2,129ft/649m south of Hard Knott Pass, and provides stirring views across Eskdale towards the rugged peaks of Bow Fell and the Scafells. South of Harter Fell, and bounded by the Duddon and the Esk, runs a range of broad, undulating and lonely hills ending with Black Combe, above Whicham.

The entire walk is twenty miles, but two roads cross the hills conveniently dividing the route into three sections. These sections are distinctive and make excellent mini-expeditions in themselves although, if conditions and fitness allow, the entire itinerary is strongly recommended. Thus we have the very rough Harter Fell protected by rocky outcrops and overgrown boulder fields, a stretch of coarse moor grass and bog on the flattish fells south of Devoke Water and, finally, the massive whale-back of Black Combe with its heavily eroded escarpment on the east side and its unbroken views westwards over the Irish Sea.

The steep slopes of Harter Fell can be tackled from any convenient point near the base of Hard Knott Pass. Pause at the top of this proud peak to enjoy the panoramic view of southern Lakeland, and then make your way over the peat hags of Green Crag and the prehistoric settlement on Great Worm Crag, to meet the Ulpha to Eskdale Green road near Devoke Water.

From the track on the east side of Devoke Water, it is a wet and boggy ascent to gain the outcrop of Yoadcastle on Woodend Height, and several miles of similar going must be endured as you wind your way south. Yet these desolate fells are full of interest: the tiny Holehouse Tarn below Stainton Pike, an eighteen-foot-high standing stone on Whitfell, numerous Bronze Age hut circles, and the extraordinary tors on Kinmont Buck Barrow.

Enthusiastic historians may wish to detour two miles to see the Neolithic stone circle at Swinside, but most walkers will continue south over Swinside Fell, Stoupdale Crags and Black Combe.

Thrusting up between the sea and the Duddon Estuary, Black Combe is a considerable influence on West Cumbria. The hill inspired Norman Nicholson, the Millon poet who died in 1987:

'Every
Inland fell is glinting;
Black Combe alone still hides
Its bald, bleak forehead, balaclava'd out of sight.'

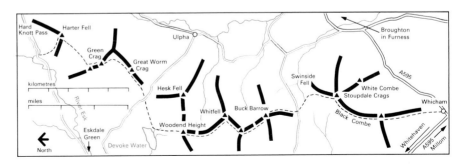

SNAEFELL AND THE MANX HILLS

Map *OS Sheet 95* **Start/Finish** *The Hibernian (459912)/Port Erin (459912)* **Distance/Time** *27 miles/44km, 14 hrs*

Grading *A long but easy walk, mainly over grassy or heather-clad hills.*
Escape Routes *Numerous. The route is never more than 2 miles from a road.*
Transport *Bus services: Douglas/The Hibernian/ Ramsey and Douglas/Castletown/Port Erin. Steam train (summer): Port Erin/Douglas. Electric tram (summer): Douglas/Ballaglass Glen.*
Accommodation *Varied accommodation throughout the island. No Youth Hostels now open.*

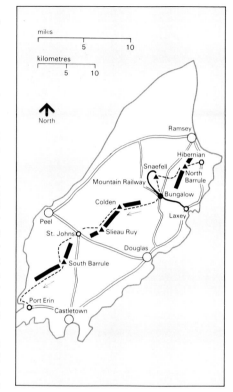

A view of the distant hills of the Isle of Man can be the highlight of a day's walk over the tops of Snowdonia or the Lake District. Occasionally, from Black Combe or Coniston Old Man, Snaefell rises above a silvery sea, wreathed in mist, and you can imagine yourself as Professor Challenger in Conan Doyle's *The Lost World*.

The Isle of Man, once a Viking stronghold, is now a holiday island noted more for its TT and Grand Prix motor cycle races than hill walking. But go out of season and you can walk for 27 carefree miles along the high spine of the island, tramping over grass and heather, and enjoying views down to lonely wooded valleys as well as across the blue sea to distant horizons.

In this itinerary we combine bracken-covered slopes with open moorlands of heather and peat, outcrops of slate, prehistoric remains, a Victorian mountain railway, Europe's largest water-wheel and a magnificent stretch of cliff-girt coastline.

The walk starts at The Hibernian, just south of Ramsey in the north of the island, and follows a path over the smoothly contoured slopes of North Barrule. Beyond Clagh Ouyr drop to a col and then climb to Snaefell's summit, 2,036ft/621m. An electric tramway runs up Snaefell from Laxey; this was the first mountain railway to be built in Britain, in 1895, beating the Snowdon Mountain Railway by a few months. From the summit you can look down to the Laxey Glen, site of a gigantic water-wheel known as *Lady Isabella*.

Keeping to the highest ground cross the rather featureless, heather-covered fells of Beinn-y-Phott, Colden and Slieau Ruy and descend to St John's. On Tynwald Hill, on the edge of St John's, the Manx parliament has met for over 1,000 years; it continues to do so, annually, on July 5th.

Proceed south over Slieau Whallian to South Barrule, which carries an Iron Age fort, and then head west to Cronk ny Arrey Laa over-looking the rugged western seaboard. At Sloc Gap you pass a collection of ancient hut circles, and then you climb to 1,000ft above the sea before dropping again to Fleshwick Bay.

The final three-mile stretch climbs to Bradda Hill, which looks south to the Calf of Man, and then follows a path along the towering cliffs of Bradda Head before entering the picturesque town of Port Erin.

WEARDALE: THE FORGOTTEN CORNER OF ENGLAND

Map OS Sheets 87 and 91   *Start/Finish* Ireshopeburn (865387)   *Distance/Time* 19 miles/31km, 8-9 hrs

---

Grading *A long walk over undulating, heather-clad moorlands.*
Escape Routes *From Burnhope Seat head W for 1 mile to reach the B6277.*
Transport *Bus service: Bishop Auckland/Stanhope/ Cowshill.*
Accommodation *Hotels at St. John's Chapel. B & B locally. Youth Hostels at Langdon Beck, Alston and Edmundbyers.*

The Northern Pennines are drained to the east by three great rivers: the Swale, the Tees and the Wear. Proceeding north the dales become progressively more barren, open and unspoilt, and walkers who enjoy striding over trackless upland country will find their Mecca in the bleak fells of Upper Weardale.

Weardale is very much a working dale, making few concessions to the visitor. Grouse shooting, once the mainstay of the moors is now on the decline, hill farmers are struggling and the uplands are reverting to the wild.

Yet Weardale has a history of prosperity. In the eighteenth century the London Lead Company mined galena, a silver-rich ore of lead, and communities sprang up. The impact was considerable with the construction of roads, shafts, crushing mills and reservoirs. Flues, up to a mile long, were run up the hillsides to disperse poisonous fumes from the smelters.

The industrial history of Upper Weardale adds a distinctive flavour to a walk on the fells: the hillsides are pock-marked by old scars, exposed minerals abound beside the gills and down in the dale archaeological trusts are restoring important relics.

In this circular walk round the head of Weardale you experience the charm of the dales and the exhilaration of high, lonely moorlands in a forgotten corner of England.

From Ireshopeburn leave the bluebells and bracken and take the track leading towards Great Stony Hill. You are soon amongst the heather, bilberry and cloudberry bushes, while larks, pipits, dunlins, curlews and plovers keep up their song; the latter being known locally as Pennine Whistlers.

As you walk west towards Scaud Hill and Burnhope Seat the mass of Cross Fell fills the view south across Upper Teesdale. You can pick up amethyst-tinged specimens of fluorite from abandoned spoil heaps. Wild thyme and spring sandwort seem to thrive on the lead-poisoned mounds and, growing in profusion, they provide a splash of colour.

At Burnhope Seat, 2,452ft/747m, the broad ridge swings north and leads over Dead Stones and Knoutberry Hill to the Alston road at Kill-hope Cross. At 2,056ft this is the highest classified road in England. Just below, in the dale, stands the 34ft diameter Killhope Water Wheel.

Return to Ireshopeburn over the swelling moors of Slate Hill, Killhope Law with its massive cairn, and Black Hill. You meet a grassy path at Race Head, dotted with mountain pansies while wild raspberries tangle in the hedge.

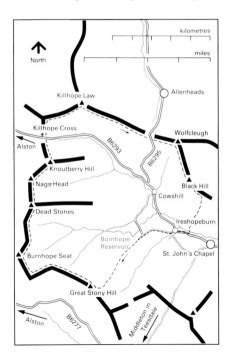

HIGHEST PENNINES:
UPPER TEESDALE AND CROSS FELL

Map OS Sheets 91 and 82 (Outdoor Leisure 31)   **Start/Finish** Middleton in Teesdale (946253)/Alston (717465)
Distance/Time 35 miles/56km, 12 hrs

Grading A very long walk over the highest of the
Pennine fells. Some stretches of rough moorland but
in general the going is good.
Escape Routes From High Cup Nick a good path
descends S to Dufton. From Cross Fell summit
descend W to Kirkland.
Transport Bus services: Alston/Haltwhistle/Carlisle;
Darlington/Middleton in Teesdale; Middleton in
Teesdale/Alston (infrequent).
Accommodation Hotels and B & B in Middleton in
Teesdale and Alston. Youth Hostels at Langdon
Beck, Dufton and Alston.

This long and magnificent walk takes in some
of the best fell country that England has to
offer. From Middleton in Teesdale it proceeds
up the delectable valley of the upper Tees,
before climbing up to the Pennine Ridge and
traversing Cross Fell, at 2,930ft/893m, the
highest summit on the backbone of England.
The walk ends at Alston in Cumbria, the
highest market town in England.

Much of the walk comprises the wildest
section of the Pennine Way, Britain's oldest
and finest long-distance footpath, which still
has no rival.

Take the path running along the south bank
of the River Tees from Middleton. In spring the
meadows are ablaze with violets, primroses,
wood anemones, cowslips and bluebells.

Beyond Winch Bridge the scenery becomes
wilder, and as you push your way through
scrub juniper you can hear the roar of High
Force, where the Tees plunges 70ft into a dark
whirlpool enclosed in an amphitheatre of
black cliffs. Further on you pass under a line of
broken cliffs called Falcon Clints and then the
Maize Beck joins the Tees from the west. At this
point a cataract of white water comes into
sight; this is Cauldron Snout where the Tees
roars down a narrow gorge of Whin Sill rock.

Cauldron Snout and Cow Green Reservoir,
above, are in a National Nature Reserve. Here,
arctic flora grows on the rare sugar limestone,
unique flora which survived the last ice age.

Head west now, through Birkdale Farm, to
the Maize Beck. In wet weather don't risk a
crossing but use the bridge situated a mile
further upstream; a walker was drowned at
this point several years ago.

Skirt the top of High Cup Nick, a spectacular
geological phenomenon where the ground
falls away into a vast chasm, and make for
Knock Fell which overlooks the fertile Eden
Valley. Now wonderfully high, open and
bracing walking takes you past the radio masts

on Great Dun Fell to Cross Fell, a bleak, stony
plateau with a much-needed stone wind-break
on the summit. The views west to the Lake
District are extensive.

Descend northwards, following a line of
cairns, to Greg's Hut and meet a path running
down to Garrigill in the South Tyne Valley.
Old mine workings abound and purple
crystals of fluorspar, or Blue John, litter the
ground.

The walk ends as it started, with a pleasant
riverside stretch of four miles into Alston.

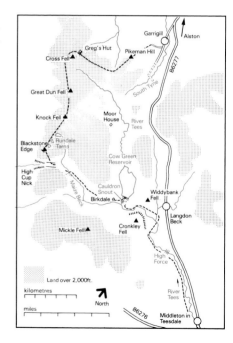

THE SWALEDALE WATERSHED

Map OS Sheets 91 and 98 (Outdoor Leisure 30)   **Start/Finish** Thwaite (892982)
Distance/Time 30 miles/48km, 12-13 hrs

Grading A long and difficult walk over high, open
fells. Much of the way is trackless, crossing coarse
grass, deep heather and peat hags.
Escape Routes Roads are crossed at Birkdale, Tan
Hill and Muker.
Transport Railway station at Darlington. Daily bus
service: Darlington/Richmond/Reeth/Muker and
Gunnerside, continuing to Keld on Tues and Sat.
Accommodation Hotels and B & B at Muker,
Gunnerside, Reeth and Richmond. Youth Hostels at
Keld and Grinton Lodge.

Take the road west from the historic town of
Richmond and you will discover a corner of
England little changed over the centuries. The
road up the dale winds between hedges of
blackthorn, hazel and oak, the bridges are
hump-backed, every house is stone built and
many have narrow mullioned windows and
stone-slabbed roofs.

The hay meadows are bright with flowers
(spraying is rare): clover, buttercup, cranesbill,
vetch, bedstraw and birdsfoot trefoil. Higher
up the valley side, above the lush gills, heather
and rough moorland take over and in several
places remnants of the lead mining industry
are visible. The ancient trackways and spoil
heaps are now overgrown, the smelt mills and
chimneys tumbled down and lichen-covered.

The head of Swaledale is surrounded by
high fells, seamed by gullies and gills which
carry down the water in falls and cascades and
through deep gorges.

A circular walk over the high tops of the
Swaledale watershed involves thirty tough
miles and, although the Pennine Way and the
Coast to Coast Walk cross the watershed, the
fells are mostly quite barren and trackless.

From Thwaite the Pennine Way leads easily
to Great Shunner Fell, 2,340ft/716m, the
highest point of the day. Thereafter it is a relief
to leave the eroded track and forge your own
way across the unspoilt Pennine country of
Hugh Seat and High Seat, stealing a glance

over the broken crags of Mallerstang Edge to
the Settle–Carlisle railway in the valley below.

Having crossed the B6270 and fought through
the bogs of Rollinson Haggs, you arrive at the
massive cairns on Nine Standards Rigg. Ahead
lies Brownber Fell and a stretch of appallingly
tough moorland: the heather is as coarse and
thick as barbed-wire, the peat hags are as deep
as elephant traps and the black bogs suck
hungrily at your boots.

Don't despair for your exertions are soon
rewarded by the providential arrival of the Tan
Hill Inn, at 1,732ft the highest hostelry in
England. Thereafter the going becomes easier
as rolling, heather moorlands rise to Rogan's
Seat. Beyond this rather featureless fell you
pick up a path heading south into Swinner
Gill, a lovely deep, green valley bedecked with
flowers and fringed with crags.

Cow-grazed pastures lead into the charming
dales village of Muker, where refreshments
may be obtained. A narrow, tree-lined path
runs beside the Muker Beck back to Thwaite.

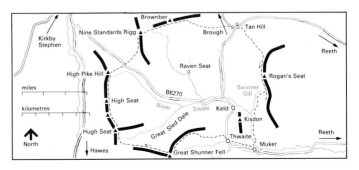

WILD BOAR FELL AND THE HOWGILLS

Map OS Sheets 91, 97 and 98   **Start/Finish** Kirkby Stephen (775086)/Sedbergh (657922)
Distance/Time 23 miles/37km, 9-10 hrs

Grading Easy walking over rolling, grassy fells.
Wild Boar Fell is rougher than the Howgills.
Escape Routes The fells are easily descended to the
valley from any point except above the escarpment
overlooking Cautley Spout.
Transport Bus service: Kirkby Stephen/Sedbergh.
Accommodation Hotels and B & B at Kirkby Stephen
and Sedbergh. Youth Hostels at Kirkby Stephen,
Hawes and Kendal.

This fine walk links the two Cumbrian towns of Kirkby Stephen and Sedbergh; crossing the wild and lonely massifs of Wild Boar Fell and the Howgill Hills.

These two upland areas are separated by the valley of the Rawthey and their features are different. The Wild Boar Fell country is characterised by gentle, rolling hills, outcrops of millstone grit and eroded patches of shale and scattered boulders. The Howgills are smoothly sculptured grassy hills enclosing steep valleys. They are ideal walking country because of a notable absence of walls and fences above 700ft.

Take the Sedbergh road out of Kirkby Stephen and, after a mile, turn left for Wharton Fell. Once on the open hillside make for the abrupt rocky nose, known as the Nab. The ridge becomes rougher and more stony, but it gives wonderful views east to the broken escarpment of Mallerstang Edge, rimming the most pastoral of dales.

Wild Boar Fell's trig. point at 2,324ft/708m lies west of the cliffs, but the best route follows the edge of the crags to a cluster of cairns on the south side.

Continue over the mound of Swarth Fell to the cairn on Swarth Fell Pike, then swing right and descend Ulldale, down which flows the infant River Rawthey. The path follows the river as it rushes through ravines and over waterfalls and cascades to Rawthey Bridge on the A683.

Follow the road for a mile to the Cross Keys Inn, where you turn off and ascend the path on the right of the beck to Cautley Spout. This waterfall is one of the finest in England and the setting could hardly be bettered. The water, descending in a series of leaps, has worn a deep groove in the rounded shoulder of the fell, while on the south side the loose cliffs of Cautley Crag contrast the grassy slopes of Great Dummacks.

A rather indistinct path continues west to The Calf, at 2,220ft/676m the highest point in the Howgills. Now walk south to the large cairn on Calders, skirt the pointed summit of Arant Haw and bear left for Winder. Winder overlooks Sedbergh, the Sedbergh School song is named after it, and it is a marvellous viewpoint for the Lune Valley and Morecambe Bay.

From Winder take the path which runs down to Lochbank Farm. This gives access to Howgill Lane, just a few minutes' walk from Sedbergh's main street.

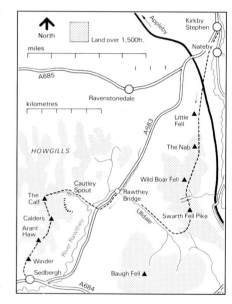

INGLEBOROUGH, PENYGHENT AND WHERNSIDE

Map OS Sheet 98 (Outdoor Leisure 2)   **Start/Finish** Ribblehead (765793)   **Distance/Time** 23 miles/37km, 9-10 hrs

> **Grading** A well defined walk, over mainly grassy hills, which has become a North of England classic.
> **Escape Routes** The walk crosses roads at Chapel le Dale and Horton in Ribblesdale.
> **Transport** Railway stations at Ribblehead and Horton in Ribblesdale. Bus services: Ingleton to Skipton, Lancaster and Kendal; Hawes/Leyburn/Darlington.
> **Accommodation** Hotels in Horton, Hawes and Ingleton. B & B locally. Youth Hostels at Hawes, Ingleton and Stainforth.

In the heart of the Yorkshire Dales, standing on a great plinth of Carboniferous limestone, rise the separate gritstone mountains of Penyghent, Ingleborough and Whernside. These mountains are mainly rounded, except in their upper parts where weathering has produced escarpments and boulder-strewn slopes. The valleys are fertile, provide good grazing, and are characterised by networks of limestone walls which appear dazzling white in the sunshine. Caves and potholes abound. In early summer the grass is green and lush and the flowers at their most colourful; the air is full of the cries of larks, curlews, redshanks, peewits and golden plovers.

The 'Three Peaks' round has long been a classic walk and it is on the fell runners' calendar, the race being run on the last Sunday in April. Inevitably commercialisation has crept in, and walkers can 'clock in' and obtain a certificate of achievement at the Penyghent cafe in Horton if they complete the round inside twelve hours.

From Ribblehead walk beside the great viaduct, now surely part of our heritage, and continue along the east side of the railway until you reach Blea Moor tunnel. Cross the line by an aqueduct and strike up the hillside towards the north ridge of Whernside, passing two spectacular waterfalls in Force Gill.

Whernside is a long 'whale-back', and although it is the highest of the Three Peaks, at 2,415ft/736m, it has the least character. It provides excellent views, however, of the Lake District, the Howgills, Morecambe Bay and even to Blackpool Tower.

Descend muddy slopes to Bruntscar, follow the lane to the Hill Inn, and locate the Ingleborough footpath which is signed to Great Douk Cave. After a steep pull up to the saddle under Simon Fell, you soon arrive on Ingleborough's flat table-top, where there are traces of an Iron Age fort built by the Brigantians.

Retrace your steps, traverse Simon Fell by an excellent path and walk through a dry depression known as Sulber Nick to reach Horton.

The Penyghent path starts from Brackenbottom and skirts the south end of the prominent fringe of crags; this is one of the worst-eroded sections of the walk and extensive repairs are being carried out here by the National Park Authority.

The final leg of the walk takes a winding and complex route, via farms at High Birkwith and Nether Lodge to meet the Ribblehead road near Ingman Lodge.

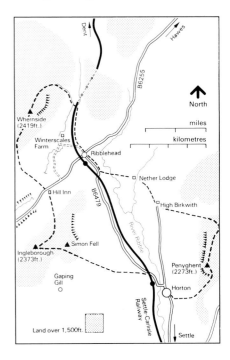

PEN HILL AND BUCKDEN PIKE

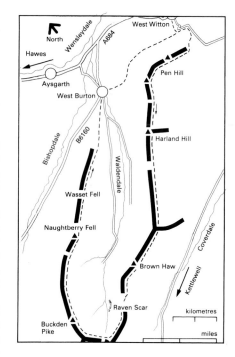

Map OS Sheets 98 and 99 (Outdoor Leisure 30)   **Start/Finish** West Witton (058884)
Distance/Time 22 miles/35km, 8-9 hrs

Grading A rough walk over high Pennine moorland.
Escape Routes Numerous easy descents into
Coverdale, Waldendale or Bishopdale. An overnight
stop could be made at Buckden or Kettlewell.
Transport Railway station at Darlington. Bus
service: Richmond/Leyburn/West Witton/Hawes,
with connections from Darlington, Ripon and
Northallerton.
Accommodation Hotels and B & B at West Witton,
Aysgarth and West Burton. Youth Hostels at Aysgarth
Falls, Hawes, Kettlewell and Ellingstring.

Pen Hill stands proudly at the gateway to
Wensleydale, and its conspicuous flat top and
sharp escarpment make it easily identifiable
from the North York Moors. For centuries it
has been used as a beacon in times of national
peril or rejoicing.

The hill walker should not look at Pen Hill
in isolation, for it marks the end of a long and
broad ridge of high fells running north from
Buckden Pike above Wharfedale. This ridge is
wild, lonely and trackless and it makes a vastly
superior ascent of Buckden Pike than the
trade-route from Starbotton. A return can be
made north-west to the delightful dales village
of West Burton. This horseshoe walk encloses
sleepy, rural, undiscovered Waldendale. Where
else in the Yorkshire Dales can you walk

eighteen peaceful miles over high fells without
crossing a single road? This is a walk for the
connoisseur of the old Yorkshire Dales,
before the coming of the trail riders, the fell
runners and the charabancs. It is quite perfect.

Access onto the east ridge of Penhill Beacon
is gained from Penhill Farm, a pleasant walk
up a winding lane from West Witton. After
passing the OS pillar and various cairns you
should follow the escarpment edge westwards,
and then head south through thick heather
and coarse grass to Height of Hazely.

The way ahead is now revealed over Harland
Hill and Brown Haw to the distant blue outline
of Buckden Pike. Far below, on either side, the
farms, patterned fields and woods of Waldendale and Coverdale can be seen. This is
magnificent Pennine country where a breeze
blows constantly, ruffling the wool of the
Swaledales and bearing away the curlew's cry.

The high ground can be followed over North
Moor and Windle Side to meet the north-south
ridge of Buckden Pike near the memorial
cross. Alternatively, you can descend to Raven
Scar and take a more direct route to the Pike.
Buckden Pike is one of the finest viewpoints in
the Pennines and a complete panorama is

enjoyed with Penyghent and Ingleborough
prominent to the west.

Open, featureless fells lead gradually north
over Naughtberry Fell and Wasset Fell to the
picture postcard village of West Burton. An
attractive 'green lane' enclosed by limestone
walls and overhung with ash trees, contours
Pen Hill at about 1,000ft, returning you to West
Witton. A more delightful last lap of the walk
cannot be imagined.

GREAT WHERNSIDE AND BUCKDEN PIKE

Map *OS Sheet 98 (Outdoor Leisure 10)*   **Start/Finish** *Conistone (982675)/Buckden (942772)*
Distance/Time *15 miles/24km, 6-7 hrs*

Grading *A mainly easy walk over high fells. Certain stretches have coarse tussocky grass, others can be boggy.*
Escape Routes *The route crosses the Kettlewell–Coverdale road, otherwise the fells may be descended easily in almost any direction.*
Transport *Bus service: Skipton/Grassington/ Kilnsey/Kettlewell/Buckden.*
Accommodation *Hotels at Buckden, Kettlewell, Kilnsey and Grassington. B & B locally. Youth Hostels at Aysgarth Falls, Kettlewell, Linton and Malham.*

Great Whernside is a long whale-back which rises high above Pateley Bridge in Nidderdale and dominates the eastern Pennines. It is a fell neglected by the hordes, yet it can offer a day which combines vigorous exercise with the charms of the Yorkshire Dales.

Wharfedale runs under the western slopes of Great Whernside, a dale which represents the Dales at their most delightful. Grey stone houses and barns, green pastures, well-groomed sheep, drystone walls and clear rivers. Startlingly white Carboniferous limestone thrusts out, forming escarpments, outcrops and boulder-fields and encouraging good grasslands and grazing.

The hill walker experiences an abrupt change of landscape as he climbs out of the dales and up the fells. At about 1,200ft the limestone is overlaid by gritstone and impervious clays, thus the high ground becomes acid and waterlogged and coarse grass, peat and bilberry predominate.

From the hamlet of Conistone take the narrow lane past the church and then branch right up Mossdale, an open valley leading into the heart of Great Whernside. The gentle limestone landscape is left behind and you enter a world of cotton-grass and curlews, skylarks, peewits, rabbits and old mine workings.

Just before Mossdale Head ford the beck and strike out onto the broad south-east ridge of Great Whernside. Watch out for some severely eroded gullies, some 30ft deep with steep sides like elephant traps.

The three miles to the summit are the roughest and toughest of the day, but are in the best traditions of British fell country. Open views, expansive skies, coarse moorland, the croaking of grouse and the calling of plovers, and a stiff breeze in your hair. It is a walk reminiscent of the high Cheviots and the hills of Peebles-shire.

Drop down from the 2,310ft/704m summit of Great Whernside, to the road between Wharfedale and Coverdale at a line of Iron Age fortifications.

Buckden Pike, which rises ahead, is an altogether much easier proposition. The grass is less coarse and a path of sorts runs beside a wall to aid navigation. High on the summit ridge you pass a white stone cross, erected in memory of five Polish airmen who perished here in January 1942.

It is a gentle descent into Wharfedale, and no doubt you will welcome the re-emergence of the limestone. Make for the village of Cray and then contour the hillside, entering Buckden through the leafy Rakes Wood.

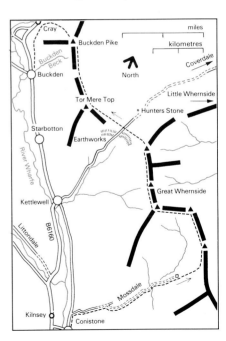

MALHAM COVE AND GORDALE SCAR – A BOTANIST'S PARADISE

Map OS Sheet 98 (Outdoor Leisure 10)   *Start/Finish* Malham (900628)   *Distance/Time* 7 miles/11km, 5 hrs

> **Grading** *An easy walk through spectacular limestone scenery. The scramble through Gordale could be tricky in wet weather when the beck is in spate.*
> **Escape Routes** *Numerous.*
> **Transport** *Railway stations at Settle, Skipton and Gargrave. Bus service: Skipton/Gargrave/Malham.*
> **Accommodation** *Hotels and B & B in Malham. Youth Hostels at Malham, Linton and Kettlewell.*

Malham, showpiece of the Yorkshire Dales, is the focus of this popular and ever-fascinating walk. In spring the landscape is a kaleidoscope of colour for the meadows are not sprayed and a myriad flowers bloom. Carboniferous limestone dominates the scenery of this region: the great cliffs of Gordale and Malham, the extensive pavements fissured by grykes, the bluffs and outcrops and the criss-cross network of dry-stone walls all reflect the sunlight with dazzling intensity.

From the south end of Malham village take the waymarked path beside the beck and through meadows to Janet's Foss, here the Gordale beck cascades over a moss-covered tufa screen into a deep pool set in sombre woodlands. A delightful spot, associated with fairies by earlier generations.

Cross the road and walk towards the lime-stone gorge of Gordale Scar which has a cathedral-like quality. You may see climbers clinging to the vertical walls, and you will certainly see stunted yew trees growing out of the crevices.

Clamber up beside the splendid 30ft waterfall to enter the wild upper reaches of the gorge. The harsh cry of jackdaws can be heard above the roar of the water.

Scrambling up a bank of loose scree you emerge above a valley flanked by limestone pavement. The grykes hold many woodland species: wood sorrel, dog's mercury and herb robert, while the turf is decorated by violets, birdsfoot-trefoil, thyme, bedstraw and fairy flax.

Cross the ancient Mastiles Lane to reach Malham Tarn, which is managed by the Field Studies Council who own the impressive house above the shore. The tarn has no visible inlet, it is fed by streams which well up from the bottom.

The outflow stream is followed to Water Sinks, a jumble of boulders where, in dry weather, the water disappears underground. Walk on down the dry valley below Comb Scar to the top of Malham Cove.

Peer over this 360ft cliff, over which the stream once tumbled, and then descend the specially constructed stairway to the fields at its base. Tests have shown that the stream issuing from under the cliff is the infant River Aire, and not that which disappeared at Water Sinks. The rare tall blue flower, Jacob's ladder, grows on the screes nearby; it was discovered here 300 years ago by John Ray, 'father' of British botany.

You can afford to linger awhile in this idyllic spot because Malham is close-by.

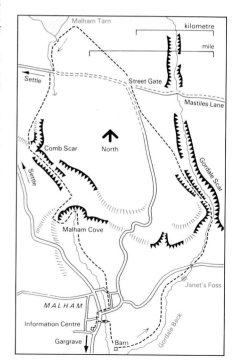

WHARFEDALE – A TASTE OF THE DALES WAY

Map *OS Sheets 98 and 104 (Outdoor Leisure 10)* **Start/Finish** *Ilkley (110482)/Kettlewell (972723)*
Distance/Time *24 miles/39km, 8-9 hrs*

Grading An easy riverside walk, mainly on footpaths.
Escape Routes Numerous. The walk can be conveniently terminated at Grassington, after 17 miles.
Transport Railway station at Ilkley. Bus services: Leeds/Ilkley; Ilkley/Kettlewell; Skipton/Kettlewell.
Accommodation Hotels and B & B at Ilkley, Grassington and Kettlewell. Youth Hostels at Kettlewell and Linton.

The Dales Way is a long-distance footpath which runs from Ilkley to Windermere. The first 24 miles of the walk, described here, follows the River Wharfe up into the best of the dales' limestone country at Kettlewell, whence a bus will return you to your starting point.

Wharfedale, with its woods, green meadows, stone barns, picturesque villages and lively river is the showpiece of the Yorkshire Dales. Certain popular attractions, such as Bolton Priory and Grassington, will be crowded in the summer months, but few tourists stray far from the road and you will be able to fully enjoy the peace of this exquisite dale.

The path from Ilkley proceeds rather mundanely alongside the River Wharfe until it crosses the A59. Then, quite suddenly, you round a bend and behold Bolton Priory, built in rich limestone on a promontory of parkland while woods, rocky brows and open moorland form the perfect backdrop. The ruined Priory, dating from 1151 and rising beside the river in the most romantic of settings, inspired Turner, Ruskin and Wordsworth.

Cross the river and continue north through shady woods of oak and ash which give fleeting, but graphic, views back to Bolton Priory. You meet the river again at the Strid, a notorious gorge where the full force of the water rushes between two rocks, not more than six feet apart. Several visitors have drowned while trying to jump the Strid, for the take-off and landing rocks are slippery and treacherous.

Having left the woods the river runs through open, pastoral scenery, passing under ruined Barden Tower and rushing headlong over rapids near Appletreewick. Burnsall comes next, the most charming dales' village imaginable, and another three miles through the meadows sees you in Grassington.

Here the green fields and white limestone appear their most vivid. The pastures, which reach up the sides of the dales, were reclaimed from acid moorland in the eighteenth and nineteenth centuries by massive applications of lime. Nowadays, the obsolete lime kilns are a common feature of the landscape, they merge perfectly into the hillsides without being at all intrusive.

Take the high path above Grass Wood to the rocky terraces above Conistone. Look west across the dale to Kilnsey Crag, and marvel at the feat of Mark Leach who free-climbed its vast overhang in 1988.

The path continues traversing the western slopes of Great Whernside (chapter 113) before dropping to Kettlewell.

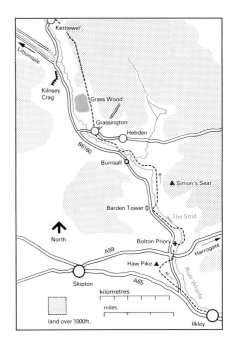

WARD'S STONE, FOREST OF BOWLAND

Map OS Sheets 97 and 102   **Start/Finish** Tarnbrook (587556)   **Distance/Time** 10 miles/16km, 4 hrs

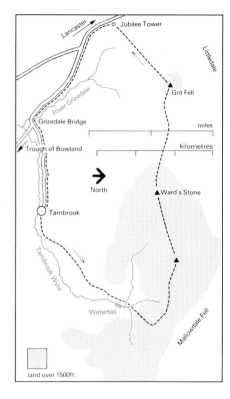

land over 1500ft.

Grading Easy under good conditions. In mist the route, which under landowner's instructions must be strictly adhered to, could be difficult to follow.
Escape Routes The S side of the fells may be descended easily to the road.
Transport Railway station at Lancaster. Bus service: Lancaster/Abbeystead.
Accommodation Hotel at Bay Horse. B & B at Dolphinholme. Youth Hostels at Slaidburn and Earby.

How many drivers, powering up the M6 north of Preston on a sparkling morning, have their spirits lifted by the smooth, folded hills of the Forest of Bowland? These hills are walking country *par excellence*; the constant breeze off the Irish Sea ripples the grass and heather, clear streams course down deep valleys and there are few enclosures. The north-western area of Bowland is Pennine in character with coarse, tussocky moor-grass, peat and gritstone outcrops. Its smooth contours were caused by the glaciers which moved south from the Lake District mountains during the last ice-age.

Sadly, the Forest of Bowland suffers some of the worst access restrictions to be found in Britain. Only a few routes are available to the general public, one of which, a circular walk over Ward's Stone, the highest hill in Bowland

at 1,836ft/561m, is described here.

On the north side of the Trough of Bowland the road crosses the Tarnbrook Wyre at Lee Bridge. Park at the bridge and walk up the dale to the hamlet of Tarnbrook, which was once a centre for felt hat and glove making.

From Tarnbrook take the path which runs above the stream, gradually contouring round the side of Tarnbrook Fell to meet the stream again at a waterfall. A line of posts now guide you north to a broad ridge, where a path from Wolfhole Crag comes in from the east. Here you turn west across the windswept, peat-hagged moorland until you reach the plateau of Ward's Stone.

There are two summits on the plateau, each sporting a collection of gritstone boulders and each carrying an OS pillar. The most easterly summit is the highest by three feet.

Approaching from the east you first meet a single boulder known as the Queen's Chair, and then two distinct piles of boulders called the Grey Mare and Foal.

Ward's Stone is one of the Pennine's most remote and isolated summits, and the characteristic outlines of Ingleborough and Penyghent are most prominent to the north.

The so-called 'Access Strip' continues west for two miles to Grit Fell and another line of boulders. Here the waymarked path turns south-west, below Clougha Pike, crosses the head waters of the Grizedale river and meets the road again at the Jubilee Tower. It is now only a short distance down the hill to Lee Bridge.

WOLF FELL AND FIENDSDALE

Map *OS Sheet 102*   **Start/Finish** *Chipping (623433)*   **Distance/Time** *19 miles/31km, 7-8 hrs*

Grading *A magnificent walk over wild upland country. In bad weather route finding on the bleak, exposed moors above Fiendsdale could be difficult.*
Escape Routes *The walk may be cut short at the Trough of Bowland.*
Transport *Railway station at Preston. Bus service: Preston/Longridge/Chipping.*
Accommodation *Hotels at Chipping, Longridge and Clitheroe. B & B locally. Youth Hostels at Slaidburn and Earby.*

The Pennine Chain thrusts out a limb to the west, producing a distinct area of wild uplands having its own history, traditions and character. This is the Forest of Bowland.

Although the Forest of Bowland is a designated Area of Outstanding Natural Beauty it is still relatively undiscovered. Over the years it has gained a sad reputation as a no-go area and even now only certain parts have free access. Lancashire County Council has won access agreements for Clougha Fell, Fair Snape Fell, Wolf Fell and Saddle Fell, but the penalty exacted is harsh: yellow marker posts, brutal fences, official notices and the channelling of walkers along fixed routes.

In spite of the access restrictions walkers can enjoy several wonderfully wild and diverse expeditions. Not only does Bowland offer

bleak and rugged fells, but it is surrounded by picturesque old villages, hay meadows, woods, valleys and bubbling streams. Iron Age man, the Romans, Angles and Norse all settled in Bowland and it became a Royal Forest under the Normans.

From Chipping, a delightful village set under the southern slopes of the fells, take the lane which runs beside the chair factory and make your way up the broad ridge of Saddle Fell. There, the inevitable fence, stile and access notice awaits you but, once you have crossed the peat-hagged plateau and reached Fair Snape Fell, you can walk unrestricted.

To the north you can look over Ward's Stone to the Yorkshire Three Peaks, while to the west Heysham Nuclear Power Station broods menacingly over the Lune estuary.

Be sure to make the one-mile detour south to Parlick, for it is a magnificent walk along the broad ridge with lonely coombs on either side. Parlick's summit gives a bird's-eye view over the chequered fields, hill farms and villages of the Ribble valley.

Return to the 1,707ft/520m summit of Fair Snape Fell, follow the fence north and then descend the astonishing valley of Fiendsdale.

Without warning the fell falls away into an almost bottomless ravine with steep, and in places precipitous sides.

Ford the Langden Brook with care and walk down the valley to the Trough of Bowland, where crystal-clear streams and inviting coombs run deep into green, steep-sided, fells.

With access being denied to Totridge Fell, take the pleasant low-level route, through woods and meadows, back to Chipping via the farms of Dinkling Green and Lickhurst.

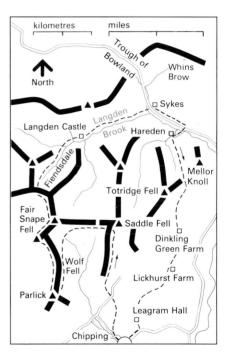

THE LYKE WAKE WALK

Map OS Sheets 93 and 94 (Tourist Map/Outdoor Leisure 26, 27)   **Start/Finish** Osmotherley (459998)/
Ravenscar Hotel (981019)   **Distance/Time** 40 miles/64km, 13-14 hrs

Grading A very long walk over undulating heather-
clad moors. There is now a path over the entire route.
Escape Routes The route crosses several roads.
From high ground both N and S facing dales lead
gently down to lower ground.
Transport Bus services: Northallerton/Teeside;
Leeds/Osmotherley/Middlesbrough; Ravenscar/
Scarborough.
Accommodation Hotels and B & B in Osmotherley
and Ravenscar. Youth Hostels at Osmotherley,
Helmsley, Wheeldale, Boggle Hole, Whitby and
Scarborough.

This now classic 40-mile marathon walk crosses the whole of the North York Moors, from Osmotherley in the west to Ravenscar on the east coast. It includes most of the highest tops of the Cleveland Hills. The walk is a natural line and was first completed by Bill Cowley in 1955. Now the Lyke Wake Walk is a household name and thousands of crossings are made every year. In fact the walk has come to be recognised as a physical fitness and endurance test for macho outdoor types, and a crossing in under 24 hours entitles you to wear the Lyke Wake tie, a black tie embellished with silver coffins.

The moors on the line of the walk carry many Bronze Age burial mounds, and this gave Bill Cowley the idea of naming the walk after the Lyke Wake or coffin trail. The very old dialect verse, the 'Cleveland Lyke Wake Dirge', has been adopted as the song to be chanted as walkers or dirgers tramp the moors by night.

Take the Swainby road out of Osmotherley and, after a mile, turn east up a muddy track leading through woods into Scugdale. As you climb the rounded hills of Carlton Bank and Hasty Bank the view north unfolds: at night a blaze of lights, flares and sparks emanating from industrial Tees-side and, in daylight, the impertinent, sharply-pointed hill of Roseberry Topping.

Scramble through the sandstone outcrop known as the Wainstones, descend to the road near Chop Gate and climb heathery slopes to Urra Moor, at 1,490ft/454m, the highest point on the Cleveland Hills. It is always a relief to meet the old Rosedale Railway, built in the 1860s, where you can swing along the level track of cinders.

After rounding Farndale Head turn left to meet the Blakey Ridge road near Ralph Cross. Extensive and sweeping heather moors are crossed by Shunner Howe and, on Wheeldale Moor, areas of eroded clay bear witness to the disastrous fire of 1976.

Cross the paved Roman Road, then Wheeldale Beck by stepping stones, and climb to Simon Howe where you are confronted by the radar domes on Fylingdales Moor.

A good path skirts the radar station, climbs to Lilla Howe and then descends to Jugger Howe beck. Just three more miles now, and you can walk triumphantly into Ravenscar and peer over beetling cliffs to creamy rollers pounding the rocks below.

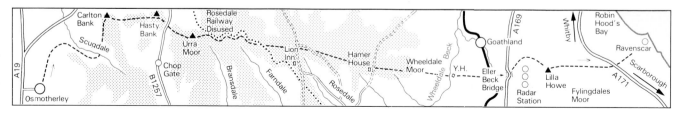

BLACK HAMBLETON BY THE DROVE ROAD

Map OS Sheet 100 (Tourist Map/Outdoor Leisure 26) **Start/Finish** White Horse car-park, Kilburn (515812)/
Osmotherley (456973) **Distance/Time** 14 miles/23km, 5-6 hrs

Grading An easy walk along a good path, but the route follows a high moorland escarpment which is exposed to the elements.
Escape Routes Numerous. Metalled roads cross the route at Sutton Bank, Sneck Yate Bank, Kepwick and Oak Dale.
Transport Bus services: Ripon/Kilburn/Scarborough; Northallerton/Osmotherley/Tees-side; Leeds/Osmotherley/Middlesbrough.
Accommodation Hotels and B & B in Kilburn and Osmotherley. Youth Hostels at Helmsley and Osmotherley.

Stand beside the indicator on Sutton Bank and look west across the Vale of Mowbray to the Pennine Chain. Then turn to the south and gaze beyond the crumbling yellow limestone of Roulston Scar to York Minster, the dominant feature on this broad landscape. From this perch in the Hambleton hills Wordsworth watched the sun go down on his wedding day, and James Herriot claims the view to be the finest in England.

The west-facing escarpment of the North York Moors extends for 14 miles and provides a walk of compelling interest, breathtaking views and a feeling of freedom and space. Close at hand exists a wealth of lovely abbeys, churches, castles and villages, as well as a host of other historical sites and stimuli for the geologist, botanist and natural historian.

Start from the car-park at the base of the Kilburn White Horse and climb the steep path to gain the crest of the hill. The White Horse has no great antiquity, being cut in 1857 at the suggestion of Thomas Taylor. Follow the path which hugs the cliff-edge above the crumbling Jurassic limestone of Roulston Scar. The cliffs funnel the west winds into strong up-currents, and you may see gliders soaring above. The airfield on the right is the home of the Yorkshire Gliding Club.

North of Sutton Bank the route follows the Cleveland Way over the top of Whitestone Cliff, a superb rock face giving steep routes of over 100ft. Below the cliff lies the mysterious dark lake of Gormire, steeped in legend and reputed to be bottomless.

Continuing north along the escarpment the banks are bright with primroses, cowslips and violets, while honeysuckle tangles over the rocks. Below nestle the villages of Thirlby, Boltby and Cowesby, the suffix '-by' being Danish for settlement.

You meet the historic drove road near Sneck Yate Bank, and follow it over the heather-clad hills of Black Hambleton. The road was used by prehistoric man, the Romans and the cattle drovers from Scotland making for the lucrative fairs at York and Malton.

Having descended from the blowy moors of Black Hambleton you branch left through Oak Dale to the peaceful old village of Osmotherley, near the Carthusian Priory of Mount Grace. As the sun sinks, down a pint at one of the three old inns in the village. A fitting end to one of Yorkshire's great walks.

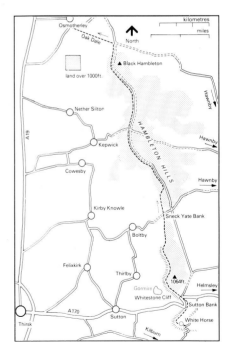

THE NORTH YORK MOORS FROM NORTH TO SOUTH

Map *OS Sheets 93, 94 and 100 (Tourist Map/Outdoor Leisure 26)*   **Start/Finish** *Newton (570129)/ Lastingham (730904)*   **Distance/Time** *25 miles/40km, 9-10 hrs*

Grading *A long but easy walk through upland dales and across rolling, heather-clad moors.*
Escape Routes *The walk may be cut short at Westerdale, the Lion Inn on Blakey Bank or Rosedale Abbey.*
Transport *Railway station at Great Ayton. Bus service: Great Ayton/Middlesbrough. No bus service to Lastingham.*
Accommodation *Hotels and B & B at Great Ayton, Lastingham and Hutton-le-Hole. Youth Hostels at Westerdale, Helmsley and Lockton.*

The North York Moors are bounded on the west side by the Hambleton Hills and a limestone escarpment falling 600ft to the Vale of Mowbray, while on the east the North Sea pounds even higher cliffs and headlands, which descend in places to tiny fishing villages and smugglers' coves.

To the north and south the moors are intersected by sheltered wooded valleys, where settlements of Mesolithic and Bronze Age man, the Romans and the Vikings have been discovered. In the twelfth century Cistercian and Carthusian monks built glorious abbeys in choice sites on the fringes of the moors.

A north-south crossing of the moors from Roseberry Topping to Lastingham combines the delights of open moorland, wild upland valleys, sleepy pastoral dales and charming stone-built villages. It should not be seen as a challenge walk, to be completed head down and teeth gritted, but as an excursion through some of Yorkshire's most richly varied hill country.

On the north side of the moors a cap of hard rock has protected the isolated hill of Roseberry Topping from erosion, and this pointed feature is much loved by the population of Tees-side. From the Topping the Cleveland Way is followed round to Captain Cook's Monument on Easby Moor and a descent made to Kildale.

While the Cleveland Way continues over Ingleby Moor, we proceed south to Baysdale where the grey farmhouse, nestling above the beck, was built on the site of a Cistercian nunnery. A contour path runs round into Westerdale, crossing Great Hograh beck by a beautifully constructed pack-horse bridge.

Westerdale is the loveliest of upland valleys, bedecked in spring with primroses, wood anemones, violets, cowslips, bugle and harebells. Esklets, at the valley head, is the site of a monastic grange once owned by the monks of Rievaulx.

A wide track zig-zags up to meet the old Rosedale Railway, and the next seven miles is flat, fast walking along this ancient cinder track which was in regular use until 1928. After rounding the head of Farndale it winds along the west side of Rosedale to the terminus at Bank Top, where some old kilns remain from the era of ironstone mining.

Head south across the heather to Ana Cross, a stone monument of obscure origin, to enter the charming village of Lastingham; here you will find an eleventh-century church boasting one of the finest crypts in England.

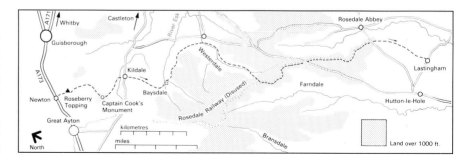

HIGH PEAK CLASSIC: MARSDEN TO EDALE

Map *OS Sheet 110 (Tourist Map/Outdoor Leisure 1)* **Start/Finish** *Marsden (048113)/Edale (123858)*
Distance/Time *25 miles/40km, 10-11 hrs*

Grading *A classic walk of the Peak District. It is long and rough and can be difficult in bad conditions.*
Escape Routes *Wessenden Head. Woodhead–Holmfirth road at Holme Moss. A628 at Woodhead. Snake Pass summit.*
Transport *Railway stations at Edale for Manchester/Sheffield and at Marsden for Manchester/Huddersfield.*
Accommodation *Hotels and B & B at Marsden and Edale. Youth Hostels at Crowden, Edale and Hagg Farm.*

The classic Peak District marathon is undoubtedly the 25-mile Marsden to Edale walk. It follows a natural north-south line over the three highest plateaux, Black Hill, Bleaklow and Kinder, and was first completed by Cecil Dawson at the beginning of the century. The first double Marsden to Edale was achieved by Fred Heardman in the 1920s. Nowadays the Peak is criss-crossed with long-distance challenge routes but none has matched the Marsden to Edale for variety. The walk is particularly satisfying in winter, when good speed can be made across the iron-hard bogs and peats, and the high plateaux are dusted with snow.

From Marsden take the Pennine Way alternative route which runs above the east side of the Wessenden reservoirs. Cross the A635 and strike south to the aptly named Black Hill, a cheerless moor of saturated peat. Now head south-west along the Pennine Way down Crowden Great Brook, passing under Laddow Rocks and Rakes Rocks, to Crowden village lying between the reservoirs of Woodhead and Torside.

Cross the dam at the west end of Woodhead Reservoir, and then a footbridge over the railway line, to gain access to Bleaklow. Head due south to the Rollick Stones and the gritstone ravine of Wild Boar Clough, which gives a wholly delightful scramble onto the eroded plateau of Bleaklow.

The traverse of Bleaklow to the Snake Pass has already been described in the Derwent Watershed Walk, as has the continuation south round the head of Ashop Clough to Kinder Scout. If this circuit has been completed, and the terrain is familiar, you may begin to look on the desolate, exposed and seamed areas of peat with some affection. Bleaklow, in particular, is unique and should be preserved. Even on the highest parts you will notice colonisation by cotton-grass, harestail, ling, bilberry, cowberry and mat grass.

Purists, however, should note that the strict north-south route of the Marsden to Edale leaves the Pennine Way at the Snake, ascends to Featherbed Top and descends to the stream in Ashop Clough. A steep, scrambling climb up through the gritstone outcrop of the Edge now brings you onto the Kinder plateau.

From the waterfall at Fair Brook head south to Crowden Head, and then drop down south-east to the infant Grinds Brook. The stream has worn a way through the peat forming an open, rocky, defile and this leads easily into Edale.

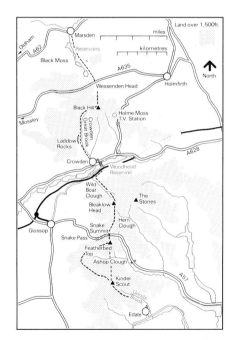

DERWENT WATERSHED WALK

Map *OS Sheet 110 (Tourist Map/Outdoor Leisure 1)*   **Start/Finish** *The Yorkshire Bridge (201849)*
Distance/Time *40 miles/64km, 14 hrs*

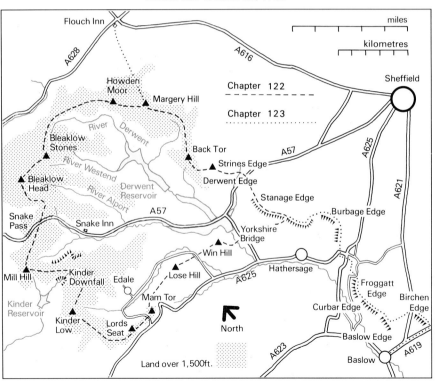

The River Derwent is fed by countless streams rising on the barren moors of the High Peak. Thus a circuit of the watershed is an exceptionally long, rough, peaty and, at times, boggy walk. The circuit has a reputation for extreme toughness, and few would dispute its membership of the growing number of worthy challenge walks in the north of England. While I have little time for challenge walks *per se*, this walk has much else to offer for it visits many of the best-loved landmarks and wildest features of the Peak.

Starting from Yorkshire Bridge, below the Ladybower dam, you climb easily to Win Hill, drop down to cross the River Noe and then climb again to Lose Hill. Next comes Mam Tor, with its Iron Age fort, and the tumulus on Lord's Seat. These early sections provide easy walking along good grassy paths, with varied and delightful views in all directions.

As you climb gradually up over Brown Knoll to the Kinder plateau the terrain becomes boggy and featureless. From the trig. point on Kinder Low you can either hug the west-facing slopes, and make straight for the waterfall of Kinder Downfall, or head north-east across the plateau to Crowden Head and then swing

Grading *A long, rough and exhausting walk over boggy and peat-hagged ground.*
Escape Routes *Numerous. Even at its most remote the route is never more than 3 miles from a road.*
Transport *Railway station at Bamford (2 miles). Bus service: Sheffield/Glossop/Whaley Bridge.*
Accommodation *Hotels and B & B at Castleton, Bamford and Hathersage. Youth Hostels at Edale, Castleton, Hathersage, Hagg Farm and Langsett.*

westwards to the Downfall. The latter route takes you past a small cairn, 2,088ft/631m, marking the true summit which is the highest point in Derbyshire.

Deep groughs must be tackled on Mill Hill and Featherbed Moss, before you cross the Snake Pass, but these are nothing to the horrors on Bleaklow which could hide an army between their black and dripping walls. Isolated and weird wind-sculptured rocks come and go on Bleaklow, but they make welcome landmarks on this stark plateau.

At Bleaklow Head leave the Pennine Way to continue northwards to the Yorkshire Dales, Cross Fell and the Scottish Border. Curve round the head of the Derwent valley, past Bleaklow Stones, and head south-east over Howden Moor and Margery Hill to Back Tor. These moorlands, high above the eastern edge of the Derwent Reservoir, make up the wildest stretch of the walk and the path is indistinct.

At Strines Inn on the A57 you can pause for a drink before toiling up to High Neb on Stanage Edge, perhaps the Peak District's finest gritstone outcrop. Yorkshire Bridge and the end of this marathon circuit lie below.

Chapter 123

Grading *A long walk over moorland and gritstone edges, much of it above 1,000ft.*
Escape Routes *At Cut Gate, Ladybower, Ringinglow road, Burbage Brook and Curbar Gap.*
Transport *Railway stations at Huddersfield, Matlock and Chesterfield. Bus services: Huddersfield/Flouch Inn; Bakewell/Baslow/Chesterfield.*
Accommodation *Hotels and B & B at Baslow, Matlock and Bakewell. Youth Hostels at Langsett, Hathersage, Eyam and Bakewell.*

THE EASTERN EDGES OF THE PEAK

Map OS Sheets 110 and 119 (Tourist Map/Outdoor Leisure 1)   *Start/Finish* Flouch Inn (197016)/Robin Hood Inn, Baslow (279721)   *Distance/Time* 25 miles/40km, 10 hrs

---

Although the Marsden to Edale is the peatiest, boggiest and most frustrating expedition in this book, black, saturated moorlands do have a certain attraction. In this route, down the eastern fringes of the Peak District, you mix high, eroded, tussocky and distinctly wet moorland with the traverse of a number of famous gritstone crags. The toughest section of the walk is completed early in the day, leaving you in a receptive mood for the much easier, more diverse and less exposed stretches further south.

The Millstone Grit of Northern England is a massive layer of rock, up to 4,000ft thick, which is thought to have been formed by the silting up of Carboniferous limestone seas. It leads to an austere landscape where high rainfall and poor drainage favour cotton-grass and reeds, while many of the outcrops themselves have become blackened by the smoke-laden air of industrial Lancashire.

Start from the Flouch Inn, west of Penistone, skirt the forestry to the west and then follow the path round Hingcliff Hill. This is an ancient track known as the Cut Gate.

Climb to the summit of Margery Hill, the highest point of the day, at 1,791ft/546m, which gives wonderful views west to its notorious neighbour Bleaklow. Proceeding south you must plod across very rough ground on Featherbed Moss, and then contour round the head of Abbey Brook to Back Tor. The moors here are too wet for heather to thrive, and cloudberry and cotton-grass predominate.

On Derwent Edge you pass the weathered rocks called the Cakes of Bread and the Salt Cellar, and then swing east along Strines Edge to meet the A57 under Stanage.

Now begins the switchback second half of the route, as you scramble over the edges of Stanage, Burbage, Froggatt, Curbar, Baslow and Birchen. All these fine crags have been used for rock climbing since the beginning of the century and many historic battles have been fought. The rounded edges of the bedding planes and joints mean that gritstone suffers a dearth of jug-handle holds. Subsequently the technique of hand-jamming developed, and gritstone climbers can always be identified by scabs on the back of their hands from the coarse-grained rock.

The large tors on Birchen Edge are known as Nelson's Monument and the Battleship Boulders. They bear the inscriptions *Victory*, *Dreadnought* and *Indefatigable*. An easy descent leads to the Robin Hood Inn and Baslow.

THE ROUND OF KINDER SCOUT FROM EDALE

Map OS Sheet 110 (Tourist Map/Outdoor Leisure 1)   **Start/Finish** Edale (123858)
Distance/Time 16 miles/26km, 6-7 hrs

Grading A tough moorland walk, very exposed in bad weather conditions.
Escape Routes Numerous. The plateau is criss-crossed with paths leading down to lower ground.
Transport Railway station at Edale for Sheffield and Manchester.
Accommodation Hotels, B & B and Youth Hostel at Edale.

Kinder Scout manages to preserve its wild nature in spite of its close proximity to many of the north's major cities. It is much more than just an elevated land mass for rock buttresses and escarpments abound, weird boulders emerge from the peat and streams race through deeply cut channels. Patrick Monkhouse, the famous Pennine walker of the 1930s, describes it as a mountain which must be taken seriously.

For this reason Kinder deserves a chapter to itself, and here I describe a sixteen-mile circuit that keeps mainly to the perimeter of the high ground. It should not be forgotten that up until 1932 there was no legal access onto Kinder. But, following the mass trespass of April 24th, 1932, after which the leaders were sent to prison, public outcry forced concessions from the landowners.

A word of warning before you set out from Edale. In winter darkness falls quickly and the deep groughs and oozing bogs make progress imperceptible; the Kinder plateau, at over 2,000ft/630m, is not the place to be benighted. Accurate compass-work is imperative and a wide margin of safety must be allowed.

The Pennine Way leaves Edale by Grinds Brook, but an alternative path climbs to the Kinder plateau via Grindslow Knoll. This path continues to the rock outcrops of Crowden Tower and the Wool Packs, before reaching the OS pillar on Kinder Low.

Keeping to the edge of the escarpment you arrive at Kinder Downfall, where the river cascades down the cliffs adjacent to the 100ft high Great Buttress. Climbing on this magnificent rock face started in the last century but, in 1910, many classic severe routes fell to Herford, Laycock and Jeffcoat.

Where the path starts to descend to Ashop Clough, head east along the broken cliffs of The Edge to the rocky prow of Fairbrook Naze. This section of the walk is well drained and airy giving wide views north, across the Snake Pass to Bleaklow.

Continue following the plateau-edge southwards over Seal Edge, and then head east along the high promontory of Blackden Edge to Crookstone Knoll, overlooking Woodlands Valley and Ladybower Reservoir.

Now, swing right round in a south-westerly direction, above Jagger's Clough, to the rocky ridge of Ringing Roger. A spur, called The Nab, runs easily down to Grindslow House and Edale.

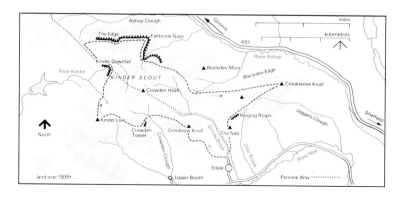

THE WESTERN PEAK AND SHUTLINGSLOE

Map OS Sheets 109, 110, 118 and 119 (Tourist Map/Outdoor Leisure 24)   **Start/Finish** Errwood Reservoir (010748); (for Shutlingsloe) the Cat and Fiddle (001719)   **Distance/Time** 21 miles/34km, 11 hrs

Grading A long walk over high and often bleak moorlands.
Escape Routes Numerous.
Transport Railway stations at Buxton, Whaley Bridge, Disley and New Mills/Newtown. Bus services: Buxton/Whaley Bridge and Buxton/Cat and Fiddle/Macclesfield.
Accommodation Varied accommodation in Buxton. Youth Hostels at Buxton and Gradbach Mill.

The people of Macclesfield are extremely fortunate to live under the shadow of Shutlingsloe, a hill of exquisite form which gives them joy at all times of the year. Patrick Monkhouse sees Shutlingsloe as an English Matterhorn, and Roger Redfern rates it a close second to Penyghent for the title of Suilven of the Pennines.

The Peak District does not fade away into the Cheshire plain with a whimper, for a line of distinctive hills make the transition an abrupt one: Shutlingsloe, Black Hill, Sponds Hill, Cats Tor and Shining Tor, the highest of them all at 1,834ft/559m.

I describe here a circular walk from the Goyt Valley, which includes the traverse of many notable hills in the Western Peak. An extension can be made to Shutlingsloe if required.

Park at the Errwood reservoir in the upper Goyt Valley. The lower, Fernilee reservoir was constructed during the 1930s and the Errwood followed in the 1960s.

The path on the west side of the valley runs pleasantly through woods and fields, and in places you can see the line of the old Cromford and High Peak Railway which opened as a horse-drawn line in 1831 to transport limestone.

From the delightful village of Taxal take the lane to Handley Fold Farm, and strike over the moor to Bow Stones which look over the National Trust-owned Lyme Hall and Park. The path south to Sponds Hill is a section of the Gritstone Trail, one of Cheshire's designated long-distance footpaths.

Cross the A5002 and head east to Windgather Rocks. This small outcrop provides low standard routes of 35ft and is ideal for beginners.

Continuing south along the broad ridge to Shining Tor the going becomes rather peaty, and exposed outcrops are passed at Pym Chair, Oldgate Nick and Cats Tor. Shining Tor gives you the classic view of Shutlingsloe and, rising haughtily above the deep defile of Wildboarclough, it looks every bit the Roseberry Topping of the Peak District.

At Shining Tor you can drop down Shooter's Clough and return to the Errwood reservoir, or extend the walk to Shutlingsloe.

If you decide on the latter, take the path south-east which meets the A537 near England's second highest inn, the Cat and Fiddle at 1,690ft. A path runs south to Cumberland Brook and Wildboarclough, whence you can climb easily to Shutlingsloe's summit and savour one of Northern England's most extensive views.

Descend north across damp moorland then through Macclesfield Forest to gain a high lane leading down to the Stanley Arms.

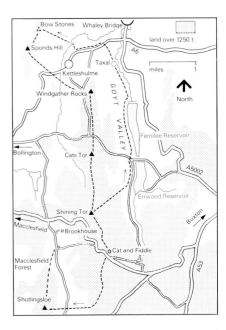

DOVEDALE FROM AXE EDGE

Map OS Sheet 119 (Tourist Map/Outdoor Leisure 24)   **Start/Finish** Dove Head Cottages beside the A53 (031683)/ Izaak Walton Hotel (144508)   **Distance/Time** 18 miles/29km, 7-8 hrs

---

Grading A long but easy walk, much of the route is along waymarked paths.
Escape Routes The walk may conveniently be cut short at Hartington which is connected by bus to Buxton and Ilam.
Transport Railway station at Buxton. Bus services: Buxton/Axe Edge/Leek; Buxton/Ashbourne and Ashbourne/Ilam (infrequent).
Accommodation Hotels and B & B at Buxton and Ilam and locally. Youth Hostels at Buxton, Hartington and Ilam Hall.

In the seventeenth century Izaak Walton and Charles Cotton spent countless happy days trout fishing on the River Dove, and these experiences are recounted in *The Compleat Angler*. They searched for the source of the Dove high up on the acid moorlands of Axe Edge and carved their initials on a slab of rock.

In this chapter we too trace the Dove from Axe Edge to the Izaak Walton Hotel near Ilam; a walk which starts amongst bog cotton and weathered gritstone, and finishes in flowery water-meadows set in a sheltered valley over-looked by woods and frowning limestone crags.

From Dove Head farm on the A53 a network of rarely used paths follow the infant River Dove to Hollinsclough. Here the dale broadens, and it is well worth making a diversion to climb the shapely and individual Chrome and Parkhouse Hills, which rise quite steeply above the north bank of the river.

At Crowdicote the impervious gritstones are weakening, and you pass through an area of black shales before limestone is reached at Hartington. On the north bank of the river you see the ramparts of Pilsbury Castle, an ancient earthwork.

Dovedale becomes more entrancing the farther south you walk. The path crosses and recrosses the river by packhorse bridges, you pass through woods and under cliffs while the river meanders down the dale, sometimes rushing headlong over weirs and sometimes forming deep, clear pools.

Narrow, wooded Beresford Dale gives way to the broader Wolfscote Dale and then, at Milldale, the incredible limestone architecture of the crags dominates the valley. This is the Dovedale beloved by Victorian romantics, writers and artists: Raven's Tor, the caves at Dove Holes, the buttresses of Ilam Tower, Pickering Tor emerging from the greenery, the Lion's Head rock, the natural arch at Reynard's Cave, the fantastic pinnacles of Tissington Spires, Jacob's Ladder and Lover's Leap.

While you are enjoying the endless variety of magnificent features, the River Dove flows serenely on. Thankfully these lower reaches of the Dove are now owned by the National Trust.

Just before the River Dove joins the River Manifold it performs an exaggerated S, and as you round the corner the conical hill of Thorpe Cloud bursts into view. Only a short detour is needed to climb this attractive hump, and the reward is a lovely view over the wooded dale and down to your destination, the Izaak Walton Hotel.

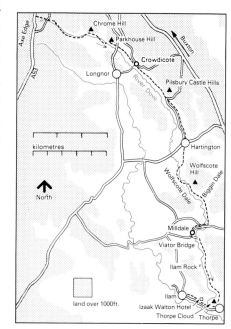

EIGHT DALES OF THE WHITE PEAK

Map OS Sheet 119 (Tourist Map/Outdoor Leisure 24)   **Start/Finish** Alport (222645)/Peak Forest (115793) or Brierlow Grange (097692)   **Distance/Time** 18 miles/29km, 8 hrs

Grading Very easy walking. The route is mainly sheltered and can be undertaken in almost any weather conditions.
Escape Routes Numerous.
Transport Bus services: Bakewell/Alport/Matlock/ Chesterfield; Buxton/Peak Forest/Castleton; Buxton/ Peak Forest/Sheffield.
Accommodation Hotels at Peak Forest and Youlgreave. B & B locally. Youth Hostels at Youlgreave, Bakewell, Ravenstor and Buxton.

Lathkill Dale in spring is sublime. The river cascades over the weirs into deep, clear pools bordered by brilliant beds of kingcups and butterbur. The leaves on the hawthorn and elm are that delicate, transient green which appears only fleetingly in springtime, and the ash buds are just beginning to burst. Limestone crags overlook the steep valley sides which are yellow with a profusion of cowslips, while in the woods bluebells, violets, forget-me-nots, red campions, ramsons and dog's mercury add to the blaze of colour.

Lathkill Dale can be linked to a string of other dales to give a long and varied walk through some of the Peak District's loveliest scenery: limestone dales with rushing rivers, woodlands, dry valleys, open pastures, mills, viaducts, lead mines, water-wheels and other relics of the industrial revolution.

The path from Alport meanders through water meadows and woods, and crosses a packhorse bridge while the river splashes over the weirs and trout leap from the pools.

A dry valley leads up to Monyash, where, in May, you will see the festival of 'well dressing'. Colourful mosaics, using petals, leaves, berries and moss, are set up on boards of wet clay beside the natural wells in the village.

Another dry valley, Deep Dale, which is bright with orchids, runs into Monsal Dale where the scenery becomes much grander. The River Wye is deep and fast, the wooded valley-sides rise steeply to over 1,000ft and towering cliffs of white limestone thrust upwards through the trees.

At Monsal Head a viaduct strides boldly across the dale. The old railway track runs right through Miller's Dale and Chee Dale forming part of the Monsal Trail.

Cressbrook Mill, built by Arkwright in 1815, is an impressive monument in grey stone at the junction of Cressbrook Dale and Miller's Dale. Here, the path runs along the water's edge under an overhanging wall of clean limestone; a popular venue with rock climbers.

At Miller's Dale village you can leave the Wye and head north into peaceful Monk's Dale, which leads into a succession of minor dales: Peter Dale, Hay Dale and Dam Dale. This route brings you to the Devonshire Arms at Peak Forest.

The alternative finish continues through the spectacular scenery and prodigious rock architecture of Chee Dale. East of Topley Pike you cross the A6, enter (another) Deep Dale and finish along the Priest's Way to Brierlow Grange.

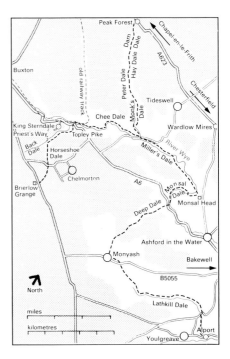

THE MANIFOLD VALLEY

Map OS Sheet 119 (Tourist Map/Outdoor Leisure 24)   **Start/Finish** Ilam Hall (133506)
Distance/Time 18 miles/29km, 7-8 hrs

> *Grading* Easy walking through rural dales and hills.
> *Escape Routes* Numerous. The walk is never more than 2 miles from a village.
> *Transport* Bus services: Derby/Buxton to Ilam or Hulme End; Ashbourne/Hartington/Hulme End/ Warslow/Buxton.
> *Accommodation* Hotels at Ilam, Hartington and Hulme End. B & B locally. Youth Hostels at Ilam Hall, Hartington and Buxton.

At Thorpe, the River Dove is fed by the considerable tributary of the Manifold, which runs south from the hills near Flash following an almost parallel course to that of its neighbour. In fact at Longnor the two rivers are less than one mile apart.

While the walk north through Dovedale keeps mostly along the river banks, the Manifold valley is best explored from above, either by contouring the valley sides or traversing the surrounding hills. Here, I describe an eighteen-mile circular walk from Ilam, which follows the north side of the valley to Hulme End and returns via Warslow and Ossoms Hill.

Unlike the Dove, in certain places the River Manifold has a habit of disappearing into its limestone bed, only to reappear further down the valley. Thus, soon after leaving Ilam, at a point below Ilam Hall, you will see the river welling up from its stony bed.

At Rushley Bridge take the track to Castern Hall and cross the fields to reach the road running down to Weag's Bridge. The prominent limestone outcrop of Beeston Tor is National Trust property, and you can detour to examine St Bertram's Cave which extends for 600ft. A collection of Saxon coins was found here in 1924.

Half-a-mile north of Weag's Bridge is another famous landmark, Thor's Cave, where troglodytes may enjoy exploring the passages and chambers. Situated high above the valley it provides excellent views of the surrounding hills.

At Wettonmill walk up from the valley, through Dale Farm, and head over Ecton Hill, the highest point of the day at 1,212ft/369m whence, looking north, you can follow the course of the Manifold towards Axe Edge. Descend again to the river bed and take the old railway track into Hulme End.

Turning for home now follow the path north of the river, which skirts Warslow and then runs due south, straight as an arrow, to Hoo Brook on the west side of Ossoms Hill. If time allows, an ascent of Ossoms Hill will provide views east across the Manifold to Ecton Hill, Wetton Hill, Thor's Cave and Beeston Tor.

Continue south through Grindon to the normally dry Hamps Valley at Lee House, then climb the steep eastern slopes to regain the high ground near Slade House. The River Manifold is crossed by a footbridge south of Rushley to regain the path through the Ilam Hall estate.

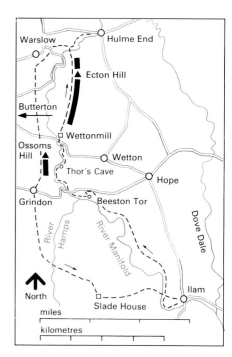

THE ROACHES AND AXE EDGE

Map OS Sheets 118 and 119 (Tourist Map/Outdoor Leisure 24)   **Start/Finish** Upper Hulme (013609)/Buxton (059734)
Distance/Time 14 miles/23km, 6 hrs

> **Grading** A fine day's walk along rock escarpments, moorland edges and through a beautiful river valley.
> **Escape Routes** Numerous. The route is never far from a minor road or a village.
> **Transport** Railway station at Buxton. Bus services: Buxton/Upper Hulme/Leek; Hanley/Upper Hulme/Sheffield.
> **Accommodation** Hotels and B & B at Buxton and in the surrounding villages. Youth Hostels at Buxton, Gradbach and Meerbrook.

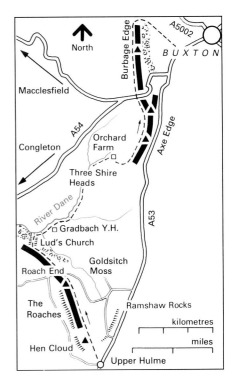

The unchanging steadfastness of the sculptured boulders and gritstone outcrops of Northern England is reassuring. They stand firm and aloof from the turmoil of life in the valleys, and serve as focal points on the sweeping moorlands of the High Peak. They provide roughly textured rock for climbers to caress and natural markers for hill walkers to aim for on marathon expeditions over the uplands.

Although the rock can appear rich, warm and friendly in the slanting sunshine of a summer evening, I associate the outcrops with a bitter winter wind, when the ice on the pools is splintered and the black peat is frozen into corrugated iron.

From Upper Hulme an easy scramble takes you to Hen Cloud which gives just a taste of the pleasures to come. Keep to the firm gritstone edge of the escarpment, and enjoy the spacious views south towards Leek and the meadows and woods surrounding the Tittesworth Reservoir.

Thick woods cloak the western edges of The Roaches, and a natural hollow above the crags harbours a tiny tarn, Doxey Pool. The highest crags are towards the south end of The Roaches, where they reach a height of nearly 100ft and form two tiers. Proceeding north, height is gradually gained until you reach the OS pillar at 1,658ft/505m, where you head down to Roach End and the path through Gradbach Wood to Lud's Church.

Lud's Church is one of the wonders of the Peak, a deep fissure which opened up as a result of a great mass of Roaches' gritstone landslipping on its underlying bed of shale. The name is thought to derive from Walter de Ludank, a follower of Wycliffe who, in the fourteenth century, used the cleft as a retreat.

Proceed north along the banks of the River Dane to Gradbach Youth Hostel, and continue upstream to the packhorse bridge at Three Shire Heads, an idyllic spot with waterfalls and deep, clear pools. A cobbled trackway leads north-east to Orchard Farm, after which you gain the open, windswept moorland on Axe Edge.

After crossing the minor road to the Cat and Fiddle Inn, you climb to the 1,807ft/551m summit of Axe Edge Moor enjoying huge views south and east to the valleys of the Dove and Manifold. Keep above the trees on Burbage Edge and then descend to Tunnel Farm, finally entering Buxton across the golf course.

THE LONG MYND AND STIPERSTONES

Map OS Sheets 137 and 126   **Start/Finish** Little Stretton (433911)/Stiperstones (363005)
Distance/Time 12 miles/19km, 5 hrs

> **Grading** An easy and delightful walk through rural valleys and along exposed ridges.
> **Escape Routes** Numerous. The Stiperstones may be omitted by finishing the walk at Ratlinghope.
> **Transport** Railway station at Church Stretton. Bus service: Church Stretton/Little Stretton.
> **Accommodation** Hotels at Church Stretton, Little Stretton and Stiperstones. B & B locally. Youth Hostels at Bridges (near Ratlinghope) and Wilderhope.

Church Stretton divides the sharp, rocky hill of Caer Caradoc from the smoothly swelling mass of the Long Mynd. Whereas Caer Caradoc is Pre-Cambrian volcanic, the Long Mynd is formed from shales and sandstone. West of the Long Mynd runs another high ridge, the Stiperstones, which thrusts up exposed clusters of weathered quartzite.

The hills east of Church Stretton are explored in chapters 131 and 132, and here we head westwards up one of Long Mynd's lost valleys to its broad plateau, cross the valley of the East Onny River and finish amongst the rocks of the Stiperstones.

Several isolated valleys run deep into the Long Mynd. Steep slopes of bracken, bilberry and heather rise up from clear streams to the main ridge, which is criss-crossed with old trackways and dotted with tumuli. This is rural England at its loveliest, particularly in spring when the blackthorn in the sheltered valleys is in bloom, and the air is sweet with may.

Callow Hollow, one of the most delightful valleys, is entered along a path from Little Stretton. You pass a waterfall and then the path strikes up grassy slopes on the north side, by-passes an earthwork under Round Hill, and descends to Ashes Hollow. As you climb again to higher ground take the left-hand valley which meets the plateau near Pole Cottage.

The road running along the top of the Long Mynd is Port Way, a Bronze Age track used later by drovers taking their cattle to market in Shrewsbury.

Cross the road and climb to Pole Bank, 1,695ft/516m, which gives distant views to Snowdon, Cadair Idris, the Malverns and the Brecon Beacons. Just to the east of the OS pillar is Boiling Well, a small spring which marks the source of the Ashes Hollow stream. Further east, across the very popular Cardingmill Valley, rises the conspicuous Iron Age hill fort of Bodbury Ring.

Descend Wild Moor by the Mott Road, passing a tumulus on the way, to the lovely old village of Ratlinghope, set in the heart of the hills.

Take the lane running north from Ratlinghope through Gatten and The Hollies to the windswept ridge of the Stiperstones. At 1,759ft/536m, this gives fine views south to Corndon Hill and the Radnor Forest. Several rock outcrops sprout from the heather, the best known being the Devil's Chair and Cranberry Rock.

A good path descends north-west to the Stiperstones Inn.

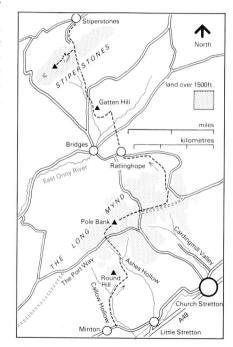

CAER CARADOC

Map OS Sheet 137   *Start/Finish* Cardington (505952)   *Distance/Time* 10 miles/16km, 4-5 hrs

Grading An easy walk over rolling, grassy hills.
Escape Routes Numerous. The hills may be descended almost anywhere.
Transport Railway station at Church Stretton. Bus service (Boulton's): Cardington/Church Stretton/ Ludlow/Shrewsbury.
Accommodation Hotels at Church Stretton and Cardington. B & B locally. Youth Hostels at Wheathill, Wilderhope and Ludlow.

Shropshire's wooded and pastoral countryside stamps it as a very English county, yet it has a sprinkling of individual hills as high and untamed as if they had spilled over from across the Welsh border.

The Wrekin, The Lawley, Caer Caradoc and Hope Bowdler are hog-backed hills which run north-south, parallel to the Church Stretton fault, and they bear a striking resemblance to the Malverns further south. Both ranges were formed by upthrust of Pre-Cambrian Uriconian lavas, some of the oldest rocks in England and Wales. Unlike the Malverns though, the Shropshire hills are wild, unspoilt by man and rarely visited.

There is some outcropping, particularly on Caer Caradoc, but the hills are mostly covered with grass, bracken, heather and bilberry,

giving rich colouring. Sheep are free to graze, walking is easy over the close-cropped grass and access is unrestricted.

Tucked away on the east side of the Church Stretton hills lies the peaceful village of Cardington. Here, the Royal Oak makes a convenient and hospitable base for the circuit of The Lawley, Caer Caradoc and Willstone Hill, a walk which can be accomplished comfortably between lunch and dinner.

Take the narrow lane to Chatwall and then cut across fields to the woods on Hoar Edge. Now the long, undulating crest of The Lawley bursts into view, its smooth ridge rising stepwise to the summit.

Access is gained through a wicket gate at the north end of the ridge and springy turf makes for a delightful ascent. The bulky Long Mynd cuts off the view westwards, but the Wrekin is prominent on the north Shropshire plain.

Caer Caradoc thrusts up steeply and, with its bold outline and fringe of rocks, it resembles a giant wart. Its height, 1,505ft/459m, and abruptness make it a natural stronghold and the earthworks of a prehistoric camp, thought to have been used by Caractacus in AD50, are visible on the upper slopes.

Weathered outcrops of rock provide interesting features on the summit of Caer Caradoc; useful as windbreaks, seats or tables for a picnic lunch.

Across the dry Wilderness Valley, on the east side, Willstone Hill carries an impressive rock outcrop, incorporating a spectacular perched block, called the Battlestones. From the summit of Willstone Hill the tower of Cardington's Norman church can be seen through the trees, and half-a-mile of winding country lane brings you back to the Royal Oak.

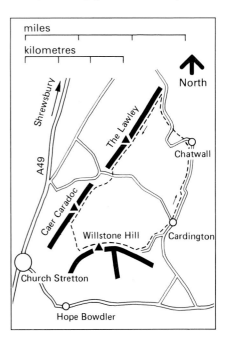

BROWN CLEE HILL

Map OS Sheet 137   Start/Finish Clee St Margaret (565844)   Distance/Time 8 miles/13km, 3-4 hrs

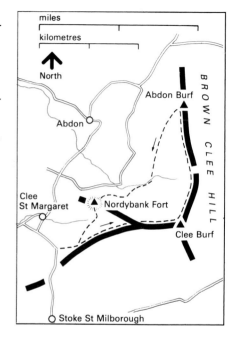

> **Grading** An easy half-day's walk with plenty of historical interest and wide views.
> **Escape Routes** W down the Five Springs valley from the col between Clee Burf and Abdon Burf.
> **Transport** Railway station at Ludlow. Bus service (Whittle's): Ludlow/Clee St. Margaret.
> **Accommodation** Hotels in Ludlow. B & B at Clee St. Margaret. Youth Hostels at Wheathill, Wilderhope and Ludlow.

Down the east side of Shropshire runs Wenlock Edge, a sixteen-mile-long limestone escarpment which was immortalised by Housman in *A Shropshire Lad*. Although Wenlock Edge can provide a pleasant walk in spring, when the woods are carpeted by primroses, wild daffodils and great swathes of bluebells, it is criss-crossed by roads and lacks the aura of wildness necessary for inclusion in this book.

However, east of Wenlock Edge, Brown Clee Hill rises to the considerable height of 1,790ft/ 540m, a superb, open hill of heather and boulders, the home of curlews and buzzards. Amazingly, Brown Clee Hill is only twenty-five miles from the centre of Wolverhampton, and the tower blocks and smoke-haze of the industrial West Midlands can be seen clearly from the summit. Thankfully, the urban sprawl

stops short of the River Severn, allowing the hill to rise from unspoilt countryside.

From Clee St Margaret take the road towards Stoke St Milborough and, after half-a-mile, turn off along a broad green path leading to Clee Burf which is one of three prehistoric forts on Brown Clee Hill.

The path follows a line of beech trees and, near the top of the hill, it passes a disused quarry and some bell pits. The rocks of Brown Clee Hill are more recent than those of the Church Stretton hills and Wenlock Edge, they are Old Red Sandstone capped with lava which has prevented erosion of Coal Measures. Brown Clee has a long industrial history: coal, iron, limestone, basalt and copper have all been mined.

Follow an old wall on the edge of another magnificent stand of old beeches, cross an area of coarse grass and reeds and plough straight through the deep heather to the radio mast. Set low down in the heather is a stone memorial to twenty-three Allied and German airmen, who died in various accidents on Brown Clee Hill during the last war.

The hill is the highest in Shropshire and the top is the site of a second hill fort, Abdon Burf.

A shallow pond lies near the OS pillar from where wonderful views into Wales may be obtained, extending from Cadair Idris to the Radnor Forest.

A path leads down to a sheltered valley below Five Springs and, at the terminus of an old mineral railway, you can head for home via the fascinating earthwork of Nordybank Hill Fort.

HIGH DYKE

Map OS Sheets 137 and 148   **Start/Finish** Knighton (285725)/Blue Bell Inn on A489 (248932)
Distance/Time 20 miles/32km, 8-9 hrs

Grading A long and undulating walk over rolling
uplands. There is a well-marked path along the entire
route.
Escape Routes Numerous. The walk can
conveniently be left at the village of Newcastle, near
the river Clun, this is about the half-way point.
Transport Railway stations at Knighton, Newtown
and Welshpool. Bus services: Newtown/Montgomery;
Welshpool/Montgomery.
Accommodation The Blue Bell Inn. Varied
accommodation in Knighton and Montgomery. Youth
Hostels at Clun and Ludlow. Several farmhouses on
Offa's Dyke offer accommodation.

The Romans never extended their influence far
into Wales, and when they left Britain in the fifth
century the adjoining kingdom of Mercia could,
likewise, make little impression on the growing
strength and independence of the Celts.

However, in 757 Offa won the throne of
Mercia and decided to delineate his western
boundary by building a dyke. This extraordinary embankment was planned to run
from Prestatyn to the Severn and, whenever
possible, it was built on west-facing hills and
ridges. The large gap in the Dyke in Herefordshire coincided with an escarpment of sandstone and thick, impenetrable forest, thus no
artificial barrier was necessary.

Today Offa's Dyke runs through the magnificently diverse Welsh Border country of high
hills, winding rivers, remote valleys, forests
and castles. It made a natural line for a long-
distance footpath (168 miles) and it was
officially opened by Lord Hunt of Llanfair
Waterdine in 1971.

Here I describe a 20-mile section, through
the ancient Clun Forest about mid-way along
the walk, and one where the Dyke itself is well
preserved.

From Knighton the waymarked path crosses
the River Teme and climbs to Panpunton Hill.
From here the distinctive hump and ditch of
the Dyke stretches north-west, straight as an
arrow for six miles, to the River Clun. You
traverse Llanfair Hill, 1,408ft/432m, the highest
point on the Dyke giving views to the Long
Mynd, Radnor Forest, the Black Mountains and
deep into the foothills of the Cambrian
Mountains. The walking is fast and open with
just a few Kerry Hill sheep for company.

Continuing north out of the Clun Valley you
pass the famous Hergan misalignment, where
two gangs of Dyke builders failed to meet and
a kink was needed to join the sections. The
Dyke switchbacks over the Kerry Hills,
descends to the tiny church at Churchtown,

crosses the River Unk and its various tributaries
and re-enters Wales (Powys) near Hazel Bank.

This is another unusually well-preserved
section of the Dyke, where the drop from the
crest of the bank to the bottom of the ditch on
the west side can be thirty feet.

You gradually lose height to farms, fields
and lanes in the wide valley of the Caebitra
river. The Dyke runs through the grounds of
Mellington Hall, and your day's walk can be
ended conveniently at the Blue Bell Inn, on
the A489 three miles south of Montgomery.

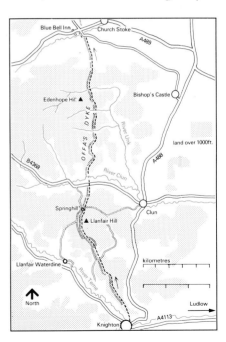

THE MALVERN HILLS

Map OS Sheet 150   **Start/Finish** The Winter Gardens, Great Malvern (776459)/Rye Court (776357)
Distance/Time 11 miles/18km, 5 hrs

Grading A very easy hill walk along good paths.
Escape Routes Roads cross the hills at Wyche, Wynds Point and Hollybush.
Transport Railway station at Malvern. Bus services: Malvern to Worcester, Birmingham, Bristol and Gloucester.
Accommodation Varied accommodation in Malvern. Youth Hostel at Malvern Wells.

The Malvern Hills have been an inspiration to many: Stanley Baldwin described them as the most beautiful silhouette in England, Sir Edward Elgar would take breaks from composing to walk along their broad ridges, they set the scene for Langland's fourteenth-century poem *Vision of Piers Plowman* and Wilfred Noyce rated the Worcestershire Beacon as lovelier than many a 20,000ft Tibetan peak.

Malvern has changed little since its development as a Victorian Spa. It is still a graceful and stylish town with an ancient Priory Church built of rich stone, and Winter Gardens where you can sip tea amongst the flowers and listen to the band.

From North Hill the hills stretch south for over seven miles. The ridge is close-cropped turf while the slopes are either wooded or covered with bracken, gorse, fox-gloves and rose-bay willow-herb. A few outcrops emerge, the rather crumbly rock being the oldest in England, at over 650 million years.

Take the path to the North Hill, crossing a wide drive built for Lady Howard de Walden in the last century. Head south for the Worcestershire Beacon, making a slight detour to St Ann's Well where pure water gushes through a dolphin spout into a marble bowl.

Worcestershire Beacon, 1,395ft/425m, is a wonderful viewpoint for the hills of South Wales, Shropshire and the Mendips. Looking east there is no higher ground until the Urals. The beacon was used as an Armada warning in 1588 and, more recently, to celebrate the Royal Wedding in 1981.

Proceeding south it is an extraordinary experience to be walking along a mountain ridge in a civilised suburban setting. Below the ridge are grand Victorian houses with Gothic features, many having large gardens and tennis courts.

The next prominent hill is the Herefordshire Beacon with its Iron Age fort. The terraced earthworks can be seen from afar and, as you approach the Beacon, the details of the ramparts and ditches, constructed in the fourth century BC, become clear.

Further south another earthwork, Red Earl's Dyke, is passed, followed by Midsummer Hill overlooking the obelisk in Eastnor Park. On the south side of Raggedstone Hill you will discover a tiny hamlet of half-timbered seventeenth-century houses called Whiteleaved Oak.

Chase End Hill marks the southernmost limit of the Malvern Hills; it overlooks the M50 and the tranquillity of this gentle and most beautiful walk is at once shattered.

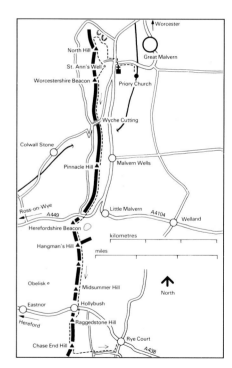

THE WYE VALLEY AND THE FOREST OF DEAN

Map OS Sheet 162 (Outdoor Leisure 14)   **Start/Finish** Monmouth (508130)/Welsh Bicknor Youth Hostel (591177)   **Distance/Time** 12 miles/19km, 5-6 hrs

> **Grading** Easy walking along forest and riverside paths.
> **Escape Routes** Numerous.
> **Transport** Bus services: Ross-on-Wye/Lydbrook/ Coleford; Ross-on-Wye/Monmouth.
> **Accommodation** Hotels at Monmouth and Symonds Yat. B & B locally. Youth Hostels at Monmouth and Welsh Bicknor.

The river Wye winds a sinuous course north from Monmouth to Welsh Bicknor. For much of the way it is overlooked by tree-clad hills, which mark the westernmost extremity of the ancient Forest of Dean. Outcrops of both sandstone and limestone break out above the river and contribute to the untamed nature of the valley.

Accommodation is available at both ends of the walk, or local transport can be used to return to the starting point.

From Wye Bridge on the east side of Monmouth take the footpath waymarked 'Wye Valley Walk' along the north bank of the river, and walk downstream to Redbrook. At the Bush Inn look out for another sign to The Buckstone; this path climbs through woods to a trig. point, 751ft/229m, and a large boulder which is a popular viewpoint west over the

Wye, Monmouth and the Black Mountains of South Wales.

The path now descends northwards, crosses the A4136 near Staunton and re-enters woodlands, emerging briefly at the Suckstone, a gigantic block of sandstone estimated to weigh 12,000 tons. Beyond, you pass under sandstone cliffs called the Near Hearkening Rocks and zig-zag down to Biblins Bridge over the River Wye. There is a maze of paths, woodland ridges and forest trails in this area and it is best to proceed in stages, from landmark to landmark.

Cross the suspension bridge and walk downstream to the Seven Sisters, a line of limestone buttresses rising high above the trees. A path traverses below another line of cliffs and then ascends to King Arthur's Cave. Continue along a minor road to Great Doward Hill and then descend again to the Wye at Symonds Yat.

The Symonds Yat ferry is of the simplest design: a rope slung from bank to bank to guide the boat and provide propulsion. Turn right on the far bank, and then left at the Forest View Hotel. A path climbs steeply through beech woods to the Yat Rock.

The Wye, whose source is high on the

slopes of Plynlimon, is the most gracious of rivers. When seen from Yat Rock, meandering through the lush water meadows and richly wooded, undulating hills of Hereford and Worcester, it exemplifies the most peaceful of English pastoral landscapes.

Descend through the woods to the river and follow an excellent track along the south bank for two miles. Cross a disused railway bridge to reach the north bank and Welsh Bicknor.

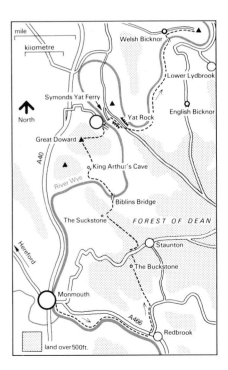

A COTSWOLD CLASSIC

Map OS Sheet 150   *Start/Finish* Fish Hill Quarry (120369)   *Distance/Time* 11 miles/18km, 4-5 hrs

Grading Easy walking through gentle hills.
Escape Routes Numerous. The route passes through several Cotswold villages.
Transport Railway stations at Evesham and Moreton-in-Marsh. Bus services: To Broadway from Stow-on-the-Wold, Stratford, Evesham and Moreton-in-Marsh.
Accommodation Varied accommodation in Broadway. Youth Hostels at Cleeve Hill and Stow-on-the-Wold.

The Cotswolds are not so much a range of hills as a long west-facing escarpment of oolitic limestone. The limestone beds dip to the east and streams have carved valleys which divide the scarp into more distant masses. The highest point is Cleeve Hill at 1,075ft/330m.

The Cotswold scene is idyllic and timeless: broad-eaved cottages of honeyed stone, roofed with thatch or stone tiles which merge perfectly into the landscape of clear streams, sloping fields of lush grass grazed by sheep, dry-stone walls and beech woods.

The last ice age did not reach the Cotswolds, thus man has lived and worked in the hills uninterrupted for thousands of years. He has left his mark in many places: long barrows, round barrows, hill forts, Roman villas, Norman churches and the present villages which date from the wool trade in the Middle Ages.

On the circular walk described here we traverse a northern section of the scarp, amble through cool woodlands, explore several cosy and delightful villages and visit a hill fort and a folly.

Start from the car-park at the top of Fish Hill on the A44 just east of Broadway. Take the Nature Trail which runs down the hill to enter the wide main street of the lovely old village of Broadway, which contains a wealth of ancient buildings including the Lygon Arms, a coaching inn of world renown.

A path runs across the fields below Buckland, passes through Laverton and leads you to the picturesque and uncommercialised village of Stanton. Here you meet the well-established Cotswold Way which leads on to Stanway, another peaceful village. Stanway House, on the village outskirts, is a Renaissance mansion once owned by Thomas Dover, who rescued Alexander Selkirk from the island of Juan Fernandez in 1708 and thereby inspired Defoe to write *Robinson Crusoe*.

The waymarked path now climbs up to Shenberrow Hill Fort, 900ft up on the Cotswold scarp and a notable viewpoint. It then slowly descends towards Broadway but, at the coppice you should climb up to the obvious landmark of Broadway Tower. This amazing folly was built on Broadway Beacon, the second highest hill in the Cotswolds at 1,024ft/312m, by the Earl of Coventry in 1799. It is a magnificent viewpoint for the Malverns, the Wrekin and the Black Mountains.

Broadway Tower now stands in a Country Park and an excellent path runs on to Fish Hill.

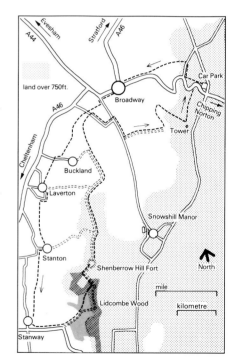

THE ANCIENT FOOTPATHS OF THE CHILTERNS

Map OS Sheets 165 and 175   *Start/Finish* Stokenchurch (759964)/Nettlebed (702870)
Distance/Time 12 miles/19km, 4 hrs

Grading Easy walking through woods and over commons and gentle hills.
Escape Routes Numerous.
Transport Bus services: London (Victoria)/Stokenchurch/Oxford; London (Victoria)/Nettlebed/Oxford.
Accommodation Hotels and B & B in Stokenchurch and Nettlebed. Youth Hostels at Oxford, Bradenham and Streatley.

The landscape of the Chilterns is very aesthetically pleasing: rolling chalk hills often crowned with clumps of beech trees, sheep pastures, open dry valleys with nestling villages and wide undulating fields which show white after ploughing. The Chilterns' soil is thin and the scars of small quarries dot the scarps but, where downland has been allowed to lie undisturbed, flowers proliferate.

The Buckinghamshire and Oxfordshire Chilterns are particularly accessible to London and other large centres of population and, for protection, they have been designated an Area of Outstanding Natural Beauty. Throughout history a network of paths and bridleways have linked the hamlets and villages of the Chilterns, and today the hills are generously supplied with rights-of-way.

Here I describe a walk through the most unspoilt part of the Chiltern Hills, from Stokenchurch to Nettlebed. The path, throughout, has been waymarked by volunteers from the Chilterns Society.

Leave Stokenchurch by the footbridge over the M40 motorway, cross the minor Ibstone road and head west over fields, through woods and across valleys to Bald Hill, which is a Nature Reserve.

Descending through another wood you meet the broad Icknield Way, part of the Countryside Commission's Ridgeway Path which runs 90 miles from Avebury to Ivinghoe Beacon. Follow the Icknield Way south for a mile-and-a-half under the wooded edge of the Chilterns. Barley has been grown in the fields on each side of the Way since Bronze Age times.

Just below Pyrton Hill the Icknield Way meets the Oxfordshire Way, a long-distance path linking the Chilterns with the Cotswolds. Turn left up the bridleway and climb Pyrton Hill to regain the Chiltern escarpment. You can look southwest across the Thames Valley to the Berkshire Downs (chapter 138) and west to the spires of Oxford and the low line of the Cotswolds.

Your path now leads to the sprawling village of Christmas Common, whence an unsurfaced lane passes Hollandridge Farm and descends to Stonor. Peer through the gates of the thirteenth-century Stonor House and watch the deer grazing under the trees in the park.

Now head west again, from a point near the inn, climbing to Russell's Water Common at Maidensgrove. Follow the top edge of a wood and skirt south of Westwood Manor Farm, finally passing through another wood to reach Nettlebed Common. Windmill Hill above Nettlebed, 692ft/211m, is an apt reminder of your elevated position in the Chilterns.

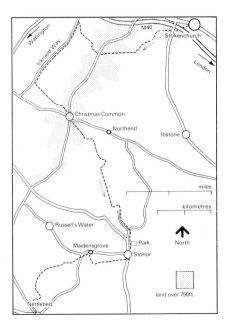

THE RIDGEWAY OVER THE BERKSHIRE DOWNS

Map OS Sheet 174 *Start/Finish* The Ridgeway S of Ashbury (273844)/Gore Hill (491835)
Distance/Time 16 miles/26km, 5 hrs

Grading An easy walk maintaining a fairly constant height.
Escape Routes Numerous.
Transport Railway stations at Swindon, Newbury and Didcot. Bus services: Swindon/Ashbury; Oxford/Chilton/East Ilsley/Newbury.
Accommodation Hotels at Ashbury, Compton and West Ilsley. B & B locally. Youth Hostels at Streatley.

The chalk uplands of the Berkshire Downs are divided from those of the Chilterns by the Thames Valley. For about six miles the Thames flows through the Goring Gap where the chalk has been cut right through to the clay, producing steep valley sides which are now well-wooded and very lovely.

For this walk we seek a section of the Ridgeway Path running south of the Thames, along the rolling downs of Berkshire between Ashbury and Gore Hill.

In addition to providing a principal artery for communications, the Ridgeway and its environs were extensively settled by early man and numerous prehistoric sites have been preserved, particularly on the higher ground where they have not been destroyed by ploughing. It is a sobering thought that the Ridgeway was used in the Old Stoneage era,

before Britain became an island and well before Stonehenge was built.

For a west to east crossing you meet the Ridgeway just south of Ashbury and, after a mile, arrive at Wayland's Smithy. Here a stand of beech trees encompasses a Neolithic long barrow, or chambered tomb, built of great sarsen (sandstone) boulders. It was probably constructed about 2,700BC. A legend, which has been traced back for at least 1,000 years, tells of the Saxon god Wayland who would shoe your horse if you left it at the smithy.

The rutted Ridgeway takes you on, for another mile, to Whitehorse Hill on which is built an Iron Age fort, Uffington Castle. On the face of the hill, cut through the turf to the chalk underneath, is the White Horse of Uffington. This huge horse, 365ft long, was cut about 50BC and is the most dramatic example of Iron Age art in Britain.

Dispensing with ancient relics for a while, you can stride out over the springy turf without a care in the world enjoying a wide vista north over the Vale of the White Horse, although your musings may be spoilt by the dominating edifice of Didcot power station.

At the Devil's Punchbowl the rippling downs descend to a deep fold and soon after you pass the perimeter of Segsbury Fort, another Iron Age earthwork.

After crossing the B4494 you reach Grim's Ditch, a prehistoric ditch of dubious design running just north of the Ridgeway, and you follow this over East Hundred Down and Bury Down to the A34 at Gore Hill.

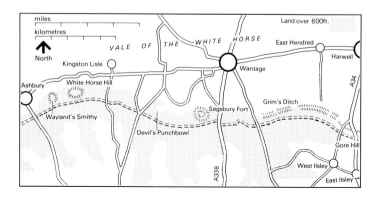

A HISTORIC EXCURSION OVER THE WILTSHIRE DOWNS

Map OS Sheet 173   *Start/Finish* Avebury (102699)   *Distance/Time* 12-14 miles/19-23km, 5-6 hrs

---

Grading Generally easy walking, no steep gradients, but overgrown in some places.
Escape Routes Numerous.
Transport Railway station at Swindon. Bus service: Swindon/Avebury/Devizes.
Accommodation Hotels and B & B at Avebury and surrounding villages. Youth Hostels at Inglesham and Salisbury.

South of Avebury there is an area of about 25 square miles of downland which contains the greatest concentration of prehistoric remains in Britain.

The fourteen-mile excursion described here uses these historic sites as reference points, where some feelings for the life and experiences of man over many thousands of years can be absorbed. I hope that first-time walkers in this area will return to explore the individual sites at leisure, and to give them the detailed study they deserve.

For a combination of physical exercise and compelling interest almost every step of the way, this walk is unique.

Start from Avebury and, to set the mood of the day, take a quick walk round the high circular earthwork, within which are several smaller circles of gigantic sarsen stones. A track leads south, across the fields to Silbury Hill which is so huge that it looks natural; in fact it is the largest man-made earthwork in Europe, 130ft high and covering five acres. Successive excavations over the centuries have discovered its method of construction, but no artefacts have ever been found.

Crossing the A4 and the River Kennet you soon arrive at West Kennett Long Barrow, a chambered tomb 350ft long in which 46 people had been buried, the internments extending over a long period of time.

Take the path to East Kennett where you meet the Ridgeway Path, just eleven miles west of Ashbury where the Berkshire Downs' walk commences (chapter 138). Follow the Ridgeway south for two miles until it crosses the Wansdyke, a hugh earthwork consisting of a bank and ditch which runs fifty miles from Inkpen to the Bristol Channel. The Wansdyke is thought to have been built in the fifth century to discourage Saxon invaders from the north.

Walk west along the Wansdyke to Morgan's Hill, passing many much earlier tumuli and barrows on the way. The highest point of the day is reached on this section of the walk, 964ft/294m, on Tan Hill which gives lovely views over the Vale of Pewsey and down to the Kennet and Avon Canal.

Head eastwards along the Roman Road (London to Bath) and then strike north to visit the Iron Age fort of Oldbury Castle, the prominent Landsdowne Column and the eighteenth century Cherhill White Horse. Cross the A4 and make a detour to the intriguing Neolithic camp on Windmill Hill before returning to Avebury.

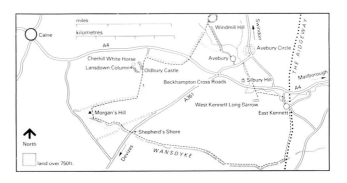

THE NORTH DOWNS FROM GUILDFORD TO BOX HILL

Map *OS Sheets 186 and 187*   **Start/Finish** *Guildford (996493)/Box Hill (179512)*   **Distance/Time** *12 miles/19km, 4 hrs*

Grading *Easy open walking, mostly along paths.*
Escape Routes *Newlands Corner (A25) after 3 miles.*
Numerous minor paths lead S to the A25 and
E towards Dorking.
Transport *Railway stations at Guildford and Dorking.*
Bus service: London Victoria, Marble Arch and Kings
Cross to Guildford and Dorking; Guildford/Dorking
Nos 425 or 439.
Accommodation *Hotels and B & B in Guildford,*
Dorking and surrounding villages. Youth Hostels at
Tanners Hatch and Holmbury St. Mary.

Greater London sits in a basin, where the surface soil is clay but the underlying rock is chalk. The outer rim of the chalk basin breaks out onto the surface forming the Chilterns on the north side and the Hog's Back and the North Downs to the south. The Thames has cut its way into the basin at the Goring Gap.

In chapter 137 we explored the Chiltern Hills and here we turn to the North Downs, where the chalk is more steeply inclined than in the Chilterns producing a pronounced ridge of high, bare scrubland overlooking the Weald of Kent and Sussex. Stone implements made of chert have been discovered along the North Downs, indicating that the downs were inhabited by Mesolithic man about ten-thousand years ago.

A footpath, designated by the Countryside Commission as the North Downs Way, runs along the top of the downs and, in places, it coincides with the Pilgrim's Way. This latter path, from Winchester to Canterbury, was popular in the Middle Ages with pilgrims going from the then capital of the kingdom to the holy shrine of Thomas à Becket.

This twelve-mile walk over the downs, between Guildford and Box Hill, combines some of the finest sections of both major footpaths, while a frequent bus service from Dorking will return you to the starting point at the end of the day.

From Guildford Castle climb to the edge of Chantries Wood where pine trees grow, and follow a sandy path to the extraordinary Church of St Martha, built in the Norman style in 1840.

Turn north through beech and yew trees to the popular picnic spot at Newlands Corner on the A25. The North Downs Way now runs east for ten miles to Box Hill, crossing minor roads, scrubland, open commons and woods. Generally it keeps to the south side of the highest ground, thus providing lovely views to Leith Hill, the highest hill in Surrey, and across the Weald to the South Downs.

On Hackhurst Downs the Pilgrims' Way comes in from the south and it passes darkly through a stand of yews before reaching St Bartholomew's Church on Ranmore Common, whose spire is a conspicuous landmark.

Descend from the downs, cross the River Mole by stepping stones, and climb steeply to Box Hill, 563ft/172m. Here you can enjoy one of the most magnificent views in south-east England before heading south for Dorking.

THE SEVEN SISTERS AND THE LONG MAN OF WILMINGTON

Map OS Sheet 199   **Start/Finish** Duke's Drive, Eastbourne (599971)   **Distance/Time** 20 miles/32km, 7-8 hrs

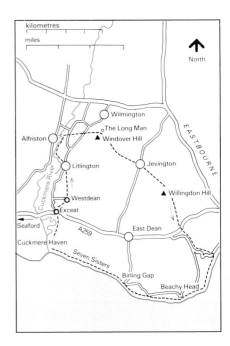

> **Grading** A long but easy walk over rolling downland.
> **Escape Routes** Numerous.
> **Transport** Railway station at Eastbourne. Bus service: Eastbourne/Beachy Head/Birling Gap/Exceat/Seaford/Alfriston.
> **Accommodation** Varied accommodation in Eastbourne and the surrounding villages. Youth Hostels at Beachy Head and Alfriston.

In a little over an hour from central London you can be at Eastbourne, tasting the tangy sea air and lacing your boots in readiness to tackle a 20-mile circuit, including the finest stretch of coastal scenery in south-east England and a sweep of historic, undulating downland.

From Eastbourne take the cliff-top path towards Beachy Head. Immediately you are in another world. The traffic fades away behind you, the chalk cliffs gleam brilliantly white in the sunshine and, walking on the springy turf, you hardly notice the switchback course of the path.

In summer the downs are bedecked with flowers like an alpine meadow: centaury, thyme, viper's bugloss, yellow rattle, rest-harrow, eyebright, scabious, knapweed and betony, to name just a few. In spring several varieties of orchid can be found.

At Beachy Head the cliffs plunge vertically for 520ft completely dwarfing the lighthouse, a mere 142ft, which is built on a plinth a short way out from the shore. Layers of flint can be seen protruding from the chalk, and holes and ledges provide homes for rock pipits and jackdaws. A museum of natural history is sited near the cliff-top.

Passing the stump of the old Belle Tout light-house, built in 1831, descend to Birling Gap. The *pièce de résistance* lies ahead, two exhilarating miles over the rounded chalk cliffs of the Seven Sisters.

In summer you enjoy the wide vista of bottle-green sea set against the beetling chalk cliffs. Waves grind the shingle beaches, the aroma of sun-warmed turf rises into the still air and the sails of the yachts hang loosely.

At Exceat you turn inland, replacing the seascape with woods, dry valleys and the picturesque villages of the Sussex Weald.

Walk through Friston Forest, past Westdean and Litlington, to the Cuckmere river and Alfriston. This village has several excellent inns and is a good place for tea. Cross the footbridge and climb up to Windover Hill and the Long Man of Wilmington. The giant figure cut out of the turf is 226ft long and something of a mystery to historians, although it is thought to be Romano-British in origin.

Follow South Downs Way indicators as you stride freely over the fields to Jevington, and its Saxon church with flint walls and tiled roof.

A leafy lane now leads to Willingdon where, quite suddenly, you find yourself back in civilisation with Eastbourne sprawling below.

THE DORSET COAST AND THE PURBECK HILLS

Map OS Sheets 194 and 195 (Outdoor Leisure 15) **Start/Finish** Corfe Castle (959824)/Hardy Monument (613877)
Distance/Time 27 miles/43km, 8-9 hrs

> **Grading** A long and varied walk along cliffs and over
> rolling downland.
> **Escape Routes** Numerous.
> **Transport** Railway stations at Poole and Wareham.
> Bus service: Poole/Wareham/Corfe Castle/Swanage.
> **Accommodation** Hotels and B & B abound in the
> area. Youth Hostels at Swanage, Lulworth Cove,
> Litton Cheney and Bridport.

The extensively folded chalk ridge, which runs from the Needles on the Isle of Wight through Foreland Point to Lulworth Cove and White Nothe, gives us the high downlands of the Purbeck Hills and the gleaming white cliffs stretching from Worbarrow Bay to Durdle Door.

In Jurassic times Purbeck was a freshwater lagoon which laid down beds from shells of the snail *Paludina*. This is the famous Purbeck Marble, a dull green rock much in demand for building and decoration.

The walk described here, from Corfe Castle to the Hardy Monument, combines the best of downland and coastal scenery with visits to several notable historic sites. One word of warning: the Lulworth section of the walk passes through Ministry of Defence land and you should check to see that the ranges are

clear, by phoning Bindon Abbey 462721, before setting out.

Corfe Castle is a Saxon hill-top ruin, which overlooks the charming village in the best romantic tradition. Walk up to the tumuli on West Hill and head west along Knowle Hill to Creech Barrow, which gives panoramic views over the Dorset coast and even to your destination, the Hardy Monument. A short stretch of road now leads to Povington Hill, 623ft/191m, another spectacular viewpoint.

Turn off left into the range area and climb up to Flower's Barrow, an Iron Age fort on Rings Hill which is cut away on the south side

into a cliff above Worbarrow Bay.

The tiny circular cove of Arish Mell is completely spoilt by barbed-wire fencing and it is a relief to traverse Bindon Hill to Lulworth. On the east side of the cove descend to the Fossil Forest, to marvel at the fossilised tree stumps, 200 million years old.

Lulworth Cove is an oval inlet surrounded by chalk cliffs of grossly contorted strata, capped with green turf. It is best viewed from the west side.

Continuing west you pass Stair Hole, a huge roofless cave, and then Durdle Door where a sheer arched cliff rises from the shore.

Leave the coast at Ringstead Bay and walk through Upton to White Horse Hill. The gigantic equestrian figure, which was intended to represent George III, was cut from the turf in 1808.

Cross the A354 and climb Corton Down and Bronkham Hill which carry an extraordinary array of tumuli. Black Down, 777ft/237m, and the monument to Admiral Sir Thomas Hardy, rise close by.

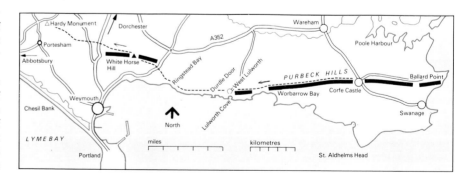

THE MENDIP HILLS

Map OS Sheet 182 **Start/Finish** Compton Martin (545571) **Distance/Time** 15 miles/24km, 6 hrs

> **Grading** An easy walk through upland valleys, woods and along limestone escarpments.
> **Escape Routes** Numerous.
> **Transport** Bus services: Bristol/Compton Martin; Bath/Compton Martin/Weston-super-Mare.
> **Accommodation** Hotels in West Harptree. B & B locally. Youth Hostel at Cheddar.

About 350 million years ago the dramatic earth movement known as the Armorician oregony produced the Pennine Chain, the Malverns, the folded cliffs of Gower and the Mendip Hills of Somerset.

In the Mendips the underlying rock is hard, crystalline Carboniferous limestone and the hills are similar to the Derbyshire Peak District. Thus we find a plateau rising to over 1,000ft, boasting the usual limestone pavements with grykes, dry valleys, cliffs, chasms, gorges, woods and excellent grazing land enclosed by dry-stone walls.

In this circular walk of fifteen miles you have the opportunity to sample most of the characteristic features of this small, but charming, area of upland Britain.

From the village of Compton Martin, lying under the northern ramparts of the Mendips, take the lane which runs up into a combe, passes through a quarry and a wood, and then breaks out onto high, open ground at Hazel Farm.

Follow the narrow lane west for a mile to Warren Farm, and then drop down through a wood to a reedy lake and a collection of spoil heaps. This is the lead mining centre of the Mendips where lead and silver have been extracted since Roman times. Roman dwellings and even an amphitheatre have been discovered here, although the flues and spoil heaps which you see today date from the nineteenth century.

Continuing downhill you walk through Velvet Bottom, a dry valley that is riddled with old mine workings, to Black Rock Gate on the edge of the Mendip escarpment. Wonderful views across Somerset open up, to the Bristol Channel, Exmoor, the Quantocks and the Blackdowns.

Below your feet Cheddar Gorge falls sheer for 400ft. Cheddar is a narrow, dry, limestone chasm cut by running water. It was left dry when the stream found an alternative course underground, and one theory is that it was formed by the collapse of the roof of a line of caverns. Caves in the side of the Gorge have yielded extensive evidence of habitation by man since the Stone Age.

Return to Black Rock Gate, skirt west of Long Wood and stride through the heather to Black Down Beacon, 1,054ft/325m, the highest point on the Mendips. Views extend north across the Bristol Channel to the Brecon Beacons.

A drove road now leads back eastwards to the mine workings at Charterhouse. Head north beside the lake to Ubley Hill Farm and descend wooded slopes to the road near Compton Martin.

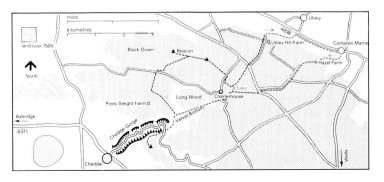

THE QUANTOCKS

Map OS Sheet 181   **Start/Finish** Holford (157411)   **Distance/Time** 12 miles/19km, 5-6 hrs

William and Dorothy Wordsworth stayed at Alfoxden Park under the Quantock Hills from 1797 to 1798, principally to be near Coleridge who was living at Nether Stowey and working on *The Ancient Mariner*. They walked extensively in the hills and Dorothy wrote, 'There is everything here; sea, woods wild as fancy ever painted, brooks clear and pebbly as in Cumberland, villages so romantic.'

Today the Quantocks have changed little, although regrettably the Forestry Commission have planted out several lovely combes. You will find oak woodlands, avenues of beech trees, overgrown combes with tumbling streams, high moorlands of bilberry and heather, prehistoric roads, tumuli, gritstone outcrops, wild ponies, deer and sweeping views from the bare spine of the hills. The highest point is Will's Neck, in the south, at 1,261ft/384m.

From the village of Holford take the path which climbs steadily up through the cool woods of Holford Combe, skirts to the west of Dowsborough Iron Age fort and meets the Crowcombe to Nether Stowey road.

A broad track known as Dead Woman's Ditch leads south into Quantock Forest. Here you descend to Rams Combe, head eastwards alongside the stream, and then double back west up Quantock Combe. You emerge from the forest just below Triscombe Stone, on the south end of the main ridge near Will's Neck.

As you walk down the old drove road, running north-west along the escarpment between lines of beech trees to Crowcombe Park Gate, you will appreciate the expansive views westwards to the Brendon Hills and Dunkery Beacon on Exmoor.

Beyond the Crowcombe road you enter a more open, barren landscape, where the path runs through heather with just a few stunted trees. A landscape common to scores of chapters in this book, where the breeze always blows and you fill your lungs with the purest air. On either side of the path you will notice strange mounds and lumps indicating tumuli and barrows, while the gleaming OS pillar perched on Beacon Hill beckons you on to the northernmost extremity of the ridge.

Beacon Hill looks out to the Bristol Channel and you can pick out the islands of Steep Holm and Flat Holm, although the nuclear power station at Hinkley Point tends to dominate the view.

Retrace your steps for 500m and then follow the path which descends Lady's Edge into Hodder's Combe, another delectable wooded combe which runs down into Holford.

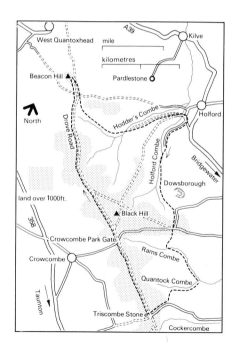

THE EXMOOR COAST PATH

Map OS Sheets 180 and 181 (Tourist Map)   *Start/Finish* Minehead (971470)/Combe Martin (576473)
Distance/Time 35 miles/56km, 2 days with overnight stop

Grading A magnificent coastal walk along a
switchback, narrow and at times exposed path.
Escape Routes Numerous. The route passes through
several villages.
Transport Railway stations at Taunton and
Barnstaple. Bus services: Taunton/Minehead; Exeter/
Minehead; Combe Martin/Ilfracombe/Barnstaple.
Accommodation Varied accommodation in
Minehead, Lynmouth and Combe Martin. Youth
Hostels at Minehead, Lynton, Exford and Ilfracombe.

The path between Minehead and Combe
Martin is a mere 35-mile section of the South-
West Peninsula Coast Path. Every step of this
walk should be savoured, for it offers a unique
combination of seascape, with moorlands,
wooded valleys and rushing streams. Allow
two days with an overnight stop at Lynmouth,
then you will have time to visit the fascinating
places you pass en route: old churches, inns,
lighthouses, harbours, smugglers' coves, beacons and villages.

The hills of Exmoor shelter the coast from the
winter gales and vegetation grows profusely.
At times the path runs through dank, mossy
woods of oak, elm and sycamore, at others it
winds between banks of brilliant rhododendrons and, when it passes through the pretty
villages of Bossington, Porlock Weir and

Lynmouth, palm trees can be seen.

For me the walk is memorable for the
narrow path, which clings precariously to the
steep hillsides, leading you dizzily above the
rocky shore hundreds of feet below.

From the elegant resort of Minehead climb
to Selworthy Beacon and gaze across the
gently rolling Brendon Hill to the Quantocks,
and away north to the Welsh coast.

Crunch along the shingle of Porlock Bay,
enjoy a drink at an old inn in Porlock Weir and
then climb through oak woods to the tiny
medieval church of Culbone, which was used
in the set for the film *Lorna Doone*.

Culbone Wood is skirted by a higher line

but the path then descends under Sugarloaf
Hill, passes Glenthorne House and takes a
rhododendron alley to gain steep slopes
below Desolate. From the intricate Chaddow
Combe zig-zags lead up over Foreland Point
for the descent to Lynmouth.

Lynmouth has been almost completely re-
built since the tragic flood of 1952, and you can
take the ingenious water-driven cliff railway to
gain the path through the Valley of Rocks, which
is overhung with rock towers and pinnacles.

The path crosses the steep slopes west of
Woody Bay, descends to Hunter's Inn and then
reascends to a fine traversing line out above the
wild inlet of Heddon's Mouth. Four miles of
exhilarating walking ends with a steep descent
into Sherrycombe and thence out around
Great Hangman, which casts 1,000ft cliffs
straight into the sea. The area is reminiscent of
Slieve League and demands a head for heights.

The path now hugs the cliff edge all the way
into Combe Martin, a village established in the
thirteenth century as a silver mining centre.

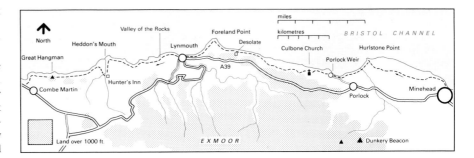

THE DUNKERY CIRCUIT

Map OS Sheet 181 (Tourist Map/Outdoor Leisure 28)   **Start/Finish** Horner (898455)
Distance/Time 11 miles/18km, 6 hrs

Grading A high and exposed moorland walk. Not recommended to inexperienced parties in bad conditions.
Escape Routes From minor roads near Lang Combe Head and Thurley Combe, return to Horner or Porlock.
Transport Bus services: Porlock/Minehead and Porlock/Lynton.
Accommodation Hotels and B & B in Porlock. Youth Hostels at Exford, Minehead and Lynton.

Dunkery Beacon, 1,706ft/519m, is the highest point in the Exmoor National Park. It is owned by the National Trust and walkers are free to wander at will over its windswept slopes.

For nearly 1,000 years Exmoor was a royal hunting preserve. In 1815, however, it was sold to John Knight who reclaimed much of the moor, below the 1,000ft contour, by liming and drainage.

Although a minor road passes within a mile of the Beacon, few motorists leave their cars and climb to the summit trig. point to enjoy the view. It has been used as a beacon since the fourteenth century and, at Queen Victoria's Jubilee celebrations in 1897, forty-four other beacons were sighted, including those on the hills of South Wales and the Worcestershire Beacon on the Malvern Hills. Outside the

holiday period your only companions are likely to be red deer, wild ponies, sheep, grouse, kestrels and ravens.

The charm of Exmoor lies in the juxtaposition of exposed hills and steep slopes of bracken and heather with deep wooded valleys.

This wild and sometimes savage scenery is the setting for R. D. Blackmore's *Lorna Doone*, and he researched old Exmoor legends while he was writing the book. Samuel Taylor Coleridge walked over Exmoor in 1795 and thereby found the inspiration to write *Kubla Khan*.

Here, I describe a circular itinerary which combines an ascent of Dunkery Beacon with wild combes and deciduous woodlands, thereby making full use of this extraordinary diversity of landscapes.

From Horner take the waymarked path to Webber's Post and then climb Dicky's Path to the summit of Dunkery Beacon. As you gain height look back across the valley to the church and white-washed thatched cottages of Selworthy; an olde worlde village, said to be the most beautiful in England.

Without losing height, walk west through the heather for a mile to the group of Bronze Age burial mounds known as the Rowbarrows.

A well-beaten path descends in a north-westerly direction to the unfenced road over Wilmersham Common. Cross the road and strike out over the heather towards Nutscale Reservoir, until you meet a path which runs over Tarr Ball Hill to Lucott.

The last leg of the walk follows the stream of Horner Water as it winds through woods of sessile oak, ash, beech and birch with the occasional sycamore, hazel, alder and rowan. You may be lucky enough to see dippers and kingfishers.

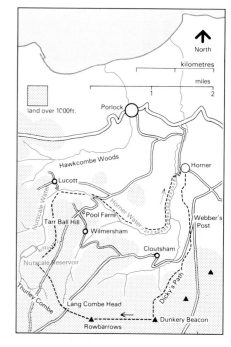

6   Little Hell Gate and the Napes crags
f Great Gable seen from the slopes of
ngmell (Chapter 98). Photo: Jerry Rawson

17 The Howgills in winter – descending Arant Haw heading towards Winder (Chapter 110). Photo: John Gillham

18　The view west to Penyghent from Brackenbottom
Scar (Chapter 111). Photo: Phil Iddon

19 Looking south from Chrome Hill to Park House Hill
and Dovedale (Chapter 126). Photo: Ken Wilson

0   Heading south along the Malvern ridge from
Worcestershire Beacon (Chapter 134). Photo: Marion Teal

21   The Dorset Coast Path above Durdle Door (Chapter 142). Photo: Andy Hosk

22 The Cornish Coast – east of Cribba Head near Penberth Cove (Chapter 151). Photo: Marion Teal

23 The Brecon Beacons – looking east to Cribin from Pen-y-Fan (Chapter 178). Photo: Phil Iddon

24 The view from Moel Cynghorion across the head of Cwmbrwynog and Clogwyn Du'r Arddu to the western slopes of Snowdon (Chapter 161). Photo: Jerry Rawson

THE MOORS AND TORS OF EASTERN DARTMOOR

Map OS Sheet 191 (Tourist Map/Outdoor Leisure 28)   *Start/Finish* Widecombe-in-the-Moor (718769)
Distance/Time 14 miles/23km, 7 hrs

Grading A varied walk exploring some of Dartmoor's impressive granite tors. Some tough going over rough heather moorland and boulder fields.
Escape Routes Numerous. The route crosses several roads.
Transport Railway stations at Exeter and Newton Abbot. Bus services: Exeter/Moretonhampstead/ Bovey Tracey; Widecombe/Bovey Tracey/Newton Abbot (infrequent).
Accommodation Hotels at Bovey Tracey and Haytor Vale. B & B at Widecombe. Youth Hostels at Steps Bridge (Dunsford) and Bellever.

I have included three Dartmoor walks in this book. Both the north-south crossing and the expedition to Cranmere Pool explore the principal areas of high and wild moorland, and they capture the unique sombre atmosphere of Dartmoor, an atmosphere which makes it the most inscrutable and mystical area of England.

In this chapter I describe an itinerary on the eastern moors, between Bovey Tracey and Postbridge, which combines the best of the desolate moorlands with impressive rock features and fascinating historical sites.

The walk is centred on the old Dartmoor village of Widecombe-in-the-Moor, where a perpendicular-style church with a magnificent hundred-foot-high tower presides over a collection of cottages and a fourteenth-century inn. Note that the village is best avoided on the second Tuesday in September, when Old Uncle Tom Cobley and All come to Widecombe Fair.

You start the walk in style, by striding out along springy turf on the spine of Hamel Down. Various barrows and standing stones are passed on the way north to Hameldown Tor at 1,732ft/529m.

A path runs down through the heather to Grimspound, the finest Bronze Age relic on Dartmoor. An ancient wall of enormous granite blocks, built for stock about 3,000 years ago, forms an enclosure for twenty-four hut circles. Mercifully, the site has been quite undeveloped. It is a moving experience to approach Grimspound through wet, clinging mist and be confronted by the massive, lichen-encrusted boulders, left where they had fallen thousands of years ago.

Follow a line of posts on King Tor, which were erected in 1940 to deter German gliders from landing on the moor, and descend through trees to the road under Hayne Down. Wind through the weird granite tors on the Down, cross a bracken-filled valley and climb

to Hound Tor, whose silhouette is said to resemble a pack of hounds.

Very rough country leads on to Grea Tor where granite rails can be seen through the heather, for the stone was used in the construction of London Bridge.

A long sweep round to Haytor Rocks, Saddle Tor, Rippon Tor (which gives views across Devon from the Teign to the Bristol Channel) and Top Tor brings you back to Widecombe. Almost every feature on this most varied walk has historical significance, and you should consult the appropriate guidebook for details.

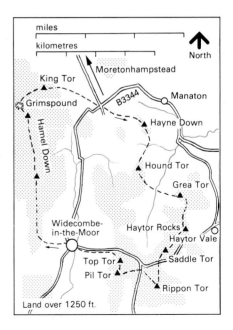

NORTH TO SOUTH ACROSS DARTMOOR

Map *OS Sheets 191 and 202 (Tourist Map/Outdoor Leisure 28)*   **Start/Finish** *Belstone (620933)/Bittaford (653569)*
Distance/Time *25 miles/40km, 14 hrs*

Grading *A marathon walk over rough and boggy moorland.*
Escape Routes *Main roads are crossed at Postbridge and Dartmeet.*
Transport *Bus services: Exeter/Sticklepath/ Okehampton; Ivybridge/Plymouth.*
Accommodation *Hotel at Ivybridge. B & B at Sticklepath. Youth Hostels at Gidleigh, Bellever and Plymouth.*

Walkers who relish a tough leg-stretcher over high moorlands, which are bristling with historic and interesting features, will not be able to resist a crack at the north-south traverse of Dartmoor. There are a great many possible routes for this traverse, because Dartmoor is an extensive area, but Len Copley recommends the 25-mile Belstone to Bittaford crossing, which can be completed in a long day.

From Belstone, cross the river Taw near Birchy Lake and climb to the Bronze Age cairn on Cawsand Beacon, which gives excellent views of the way ahead. High ground now runs south to Wild Tor, the broad ridge bisecting the notoriously treacherous soft ground of Taw Marsh, Raybarrow Pool and Gallaven Mire.

Wild Tor contains one of Dartmoor's famous letter-boxes, complete with visitor's book and rubber stamp. This tradition started in the nineteenth century, and has since generated much interest; each visitor should post the cards he finds in the box and, in turn, leave his own for the next-comer.

As you climb slowly to Hangingstone Hill you enter one of the bleakest regions of Dartmoor, and you remain on an exposed plateau as you continue south between the upper reaches of the North Teign and East Dart rivers. After passing the ruins of Staffs House, once used by peat cutters, you meet the river at Sandy Hole Pass and follow the bank to Beehive Hut and Postbridge.

The second half of the walk starts with a short climb through trees, before you break out onto open ground at the summit of Bellever Tor. Nearby Dartmeet is popular with tourists and the next two features, Huccaby Tor and Combestone Tor, mark a temporary return to civilisation, but more wild moorland lies ahead.

From Ryder's Hill you can see spoil heaps from the old Redlake China Clay Works, and the descent leads to an area with several derelict industrial monuments: a china clay pit, tinners' huts and the track of the Redlake Railway.

Watch out hereabouts for 'quakers', which are ooze-filled depressions in the granite, having a green crust on top. A fall into a 'quaker' is at best unpleasant and at worst highly dangerous.

Although the old railway track leads to Bittaford, it is more enjoyable to take the elevated route, passing a plethora of Bronze Age remains on Three Barrows, Piles Hill and Ugborough Beacon.

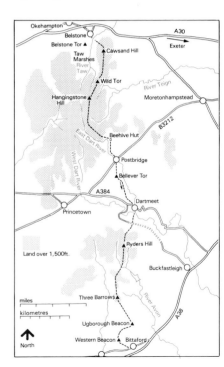

A VISIT TO CRANMERE POOL

Map *OS Sheet 191 (Tourist Map/Outdoor Leisure 28)*   **Start/Finish** *Postbridge (645790)*
Distance/Time *17 miles/27km, 7 hrs*

*Grading A long and rough walk over remote moors.
Can be serious in bad conditions. Before leaving
Postbridge phone Okehampton 2939 to check that
the firing ranges are open.*
*Escape Routes The military road one mile N of
Cranmere Pool.*
*Transport Infrequent bus service: Plymouth/
Postbridge/Moretonhampstead.*
*Accommodation Hotel at Postbridge. Youth Hostel at
Bellever.*

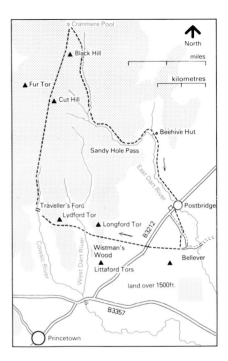

In this chapter we venture into the wild heart of Dartmoor to seek the legendary and elusive Cranmere Pool. The route runs right up to the boundary of the Okehampton artillery range, which is indicated by warning notice boards and red flags.

In common with many walks in this book, Man's impact on the landscape throughout the ages is very evident and adds considerably to the day's interest and enjoyment.

Start from the National Park Centre at Postbridge, and walk downstream past the world-famous medieval clapper bridge. Follow the path which runs to the edge of Bellever Forest and then climbs up through the trees, heading westwards to the B3212. It crosses the road, then another clapper bridge, and passes north of the Powder Mills. These mills employed over a hundred men in the nineteenth century, the powder being ground by water-driven stone wheels, but closed when dynamite was discovered.

After another mile you look down to Wistman's Wood in the valley of the West Dart. This oak wood has survived remarkably well at a height of 1,350ft, though the trees are gnarled and stunted and covered with thick layers of moss and lichen.

Ford the river, climb up to Lydford Tor and descend to Traveller's Ford on the Cowsic River. Now you leave the path and strike north onto wild moorland on Cowsic Head. For two miles the landscape is open and featureless, but you should regain your bearings on Cut Hill, 1,980ft/603m, which has the reputation of being the most remote spot in England, south of Northumberland.

If you continue walking north over Black Hill you arrive at the day's objective, Cranmere Pool, a depression in the boggy ground which only holds water after heavy rain. You will, however, be able to visit the most exclusive letter-box in the country and stamp your card.

The tradition of Dartmoor letter-boxes was started in 1854 by the guide James Perrot, who left a screw-top jar at Cranmere Pool. On this walk you pass close to another remote letter-box, at Fur Tor one mile west of Cut Hill.

Before leaving Cranmere Pool, if the weather is misty, look around for the resident ghost, a swarthy dwarf named Benjie Gear.

Head gently downhill in a south-easterly direction to East Dart Head, and follow the river through the artificially produced gorge at Sandy Hole Pass to the Beehive Hut and Postbridge.

THE GRANITE TORS OF BODMIN MOOR

Map OS Sheets 200 and 201   **Start/Finish** Camelford (106837)/Minions (261712)
Distance/Time 16 miles/26km, 8 hrs

> **Grading** A long walk over high and exposed moorlands. In places the going is very rough and in wet weather it can be boggy. Route finding difficult in mist.
> **Escape Routes** The walk may be terminated at Jamaica Inn on the A30 or at Tressellern Farm.
> **Transport** Bus services: Bude/Camelford/Newquay; Minions/Liskeard; Upton Cross/Liskeard. Train Liskeard/Bodmin, thence bus back to Camelford.
> **Accommodation** Varied accommodation in Camelford. Youth Hostel at Tintagel.

Even in the height of summer Bodmin Moor is deserted, for the holiday crowds flock to the sandy bays of Cornwall's rugged coastline. However, relics found on the moor show that it was extensively inhabited by Stone Age man, the Beaker people, Bronze and Iron Age man. It has associations, too, with King Arthur, legendary tribal chieftain of the Dark Ages. Early in the eighteenth century copper mining brought railways, chimneys and engine houses but, with the advent of cheap, imported copper, the industry soon collapsed.

Today, Bodmin Moor is wild, open country, characterised by extensive outcropping of granite, part of a chain stretching from Dartmoor to the Scilly Isles. Traditional Cornish enclosures, constructed of boulders and turf and now covered with a thick tangle of blackberry and honeysuckle, abound on the lower ground and add greatly to its enchantment.

From Camelford a narrow, tree-lined lane runs straight as an arrow towards Rough Tor. At the road-end a stone monument marks the spot where Charlotte Dymond was murdered by her crippled lover, Mathew Weeks, in 1844. Beyond the monument rise huge and startlingly white spoil heaps from the Stannon china clay works.

Rough Tor, like most Bodmin tors, is eroded into rounded plate-like formations. Harder stones, rolling in hollows, have produced scoops and pockets which fill with rain water.

Further south Brown Willy, 1,377ft/420m, is the highest point on the moor and the barren and marshy east side is grazed by semi-wild ponies.

The A30 trunk road is crossed a mile north of Jamaica Inn, immortalised by Daphne du Maurier's historical novel of that name.

Fox Tor gives a wonderful view south to the turreted outlines of Trewortha and Kilmar Tors while, closer at hand, two tumuli and a circle of nine standing stones emerge from the heather.

It is a fight to gain Trewortha Tor, for it is guarded by deep bracken, heather, bilberries, brambles, gorse and a chaos of fallen granite blocks. On the western tor a deep, smooth, cradle-like depression is known as King Arthur's Bed.

Granite sleepers from the 1840s lie in the heather south of Kilmar Tor, but perhaps the most astonishing feature is the Cheesewring, a stack of immense granite dinner plates piled high on Stowe's Hill. The name derives from a cider press and when the cock crows the top stone is said to rotate three times.

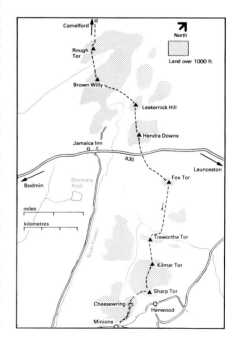

LAMORNA COVE TO PENDEEN WATCH

Map *OS Sheet 203*   **Start/Finish** *Lamorna Cove (450243)/Pendeen (382344)*   **Distance/Time** *21 miles/34km to Pendeen or 26 miles/42km to Zennor, 2 days*

Grading *A long and varied walk, which follows a waymarked path hugging the edge of a rugged and fascinating stretch of coastline.*
Escape Routes *Numerous.*
Transport *Railway stations at Penzance and St. Ives. Bus services: Penzance/Lamorna; Penzance/St Just; St. Just/Zennor/Pendeen/St. Ives.*
Accommodation *Varied accommodation abounds. Youth Hostels at Penzance and Land's End.*

From Poole Harbour to Minehead the South-West Way runs through the finest coastal scenery that England can offer. Notwithstanding the chalk cliffs of Dorset, the wooded valleys of South Devon and the high moorlands of Exmoor, most walkers agree that the highlight is the Cornish coast. The granite headlands which have been sculptured by Atlantic rollers for thousands of years, the smugglers' coves where the breakers send foam racing across firm sands and the tangle of bushes and flowers on the cliff-tops, together provide the most lasting memories.

A two-day walk from Lamorna Cove to Pendeen Watch guarantees a stirring experience under a variety of conditions. In summer the sun sparkles off a brilliantly coloured landscape and, during a winter storm, the waves thunder

with frightening ferocity and the scene can become a maelstrom of blinding spray.

From Lamorna Cove, with its quaint cottages and wooded valley, take the cliff path to Tater-du lighthouse. At Penberth Cove you pass a row of fishermen's stone cottages and then scramble to the headland where Logan Rock looks out across Porth Curno bay. This famous rocking stone was dislodged by a Lt Goldsmith in 1824 but, following a public outcry, the Admiralty ordered him to replace it at his own expense.

The Minack open-air theatre was hewn out in Greek style from the granite above Porth Curno. Plays are performed regularly during the summer months, and it is an unforgettable experience to attend a performance to the background of breaking waves, while the sun slowly sinks in the west.

Porthgwarra's tiny harbour comes next, and then you round the sheer cliffs of Tol-Pedn-Penwith before descending to Nanjizal Bay where the hulk of the steamship 'City of Cardiff' has remained since 1912.

As you hasten round Land's End waves boil over the wicked offshore rocks of the Longships, Shark's Fin, Armed Knight, Kettle's Bottom and the Peal.

Sheer cliffs and an exposed bay await you at Sennen Cove and then you are away, heading north to Cape Cornwall with its melancholy relics from the tin mining industry.

You are now approaching Pendeen Watch and the best rock-climbing area in Cornwall, for the cliffs bristle with exciting features: flying buttresses, razor ridges, roofs, slabs and walls. If time allows, an extension of the walk eastwards for five miles along this magnificently contorted coastline to Zennor is highly recommended.

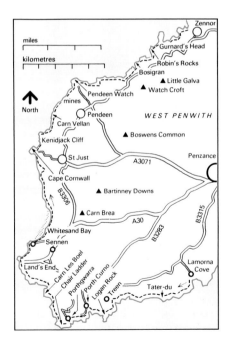

THE CLWYDIAN HILLS

Map *OS Sheets 116 and 117* **Start/Finish** *Bodfari (093701)/Llandegla (196525) or Llangollen (215419)*
Distance/Time *12 miles/19km to Llandegla (5 hrs) or 20 miles/32km to Llangollen (8 hrs)*

Grading An easy walk along a waymarked path over
mainly grassy hills.
Escape Routes Numerous.
Transport Bus services: Mold/Bodfari/Denbigh;
Llangollen connected to Chester, Oswestry, Corwen,
Wrexham and Ruabon.
Accommodation Hotels and B & B in Bodfari,
Llandegla and Llangollen. Youth Hostels at
Llangollen and Maeshafn.

The Clwydian hills run south from Prestatyn to
Llandegla, forming a distinct feature which has
been used by man as a natural defence
throughout the ages.

The line of hills is steeply scarped to the
west, and they look over the pastoral landscape
of the Vale of Clwyd to the distant mountains of
Snowdonia. Each hill is ringed by an Iron Age
hill fort built, possibly, by the Deceangli tribe
as a defence against the Romans. Although the
Offa's Dyke footpath runs along the top of the
Clwydian hills, the actual line of the Dyke is
further east, near Mold.

Thus the Clwydian hills provide a roller-
coaster walk along a broad ridge of heather,
gorse, bracken and bilberry, mostly well
above the creeping canopy of forestry. Here I
have extended the walk by eight miles, to

finish at Llangollen, in order to include the
delights of the bare, white limestone escarpment of Eglwyseg Mountain, a welcome change
from the underlying slates of the Clwydian hills.

From Bodfari take the path to the summit of
Moel y Parc which carries a TV mast. Easy,
open, undulating walking stretches south over
the hill forts of Penycloddiau and Moel Arthur
to the ruined tower on Moel Fammau. The
tower was built on the highest of the Clwydian
hills, at 1,818ft/554m, in 1810 to commemorate
the jubilee of George III. It is now a wonderful
viewpoint for the Berwyns, the Denbigh moors
and the southern Pennines, but its popularity
with picnickers is causing serious erosion.

Skirt the upper edge of the Clwyd Forest and
head south for Foel Fenlli, another hill fort,
overlooking Ruthin. The path now contours
the western slopes of Moel Gyw and Moel Llanfair, climbs to the OS pillar on Moel y Waun and
descends to fields just west of Llandegla.

The final leg of the expedition follows the
Offa's Dyke path south from Llandegla, which
passes through Hafed Bilston and then crosses
an exposed moor carrying a ruined tower. The
correct route over the moor to World's End is
waymarked with stakes.

The great, broken limestone crags of Eglwyseg Mountain, 1,677ft/511m, face west and the
path meanders beneath them, through rich
pastureland dotted with boulders and brightly
coloured flowers. Below Creigiau Eglwyseg
the path joins a narrow lane, only to branch
south after a mile to pass the ruined Castell
Dinas Bran, cross the Shropshire Union Canal
and the river Dee, and enter the fascinating,
historic town of Llangollen.

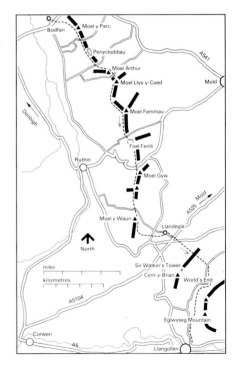

MWDWL-EITHIN AND THE DENBIGH MOORS

Map OS Sheet 116   *Start/Finish* Cerrigydrudion (953488)/Llansannan (933658)
Distance/Time 16 miles/26km, 7-8 hrs

Grading A surprisingly tough walk through deep heather and across trackless moors.
Escape Routes The walk may be terminated after crossing Mwdwl-eithin, at the A543.
Transport Bus services: London/Holyhead route along the A5 through Cerrigydrudion; Llansannan/Denbigh/Abergele/Rhyl.
Accommodation Hotels and B & B in Cerrigydrudion and Llansannan. Youth Hostels at Maeshafn, Cynwyd and Capel Curig.

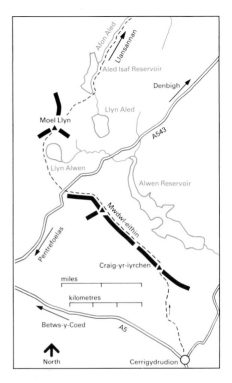

The eastern Denbigh moors have suffered at the hands of Man, for the hills have been cloaked in conifers and the valleys dammed and flooded. The great forests of Clocaenog and Mynydd Hiraethog stretch monotonously north, to the bare outline of Moel Fammau and the Clwydian hills beyond Ruthin.

But Mwdwl-eithin and the wild moors to the west are still untouched by the plough, and give a tough walk which may be extended down the secret Afon Aled valley to Llansannan.

From Cerrigydrudion make your way through fields and bracken to the outcrops on Craig-yr-iyrchen. Now forge your way through waist-deep heather and across rough bouldery ground to the 1,742ft/532m summit of Mwdwl-eithin. The open position is invigorating and the views magnificent.

The wall of the Snowdonia mountains forms an impressive backcloth, while south across the A5 rise Carnedd y Filiast and the distant Arans. North, beyond the blue waters of the Alwen Reservoir, the gaunt, derelict shooting lodge of Gwylfa Hiraethog is the only feature on a barren landscape. Perched at the focal point of the walk I found this ghostly ruin unnerving; it always seemed to be watching me, like an evil eye.

A mile of tussocky grass leads to the A543 north of Bwlch Gwyn, whence it is best to keep to the high ground on Pen yr Orsedd to reach Llyn Alwen. Climb Moel Llyn to appreciate the beautiful situation of Llyn Alwen, set below in a fold in the hills, with a deserted cottage and a stone boathouse adding to its charm.

Walk to the bridge at the northern end of the Aled Isaf Reservoir and enter the hidden world of the Afon Aled valley.

The valley is deep, with precipitous sides in its upper reaches, and is well wooded with deciduous trees. It is one of the gems of the Principality and is seen to its best advantage when approaching from the bleak moorlands to the south.

Except in the vicinity of Llansannen, there are no paths beside the river and you must keep to the open, heathery slopes above the tree level.

The last mile of the walk keeps to the east bank of the river, under a canopy of oaks, beeches and alders. When the sun streams through the branches, and glances off the lively water, the scene is perfection. You could only be in Wales.

THE ABER FALLS AND THE NORTHERN CARNEDDAU

Map *OS Sheet 115 (Tourist Map/Outdoor Leisure 16, 17)* **Start/Finish** *Bont Newydd (662720)*
Distance/Time *13 miles/21km, 6-7 hrs*

Grading *An easy mountain walk over flattish hills. Route-finding problematical in mist.*
Escape Routes *W from Garnedd Uchaf to Bethesda via Afon Caseg valley. From Drum W to Llyn Anafon and Bont Newydd.*
Transport *Railway station at Llanfairfechan. Bus service: Conwy/Aber/Bangor.*
Accommodation *Hotels and B & B in Bangor, Conwy, Llanfairfechan and Penmaenmawr. Youth Hostels at Bangor, Penmaenmawr, Roewen and Idwal Cottage.*

The spacious plateaux, broad ridges, boulder fields, crags and deep cwms of the Carneddau provide, perhaps, the best walking in Wales.

Five mountains in the Carneddau are classed as separate three-thousanders and receive some attention from Munro baggers, while discerning climbers visit Craig yr Ysfa to tackle magnificent routes such as Amphitheatre Buttress, Great Gully, Mur-y-Niwl and Pinnacle Wall. Apart from these intrusions the hills are mostly deserted.

However, the northern Carneddau, over-looking Conwy Bay and the Menai Straits, is an area of wild and desolate hill country which can provide a varied and fascinating expedition. These hills form a perfect horseshoe surrounding the headwaters of the Afon Anafon and Afon Goch which meet at Bont Newydd.

From Bont Newydd the path to the Aber Falls runs beside the sparkling Afon Rhaeadr-fawr, passing through woods of oak, hazel, alder, willow, ash and birch.

Beyond the woods the river has cut deeply into the Carneddau massif until, on meeting hard granophyre, it has formed the Aber Falls. Here, the river plunges 150ft down the rocks in a cascade of white foam.

Walk west to the smaller fall, Rhaeadr-bach, and then climb steeply to the summit of Moel Wnion, which gives views extending from the Great Orme across Conwy Bay, Puffin Island and Anglesey to the hills of Lleyn.

Fine open walking leads south to Drosgl, another rounded hill strewn with rough, grey boulders. The pile of stones on the summit is a Bronze Age burial mound, similar to those found on Moel Wnion and Drum. Looking south, beyond Yr Elen, a dramatic view is obtained into Cwm Llafar, ringed by the great circle of cliffs, Ysgolion Duon – the Black Ladders.

Cross the extraordinary Bera Mawr and Bera Bach, which are turrets of rock splinters piled at crazy angles, and continue to Garnedd Uchaf on the main spine of the Carneddau. Swing round north to Foel-fras, at 3,091ft/942m the final peak of the Welsh 3,000s circuit and scene of many acts of jubilation.

A gradual descent round the head of Llyn Anafon leads to Drum and Foel-ganol, a series of shapely hills with delightful sharp ridges having almost downland quality. As you scramble down the loose west ridge of Foel-ganol to the lane near Bont Newydd, you enjoy a bird's-eye view over the glistening expanse of Lavan Sands between Llanfairfechan and Beaumaris.

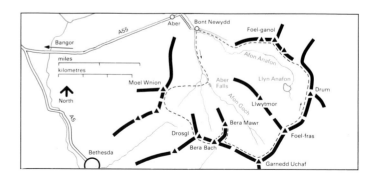

THE CWM EIGIAU HORSESHOE OF THE CARNEDDAU

Map OS Sheet 115 (Outdoor Leisure 16, 17)   *Start/Finish* Cwm Eigiau roadhead (732662)
Distance/Time 9 miles/14km, 5 hrs

Grading A tough mountain walk which includes the ascent of the second highest peak in Wales.
Escape Routes From Bwlch Trimarchog S to the Ogwen Valley. From Pen yr Helgi Du descend to the Ffynnon Llugwy Reservoir.
Transport Railway station at Dolgarrog between Betws-y-Coed and Llandudno Junction. Bus service: Llanrwst/Dolgarrog/Conwy.
Accommodation Hotels in Betws-y-Coed and Llanrwst. B & B in Dolgarrog and Tal-y-Bont. Youth Hostels at Rowen and Capel Curig.

The quickest way onto the eastern Carneddau takes the access road from the Ogwen Valley to the Ffynnon Llugwy reservoir, and then breasts the west ridge of Pen yr Helgi Du above Craig yr Ysfa. But this is a dreadfully uninspiring approach to a magnificently wild and rocky range of mountains.

If you walk into Cwm Eigiau from the north, you have the whole cirque of crags, hollows, inner cwms, spurs and ridges ahead of you, topped by the shapely summits of Pen yr Helgi Du and Pen Llithrig-y-wrach, an inspiring sight which will raise your spirits.

From the Conwy Valley drive up the narrow road to Llyn Eigiau, the scene of tragedy in November 1925 when the dam burst and sixteen people were drowned. Wind your way through the rocky bluffs onto the long north ridge of Pen Llithrig-y-wrach, walk easily over its rounded, grassy summit and descend to Bwlch Trimarchog.

Now climb steeply up to Pen yr Helgi Du, which commands wonderful views north down Cwm Eigiau, south down to the Ffynnon Llugwy reservoir and away across the A5 to a whole panorama of peaks extending from Moel Siabod to the Glyders, Tryfan and Y Garn.

Continuing round Cwm Eigiau the ridge narrows, steepens and becomes rocky, while the exposure is heightened by dramatic views to the cliffs of Craig yr Ysfa, home of some of Snowdonia's greatest, classic rock climbs.

The ridge now bends away from Craig yr Ysfa and climbs to the broad summit of Carnedd Llewelyn.

Although Wales' second peak, only 100ft lower than Snowdon, Carnedd Llewelyn could not be more different. It tops an extensive, stony plateau, solitude is the norm and the foreground precludes any outstanding views, save to the west where the sun glints on Conwy Bay.

If, however, you have time to walk a short distance from the summit cairn, you can obtain stirring views into Carnedd Llewelyn's four cwms: Eigiau, Llugwy, Gaseg and Llafar; the latter ringed by the notorious cliff, Ysgolion Duon or the Black Ladders.

A cairned path runs north from Carnedd Llewelyn to Foel Grach, but you must take the ridge north-east, overlooking the lakes of Dulyn and Melynllyn, which are set deeply in dark cwms. Where the east-facing crags peter out drop down the slopes to reach the northern tip of Llyn Eigiau and the roadhead.

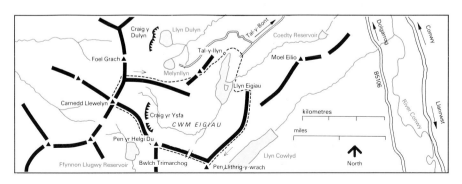

TRYFAN AND THE BRISTLY RIDGE

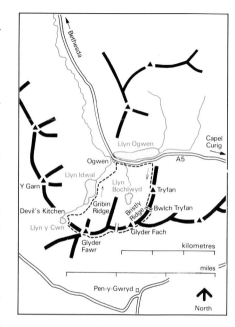

Map *OS Sheet 115 (Tourist Map/Outdoor Leisure 17)* **Start/Finish** *Car-park by Llyn Ogwen (659602)*
Distance/Time *7 miles/11km, 5 hrs*

Grading *A short but rough walk involving some scrambling over fine rocky ridges.*
Escape Routes *From Bwlch Tryfan W to Llyn Bochlwyd and Ogwen. From Glyder Fach descend S, almost anywhere, towards Pen-y-Gwryd.*
Transport *Railway stations at Bangor and Betws-y-Coed. Bus service: Bangor/Bethesda; Betws-y-Coed/Capel Curig/Bethesda.*
Accommodation *Hotels in Capel Curig and Bethesda. B & B in the Ogwen Valley. Youth Hostels at Capel Curig and Idwal Cottage.*

When driving west from Capel Curig along the A5, you round the shoulder of Gallt yr Ogof to be confronted by the serrated outline of Tryfan. The impact is electric, you rub your eyes in disbelief at this stark wedge of rock rising 3,000ft into the clouds. Even when you know and love Tryfan, and are eagerly awaiting the view, it always exceeds your wildest expectations. Only the view of Suilven seen from Elphin makes as dramatic an impression.

Tryfan is equally fine to climb; whether you enjoy one of the classic east face rock routes, or a scramble up the exciting north ridge. Here we take the latter route, continue south over more bare rock to the windswept plateau of the Glyders and then descend beside the

Devil's Kitchen to the wilds of Cwm Idwal. Despite its modest length this is one of the top quality expeditions in this book, where absorbing interest is maintained from beginning to end.

A cairned path winds up through the heather on the lower section of the north ridge, but then bands of rock block your way and you must pick your own route. You can swing up on jug handles, bridge short chimneys or avoid the difficulties altogether. This is not a very serious route and every move can be enjoyed.

Tryfan's summit is announced by two huge rocks called Adam and Eve. When dry it is very simple to jump from one to another, but an iron nerve is needed for a slip would be disastrous.

Descend the west side of the ridge to Bwlch Tryfan and scramble up the rocky Bristly Ridge, which is composed of rock slivers and needles stuck in at all angles. This deposits you on the plateau of the Glyders and you should walk across from Glyder Fach to Glyder Fawr, the highest at 3,279ft/999m. En-route you pass an extraordinary collection of rock spikes called Castell y Gwynt (Castle of the Winds).

Llyn y Cwn under the west side of Glyder Fawr, drains north down the precipitous chasm of the Devil's Kitchen. A cairned path running north-east from the Llyn zig-zags down steep slopes beside the Devil's Kitchen to Cwm Idwal. Don't attempt any other route for this is a dangerous area.

Follow the excellent path which runs between Llyn Idwal and the famous Idwal Slabs and meets the A5 at Ogwen.

THE GLYDERS FROM PEN-Y-GWRYD

Map *OS Sheet 115 (Outdoor Leisure 17)* **Start/Finish** *Pen-y-Gwryd Hotel (660559)*
Distance/Time *6 miles/10km, 5 hrs*

> **Grading** *A rough mountain walk which is straightforward in good conditions.*
> **Escape Routes** *The S slopes of the Glyders, although steep and rocky in places, may be descended almost anywhere.*
> **Transport** *Railway stations at Bangor and Betws-y-Coed. Bus services: Caernarfon/Pen-y-Gwryd; Beddgelert/Pen-y-Gwryd.*
> **Accommodation** *Pen-y-Gwryd Hotel. B & B in Capel Curig, Llanberis and Beddgelert. Youth Hostels at Pen-y-Pass, Llanberis and Capel Curig.*

When the Glaslyn copper mines were being worked in the nineteenth century, miners from Bethesda would walk home over the mountains at weekends. Thus we have Miners' Tracks on both Snowdon and the Glyders.

A very pleasant, and not too arduous, excursion takes the Miners' Track from Pen-y-Gwryd to the rocky plateau of the Glyders, and returns down the southern slopes of Glyder Fawr, by-passing Pen-y-Pass and Llyn Cwm-y-ffynnon. The walk is unique for the unsurpassed views it provides of the Snowdon range, while from the north-facing cliffs of the Glyders you look down to the wildest of Welsh scenes: Tryfan, Cwm Bochlwyd, the Gribin, the 'Nameless Cwm' and Cwm Idwal. In many ways the Glyders exemplify the rough and

rocky nature of Snowdonia and, although they are not popular tourist mountains, they are extremely highly rated and remain firm favourites with connoisseurs of Snowdonia.

From just east of the Pen-y-Gwryd Hotel a stile gives access to the Miners' Track. This path is maintained by the National Park and it takes the optimum route through the heather and boulders to the eastern shoulder of Glyder Fach, just above Llyn Caseg-fraith.

Follow the broad ridge round the head of Cwm Tryfan to the top of Bristly Ridge. This splintered, serrated ridge looks at its best from here, complemented by the towers and buttresses of Tryfan in the background. Chapter 156 describes this exciting scramble.

A chaotic collection of spiky rocks are jumbled together on Glyder Fach's plateau, and you must clamber over them to reach the true summit. The famous cantilever, along which it is perfectly safe to walk, was first described by Thomas Pennant over 200 years ago.

The path west to Glyder Fawr passes the extraordinary rock blades called Castell y Gwynt, drops to Bwlch y Ddwy Glyder, rounds the top of the Gribin and looks down the secret 'Nameless Cwm' to Llyn Idwal.

Glyder Fawr, at 3,279ft/999m, is the highest, though less spectacular, of the Glyders. However, it gives exceptionally fine views across the Llanberis Pass to Snowdon and across Ogwen to the line of the Carneddau.

Descend southwards from Glyder Fawr along a path that is both cairned and blazed with red paint. This leads to Pen-y-Pass but, at Llyn Cwm-y-ffynnon, you should turn eastwards, negotiate some rocky bluffs and descend tussocky grass to Pen-y-Gwryd.

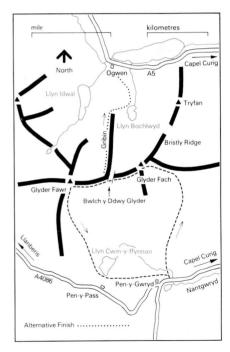

THE WELSH THREE THOUSANDERS

Map OS Sheet 115 (Tourist Map/Outdoor Leisure 16, 17)   **Start/Finish** Snowdon summit (609544)/Foel-fras (697682)
Distance/Time 24 miles/39km, 11-13 hrs in good conditions

> **Grading** The classic marathon walk of Snowdonia. A
> preliminary recce is strongly advised for the route is
> complex.
> **Escape Routes** The walk crosses main roads at
> Nant Peris and Ogwen.
> **Transport** Railway stations at Bangor and Betws-y-
> Coed. Bus services: Caernarfon/Nant Peris;
> Caernarfon/Pen-y-Gwryd (summer only).
> **Accommodation** Varied accommodation throughout
> the area. Youth Hostels at Llanberis, Pen-y-Pass,
> Capel Curig and Idwal Cottage.

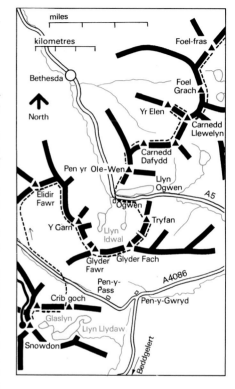

The fourteen Welsh 3,000s (or fifteen if you
count Garnedd Uchaf) make a remarkably
compact cluster of mountains in North Wales.
Their ascent can be accomplished with much
less expenditure of energy than the four
Lakeland 3,000s, in fact twelve hours is not an
unrealistic target for a fit party.

Traditionally, the Lakeland round is a circuit
starting and finishing at Keswick but, since it is
not possible to make a satisfactory circuit
which includes all the Welsh peaks, the
accepted expedition goes from the summit of
the first peak to the summit of the last.

The Welsh 3,000s excursion received much
publicity when it was highlighted in Thomas
Firbank's classic book *I Bought a Mountain*.
One's imagination is fired by the stirring
account of Esme Firbank limping through
thick white mist on the Carneddau, to complete
the marathon in the astonishing time of
9 hours 29 minutes in the 1930s.

It is usual to start from the top of Snowdon at
dawn and hasten over Crib-y-ddysgl, the rock
pinnacles and the knife-edged ridge to Crib-
goch. You should stay on the ridge as it curves
round Cwm Glas, by-passes the cliff of Dinas
Mot and reaches the Llanberis Pass.

From Nant Peris it is an exhausting pull up
to Elidir Fawr, but then easy grassy slopes lead
over Y Garn and down to Llyn y Cwn. The next
stretch is very rough going: up to and across
the plateau of the Glyders, down the screes
beside Bristly Ridge to Bwlch Tryfan and then
a scramble over the rocks to Adam and Eve.
Head north-west from Tryfan's summit to
meet, with luck, a scree gully running down to
the grass and heather under Milestone Buttress.

Throughout your descent of Tryfan the appallingly steep slopes of Pen yr Ole-Wen have
been mocking you across the valley. Once
attained, however, the ridge to Carnedd
Dafydd and Carnedd Llewelyn, with its views
down to wild cwms, provides the best high-
level walking of the day.

Just before you reach Carnedd Llewelyn,
Wales' second peak, at 3,485ft/1,064m, make a
there-and-back sortie to the north-west to bag
Yr Elen. Easy going over the gently undulating
and bouldery hills of Foel Grach and Garnedd
Uchaf lead to Foel-fras and the completion of
the walk. Keep some energy back for the long
walk out to Bethesda or Aber.

THE SNOWDON HORSESHOE

Map OS Sheet 115 (Outdoor Leisure 17)   **Start/Finish** Pen-y-Pass (646557)   **Distance/Time** 8 miles/13km, 7-8 hrs

---

Grading *A classic mountain walk with some scrambling along the Crib-goch ridge. In full winter this is a serious mountaineering expedition.*
Escape Routes *N or S from Bwlch Goch. Down the railway track from Yr Wyddfa. S from Bwlch y saethau.*
Transport *Railway stations at Bangor and Betws-y-Coed. Bus services: Caernarfon/Nant Peris; Caernarfon/Pen-y-Gwryd (summer only).*
Accommodation *Varied accommodation throughout the area. Youth Hostels at Pen-y-Pass, Llanberis and Capel Curig.*

Every visitor to North Wales waxes lyrical over Snowdon and, when viewed from the east, it has been described as the perfect mountain. It is hard to disagree when you see the immense, sharp cone of Yr Wyddfa, supported by the rocky shoulders of Lliwedd and Crib-y-ddysgl, plastered white with snow and rising into a blue sky. Moreover, the arms of Crib-goch and Gallt y Wenallt, in classic glaciological fashion, enclose a wild cwm containing an upper and a lower lake. In England and Wales Snowdon has no peer and it would hold its own amongst the grandest peaks of the Scottish Highlands.

The Snowdon Horseshoe is the complete mountaineering route, combining airy and exhilarating rock scrambling with easy ridge walking and, of course, an ascent of the highest point in England and Wales. From each peak on the Horseshoe you enjoy extensive views of the mountains of North Wales, the Menai Straits, Cardigan Bay and, on a clear winter's day, Scafell Pike, Snaefell on the Isle of Man and the Wicklow mountains in Eire.

The Horseshoe is not a route for the novice walker, it requires a steady head and some rock scrambling ability. In winter conditions full equipment including rope, ice-axe and crampons will be needed.

From Pen-y-Pass take the recently reconstructed path to Bwlch Moch where the Pyg Track branches off towards Glaslyn. From here various scrambly paths lead up towards the sharp cone of Crib-goch; where possible keep to the rather indistinct ridge.

You step straight from Crib-goch's summit onto the rocky knife-edge, but the rock is firm and the confident walker will stroll nonchalantly along the crest, enjoying the thrill of exposure. The timid can find footholds just off the crest and use the edge as secure handholds.

The ridge swoops and dives, sometimes levelling out into broad saddles and sometimes sprouting towers and pinnacles, all of which can be climbed direct.

After Crib-y-ddysgl the difficulties are over and you soon meet the railway track and the hideous hotel on Snowdon's summit, at 3,560ft/1,085m.

A horrid, steep and loose descent must now be made to Bwlch y saethau, but then a superb rocky path, on the edge of Lliwedd's huge cliffs, restores the quality. A worn path now runs down to the Llyn Llydaw causeway and the rough road to Pen-y-Pass.

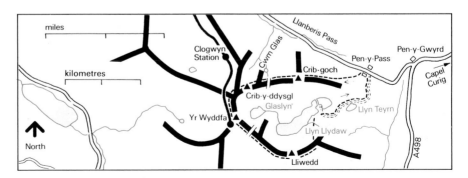

SNOWDON BY THE MINERS' TRACK

Map OS Sheet 115 (Outdoor Leisure 17)   **Start/Finish** Pen-y-Pass (646557)/Beddgelert (591481)
Distance/Time 16 miles/26km, 8 hrs

> **Grading** A high but straightforward mountain
> traverse. In winter the expedition can quickly become
> much more serious.
> **Escape Routes** From Snowdon's summit descend
> the railway track to Llanberis.
> **Transport** Railway stations at Bangor and Betws-y-
> Coed. Bus services: Caernarfon/Beddgelert;
> Porthmadog/Beddgelert/Llanrwst; Caernarfon/
> Pen-y-Pass.
> **Accommodation** Varied accommodation throughout
> the area. Youth Hostels at Pen-y-Pass, Llanberis,
> Capel Curig and Bryn Gwynant.

Unusually, this traverse of Snowdon makes minimum use of the sharp, spoke-like ridges which emanate from Yr Wyddfa. Instead, it follows man-made tracks, some ancient and some modern, which have been specially constructed in Cwm Dyli and Cwm y Llan, to facilitate access to Snowdon's summit.

Starting from Pen-y-Pass take the broad Land Rover track round into Cwm Dyli. Originally built to service the extensive Cwm Dyli copper mines – in their heyday in the late nineteenth century – it is now used by Electricity Board engineers who tap Llyn Llydaw via a hideous pipeline which runs down to the upper Gwynant valley.

Although quite extensive mining relics can be seen in Cwm Dyli, they are dwarfed by the stupendous scenery: the cone of Yr Wyddfa presides over the broad expanse of Llyn Llydaw and the dark, mysterious Glaslyn, while the cwm is enclosed by the mighty arms of the Crib-goch ridge and Y Lliwedd.

A row of derelict miners' cottages border Llyn Teryn and then you arrive at the shore of Llyn Llydaw. Unless the water level is very high you can cross the causeway to reach the broad Miners' Track; if you are unlucky you will have to detour round the lake.

On the north side of Llydaw you pass a crushing mill, and then the track steepens to reach Glaslyn, brooding under the towering face of Yr Wyddfa. The Miners' Track zig-zags up excruciatingly steep bouldery slopes to meet the Snowdon Mountain Railway just under the summit. For years thousands of boots eroded this path and turned it into a treacherous mud-slide. Recently, however, the Snowdonia National Park Authority has carried out a major reconstruction of the path which is rather raw but will, I am sure, soon merge into the landscape.

The descent from Snowdon is via the Watkin Path to Nantgwynant. This pony track was built by Sir Edward Watkin and opened by Gladstone in 1892. It winds up Cwm y Llan to Bwlch y saethau and then climbs the horribly loose stony slopes of Yr Wyddfa.

Unfortunately, the track up these final slopes has long since collapsed and you must descend them as best you can, taking extreme care. But, from Bwlch y saethau, the Watkin Path is a delight as it follows a lively stream cascading over rocky steps and thundering through deep gorges. It finally passes through woods above Bethania.

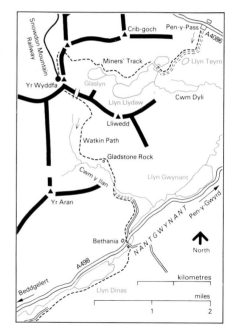

SNOWDON – LLANBERIS TO BEDDGELERT

Map OS Sheet 115 (Outdoor Leisure 17)   **Start/Finish** Llanberis (579600)/Beddgelert (591481)
Distance/Time 12 miles/19km, 6-7 hrs

> **Grading** A high and exposed mountain traverse. It can become serious in winter conditions.
> **Escape Routes** From Bwlch Cwmbrwynog descend the Snowdon Ranger track to Llyn Cwellyn. From Snowdon's summit descend the railway track to Llanberis.
> **Transport** Railway stations at Bangor and Betws-y-Coed. Bus services: Caernarfon/Beddgelert; Caernarfon/Llanberis; Llanrwst/Beddgelert/Porthmadog.
> **Accommodation** Varied accommodation throughout the area. Youth Hostels at Llanberis, Snowdon Ranger, Capel Curig, Bryn Gwynant and Pen-y-Pass.

The ascent of Snowdon appears in four chapters of this book. It is such a dominating feature of North Wales, and has played such an important role in the history of Welsh mountaineering, that any less coverage would be doing this fine peak a disservice.

In this chapter Snowdon is traversed via two relatively unfrequented ridges, and most walkers will welcome the lack of crowds and the intriguing and unusual views of well-loved landmarks which are obtained.

From Llanberis walk uphill, past the Youth Hostel, into Cwmdwythwch. Branch off right and zig-zag up the grassy north-east ridge of Moel Eilio, which is a marvellous viewpoint for Llyn Padarn, the Dinorwic slate quarries,

the Snowdon Mountain Railway, Mynydd Mawr and Caernarfon Bay.

The broad ridge winds pleasantly eastwards, rounding the fringes of crags overlooking several north-facing cwms, to Moel Cynghorion. Suddenly the dramatic west face of Snowdon is revealed, with the awe-inspiring precipice of Clogwyn du'r Arddu ringing Cwmbrwynog and guarding the graceful pyramid of Yr Wyddfa.

After a steep descent to Bwlch Cwmbrwynog, you meet the Snowdon Ranger path, which has come up from Llyn Cwellyn, and the merged paths skirt the top of the Clogwyn du'r Arddu cliffs. It is a steep pull up the west shoulder of Crib-y-ddysgl to meet the railway; loose, slatey stones litter the ground, you are exposed to the elements and there is a general air of desolation. The atmosphere does not improve on the summit of Snowdon, where jostling crowds and ugly developments further try your patience.

It is a relief to head south-west over the rocky ridge of Bwlch Main, enjoying peaceful views down to the wooded valleys surrounding Beddgelert and, away south, to Moel Hebog, the Rhinogs and Cadair Idris.

From the unnamed peak at the end of Bwlch Main a path runs off west to Llechog and Rhyd-Ddu, but you must descend due south, down a fine chunky ridge to Bwlch Maderin. Beyond the Bwlch climb steeply to the sharp peak of Yr Aran. Look back at the fabulous symmetrical cone of Yr Wyddfa, riding high above Cwm y Llan. You can just pick out the Watkin Path snaking up to Bwlch y saethau.

Drop down south into Cwm Bleiddiaid and, at Hafod-y-porth, you meet a farm track leading to the A498 west of Llyn Dinas.

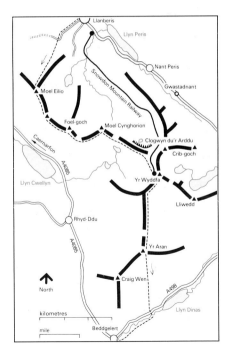

MOEL SIABOD AND MOEL MEIRCH

Map OS Sheet 115 (Tourist Map/Outdoor Leisure 17)   **Start/Finish** Capel Curig (722581)/Beddgelert (591481)
Distance/Time 14 miles/23km, 7 hrs

Grading An airy and exhilarating walk across rough
and rarely visited hills.
Escape Routes Good paths lead down to
Nantgwynant from Bwlch Ehediad and Hafodydd
Brithion.
Transport Railway stations at Bangor and Betws-y-
Coed. Bus services: Caernarfon/Beddgelert; Sherpa
service (summer only) Betws-y-Coed/Capel Curig/
Beddgelert.
Accommodation Hotels at Capel Curig, Pen-y-Gwryd
and Beddgelert. B & B locally. Youth Hostels at Capel
Curig, Llanberis, Snowdon Ranger, Bryn Gwynant
and Pen-y-Pass.

From Pen-y-Gwryd, Moel Siabod appears as an
uninviting grassy wedge, not dissimilar to
Whernside, and the majority of walkers plump
for the boulder-strewn slopes of the Glyders.

Yet the summit ridge of Moel Siabod is rimmed with crags and the mountain presents a
rugged face to the east, where a fine rocky spur
encloses the picturesque lake of Llyn y Foel.

The north-south traverse of Moel Siabod
can be continued delightfully over the craggy
outliers of Y Cribau, Moel Meirch and Craig-y-
Llan to Beddgelert, a route that gives unusual
and rewarding views across Nantgwynant to
the Snowdon massif.

From Pont Cyfyng, near Capel Curig, follow
the broad track that runs up past some disused
quarries to the east side of Moel Siabod. Skirt
round Llyn-y-Foel, weave your way through
rocky bluffs to the crest of the eastern spur,
and enjoy an airy scramble to the top of the
mountain, 2,860ft/872m.

When you have drunk in the wonderful
views of Snowdon's Cwm Dyli, and across the
desolate wastes of the Glyders and Carneddau,
head south-west and begin the long descent to
Bwlch-y-maen. The twin lakes of Llynau Di-
waunedd are tucked away below crags on the
east side of Y Cribau, a splendidly rocky and
rough hill, bristling with turrets and castles.

At the low pass of Bwlch Ehediad you cross
an ancient trackway linking Dolwyddelan with
Nantgwynant, and then you must negotiate the
ridge of Cerrig Cochion before reaching the
summit of Moel Meirch. This is difficult,
trackless terrain where patches of deep
heather, grassy hollows and crags abound, and
Moel Meirch's summit is announced by a
cluster of rock pillars.

It would be possible to continue due south
to Cnicht, only three miles away, but you
should descend westwards into the valley of
the Afon Llynedno which is one of the wildest
features in North Wales. The stream tumbles
down through a succession of gorges in the
most romantic of settings.

Cross the road at the head of Nanmor and
descend via Menlove Edwards' cottage at
Hafod-Owen to Llyn Dinas. The slopes hereabouts are suffering from a prolific spread of
rhododendrons which are causing the National
Park some concern.

From the lake-end take the path that meanders over Grib Ddu and Craig-y-Llan, where
you can marvel again at a perfect combination
of woods and crags.

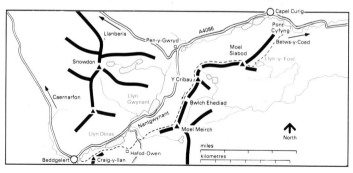

CNICHT AND THE MOELWYNS

Map *OS Sheets 115 and 124 (Outdoor Leisure 18)* **Start/Finish** *Croesor (635449)*
Distance/Time *14 miles/23km, 7 hrs*

Grading A rough walk over mixed terrain involving bogs, scree slopes and mild scrambling.
Escape Routes From Llyn yr Adar S into Cwm Croesor. From Bwlch Rhosydd either SW into Cwm Croesor or E towards Blaenau Ffestiniog.
Transport Railway station at Blaenau Ffestiniog. Bus services: Caernarfon/Beddgelert; Porthmadog/ Maentwrog/Blaenau Ffestiniog; Porthmadog/ Beddgelert (alight at Aberglaslyn).
Accommodation Hotels and B & B at Beddgelert, Maentwrog and Blaenau Ffestiniog. Youth Hostels at Ffestiniog and Bryn Gwynant.

When seen end-on, from Porthmadog, Cnicht has been likened to the Matterhorn; a rather over-generous description which has also been applied in this book to Shutlingsloe in the Western Peak. I prefer George Borrow's description, 'the conical peak impaling heaven'. But there is no denying Cnicht's impressive wedge, which makes it an obvious objective for the hill walker.

Across Cwm Croesor, to the east, rise the chunky, rocky Moelwyns. The musical name of these hills is misleading, for the Moelwyns are a complex mixture of rock faces, outcrops, lakes, abandoned slate quarries, pit-shafts and old trackways. Nevertheless, a circuit of Cwm Croesor can include both Cnicht and the

Moelwyns, where spectacular views are enjoyed all day. The hills provide a panorama of Snowdonia, in addition to the seascape of Cardigan Bay and a view down the Cambrian chain from Cadair Idris to Plynlimon.

The south-west ridge of Cnicht rises from the village of Croesor, and the path is signed through the fields until the way ahead becomes obvious. It is hard to imagine a more perfect ascent for, as you wind in and out of the outcrops, the sense of exposure increases on both sides, and the views expand. A short, rocky scramble leads you to the summit, 2,265ft/690m, whence you can look east into the heart of the Moelwyns, home of the gentle Welsh sheep and a wandering herd of wild goats.

The north-east ridge continues its sharp descent to boggy ground near Llyn yr Adar, from where you climb again to Y Cyrniau, a craggy hill overlooking three tiny, secluded lakes.

Continuing southwards over the high ground a switchback course takes you down to Llyn Terfyn, and over Moel Druman to Allt Fawr. These last-named summits command the wide Cwm Fynhadog Uchaf, which descends to Dolwyddelan, while Allt Fawr looks over the scarred and ravaged slopes, quarries and spoil

heaps above Blaenau Ffestiniog.

Scramble down the rough western slopes of Allt Fawr to Llyn Conglog and some ruined buildings. Climb steeply south to Moel-yr-hydd, descend to a broad saddle and continue to Moelwyn Mawr. Slopes of loose, slatey, boulders drop to Bwlch Stwlan, but the imposing crag guarding the summit of Moelwyn Bach can be detoured to the right; or to the left.

Return to Croesor via the long, but pleasant, west ridge of Moelwyn Bach, which avoids the almost unbroken ring of crags around the summit.

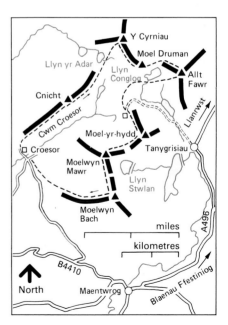

THE PENNANT RIDGES – MOEL HEBOG TO CRAIG CWM SILYN

Map OS Sheet 115 (Outdoor Leisure 17)   **Start/Finish** The chapel in Cwm Pennant (531453)
Distance/Time 15 miles/24km, 9 hrs

Grading A fine mountain walk. Rough in places with some airy scrambling which, however, can be avoided.
Escape Routes To Beddgelert or Pennant from Bwlch Meillionen or Bwlch Cwm Trwsgl. To Rhyd-Ddu from Bwlch-y-Ddwy-Elor.
Transport Bus services: Caernarfon/Porthmadog to Golan, 4 miles from the start; Caernarfon/Rhyd-Ddu/Beddgelert.
Accommodation Hotels and B & B in Tremadog and Beddgelert. Youth Hostels at Ffestiniog, Bryn Gwynant and Snowdon Ranger.

Moel Hebog is a popular tourist mountain from Beddgelert, and it combines an unusually fine view of Snowdon and Yr Aran with the romance of Owain Glyndwr, who is said to have taken refuge in a cave on neighbouring Moel yr Ogof. A cave search on Moel yr Ogof can be quite as diverting as one for Cluny's Cage on Ben Alder.

However, the ascent of Moel Hebog is best combined with a delightful, though arduous, traverse of the rough mountains ringing Cwm Pennant.

Cwm Pennant has a long history of endeavour. Today this magnificent, sheltered south-facing valley supports a few hill farms, yet ruined cottages, quarries, mine relics, stone circles,

huts and chambered cairns bear witness to man's struggle for survival in this wild corner of Wales.

From the chapel near Pont Gyfyng, climb to the grassy and gently contoured south-west ridge of Moel Hebog, 2,566ft/783m. Marvel at the view east over Cnicht and the Moelwyns, and west to Yr Eifl on the Lleyn Peninsula which can be seen dividing a great expanse of sea.

Follow a wall running down rocky slopes to Bwlch Meillionen and clamber up to Moel yr Ogof. A damp recess adjacent to the bwlch is claimed to have been used as a hiding place by the fifteenth-century chieftain Owain Glyndwr, when he was being pursued by the English.

Beyond Moel Lefn you must negotiate rocky bluffs on the descent to Bwlch Cwm Trwsgl, where you join the path through the hills from Cwm Pennant to Rhyd-Ddu. A distressing loss of height follows as you cut through the western arm of the Beddgelert Forest to the lower slopes of Y Garn.

However, ahead lies one of Snowdonia's gems, the Nantlle Ridge, which is more than adequate compensation. For five miles the rocky, airy ridge ducks and twists its way south, while precipitous cwms fall into Cwm Pennant

and the sea seems a mere stone's throw away. The flavour is akin to the Western Highlands.

The excitement starts soon after leaving Y Garn, as the ridge narrows and steepens giving a thrill of exposure. You can regain your composure on rounded Trum y Ddysgl, and marvel at the towering cairn on Mynydd Tal-y-mignedd, but the most exhilarating scramble comes on the ascent to Craig Cwm Silyn.

Follow the wall westwards to Garnedd-goch and descend via lonely Cwm Ciprwth to Cwm Pennant.

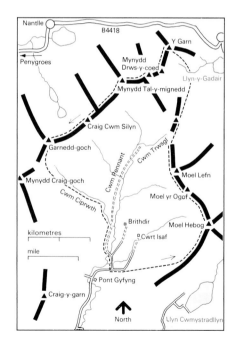

THE LLEYN PENINSULA:
THE RIVALS AND MYNYDD MAWR

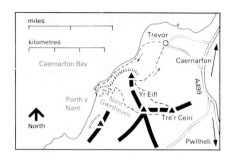

Map *OS Sheet 123*   **Start/Finish** *The Rivals – Trevor (373468)/Mynydd Mawr – Aberdaron (172265)*
Distance/Time *The Rivals – 6 miles/10km, 4 hrs; Mynydd Mawr – 8 miles/13km, 4 hrs*

> **Grading** *Easy, if steep, walking. A head for heights needed for the traverse above the sea between Trevor and Porth y Nant.*
> **Escape Routes** *Numerous. The routes are never far from roads or hamlets.*
> **Transport** *Railway station at Pwllheli. Bus services: Pwllheli/Trevor/Caernarfon and Pwllheli/Aberdaron.*
> **Accommodation** *Hotels and B & B at Pwllheli, Aberdaron and Trevor. No Youth Hostels on Lleyn.*

The Lleyn Peninsula runs twenty-five miles into the Irish Sea, dividing Caernarfon Bay from Cardigan Bay. Several groups of hills overlook the sea on the north side of the peninsula, giving short, half-day, walks which successfully combine the best of hill and coastal scenery.

Yr Eifl, The Rivals, rises south of Trevor and is conspicuous for the granite quarry which has bitten deeply into its northern flanks. A narrow path climbs to about 600ft on the west side, and then contours round the cliff-girt headland of Trwyn y Gorlech. A head for heights is needed on this exposed traverse, which is reminiscent of the Great Hangman on the Exmoor Coast path described in chapter 145.

Descend to the valley of Nant Gwrtheyrn and walk along the coast to the cottages at Porth y Nant. Climb again, through a forestry plantation, to reach the path at Bwlch yr Eifl, which leads to Yr Eifl's summit at 1,849ft/564m; a marvellous viewpoint for Anglesey, western Snowdonia, Pembrokeshire and the Irish coast.

Walk east from Yr Eifl to the Ordovician hill fort of Tre'r Ceiri (the place of the mighty), one of the best-preserved prehistoric settlements in Wales. Over 100 circular stone dwellings are arranged in rows with protective walls.

Traverse the northern slopes to the top of the quarry and return to Trevor down the incline of the disused tramway.

Two miles off the coast, off the very tip of the Lleyn Peninsula, lies the holy island of Bardsey. An abbey was founded by Cadfan on Bardsey in 516 and it is said that 20,000 saints are buried there. Once a popular place of pilgrimage, Bardsey is now a bird sanctuary and the home of seals.

A wild and hilly stretch of the Lleyn coastline overlooks Bardsey Island and Sound. From Anelog it is an easy walk up the grassy and heathery slopes of Mynydd Anelog, 628ft/191m, and beyond to the coastguard station on Mynydd Mawr.

Descend from the high ground to the inlet

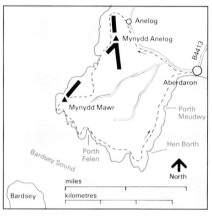

at Porth Felen and follow the cliff-edge past tiny bays at Hen Borth and Porth Meudwy to reach Aberdaron. This is a rugged and entrancing stretch of Welsh coastline, far removed from the holiday chalets and the crowds of Pwllheli. Fortunately the tip of Lleyn is owned by the National Trust, ensuring that its farms, whitewashed cottages and dreamy lanes will be preserved for future generations.

THE MIGNEINT AND ARENIG FACH

Map OS Sheets 124 and 125 (Outdoor Leisure 18) **Start/Finish** Near Pont ar Gonwy on the B4407 between
Pentrefoelas and Ffestiniog (776443) **Distance/Time** 11 miles/17km, 9 hrs

> **Grading** A rather rough and boggy walk over high
> and desolate moorland.
> **Escape Routes** From the summit of Arenig Fach
> and from Carnedd Iago easy slopes lead S to
> the B4391.
> **Transport** Railway station at Blaenau Ffestiniog. Bus
> service: Bala/Arenig hamlet (infrequent).
> **Accommodation** Hotels at Betws-y-Coed and
> Ffestiniog. B & B at Ysbyty Ifan. Youth Hostels at
> Ffestiniog, Bala and Cynwyd.

Readers of this book may correctly surmise
that the greatest variety of walking country in
these islands lies in Wales. While the rocky
ridges of Snowdonia can satisfy the most
adventurous mountain walker and scrambler,
and the grassy, folded hills of South Wales are
beloved for their gentle contours and pastoral
valleys, the largest area of cotton-grass moorland lies in Gwynedd, east of the Pentrefoelas
to Festiniog road.

Connoisseurs of the Northern Pennines will
enjoy themselves hugely on the Migneint
because the terrain is very similar. Heavy
erosion has produced peat hags and pools of
black water, while its acid nature has encouraged mat-grass, moor-grass, cotton-grass
and deer's-hair sedge.

Harold Drasdo, in *Classic Walks*, describes
his feelings on meeting a landmark on the
Migneint: 'There is a curious atmosphere,
preternatural though by no means hostile. You
tend to loiter for longer than there is good
reason. The faculties, dazed by the endless
jewelled particularity of vegetation, pool and
stream, suddenly regroup in some sort of
force field'.

There is a milestone near Pont ar Gonwy on
the B4407, which makes as good a starting
point as any for the gradual ascent of marsh
and hags to Llechwedd-mawr. Now head south
and, with luck, you will hit the lonely Llyn Serw.

As you desperately scan the Migneint for
recognisable features, you gaze longingly at the
swelling eminence of Arenig Fach, three miles
to the south-east. Yet, as you squelch your way
towards this hill, you pass, unexpectedly, the
shepherd's shieling of Cefn-Garw.

The luxury of firm ground is reached on
Arenig Fach, and its summit too springs a
pleasant surprise, by falling away on the east
side in broken cliffs fringing a sizeable lake.

If energy remains after the sapping plod
over the Migneint, the twin-topped peak of
Arenig Fawr will beckon across the Afon
Tryweryn to the south. The best ascent to its
2,800ft/854m summit is via Llyn Arenig Fawr
and the east ridge, which is quite rocky and
steep as it nears the top. Aircraft wreckage
litters the summit, which gives extensive, open
views in all directions.

Returning to the Migneint circuit, the purist
will regain his car by taking a long, curved route
from Arenig Fach over Carnedd Iago and past
Llyn y Dywarchen, thus savouring the atmosphere of this extraordinary bog to the very end.

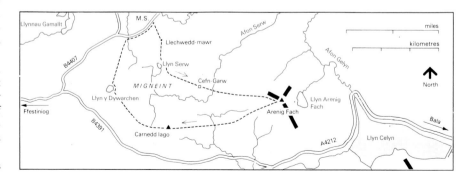

EASTERN MIGNEINT

Map OS Sheets 116 and 125 (Tourist Map/Outdoor Leisure 18)   *Start/Finish* Ysbyty Ifan (842489)/Bala (927361)
Distance/Time 17 miles/27km, 8 hrs

Grading A rather boggy walk over rough, featureless and rounded hills.
Escape Routes From Gylchedd S to Llyn Celyn. The route crosses the Bala–Cerrigydrudion road at Nantycyrtiau.
Transport Railway station at Betws-y-Coed. Bus services: London/Holyhead express to Pentrefoelas; Bala/Corwen.
Accommodation Hotels and B & B at Pentrefoelas, Cerrigydrudion and Bala. Youth Hostels at Bala and Cynwyd.

If you have already walked the Migneint – Arenig Fach circuit, described in chapter 166 of this book, you may have developed a taste or a loathing for wide expanses of desolate and saturated moorland.

Whatever your feelings, I urge you to sample the Eastern Migneint, where the watery wastes are kinder, the vegetation is more diverse and rocky outcrops emerge from firm, grassy and shapely hills. Once again this is a cheerless and unfashionable area of North Wales, where habitations are rare and you are likely to walk all day without seeing another soul.

Start from Ysbyty Ifan, where the turbulent river Conwy roars under a bridge in the centre of this sleepy village, and take the narrow lane which runs past a chapel and a row of terraced cottages, before breaking out onto the windswept moor.

The huge mass of Carnedd y Filiast, 2,194ft/ 669m, rises dark and brooding to the south, with silvery rivulets running down its every seam and fold. Half-a-mile before the deserted cottage of Cefn gwyn leave the track and paddle across a reed bed at the head of the Nant Adwy'r-Llan.

Saturated hillsides of reeds and peat bogs are meat and drink to wild walkers and the Migneint provides the largest area of this type of terrain in Wales. Ecologically it is extremely important and it has been acquired by the National Trust and designated a Grade 1 SSSI.

The ascent to Gylchedd is easy, though wet, but at Bryn Cerbyd some outcropping gives better drainage.

On Carnedd y Filiast rocks again protrude through the peat, and boulders have been used to build a substantial cairn, while the heather becomes knee-deep on the descent to Llyn Hesgyn. This wild lake is beautifully situated amongst the hills, three miles up the cwm from the Llyn Celyn dam.

Cross the B4501 to begin the second half of the itinerary, whose character is quite different from the first. A farm track leads to the empty house of Creigwen, above which open hillside rises to Garnedd Fawr. This lonely summit gives excellent views of the Berwyns, Arans, Arenigs and Mwdwl-eithin.

Walk east to Foel Goch before heading south for Bala, via the col between the rounded humps of Moel Emoel and Garw Fynydd which leads down to the valley of the Dee at Llanfor.

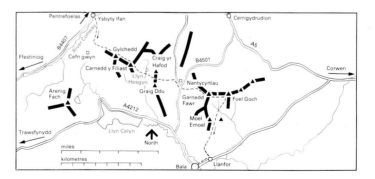

DEEPEST MEIRIONYDD: ARENIG FAWR TO RHOBELL FAWR

Map OS Sheet 124 (Outdoor Leisure 18)   **Start/Finish** Parc (875338) or Pont Rhyd-y-fen (822393)/Dolgellau (730178)   **Distance/Time** 20 miles/32km, 11 hrs

> **Grading** A long and rough walk over remote and desolate hills.
> **Escape Routes** From Blaen-Lliw to Llanuwchllyn. From Cwm yr Allt-lwyd to Pont Aber-geirw. From Ty-newydd-y-mynydd to Rhydymain.
> **Transport** Railway station at Barmouth and Blaenau Ffestiniog. Bus services: Dolgellau/Llanuwchllyn/Bala; Dolgellau/Llanfachreth (infrequent).
> **Accommodation** Hotels at Bala and Dolgellau. B & B at Llanuwchllyn. Youth Hostels at Bala, Ffestiniog and Dolgellau.

Few walkers venture into the wild, but exquisitely beautiful, no-man's-land between the Migneint and Cadair Idris. From Llyn Celyn to Dolgellau you can walk for twenty miles over rough, trackless hills and harsh moorlands, with only a few patches of recent forestry and some tumbledown farms indicating the presence of man. Yet there is no air of melancholy here, as in Cwm Pennant, rather one of hope and confidence as the hills announce themselves to a wild landscape.

The principal hills, Arenig Fawr, Dduallt and Rhobell Fawr brim with character and will be a revelation to hill walkers who rarely stray from the honey-pots.

Arenig Fawr may be approached either from the north via Llyn Arenig Fawr or, preferably, from Parc in the east. The latter route passes an old cottage at Cefn-y-maes and climbs the eastern ridge above the lake, as described in chapter 166.

Gradually descend the rocky south ridge of Arenig Fawr until gentle, grassy slopes lead to a marshy saddle under Moel Llyfnant. Follow a fence to the summit and descend to the hill road at Blaen-Lliw.

Very rough ground, composed of tussocky cotton-grass, heather and bilberry, leads due south to the outcrops on Dduallt. The stepped north ridge is always interesting as you scramble over the rocky bluffs, and enjoy ever-widening views west to the Rhinogs.

Descending the south ridge, skirt a huge block of forestry to the shieling at Ty-newydd-y-mynydd. Alternatively this can be reached from Blaen-Lliw (missing Dduallt) through the Bryn-Llin-fawr and Nant yr Helyg forests.

It is a relief to emerge from the trees on the north shoulder of Rhobell Fawr, for the creeping forest is turning much wild, Welsh moorland to green carpet. The lonely summit, 2,408ft/734m, looks across the vast Coed-y-Brenin forest to Cadair Idris and Barmouth Bay.

The descent from Rhobell Fawr to Llanfach-reth represents Wales at its most idyllic. I strolled through lush pastures, the air heady with gorse, may and foxgloves. Hazel and alder grew in the hedges and a pair of buzzards soared overhead. I delighted in the small fields, woods, rock outcrops, lichen-encrusted boulders, tiny whitewashed cottages with slate roofs, bracken, ferns and butterflies.

From Llanfachreth, with its steepled church and terraced cottages, take the waymarked Precipice Walk along Llyn Cynwch to the old town of Dolgellau.

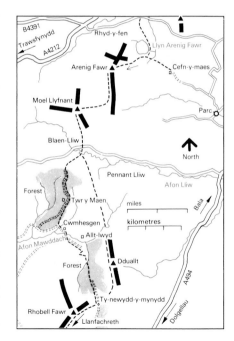

ROUGHEST WALES: THE RHINOG RIDGE

Map *OS Sheet 124* **Start/Finish** *Trawsfynydd Power Station (698384)/Barmouth (610160)*
Distance/Time *22 miles/35km, 9-10 hrs*

Grading A long and rough walk over wild mountainous country.
Escape Routes Down the Roman Steps to Cwm Bychan. SW from Bwlch Drws Ardudwy to Cwm Nantcol.
Transport Railway station at Blaenau Ffestiniog. Bus services: Porthmadog/Barmouth; Porthmadog/Ffestiniog; Porthmadog/Caernarfon/Bangor.
Accommodation Hotels and B & B at Ffestiniog and Barmouth. Youth Hostels at Ffestiniog, Harlech and Llanbedr.

If you are seeking untamed and untrammelled mountain country in Wales, you must head south of Snowdonia and the Moelwyns to the Rhinogs. Between Maentwrog and Barmouth there extends a 20-mile-long ridge of chunky mountains which are not crossed by a single road. The ruggedness of the area is due to outcrops of grit and conglomerate which are characteristic of a particular Cambrian rock known as the Harlech Dome.

Few paths can be found on the Rhinogs and the going is exceptionally tough: deep heather and bilberry bushes cover many of the boulder fields, while broken crags, rocky bluffs and screes abound. Delightful, lonely, and breeze-rippled tarns nestle in many of the rocky hollows. You will find no signposts, no 'improved' tracks and few, if any, fellow walkers save on the famous Roman Steps of Cwm Bychan.

The spine of the Rhinog ridge is gained by taking the minor road along the south side of Llyn Trawsfynydd, and climbing grassy slopes to the rock turret of Foel Penolau, on the eastern side of Diffwys. It is then only a short way to the OS pillar on Moel Ysgyfarnogod which gives a prospect of the extraordinary, contorted hills running south towards the Rhinogs.

The ridge twists and turns, rises and falls, and you are never sure that you are taking the optimum route. But it is a joy to be among wild features in such a primitive environment. The ridge overlooks Tremadoc Bay on the west side, while the swelling massif of Cadair Idris is dominant to the south, beyond the Mawddach Estuary.

South of Craig Wion the ridge curves around Cwm Bychan and then drops steeply to Bwlch Tyddiad. The Roman Steps run west from the bwlch down to Llyn Cwm Bychan. These slabby steps have been used to assist the transport of minerals and ores over the Rhinogs for aeons, probably by prehistoric man well before the coming of the Romans.

Another major pass runs between the two Rhinogs; this is Bwlch Drws Ardudwy, 1,240ft/380m, linking Cwm Nantcol with Coed y Brenin. On the south side of Rhinog Fach you descend to the exquisite Llyn Hywel, in the most romantic of settings, and then plod up to Y Llethr, 2,475ft/754m, the highest point of the day. The ground now becomes much less rough and good speed can be made across Diffwys and Llawlech to Barmouth.

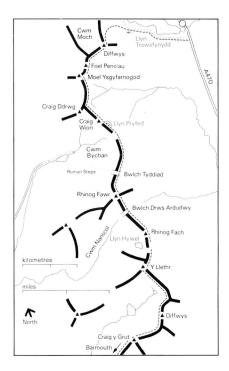

THE BERWYNS AND THE ARANS

Map OS Sheet 125   *Start/Finish* Glyndyfrdwy (148426)/Dinas Mawddwy (859149)
Distance/Time 34 miles/55km, 14-15 hrs

Grading An exceptionally long and rough walk over desolate hills.
Escape Routes From the Berwyns E down the valleys of Ceiriog, Gwynedd and Ffynnon. Roads cross the walk at Milltir Gerrig, Cwm Lloi and Ty Nant.
Transport Railway station at Blaenau Ffestiniog. Bus services: Chester/Llangollen/Bala; Blaenau Ffestiniog/Dolgellau/Dinas Mawddwy.
Accommodation Hotels and B & B in Corwen and Dinas Mawddwy. Youth Hostels at Llangollen, Cynwyd, Dolgellau and Corris (Machynlleth).

Many of the really long walks in North Wales described in this book involve the negotiation of difficult ground: rocky ridges, scree slopes, gullies and boulder fields. Thus Crib-goch, Lliwedd, the Bristly Ridge and Tryfan require careful placing of the feet and the use of the hands; a lapse in concentration could result in injury. But variety is the spice of life and there is nothing better than to swing along carefree at a good pace over high, undulating and smooth hills revelling in the huge skies and expansive views and filling your lungs with the purest air in Christendom.

The long and broad ridge of the Berwyns, which runs south-west from the A5 towards Bala Lake, will delight the freedom-loving hill walker and, by connecting these hills to the rougher and loftier Arans, a truly magnificent expedition can be devised which will match any other in the Principality.

From Glyndyfrdwy a lane runs south past an old quarry, finally petering out on the upper slopes of Moel Fferna. The Berwyn ridge now rolls away enticingly into the distance, in an uninterrupted sweep of heather. Delightful walking over the cropped moorlands can be savoured for six miles as you traverse Cerrig Coediog, Cadair Bronwen and Cadair Berwyn to Moel Sych. On the Berwyns themselves the summit ridges fall away on either side in perfect, crag-fringed cwms.

At Moel Sych the ridge divides and you should take the right-hand branch, and plough through deep heather and rocks to meet the B4391 at Milltir Gerrig.

A stretch of difficult ground lies ahead as you skirt the head of Blaen y Cwm to reach Cyrniau Nod. Since Hafod Hir, above Milltir Gerrig, is trackless deep heather it is best to approach from Point 659m on the north side.

Rough going continues as you cross Cefn Gwyntog, the Hirnant road and the Mynydd Carnedd Hywel to Ty Nant.

Ahead rise the Arans and a route via Cwm Croes and Llyn Lliwbran brings you onto the summit ridge of Aran Benllyn. As you proceed south to Aran Fawddwy, 2,970ft/907m, keep to the edge of the broken east-facing escarpment. With a lake in the cwm below and craggy features on all sides, Aran Fawddwy has a true mountain aura.

Descend the rocky spur, Drws Bach, into Hengwym which leads down into Cwm Cywarch and, eventually, to Dinas Mawddwy.

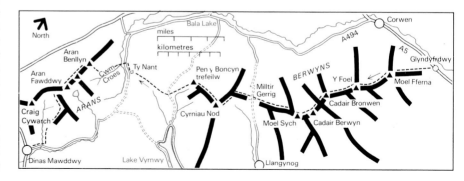

CADAIR IDRIS FROM THE SOUTH

Map OS Sheet 124 (Outdoor Leisure 23) *Start/Finish* Minffordd (733116) *Distance/Time* 6 miles/10km, 4 hrs

Grading An easy but rough walk over one of Wales' finest peaks.
Escape Routes Bwlch Cau into Cwm Cau. From col NE of Penygadair down Fox's Path to Gwernan Lake. From Twr Du col S into Cwm Cau.
Transport Railway station at Machynlleth. Narrow gauge railway: Tal-y-llyn/Abergynolwyn. Bus service: Machynlleth/Dolgellau.
Accommodation Hotels at Tal-y-llyn and Cross Foxes. Youth Hostels at Corris (Machynlleth) and Dolgellau.

Connoisseurs of the Cambrian Mountains place Cadair Idris a close second to Snowdon for rugged features and perfection of form.

In fact Cadair Idris, which rises above the Mawddach Estuary just 30 miles south of Snowdon, has much in common with her more illustrious neighbour. Both mountains are formed from Ordovician igneous rocks which resist weathering, although frost shattering has produced fields of angular boulders. The scouring action of glaciers has resulted in deep north-facing cwms, each with its own dark lake, which are divided by sharp ridges falling from a pyramidal central peak. Further down the mountains, U-shaped valleys with *roches moutonnées* are to be seen at Tal-y-llyn and Llanberis.

Here we traverse the ridges which surround Cwm Cau, Cadair's finest cwm. The walk is analogous to the Snowdon Horseshoe, although much simpler and shorter with nothing approaching the Crib-goch ridge for technical difficulty.

From Minffordd on the A487 take the path which runs through trees to the rocky south-east shoulder of Cwm Cau. The entire area is a Nature Reserve and the NCC has waymarked the path, from which you are not encouraged to stray.

As you gain height you can see right into the inner depths of the Cwm which is ringed with crags. Although the buttresses are broken, and there are no climbs to be found of the quality of those on Snowdon, you will be impressed by the massive Pencoed Pillar which juts out prominently from the face.

The path then crosses above the splendid south-facing Craig Cwm Amarch giving views down to Tal-y-llyn, beyond which the ridge narrows and steepens to the subsidiary summit of Craig Cau. After a short descent it rises to the true summit, Penygadair, 2,927ft/893m, where there is a large cairn and a stone shelter. From the summit you can enjoy views south down to

Cwm Cau, north to the cliffs of Cyfrwy overlooking Llyn y Gadair and a full 360-degree panorama over the hills and mountains of Wales, the Mawddach Estuary and Cardigan Bay.

Leave the summit along the broad ridge and head east for the outlier of Mynydd Moel. Throughout this section you can look north down rocky slopes to the very wild cwm containing Llyn Gafr. Descend mixed ground in a south-easterly direction to pick up the path of ascent near the exit stream from Llyn Cau.

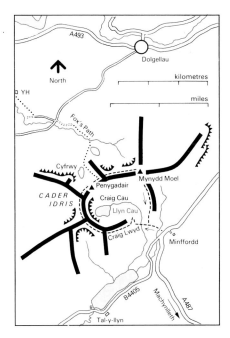

ACROSS THE DOVEY FOREST

Map *OS Sheet 124 (Tourist Map/Outdoor Leisure 23)* **Start/Finish** *Dolgellau (73C178)/Minllyn (859140)*
Distance/Time *14 miles/23km, 7-8 hrs*

Grading *An easy but exposed walk across mainly grassy and heather-clad hills.*
Escape Routes *N from the col W of Maesglasau to Penantigi Uchaf. N from Bwlch Siglen to Tyn-y-braich.*
Transport *Railway station at Barmouth. Bus services: Barmouth/Dolgellau; Dolgellau/Dinas Mawddwy (school days only).*
Accommodation *Hotels and B & B at Dolgellau, Dinas Mawddwy and Mallwyd. Youth Hostels at Dolgellau and Corris (Machynlleth).*

Those walkers who appreciate lonely cwms, broad ridges, freedom from erosion and, above all, peace and solitude, will find that the hills overlooking the Mawddach Estuary are without rival. In this book I have covered Cadair Idris, the Rhinogs, the Arans and Rhobell Fawr, and now I shall turn to the long line of hills marking the northern boundary of the Dovey Forest.

Start the walk from Dolgellau, county town of Merioneth and centre of the Gold Rush in 1862, but nowadays popular only with farmers, day-trippers and charabancs.

Walk up the lane towards Tyddyn-Ednyfed, which keeps beside the Afon Aron, and then make your way towards the rocks of Gau Graig, rounding the ridge at about 1,000ft. Scramble down the rough eastern cwm of Gau

Graig, which is thick with jumbled rocks, rowan and thorn trees and gorse, to meet the A487 Dolgellau–Machynlleth road at Point 286m.

Climb straight up the steep, grassy slopes to meet a fence which runs up to the summit of Mynydd Ceiswyn, a fine viewpoint for Dduallt, Rhobell Fawr and Aran Fawddwy. On the south side forestry plantations stretch almost to the ridge but mercifully, as you continue north to Waun-oer 2,197ft/670m, you leave the green carpet far below.

Waun-oer, like Moel Siabod, although rounded has a perfect east-facing cwm ringed by broken cliffs. It provides exceptional views

west to the bare and rocky slopes, and sublime outline, of Cadair Idris and south to Plynlimon and the Brecon Beacons.

Continue the easy, grassy walking westwards over the gently undulating hills of Cribin, Craig Portas and Maesglasau. These hills, too, have steep and precipitous faces to the north and east which fall away into deep cwms.

A considerable stream has its source on the plateau of Maesglasau, and it plunges over the edge of an escarpment into Gulcwm. In a strong wind the spray is blown straight back up the cliff in a white curtain, which in winter can change the hillside into a fairyland of hanging icicles.

A few strange-looking aerials sprout from the flat summit of Dinas, which also carries a reedy lake. The hill can be easily descended on the east side to Minllyn, down slopes of bracken and heather.

The Red Lion Inn at Dinas Mawddwy makes a convenient *rendez-vous* for your transport back to Dolgellau. Sadly there is no bus service.

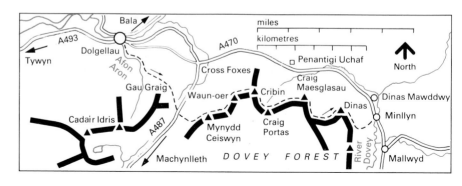

PLYNLIMON (PUMLUMON)

Map OS Sheet 135   **Start/Finish** Eisteddfa Gurig (797841)   **Distance/Time** 19 miles/31km, 6-7 hrs

Grading An easy walk over grassy and undulating hills. The peat hags and bogs could be unpleasant in wet weather.
Escape Routes Descend easy slopes E of Plynlimon to the Hafren Forest.
Transport Railway station at Aberystwyth. Bus service: Aberystwyth/Rhayader passes the start at Eisteddfa Gurig.
Accommodation Hotel at Ponterwyd. B & B locally. Youth Hostel at Ystumtuen.

As the growth of forestry marches on inexorably through the uplands of central Wales, the once proud mountain of Plynlimon is struggling to retain its dignity. Plynlimon is a complex mountain of cwms, lakes and subsidiary ridges and many of these have been stifled by the green blanket of conifers. However, Plynlimon's ten summits which exceed 2,000ft remain inviolate and all can be visited by a long day's walk across the roof of Wales.

Plynlimon (or Pumlumon Fawr) commands the vast area of central Wales bounded by Cadair Idris to the north, Cardigan Bay, Radnor Forest and the Abergwesyn Common. Its saturated spongy peat is the source of the rivers Wye, Severn and Rheidol as well as supplying the Nant-y-moch Reservoir. The blanket bog only extended to Plynlimon's summit plateau as the climate became wetter in about 1000BC. Several Bronze Age settlements have been discovered on the plateau but the later Iron Age people were driven to lower ground.

From Eisteddfa Gurig on the A44 Aberystwyth to Rhayader road a path follows the edge of a plantation and climbs up to Y Garn. You can now enjoy an easy angled, grassy and broad ridge which runs up to the summit of Plynlimon at 2,468ft/752m.

To include all the 2,000ft tops you should walk north to two subsidiary summits on the spur overlooking Llyn Llygad Rheidol, before retracing your steps and continuing east along the main backbone.

At Pen Pumlumon Arwystli turn north and cross a badly peat-hagged stretch of the plateau to visit Carnfachbugeilyn and Pumlumon Cwmbiga. A spring on the southern slopes of this (last) hill is the source of the river Severn. George Borrow drank not only here, but also at the source of the Wye and the Rheidol, on his ascent of Plynlimon in 1854. There is an amusing account of this expedition in his book *Wild Wales*. It is interesting that whereas George Borrow was much impressed by the 'mountain wilderness' of Plynlimon, Dr Johnson, writing eighty years earlier, had nothing but contempt for such landscapes.

The wide valley of the Afon Hengwm can be gained by an easy descent west from the northern end of the Plynlimon plateau. Follow the stream down to Nant-y-moch Reservoir, meet the Talybont to Ponterwyd scenic road and then, after one-and-a-half miles strike east along a forestry track which takes you back to Eisteddfa Gurig.

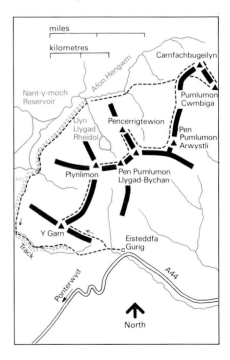

STRATA FLORIDA AND THE TEIFI POOLS

Map OS Sheet 147   *Start/Finish* Strata Florida Abbey (746657)   *Distance/Time* 16 miles/26km, 7-8 hrs

> **Grading** *A rough walk across open moorland which can be rather wet.*
> **Escape Routes** *The track from Claerwen to Strata Florida and Ffair Rhos can be taken as a convenient short cut.*
> **Transport** *Railway station at Aberystwyth. Bus services: Aberystwyth/Tregaron; Tregaron/ Pontrydfendigaid (infrequent).*
> **Accommodation** *Hotels at Tregaron and Pontrydfendigaid. B & B locally. Youth Hostel at Blaencaron near Tregaron.*

The Cistercians had an unfailing knack of choosing wild and desolate sites on which to build their abbeys. In 1164 they established a settlement at Pontrhydfendigaid (Bridge of the Blessed Ford) in the depths of Dyfed and later, when Henry II granted them all the land from the slopes of Plynlimon to the Wye at Rhayader, they built a splendid abbey at nearby Strata Florida (Valley of Flowers).

George Borrow visited the area in 1854 and reported, 'Rugged mountains formed the background of the valley, down from which came murmuring the fleet but shallow Teivi. Such is the scenery which surrounds what remains of Strata Florida: those scanty broken ruins of that celebrated monastery, in which kings, saints and mitred abbots were buried.'

Today the Abbey of St Mary is little changed from Borrow's time, but the neighbouring hills to the south are afforested with conifers, and the wild uplands to the east drain into the huge Claerwen Reservoir, which pipes its water to Birmingham.

Nevertheless, this broad expanse of bleak moorland, dotted with lakes and seamed with valleys, which is overlooked by the Abergwesyn Common hills of Gorllwyn and Drygarn Fawr, provides another demanding leg-stretcher across the ever-enigmatic uplands of Central Wales.

A narrow road runs east from the Abbey, hugging the northern banks of the Afon Mwyro, until it peters out into a rough track just beyond some waterfalls, near the farm of Gareglwyd. Strike north from the farm up slopes of bracken, tussocky coarse grass and rock outcrops to Dibyn Du, from where a watery wasteland unfolds to the north.

Head generally north-east and splash through marshlands to reach the Afon Claerddu, west of Claerwen Farm. Ford the stream with care to gain a Land Rover track, which the faint-hearted could take back to the main road at Ffair Rhos.

The intrepid walker will continue north up the saturated shoulder of Esgair Hengae to the minor elevation of Llethr Tirion which, nevertheless, overlooks a group of lonely lakes: Fyrddon-Fach and Fyrddon-Fawr.

Turning south for home you cross the Ffair Rhos track and enter another area of rather weird and marshy lakes, often mist-covered, called the Teifi Pools. Walk down the spit of land dividing Llyn Teifi from Llyn Hir and then, by skirting the north slopes of Craig Frongoch, you meet a farm track which leads in two miles to Strata Florida.

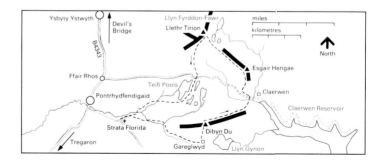

RADNOR FOREST TO LLANDEILO HILL

Map *OS Sheets 148 and 147*   **Start/Finish** *New Radnor (212608)/Erwood Bridge (090438)*
Distance/Time *26 miles/42km. 10-12 hrs*

Grading *A long walk over rolling hills. Much of the way is trackless and involves ploughing through deep heather and bracken.*
Escape Routes *Numerous. Tracks lead down to villages from many places. Roads cross the line of the walk S of New Radnor and E of Glascwm.*
Transport *Railway stations at Knighton and Llandrindod Wells. Bus services: Cheltenham/New Radnor/Aberystwyth; Knighton/New Radnor (infrequent).*
Accommodation *Hotels and B & B at New Radnor and Erwood. Youth Hostels at Knighton and Glascwm.*

The Welsh Border is crossed at Knighton and at once the lanes become narrower, the hedges higher, the gradients steeper and the villages smaller. Shropshire's rolling uplands give way to the hills of the Radnor Forest, which rise confidently to 2,000ft, dominated by the rounded dome of Whimble.

A line of slightly lesser, but very wild hills, runs south from Radnor Forest to the Wye valley at Erwood Bridge. The combination of these two groups of hills provides one of the longest and loneliest walks in the Welsh Marches.

Take the steep and narrow lane, Mutton Dingle, which runs uphill from New Radnor to Whimble, the shapeliest of the Radnor Forest hills. Skirt the shattered outcrop of Winyard Rocks and plough through deep heather and bilberry to Bache Hill, a marvellous viewpoint for the glorious hill country of the Welsh Borders, with Hengwm on Offa's Dyke prominent beyond the Lugg valley.

Head for the radio mast on Black Mixen and then contour the deep valley, Harley Dingle, to reach Great Rhos, 2166ft/600m.

A gradual descent through trees leads to a rather gloomy waterfall, with the macabre name of 'Water-breaks-its-neck', and then an avenue of chestnuts takes you to the A44 and the completion of the first loop of the walk.

Cross the A44, climb to a plantation on the west side of Castle Hill and then descend to Gilwern Brook, a swift stream running between banks of kingcups and overhung with larches and pines.

Heather slopes now lead to Gwaunceste, which commands a delectable view over the green valleys and swelling uplands rolling away to the Black Mountains. Immediately below, in a deep, wooded valley, lies the exquisite village of Glascwm, with its grey stone church standing on a knoll.

Continue over Glascwm Hill, skirt round the reedy Mawn Pools, and continue to Red Hill where the ridge turns west. Now the wiry heather gives way to a green path running through bracken between Rhulen and Llanbedr Hill, passing a picturesque outcrop above a shallow tarn.

Llandeilo Hill marks the end of the ridge and the ground falls away steeply to the north in a series of rocky steps. A wide path leads through the bracken to a farm and the ancient church of St Teil's at Llandeilo Graban, overlooking the Wye and only one mile from Erwood Bridge.

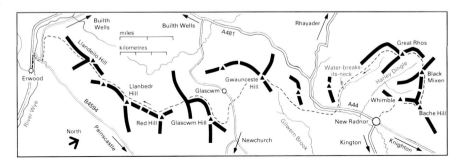

THE ABERGWESYN COMMON

Map OS Sheet 147   **Start/Finish** Ty-mawr, near Abergwesyn (863534)   **Distance/Time** 15 miles/24km, 7-8 hrs

---

Grading Rough going over high, trackless moorland. Route finding would be a problem in mist.
Escape Routes From Bwlch-y-ddau-faen, between Drygarn Fawr and Gorllwyn, descend to the Cefngarw Forest.
Transport Railway station at Llanwrtyd Wells. Postbus service: Llanwrtyd Wells/Abergwesyn.
Accommodation Hotels and B & B at Llanwrtyd Wells. Youth Hostels at Blaencaron near Tregaron, Dolgoch and Tyncornel.

Abergwesyn Common is a lost corner of Britain, tucked away in the no-man's-land between Plynlimon and the Brecon Beacons. This untamed area of high heathland, in the wildest part of Central Wales, runs west from a point just south of Rhayader to the Irfon Gorge and was bought by the National Trust in 1984.

Within the Abergwesyn Common lie 2,000ft hills, rivers, ravines, desolate boulder-strewn moorlands, ancient mine workings and natural woodlands of birch, ash and oak. Merlins and the very rare red kite are regular visitors to the Common, and the western sector has been designated a Grade 1 SSSI.

Thankfully the Abergwesyn Common will now be saved from moorland reclamation, from overgrazing and from the creeping canopy of conifers which covers much of Powys.

Llanwrtyd Wells is the base for exploring Abergwesyn Common. It claims to be the smallest town in England and Wales and was famous for its sulphur springs, now it is best known for hosting an extraordinary annual marathon: man versus bicycle versus horse.

A road runs along the River Irfon through Abergwesyn to Ty-mawr, which makes a convenient start for the walk. Follow the track to Glangwesyn farm, where you break out of the woods onto the open common. It is but a short distance further to the trig. point on Pen Carreg-dan, which reveals the whole expanse of the Common.

Since the going is appallingly tough, over tussocks of the coarsest grass, it is best to follow the Afon Gwesyn to its source high up on Drygarn. The stream has cut deeply into the bedrock, forming cascades and waterfall which provide continual diversions.

Drygarn Fawr (Three Cairns), 2,115ft/641m is a whale-back with a line of broken crags on the south side and two enormous cairns on its summit; the third lies half-a-mile to the west.

The rounded hill of Gorllwyn rises four miles to the east and no vestige of a path exists. As you plod across the marshes and reed-beds you can look north to the vast reservoirs of the Elan Valley. Although tough, this magnificent expanse of desolate moorland will prove irresistible to devotees of the Migneint.

Head south-west from Gorllwyn and cross the infant Afon Cedney to reach the black peaty ravine of the Nant Gewyn. At Esgair-gul you enter the Cefngarw forest and firm rides lead back to Glangwesyn.

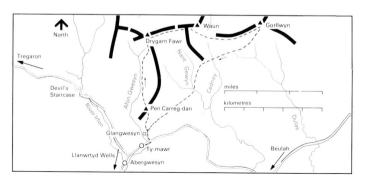

THE BLACK MOUNTAINS

Map *OS Sheet 161 (Outdoor Leisure 13)*   **Start/Finish** *Gospel Pass (236351)*   **Distance/Time** *30 miles/48km, 12 hrs*

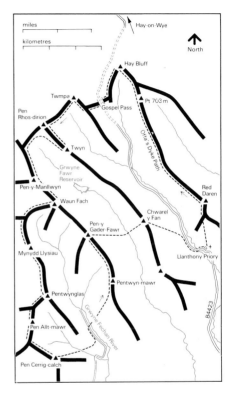

Grading A long but simple walk over rolling uplands.
Escape Routes The walk crosses roads at Cwm Farm and at Llanthony.
Transport Railway station at Abergavenny. Bus service: Abergavenny/Hay-on-Wye.
Accommodation Hotels and B & B in Hay-on-Wye. Youth Hostel at Capel-y-ffin (2 miles S of the Gospel Pass).

The Black Mountains that lie on the Welsh border near Hay-on-Wye should not be confused with Mynydd Du, the Black Mountain on the western edge of the Brecon Beacons National Park. Mynydd Du, or Carmarthen Fan, is altogether more severe with a dramatic north-facing escarpment, while the Black Mountains are soft, grassy and gently undulating hills split by deep valleys of consummate beauty. The route described here includes the ascent of all fifteen separate summits over 2,000ft in the range.

Four tentacle-like ridges emanate from the main backbone, thus it is inevitable that a circular walk will involve much ascent and descent. But this is no hardship on an expedition where the walking is always easy and the miles slip by effortlessly. This is a walk for high summer, with fleecy clouds overhead

and springy turf underfoot; allow twelve hours to complete this most attractive circuit.

The walk starts and finishes at the Gospel Pass, at a height of 1,778ft/542m, a great bonus and fillip to the morale.

Proceeding anti-clockwise Twmpa is the first summit, an easy pull up from the pass along an excellent path.

A short detour is necessary to take in Twyn, but then you can stride out south along one of the tentacles to Waun Fach, at 2,660ft/811m, the highest summit of the day.

Although the flat-topped Pen-y-Gader-Fawr is a near neighbour, its ascent is best left until the outliers, including Mynydd Llysiau and Pen Cerrig-calch, have been visited. The first major descent follows as you drop to the Grwyne Fechan valley.

Another steep descent from Pen-y-Gader-Fawr, hugging the forest edge, brings you to the Grwyne Fawr valley and the outflow-stream from the reservoir at the valley head.

Up and over Chwarel y Fan and you descend again immediately to the B4423 near Llanthony Priory. This twelfth-century ruined Augustinian priory is built in a rich red stone and its setting rivals the most romantic of the great Yorkshire

abbeys. To me this exquisite monument is the focal point of the entire walk.

A steep pull of 1,000ft brings you to Red Daren and the well-worn Offa's Dyke long-distance footpath. Just two more summits now, Point 703m and Hay Bluff, and you can turn south to the car-park at the Gospel Pass.

THE BRECON BEACONS

Map OS Sheet 160 (Outdoor Leisure 11)   **Start/Finish** Brecon (044285)   **Distance/Time** 25 miles/40km, 7-8 hrs

> **Grading** A long walk over undulating and mostly grassy hills, but with fine north facing escarpments.
> **Escape Routes** A road through the Gap leads down to Brecon.
> **Transport** Railway stations at Abergavenny and Merthyr Tydfil. Bus services: Brecon to Hereford, Abergavenny and Merthyr Tydfil.
> **Accommodation** Hotels and B & B in Brecon. Youth Hostels at Llwyn-y-Celyn (6 miles S of Brecon) and Ty'n-y-caeau (2 miles E of Brecon).

The Brecon Beacons National Park is really a loose amalgamation of four distinct hill groups in South Wales: the Black Mountain or Mynydd Du, Fforest Fawr, the Brecon Beacons and the Black Mountains. Of these the Brecon Beacons are higher, steeper and more serious for the walker in bad weather, exemplified by the frequency of accidents befalling SAS troops on winter training exercises in the area.

In summer the entire group, which includes twelve summits over 2,000ft, can be traversed in a magnificent circular walk from the town of Brecon. The ridges are mainly broad and grassy although, in many places, steep and heavily eroded escarpments fall away into north- and west-facing cwms. In winter conditions the Beacons have the feel of true mountains, and it may be necessary to cut short the expedition at The Gap, where a pass bisects the range.

Walk through country lanes from Brecon to Modrydd and take the path that leads to Pen Milan, the north-west outlier of Corn Du. Tommy Jones' Obelisk is passed on the ridge beyond, while Llyn Cwm Llwch glitters below. Corn Du provides the best views west and north, over Fforest Fawr to the Black Mountain, across the high moor of Mynydd Eppynt to Plynlimon and the distant Radnor Forest.

A quick descent and re-ascent leads to Pen-y-Fan, 2,907ft/886m, the principal summit of the Brecon Beacons. Now the view east to the Black Mountains can be appreciated. This is the heart of the range where ridges dip and swoop, and considerable faces fall away to the north providing a touch of airiness and exposure. Weathering has stripped the peat and turf from these faces revealing outcrops of Old Red Sandstone.

From the summit of Cribin descend 600ft, down the south-east ridge overlooking Cwm Cynwyn, to The Gap. The track running through The Gap was once a Roman road.

To the east side of The Gap the hills continue with Craig Cwm-oergwm, Craig Cwareli, Craig Pwllfa and a handful of outliers. These hills are altogether flatter and less dramatic than the main group of the Beacons, and the grass is more tussocky and the paths less distinct. They are less popular too and, at the end of the day, you can peacefully descend the long, easy ridge running north from Craig Pwllfa over Gist Wen down into the Usk valley and Brecon.

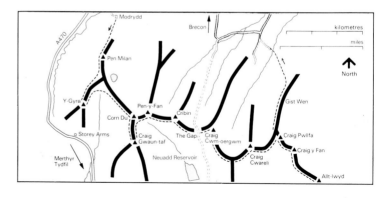

25   Cwm Cau and the Pencoed Pillar on Cadair Idris
(Chapter 171). Photo: Jerry Rawson

*26 The sharpest peaks of the Nantlle Ridge in a view
from Y Garn to the north (Chapter 164). Photo: Jerry Rawson*

27 Descending the north ridge of Tryfan
(Chapter 156). Photo: Jerry Rawson

28 On the Glencoaghan Horseshoe – Ben Baun (right),
the outlying peak of the group, seen from Bencollaghduff
(Chapter 191). Photo: Phil Cooper

29   Looking west along the Galty Ridge from Galtymore (Chapter 194). Photo: Hamish Brown

30 - The Cuillin Ridge - heading north-west fro
Sgurr Dubh na Da Bheinn towards Sgurr Alasdair ar
Sgurr Thearlaich (final chapter). Photo : Jerry Rawso

31 Abselling from the Inaccessible Pinnacle with
Coire Lagan and Sgurr Alasdair in the background
(Chapter 7/Final Chapter). Photo: Jerry Rawson

32 A rescue team sets out into a
Cairngorm whiteout. Photo: Jerry Rawson

MYNYDD DU OR CARMARTHEN FAN

Map *OS Sheet 160 (Outdoor Leisure 12)*   **Start/Finish** *Car-park three miles north of Brynamman (732185)/ Tafarn-y-Garreg (849171)*   **Distance/Time** *13 miles/21km, 6-7 hrs*

Grading   A high moorland walk over desolate and sometimes rocky country. The escarpment of Carmarthen Fan gives superb open walking with expansive views.
Escape Routes   None S of the Carmarthen Fan escarpment. From Fan Foel a steep path N to the road at Blaenau.
Transport   Railway station at Swansea. Bus services: Swansea/Glyntawe/Brecon and Ystalyfera/ Brynamman (infrequent).
Accommodation   Hotels in Brynamman and Glyntawe. B & B locally. Youth Hostels at Ystradfellte and Llanddeusant.

The loneliest mountain in the Brecon Beacons National Park is Mynydd Du. Known also as the Black Mountain or Carmarthen Fan, Mynydd Du appears as an enormous lump when seen from the valleys running south towards Swansea, yet it is a fascinating hill full of surprises.

The complex structure of the mountain, which is made up of Old Red Sandstone, Millstone Grit, Carboniferous Limestone and Coal Measures, has produced shake holes, caves, ravines, smooth rocks, boulder fields, outcrops, lakes, reed-beds, coarse moor grass and soft fescues ideal for grazing.

But the outstanding feature of Mynydd Du, which elevates the mountain into the top league in Wales, is a steep escarpment running

for four miles along the north and east sides of the plateau. From the summits of Fan Brycheiniog, 2,631ft/802m, and Bannau Sir Gaer, cliffs fall 600ft into cwms containing small and secret lakes, around which legends have been woven throughout history. The characteristic silhouette of Mynydd Du, when seen from the hills around Llandovery and the Usk valley, is one of the best-loved sights in South Wales.

From the car-park three miles north of Brynamman cross boggy ground to Garreg Lwyd and Foel Fraith. Proceeding east you pass the marshy pools of Pwll Swnd and Blaenllyn-fell to reach the long ridge of Esgair Hir.

First scoured smooth by glacial action, and then fissured and seamed by 12,000 winters, the grey gritstone rib of Esgair Hir is an extraordinary feature to emerge from the peaty moorland.

Beyond the tumuli on Twyn-Swnd you meet welcome limestone outcrops on Carreg Yr Ogof, with their associated green turf. It is thought that a cave system on Carreg Yr Ogof might run for six miles through Mynydd Du to Dan-yr-Ogof.

At Waun Lefrith the great escarpment plunges down to Llyn y Fan Fach, whose aura of mystery and romance has inspired many fables. Follow the eroded edge eastwards to the high point of Fan Brycheiniog, and then swing south over the broad scarp of Fan Hir.

Due east rises the Fforest Fawr hill of Fan Gyhirych, while to the west a desolate area of streams and hillocks culminates in the wild and deep valley of the Afon Twrch.

Descend through the farm at Dderi to meet the A4067 at the Tafarn-y-Garreg inn.

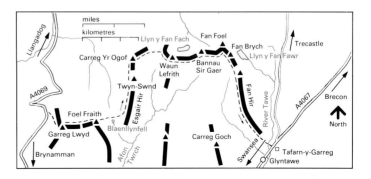

PEMBROKE: ST DAVID'S HEAD TO ST NON'S BAY

Map *OS Sheet 157*   **Start/Finish** *St David's (752252)*   **Distance/Time** *12 miles/19km, 5 hrs*

> **Grading** *An easy walk over heathland and along an indented coastline.*
> **Escape Routes** *Numerous.*
> **Transport** *Railway stations at Fishguard and Haverfordwest. Bus services: Fishguard/St. David's; Haverfordwest/St. David's.*
> **Accommodation** *Hotels and B & B in St. David's. Youth Hostels at St. David's, Trevine and Broad Haven.*

From Orkney, Cape Wrath and Slieve League to Exmoor, the Gower and Land's End we have thrilled to the traverse of switchback coastal paths, while the sea has boomed below towering cliffs sending columns of spray skyward. But here, in contrast, I describe a circular walk from St David's which ambles you across sandy bays and explores coves and prehistoric sites in the most pastoral of settings, where cultivated fields and country lanes run down to the shoreline.

St David's is the smallest city in Britain. The saint is thought to have been born at nearby St Non's and he built his first church in AD550. The present cathedral dates from the late twelfth century and is the largest church in Wales.

Take the road north from St David's and,

skirting the hill of Carnllidi, make for St David's Head, the westernmost point in Wales. The cliffs on the north side of the Head are gabbro and have become an important climbing ground. Almost on the tip of the headland you pass an earthwork, within which can be seen several stone circles and rock shelters, the remains of an Iron Age fort. Out to sea the waves cream over the rocks of Carreg-trai, North Bishop, Carreg Rhoson, Daufraich and South Bishop which carries a lighthouse.

Cross Porthmelgan cove and then stride out across the broad expanse of Whitesand Bay, one of the best surfing beaches in Wales. Continue hugging the coast around Pencarnan peninsula to Porthstinian, site of the ruined sixteenth-century chapel of St Justinian and also of a modern Lifeboat Station. Boats may be hired here to visit Ramsey Island, one mile away across the Sound, once the home of hermits but now a National Nature Reserve, a bird sanctuary and a breeding ground for Atlantic grey seals.

Easy going over turf and heather leads to Porthtaflod, the northern outpost of St Bride's Bay. Again, offshore islets, caves, inlets, coves and prehistoric remains abound. The whole of

the fascinating coastline, described in this chapter, is owned by the National Trust and you can explore at will.

At St Non's Bay a chapel has been built to commemorate St David's birth. Nearby, is the Holy Well of St Non which, according to tradition, sprang up during a storm on the night that St David was born.

A narrow lane brings you back shortly to the city of St David.

THE PRESELY HILLS

Map OS Sheet 145   *Start/Finish* Newport (058390)/Crymmych (183338)   *Distance/Time* 21 miles/34km, 8-9 hrs

Grading A long but easy walk across gently rolling hills.
Escape Routes Numerous. The B4329 from Eglwyswrw to Haverfordwest conveniently divides the route into two sections.
Transport Railway station at Fishguard. Bus services: Fishguard/Newport; Crymmych/Cardigan/Newport (infrequent).
Accommodation Hotel: the Crymmych Arms. Hotels and B & B in Newport. Youth Hostels at Pwll Deri and Trevine.

Even at the height of summer, when holidaymakers throng to every strand and cove along the Welsh coast, you will find utter peace and tranquillity in the Presely Hills. You can walk all day over these spacious uplands clothed in bracken and heather, and you can delight in the clusters of lichen-encrusted rocks, ancient standing stones, cromlechs and prehistoric hill forts. A trackway, over 5,000 years old, runs along the main Presely ridge and, when mist cloaks the hills, it is easy to imagine meeting the legendary, magical wild boar, Twrch Trwyth.

The Presely Hills are open to the salt sea air and their atmosphere is uplifting to the spirits. A brisk walk along the prehistoric trackway, when a stiff breeze is driving white clouds across a wide blue sky, is a tonic which cannot be bettered in Wales.

The recommended route starts from the coastal town of Newport, and traverses the high spine of the Presely range for 21 miles to the easternmost outlier of Freni-fawr. If transport cannot be arranged, it is possible to return to Newport by bus at the end of the day.

A lane runs south from Newport, leading to the rough slopes of Mynydd Carningli which is topped with a collection of boulders and a ruined Iron Age fort.

Descend to the lush, wooded valley of the Gwaun river at Llannerch, and then climb steep slopes to Foeleryr on the main ridge. Heading east you pass the boundary of the

Pantmaenog Forest and then detour south to Foel-cwmcerwyn, at 1,760ft/536m, the highest point in Presely. On a clear day the views extend from the Wicklow Mountains in Eire to the Lleyn Peninsula, Bardsey Island, Snowdon, Cadair Idris and Plynlimon.

Returning to the ancient trackway along the main ridge, continue east to Foelfeddau, Carnbica, Carnmenyn and the massive ramparts of Foeldrygarn hill fort. This broad ridge is sprinkled with standing stones and littered with massive boulders; the rock is spotted dolerite, or bluestone, and it was the hill of Carnmenyn that supplied Stonehenge. It is thought that the stones were dragged to Milford Haven, floated on rafts up the river Avon, and thence moved on rollers to Salisbury Plain.

This long expedition can conveniently be terminated at the village of Crymmych, but it is well worth walking the extra mile to visit the collection of tumuli on Freni-fawr, and thereby complete the ridge.

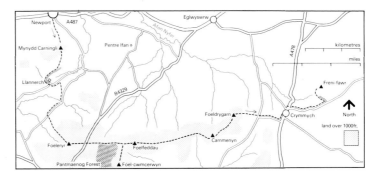

PEMBROKE: STACKPOLE QUAY TO FRESHWATER WEST

Map OS Sheet 158   *Start/Finish* Stackpole Quay (993958)/Freshwater West (885995)
Distance/Time 12 miles/19km, 6 hrs

> *Grading* An easy walk along level cliff-top paths
> giving dramatic views of natural limestone features.
> *Escape Routes* To Pembroke from Stack Rocks or
> Bosherston.
> *Transport* Railway stations at Lamphey and
> Pembroke. Bus service: Pembroke/Bosherston/
> Castle Martin (Tues and Fri only).
> *Accommodation* Hotels and B & B at Pembroke,
> Bosherston, Freshwater East and Lamphey. Youth
> Hostel at Manorbier (Shrinkle Haven).

From the Ordovician gabbro of St David's Head we arrive at the Carboniferous limestone of South Pembrokeshire. At once we meet 150ft limestone cliffs, worn into headlands, arches, stacks and blowholes, while the thick turf of the cliff-tops is decorated with as colourful a collection of flowers as can be found on the chalk cliffs of the Seven Sisters.

There are times on this walk when you could imagine you are on the Gower Peninsula, but the military presence is a constant distraction. Red flags and barbed-wire make a poor foreground to white limestone and a bottle-green sea.

From the car-park at Stackpole Quay walk to the tiny harbour, which is said to be the smallest in Britain, and then take the path towards Stackpole Head. You pass two notable blowholes and can descend natural steps to the golden sands of Barafundle Bay, where the bathing is safe.

The cliffs of Stackpole Head provide wonderful rock climbs, and there is a natural arch right at the tip of the Head through which the seas pour. Fulmars are fast taking over nesting sites from kittiwakes, guillemots and razorbills.

The next section of the walk, to Broad Haven, runs over springy turf on the edge of cliffs which plunge straight down into the sea. Broad Haven offers another expanse of firm sand, backed by dunes and marram grass. Behind the dunes lie a group of lily ponds which are the haunt of herons and kingfishers. Traces of an Iron Age camp can be discerned on the lakeside.

A line of markers guides the path round to St Govan's Chapel, and the Ministry of Defence have permitted walkers to detour to visit the Coastguard Station on St Govan's Head. On a clear day you can see across the Bristol Channel to Lundy Island and the Devon coast.

St Govan's Chapel is a minute, primitive building situated between two cliffs at the bottom of a flight of stone steps. The present chapel dates from the thirteenth century.

The path now rounds two extraordinary ravines, Stennis Ford and Huntsman's Leap, before embarking on an enthralling stretch of coastline. Arches, stacks, inlets and ancient forts come thick and fast, including the Cauldron, a blowhole of cathedral-like proportions.

Sadly, unless the MOD relents, the twin Elegug Stacks mark the point where the path turns inland, not meeting the coast again until Freshwater West.

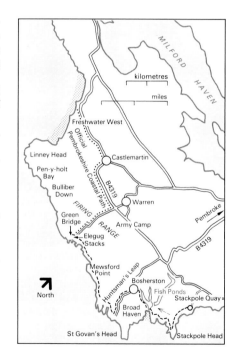

THE GOWER PENINSULA

Map *OS Sheet 159*   **Start/Finish** *Mumbles Head (629874)/Rhossili (416881)*   **Distance/Time** *21 miles/34km, 8-9 hrs*

> **Grading** *A long and fascinating walk along cliff-tops and across bays of firm sand.*
> **Escape Routes** *Numerous.*
> **Transport** *Railway station at Swansea. Bus services: Swansea/The Mumbles; Swansea/ Rhossili.*
> **Accommodation** *Hotels and B & B at The Mumbles and Rhossili. Youth Hostel at Port Eynon.*

Mumbles Head looks north across the arc of Swansea Bay to the gigantic industrial complexes at Port Talbot, but if you climb to the top of the hill and gaze west you are greeted by a different world. As far as the eye can see, stretches a wild and rugged coastline of white limestone cliffs, headlands, reefs, coves, inlets, blowholes and sandy bays. The superb Carboniferous limestone was laid down in warm seas over a period of a hundred million years, but later movements of the earth's crust buckled and folded the rock, thrusting it up into the ridge of Cefn Bryn, which overlooks the coastline of the Gower peninsula.

Springy turf grows along the top of the cliffs but tangled brambles, gorse and bracken are encroaching. The flora is outstanding with over a hundred flowering species being recorded, including the yellow whitlow-grass which grows in no other place in Britain.

In summer the sandy bays and coves are teeming with holiday-makers, but choose a sharp day in winter or early spring and you will have this magnificent coastline to yourself.

Take the narrow path which runs through gorse bushes under Rams Tor and descends to the beach at Langland Bay. Except at high tide you can walk across Langland Bay, Caswell Bay and Brandy Cove, skipping through lines of white surf as they race in over the firm sand.

Scramble up to Pwlldu Head, the highest headland in Gower, and follow the cliffs to Shire Combe Point, another of Gower's extravagant viewpoints. Prows of white limestone run out onto the sands of Threecliff Bay while, beyond the 200ft-high Great Tor, Oxwich Bay curves westwards as a two-mile-long sweep of glistening sand.

At low tide you can walk straight across the sand, scattering the oyster catchers, to the tiny thirteenth-century church of St Illtyd on Oxwich Point.

The tortured and twisted cliffs run on for five miles, to the tidal island of Worms Head, jutting out from the mainland like a hump-backed sea-serpent. In a strong breeze, with a wild sea pounding the base of the cliffs and sending plumes of spray into a blue sky, there is no finer coastal walk in Britain.

Climb to Tears Point above Mewslade Bay and, before turning inland for Rhossili, gaze back once again towards Port-Eynon Point to imprint a lasting memory of that remarkable coastline.

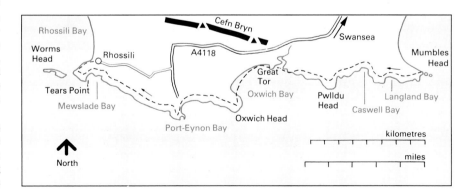

THE AGHLA – ERRIGAL HORSESHOE

Map OS 1:126,720 Sheet 1   **Start/Finish** Tullaghobegly river bridge (935260)   **Distance/Time** 12 miles/19km, 5-6 hrs

> **Grading** A straightforward mountain walk. Errigal has a fine, sharp summit ridge.
> **Escape Routes** Carefully descend S to the Creeslough–Bunbeg road from anywhere on the horseshoe.
> **Transport** Railway station at Derry. Bus services: Dublin/Letterkenny; Derry/Letterkenny/Falcarragh.
> **Accommodation** Hotels and B & B at Falcarragh and Bunbeg. Youth Hostel at Dunlewy.

The gleaming cone of Errigal throws down wide fans of frost-shattered quartzite in every direction. When the sun emerges after a heavy shower Errigal sparkles like snow and, in this respect, resembles Beinn Eighe or Conival.

On a windy day, when the islands of Inishfree Bay are ringed with surf, and the long ridge of the stark, rocky Derryveagh Mountains are outlined against a stormy sky, Errigal makes as invigorating and rewarding an ascent as any peak in Ireland.

The tourist route up Errigal climbs the broad south-east ridge from near Dunlewy Lough but, by approaching from the north, you can include Errigal and the shapely outliers of Aghla More and Beg in an extended horseshoe of Altan Lough.

Easy access is gained to the western slopes of Aghla Beg from the roadside near the northern outflow of Altan Lough. A simple walk over heather and screes leads to the cairn and a view down to a tiny, circular lake, Lough Nabrackbaddy, set high in the coum.

The Aghla hills themselves form a mini-horseshoe, for a broad and rather peat-hagged ridge leads round the rim of Lough Feeane and over a subsidiary summit to the higher Aghla More. Away to the north-east rises Muckish, a slumbering quartzite whale-back, beyond which you can glimpse Sheep Haven and the rocky promontory of Horn Head.

Drop down the steep, grassy slopes southwards from Aghla More to the head of Altan Lough, enjoying an unsurpassed view across the glen of the exposed granite outcrops on Dooish.

The outliers, Beaghy and Mackoght, guard the main cone of Errigal and they provide an enticing foretaste of what is to come. The hills and coastline of North Donegal spread out below but, once again, it will be the neighbouring Derryveagh Mountains that impress. You can look right down the Poisoned Glen of Slieve Snaght, on whose crags much early pioneering rock climbing took place.

Having passed the Glover Memorial Cairn the ridge gradually narrows and steepens and, if you keep strictly to the crest, you will have to clamber over pinnacles and blocks. The twin summits, 2,466ft/751m, are sharp and exposed and connected by a 25m-long razor-ridge.

With great care descend the north ridge, which remains very thin and airy as it overlooks Altan Lough, until it gives way to heather and screes and finally runs out onto grass.

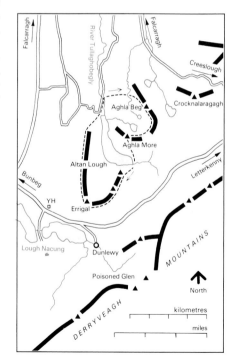

THE SPERRIN SKYWAY

Map OSNI Sheet 13 also OS 1:126,720 Sheet 13 **Start/Finish** Goles Forest (679943)/South end of Butterlope Glen (490955) **Distance/Time** 18 miles/29km, 9 hrs

> **Grading** An easy mountain walk along a series of broad and undulating summits.
> **Escape Routes** S to the Glenelly Valley by roads through the Sawel and Dart passes.
> **Transport** No public transport through Glenelly. Bus service: Omagh/Plumbridge.
> **Accommodation** B & B at Cranagh. Youth Hostel at Gortin.

The rounded, rolling Sperrin hills dominate northern Tyrone. For nearly twenty miles, between Draperstown and Plumbridge, their peat-hagged and eroded summits look down south to the sinuous Glenelly River, and west to the green water-meadows of the Foyle valley. In addition the hills command outstanding views further afield, from the Mournes to Donegal, and Sperrin Skyway is a most apt name for this walk across the roof of Ulster.

Although five summits in the Sperrins exceed 2,000ft in height, I must emphasise that these hills possess few, if any, of the rugged, rocky features which abound elsewhere in this book. The walker must be content with the considerable physical challenge of the traverse, combined with the almost guaranteed solitude to be found on these trackless fells.

From Goles Outdoor Centre on the B47

climb up alongside a forestry plantation to Mullaghsallagh, an outlying top on the southeast limb of the main Sperrins ridge. As you follow a fence onto Oughtmore you experience your first taste of the notorious Sperrin peat-hags, although I suspect that Peak District bog-trotters, accustomed to Kinder and Bleaklow, would not be too impressed.

Look back south-east to the distant blue expanse of Lough Neagh, the largest lake in Britain and Ireland, and then head west over the blanket-bog to Mullaghaneany and Meenard Mountain. Even in thick mist you are unlikely to stray far on this section of the walk, because

a westerly bearing is bound to bring you to the unfenced road which crosses the hills at the Sawel Pass, and links Learmount with the Glenelly valley.

A fence is your guide as you ascend the better drained slopes of Sawel Mountain, to reach the trig. point marking the principal summit of the Sperrins at 2,240ft/682m. Looking west, on a clear day, you can see the fine peak of Errigal (described in chapter 184) and further south the rocky Bluestacks. This stirring vista remains throughout most of the day's walk.

Dart Mountain will be appreciated for its rocky outcrops, and then you descend again to the road over the Dart Pass, which would make a convenient *rendez-vous* for a support party.

More peaty ground must be tackled before you gain the second highest point of the day on Mullaghclogha, and a final heave will take you over the rock bluffs on Mullaghcarbatagh and down over grassy slopes, skirting forestry, to Butterlope.

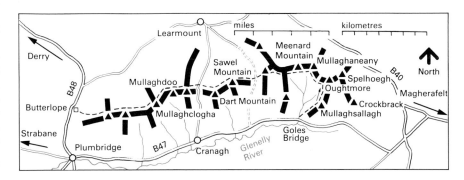

SLIEVE LEAGUE AND THE DONEGAL COAST

Map *OS 1:126,720 Sheet 3* **Start/Finish** *Bunglass car-park (560740)/Maghera (660908)*
Distance/Time *27 miles/43km, 14 hrs*

> **Grading** *A long walk along a magnificently wild and rugged coastline. Some exposed scrambling on the crest of Slieve League, but this can be avoided.*
> **Escape Routes** *Roads are met at Malin Bay, Glen Bay and Port.*
> **Transport** *Bus service: Donegal/Carrick/Glencolumbkille. No public transport to Maghera but connections at Ardara (5 miles).*
> **Accommodation** *Hotels and B & B at Carrick and Glencolumbkille. Youth Hostel at Carrick. Private hostel (Dooey) at Glencolumbkille.*

I have written enthusiastically about many exciting coastal walks but, for sheer scale of cliff and offshore scenery, combined with exposure to the full force of the Atlantic Ocean, Slieve League is unrivalled.

From inland Slieve League appears undistinguished, but on the west side the relentless pounding and sucking of the Atlantic have undermined the mountain, causing vast slabs of quartzite to peel away from the cliffs. The entire west coast of Ireland is being slowly eaten away, but nowhere is the effect more dramatic than in south Donegal.

For over two miles Slieve League throws down precipitous slopes, the maximum height being 1,972ft/601m, while to the north the rugged, indented coastline continues for a further twenty miles until the broad sands of Maghera are reached. This is a coast of islets, jagged rocks, stacks, skerries, bays, cliffs and promontories; the same coast upon which many ships of the Spanish Armada were dashed in 1588.

From Teelin drive along a narrow lane, between hedges of fuchsia, wild roses and honeysuckle, to the car-park at Bunglass. Start climbing up the ridge of Slieve League, which narrows to an exposed rocky arête called One Man's Pass; this can be by-passed to the east.

Descending west you follow the cliff edge to Trá Bán, an exquisite horseshoe bay of firm white sand ringed by sharp rock teeth, towering buttresses and arches. Walk round Malin Bay and seek accommodation at Glencolumbkille, before launching out on the second stage of the expedition.

The first objective of the second day is the massive Martello Tower on Glen Head, built above 800ft cliffs. Next comes the razor-sharp headland of Sturrall, marking the beginning of a stretch of coastline that (barring St Kilda) exhibits rock architecture unequalled in these islands. Impossibly steep fangs of rock rear out of the sea, and the islets of Toralaydan and Tormore have their green turf guarded by a ring of vertical cliffs. In bad weather white horses and thundering waves surge over the wicked black rocks, sending columns of spray high into the air.

Nowadays Port Harbour is deserted, and you must climb again to the top of 800ft cliffs before descending to Glenlough. Traverse slopes of heather and dwarf juniper round the north shoulder of Slieve Tooey, which overlooks Gull Island. Finally, an exposed sheep track runs above cliffs leading to the sand-dunes at Maghera.

THE MOURNE WALL WALK

Map OS 1:126,720 Sheet 9 – South Down also 1:63,360 Sheet 9 – Mourne Mountains   *Start/Finish* Dunnywater Bridge (354222)   *Distance/Time* 20 miles/32km, 8-9 hrs

Grading A long but fairly simple mountain walk with no navigational problems.
Escape Routes To the Hilltown–Kilkeel road from cols on the W Mourne ridge. From Hare's Gap N to Slievenaman and S to Silent Valley.
Transport Bus service: Belfast/Newcastle. Dismount at Annalong, 2 miles from Dunnywater Bridge.
Accommodation Hotels and B & B in Newcastle. Youth Hostels at Newcastle, Kinnahalla and Slievenaman. I.M.C. Cottage, The Bloat House, Annalong Valley.

It is astonishing to find a replica Great Wall of China stretching over the switchback ridges of the Mourne Mountains in County Down. In reality this dry-stone wall was built in the 1920s to enclose the water-catchment areas of the Silent Valley and the Annalong river. The labour-intensive project helped to relieve the fearful unemployment of that time.

Uniquely, walkers can enjoy a twenty-mile mountain traverse, including the ascent of nine summits over 2,000ft, in the extremely attractive granite Mourne Mountains without ever having to face navigation problems. The main ridge of the Mournes form an 'E' shape and all the summits, save one on the centre prong, are covered by this expedition. The YHA of Northern Ireland organise a competitive walk over the Mourne Wall course every year on the Sunday following Spring Bank Holiday, so be warned!

The Mournes are divided into east and west groups by the Hilltown to Kilkeel road; the west group of hills are mere grassy uplands and do not concern us, but the east group are pronounced and heather-covered with outcrops of bare granite, often in the form of tors, emerging from the ridges in several places. On the east side the slopes of Slieve Commedagh and Slieve Donard drop quite steeply into the Irish Sea, as indeed we are told in the haunting song, 'The Mountains of Mourne Sweep Down to the Sea'.

The circular walk starts and finishes at Dunnywater Bridge, and straight away you are confronted with an extremely rough and tiresome up-and-over ascent of Slieve Binnian. However, having rounded the Silent Valley reservoir, you meet the Wall on Slievenaglogh and easy walking follows over the grassy Slieve Muck and Carn Mountain.

The Wall now takes a sinuous, roller-coaster course over Slieve Meelbeg and the craggy Slieve Bearnagh before the low col of Hare's Gap is reached.

Another steep climb follows to gain Slieve Commedagh and Slieve Donard on the east ridge, the latter, at 2,796ft/852m being the highest mountain in the Mournes. The OS pillar is perched on top of a massive granite obelisk.

As you descend south over Rocky Mountain to the Annalong Valley and Dunnywater Bridge, you can avoid the rough ground by walking along the granite slabs built into the top of the Wall itself, a further use for this extraordinary man-made feature.

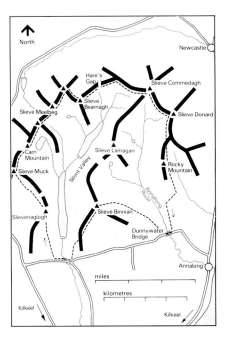

THE BENBULBIN GROUP

Map OS 1:126,720 Sheet 7   **Start/Finish** Car-park by Glencar Waterfall (761435)
Distance/Time 15 miles/24km, 6-7 hrs

Grading A long but simple mountain walk.
Good route finding is needed in misty conditions.
Escape Routes From Benbulbin descend S from
ref. 690450 or NE from ref. 700450. From
Truskmore descend TV Station access road
to Gleniff.
Transport Railway station at Sligo. Bus service:
Sligo/Glencar Lake/Cluainin.
Accommodation Hotels in Sligo. B & B locally.
Youth Hostel at Garrison.

Many of my favourite expeditions are over limestone hills. The rich springy turf, excellent drainage, water-worn features, variety of flowers and butterflies and the dazzling reflected light from the exposed outcrops put me in a benign and receptive mood.

Here, in County Sligo, we walk round the edge of a high plateau, bordered by a magnificent escarpment of white, Carboniferous limestone. The importance of the underlying rock, in determining the character of a mountain region, could not be better exemplified than by comparing the lush scenery of Benbulbin with the harsh quartzite screes of Errigal to the north, and with the acid peathags of the Nephins to the west.

From the car-park at Glencar Lake take the rough Bog Road, which climbs up through woodlands and between crags to the terrace running west above the cliffs of Tormore. Looking south, beyond the lake, the bare limestone wedge of the Castel Gal ridge fills the view; a half-day's walk for another occasion perhaps.

Where the escarpment has been breached by King's Gully (a useful escape route from the plateau), you should head north to King's Mountain and make a gradual ascent to Benbulbin. This amazing knuckle, which thrusts boldly north-west from the plateau, is sheer on three sides and extreme care should be taken in mist or high wind. Needless to say Benbulbin provides a bird's-eye view down to Sligo Bay and Inishmurray Island.

Turning eastwards, skirt the top of the Gortlaneck valley which bites deeply into the plateau and, if time allows, visit the absurd fang of Benwhiskin. Seen from the north, this graceful spire soars irresistibly into the sky making it one of Ireland's most notable physical features.

East of the Benwhiskin promontory you walk round the cliffs above the Gleniff valley, site of the legendary cave of Diarmaid and Grainne from which you can gain access to three more vast caverns.

On the plateau, set back from the cliff-edge, are relics of obsolete barytes mines, including some open shafts and an old ropeway used to carry the mineral down to Glencar Lake.

Heading north-east to Truskmore you meet the road running up to the TV station on the highest point of the day's walk at 2,120ft/646m.

Easy slopes run down southwards from Truskmore to the Bog Road and Glencar Lake.

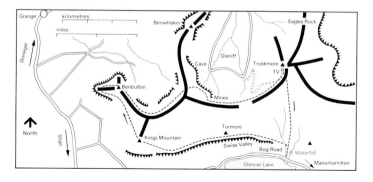

THE NEPHIN RIDGE WALK

Map OS 1:126,720 Sheet 6   **Start/Finish** The roadside S of Bangor (808203)/Mullaranny (802907)
Distance/Time 20 miles/32km, 10-12 hrs

Grading A long and arduous day's walk, only
recommended during the summer months.
Escape Routes From the col between Nephin Beg
and Glennamong, descend SE along a path to
Srahmore Lodge.
Transport Bus services: Castlebar/Bangor/Belmullet;
Castlebar/Mullaranny/Dooega.
Accommodation Hotels at Castlebar. B & B at
Bangor and Mullaranny. Youth Hostels at Mweewillin,
Pollatomish and Lough Feeagh.

Modern man has made little obvious impression on the wild, mountainous country of North Mayo. Some forestry cloaks the lower slopes, and the huge power station at Bellacorick belches smoke and steam, but closer inspection of the glens reveals traces of former occupation: ruined dwellings, acres of black, oozing bog where peat has been cut, and the bare skeletons of roots of trees, felled by early man.

The Nephin Beg range of mountains form an inverted 'Y' which is not conducive to complete coverage by the hill walker, unless he is prepared to back-track. But the western hills form the most continuous chain, with the minimum of height loss, and this route has been chosen here. In addition, these hills overlook the island-studded coastline of Co. Mayo and, being situated on a peninsula, provide expansive views to the north and south.

Once you have crossed the boggy, hag-ridden lower slopes of the Nephins you can enjoy a long day's walk over a variety of mountainous terrain: broad airy ridges, deep coums, lonely lakes and rocky outcrops. The head waters of the Owenduff River penetrate into every west-facing glen and coum producing slopes which descend abruptly to the coastal plain. Thus the walker is ever conscious of the close presence of the sea, while the hills make maximum use of their 2,000ft elevation.

This is a demanding expedition over track-less and remote hills, but the less determined can cut it short by descending from the low col, south of Nephin Beg, to a minor road at Srahmore Lodge.

From the T58 just west of Bangor, cross the Owenmore River and make for the col east of Knocklettercuss. This provides a quick, though boggy, route onto Maumykelly at the north end of the Nephin ridge.

Walk south to Slieve Cor, the highest of the day's summits at 2,369ft/722m, which gives wonderful views south to Slievemore and Croaghaun on Achill Island, and down the eastern escarpment to the tiny lake of Adana-

cleveen. From Corslieve descend steeply to Scardaun Lough and toil up the slopes ahead to Nephin Beg, 2,065ft/629m.

After another energy-sapping col has been negotiated you can enjoy the rockier peaks which ring Glennamong to the west, and also provide views of Croagh Patrick, the Pilgrims' Mountain.

Continue south-west to Claggan Mountain, overlooking Newport Bay and its myriad islets, and descend easy, grassy slopes into Mullaranny.

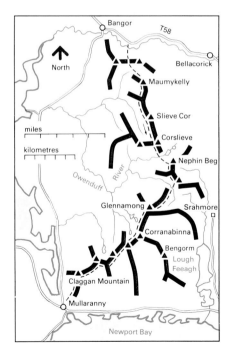

MWEELREA

> **Grading** *A magnificent mountain traverse. Mostly straightforward but rather steep on the descent from Mweelrea.*
> **Escape Routes** *From Pt. 2616ft descend SE ridge to the Owennaglogh Valley. From Mweelrea's summit descend W to the shore.*
> **Transport** *Railway stations at Westport and Galway. Bus service: Galway/Leenaun.*
> **Accommodation** *Hotel and B & B at Leenaun. Youth Hostel at Gubbadanbo (S shore of Killary Harbour).*

The ascent of Mweelrea is only a modest expedition, but the situation of this beautiful mountain, combined with its height, complexity and wealth of classical glaciated features, makes it one of the best loved in the west of Ireland.

Killary Harbour runs, fjord-like, nine miles into the mountains of Connemara, and Mweelrea stands proud on the northern slopes. Its 2,688ft/819m make it the highest mountain in Connacht. Thus Mweelrea not only looks over the Twelve Bens, Maum Turks, Sheeffry Hills and Croagh Patrick, but it also commands a wide sweep of Atlantic Ocean, with mountainous Inishturk and Clare Island dominant.

The flat, glacier-smoothed plateau of Mweelrea extends two arms to the east; these enclose the Owennaglogh valley and river which rises at two tiny lakes set in shallow coums. This chapter describes a horseshoe walk along the skyline ridge surrounding the Owennaglogh valley, which would match many of Scotland's wildest corries. Acres of grey rock fall from the high tops into the corrie, hence the name Mweelrea – Bald Grey Mountain – and care needs to be taken when attempting the traverse in bad conditions.

Start from Delphi on the south side of Doo Lough, ford the Bundorragha River and immediately begin the long haul to Ben Lugmore (Point 2,616ft), the first hill on the north side of the horseshoe.

The slopes are rough and rocky but the ridge is broad and, from its upper reaches, you can look north down 2,000ft sheer cliffs to the perfect U-shaped valley holding Doo Lough.

Descend scree slopes on the east side of Ben Lugmore to the col under Ben Bury, the ascent of which may be avoided by contouring to the south.

Easy, grassy slopes now lead to the flat top of Mweelrea, where you should pause for lunch and to admire the astonishing view. From your lonely perch it is strange to look down to Croagh Patrick and its teeming hordes, for it is

Ireland's most popular mountain and every year many thousands of pilgrims climb the rough path, to pay homage at the chapel built on its 2,510ft/765m summit.

A steep descent southwards, keeping to the edge of the great cliffs overlooking the Owennaglogh valley, brings you to a subsidiary peak, Point 1,623ft, and a low saddle. You can now either descend easily to the Owennaglogh river or surmount the final nail in the horseshoe to reach the road north of Bundorragha.

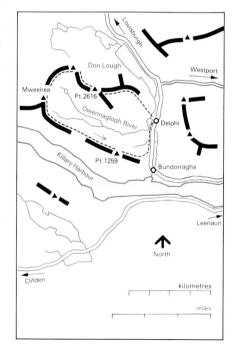

THE GLENCOAGHAN HORSESHOE OF THE TWELVE BENS

Map *OS 1:126,720 Sheet 10* **Start/Finish** *Benlettery Youth Hostel (771482)* **Distance/Time** *11 miles/18km, 7 hrs*

> *Grading A magnificent mountain walk over mainly rocky ridges. Not suitable for the inexperienced walker.*
> *Escape Routes From Maumina or Maumnageeragh descend easily down Glencoaghan.*
> *Transport Railway station at Galway. Bus service: Galway/Benlettery/Clifden.*
> *Accommodation Hotels and B & B in Ballynahinch, Kylemore, Galway and Clifden. Youth Hostels at Benlettery and Killary.*

The splendidly convoluted range of bare, quartzite mountains in western Connemara complements the wild, indented, Atlantic-buffeted coastline and makes this one of Ireland's grandest regions. Known locally as the Twelve Bens of Connemara (although few will agree on which twelve peaks should be so named), the mountains are arranged in spoke-like ridges making their complete collection in a single day a daunting task.

However, the round of Glencoaghan, which runs far into the mountains from the south, involves the traverse of at least six of the principal Bens radiating from Maumina col at the hub of the wheel. Joss Lynam, who has known Connemara for fifty years, recommends the Glencoaghan Horseshoe as the best day's introduction to the range.

Although, by the standards of many hills in this book, the Twelve Bens are not very high, Benbaun taking the prize at 2,395ft/730m, they must not be underestimated. Angular quartzite blocks are the norm underfoot, and these can be greasy when wet. In many places small cliffs and outcrops must be negotiated, and in mist it is easy to wander along subsidiary spurs which end in crags or loose screes.

The Youth Hostel at Benlettery makes a convenient starting point. Heading north, slopes of saturated bog eventually give way to heather and boulders below Benlettery's summit. Amazing views now unfold of chunky hills revealing acres of glacier-scoured rock, a scene only rivalled by the Lewisian gneiss country of North-West Scotland. Looking south you can see across Galway Bay to the Aran Islands and the Burren.

Continuing clockwise around the horseshoe, the undulating ridge brings you to Bengower and then, following a particularly craggy and scree-ridden section, Benbreen. Several minor tops must now be crossed as you round the head of a wild corrie to the low col of Maumina. Energetic walkers may wish to detour north and climb the 1,000ft, loose, south ridge of Benbaun, a worthwhile exercise if only for the most commanding view in Connemara.

Returning to Maumina, the eastern arm of the horseshoe starts with an easy climb to Ben-collaghduff. From here you can get stirring views of the eastern flanks of Benbaun falling into Gleann Eidhneach, and the colossal Inagh Crag on Bencorr which gives the longest rock climbs in Ireland.

After a tiresome ascent to Bencorr the ridge meanders over broad Derryclare, on the south-eastern slopes of which you pick up a path to Ballynahinch Lake.

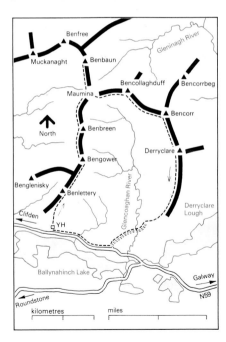

THE MAUM TURKS OF CONNEMARA

Map *OS 1:126,720 Sheet 10 and 1:63,360 Sheets 84 and 94*   **Start/Finish** *The pass 2 miles S of Maum Bridge (223179)/Leenane Hotel (997542)*   **Distance/Time** *15 miles/24km, 10-11 hrs*

> *Grading A long mountain traverse involving much ascent and descent. Much of the terrain is of rough, angular quartzite.*
> *Escape Routes Many of the cols provide easy ways down to lower ground on the E or W.*
> *Transport Railway station at Galway. Bus service: Westport/Leenane; Galway/Leenane; Galway/Maum Bridge/Clifden.*
> *Accommodation Hotels at Maum Bridge and Leenane. B & B locally. Bunkhouse at Maum. Youth Hostels at Ballinahinch and Killary Harbour.*

The Maum Turks are rocky hills of schists and quartzite, strung out in a long ridge which twists south from Killary Harbour to Maumwee Lough. Joss Lynam, guru of Irish mountaineering, reckons the scenery of pointed summits, bulging crags, stupendous coums and bare white rock to be as dramatic as anywhere in Ireland.

The Maum Turks traverse has become a test-piece of hill walking stamina, and a competitive event takes place over these hills each year in May. Although the distance is only fifteen miles, the terrain is so rough and demanding that ten hours should be allowed by the ordinary mortal; fell runners however have completed the course in five hours.

From Maum Bridge take the road running south towards Maumwee Lough and, from the highest point of the pass, climb the rocky slopes of Corcog (commonly known as Leckavrea).

The ridge now snakes over Shannakeala, a collection of tops which emerge from an eroded plateau, while rocky bluffs and small lakes abound. Descend to Maumeen Gap (pass of the birds) where a pilgrims' trail comes up from the valley to St Patrick's Well and a small chapel has been built on the site.

A steep ascent follows to Derryvoreada, which again has several summits, and then you climb to Binn idir an Da Log, at 2,307ft/703m the highest of the Maum Turks. This is a wonderful viewpoint for the Twelve Bens, Errisbeg, Cashel Hill, Mweelrea, Galway Bay, the Burren and the Aran Isles.

Another descent brings you to the pass, Mam Ochoige, and Lough Nahillion which lies under Knocknahillion. Weave your way through cliffs to climb this peak directly or contour round the north side to reach the plateau of Letterbreckaun.

Some tricky route-finding is now required. Go north-east, then north-west, then north, to locate the Maumturkmore Gap, a narrow defile running through the mountains. Another holy well, Tobar Feichin, lies just below the pass to the east.

A short climb again, and from here onwards the quartzite is left behind and the going becomes less rough. A wire fence can be followed across a featureless saddle before you climb 1,000ft to gain the last summit of the day; a nameless hill of spot height 562m. Continue north towards Killary Harbour until, at a tiny lake on the ridge, you descend straight to the Leenane Hotel.

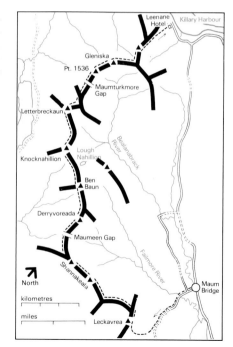

WICKLOW CHALLENGE: THE LUG WALK CLASSIC

Map OS 1:50,000 Sheet 56   **Start/Finish** Stone Cross (007203)/Seskin (907904)
Distance/Time 33 miles/53km, 12-14 hrs

> **Grading** An exceptionally long and tough marathon walk over high, mountainous terrain.
> **Escape Routes** Roads cross the line of the walk at Sally Gap and Wicklow Gap.
> **Transport** Bus services: Dublin/Stone Cross/Brittas; Dunlavin/Dublin; Baltinglass/Dublin.
> **Accommodation** B & B at Glendalough and Dunlavin. Youth Hostels at Ballinclea and Aghavannagh.

The foothills of the Wicklow Mountains run down to the suburbs of Dublin and the range stretches south for over twenty miles, culminating in Lughnaquilla, at 3,039ft/927m one of Ireland's seven Munros. The Wicklows are the largest mountain area in Ireland, and they can be seen from the Welsh hills on a clear day.

Several long-distance walks traverse the Wicklows, but none is better or more popular than the Lug Walk which, in a distance of 33 miles, succeeds in visiting most of the principal summits.

With frequent bad weather, inaccurate maps and a ridge that is often rounded and ill-defined, the Lug Walk can be a severe test of stamina and navigation. However the mountains are bisected by roads, at Sally Gap and Wicklow Gap, which divide the route into three distinct sections as well as providing

escape routes or convenient *rendez-vous* for support parties.

From Stone Cross, on L199 between Rathfarnham and Brittas, take the path which keeps left of the forestry plantation and leads to the OS pillar on Seahan. Now you have gained height the walking is open and easy and, with expansive views to enjoy, you can march happily over the heather and moor grass of Corrig and Seefingan towards the towering TV mast on Kippure.

The second section of the walk, south of Sally Gap, is more varied than the first: the summits are more defined and granite outcrops thrust up through the peat in several places. But, as you head south over Mullaghcleevaun and Tonelagee, the hillsides become wet and boggy with extensive areas of peat hags.

Down at the Wicklow Gap, Lough Nahanagan has been incorporated into a pumped water scheme by the Irish Electricity Board and pipes and access roads criss-cross the col.

Climb the stubby ridge west of the lough to gain the main east ridge of Table Mountain, and follow it round the head of Vale of Glendalough and Glenmalur to the summit itself. The slumbering giant of Lughnaquilla

now dominates the view south and this is easily ascended via the subsidiary hill of Camenabologne.

Although Lughnaquilla is mainly rounded the slopes fall away in broken escarpments on two sides. These coums are known as the North and South Prisons.

Follow a line of cairns west to Camarahill and descend easy slopes to the finish of the walk at Fenton's Pub in Seskin.

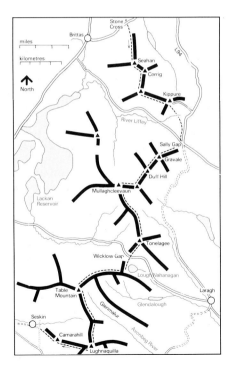

THE GALTY RIDGEWALK

Map *OS 1:126,720 Sheets 18 and 22*   **Start/Finish** *Baurnagurrahy (81522)/Caher (048250)*
Distance/Time *17 miles/27km, 7-8 hrs*

Grading A magnificent mountain walk along a high and, at times, narrow ridge. Straightforward under good conditions.
Escape Routes From Galtymore head N down steep slopes to the forest. From Galtybeg descend S to meet a turf cutter's track leading to the road.
Transport Railway stations at Waterford and Limerick Junction. Bus services: Waterford/Caher and Limerick/Caher (infrequent). No public transport to W end of ridge.
Accommodation Hotels and B & B at Caher, Glen of Aherlow and Tipperary. Youth Hostels at Ballydavid Wood and Mountain Lodge.

The Galty Mountains sit astride the boundary between Counties Limerick and Tipperary. This long ridge of gently swelling uplands is far removed, both in distance and character, from the Old Red Sandstone hills of Kerry, the bare quartzite ridges of Connemara or the limestone escarpments of Sligo.

Topographically, the Galtees are famous for supporting one of Ireland's seven coveted Munros, but hill walkers will also relish the opportunity of striding along seventeen miles of relatively isolated grassy ridge, running high above the pastoral Glen of Aherlow.

In the absence of satisfactory local transport, the best way of accomplishing this expedition is to obtain accommodation in Caher and proceed to the start at Baurnagurrahy by taxi. You can then traverse the Galty ridge from west to east, dropping down into Caher at the end of the day.

From Baurnagurrahy farm, follow the edge of a forestry plantation, which leads to the upper slopes of Temple Hill and a rocky spur just below the summit. You are now at a height of 2,579ft and, remarkably, you rarely drop much below this height throughout the day.

Descend to some old peat workings on the col under Lyracappul, climb to the summit and enjoy the feeling of space provided by the steep northern slopes which sweep down to Glen of Aherlow. A wall now guides you over Carrignabinnia and Slievecushnabinnia to the western slopes of Galtymore, whence you can peer over north-facing cliffs to Lough Curra.

Galtymore, 3,018ft/920m, carries a Celtic Cross and, in clear weather, views extend from the Shannon estuary in the north-west to the sea in the south.

Fast walking over these smooth, bare mountains continues as you wind your way eastwards, descending to a peat-hagged saddle under Galtybeg. Nestling below steep, north-facing crags is tiny Lough Diheen where, legend tells us, St Patrick banished a mischievous serpent.

To the north-east of Galtybeg another shallow coum holds Lough Borheen, above which the ridge divides. You must head due east, over the rock outcrops of O'Loughnan's Castle, to the plateau of Greenane overlooking Lough Muskry, the fourth lake of the day.

The Galty ridge now broadens and becomes less distinct. In general keep to the highest ground and make for Slieveanard, the eastern-most outlier which is afforested on its lower slopes. Select a convenient fire-break for your descent to the N24 just north of Caher.

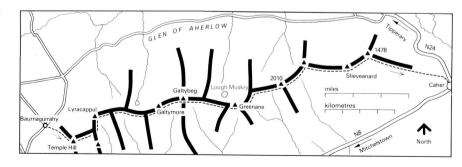

THE KNOCKMEALDOWN RIDGE WALK

Map OS 1:126,720 Sheet 22   **Start/Finish** Goat's Bridge (008104)   **Distance/Time** 14 miles/23km, 7 hrs

> **Grading** An easy mountain walk along broad heather-clad ridges.
> **Escape Routes** Descend W from Sugarloaf Hill to the L34 road at the Gap.
> **Transport** Railway station at Clonmel. Bus services: Clonmel/Clogheen/Cork; Clonmel/Newcastle/ Clogheen.
> **Accommodation** Hotels in Clonmel and Dungarvan. B & B locally. Youth Hostel at Lismore.

Many of the Irish walks chosen for this book involve long traverses of desolate, peaty hills. On the lower ground black bogs and marshlands tug at your boots, and you must become reconciled to wet feet early on in the day. Nevertheless, the rewards are commensurate: trackless hills, lonely summits, hidden coums and ruffled lakes.

In contrast the Knockmealdown Ridge, on the border of Co. Waterford and Co. Tipperary, gives firm going over dry, cropped heather. The underlying rock, which outcrops in places, is the same Old Red Sandstone which we have met on the mountains of Co. Kerry.

Seven hours should be allowed for this comparatively modest expedition, which should give you plenty of time to enjoy Knockmealdown's position between the Galtees to the north and the Comeragh/Monavullagh Mountains to the west. An organised walk over the Knockmealdowns is held annually in September.

From the car-park just south of Goat's Bridge follow a forest ride which is signposted to the Liam Lynch Monument. A tower in a clearing commemorates the spot where Lynch was shot by Irish Free State troops in 1923.

Climb up through the plantation to gain the summit of Crohan West, and continue south beside an old wall to Knockmeal. You must descend to a col right down at the treeline before climbing again to Knocknafallia, which overlooks the Cistercian monastery of Mount Mellary.

Turn north again now for the flattish hill of Knocknagnauv and then descend steeply, following the ditch which forms the county boundary, to the track running over the col between the west and east Knockmealdowns.

It is a steep climb up the eastern spur of Knockmealdown Mountain to the summit at 2,609ft/795m. A wide corrie, rimmed with broken crags, drops eastwards from the summit, greatly enhancing the feeling of spaciousness as you survey the scene below. The green, fertile plains of Lismore and the Blackwater River lie to the south while, further to the east, you can see the coast at Dungarvan Harbour.

Knockmoylan, or Point 2,521ft on the map, is a subsidiary top by-passed on the west side as you walk easily north to Sugarloaf Hill. This individual outlier overlooks The Gap, where a narrow motor road divides the Knockmealdowns from Knockshanahullion.

Retrace your steps south, climb Knockmoylan, and descend the long north-east ridge over Roche's Hill to Glengalla River and the forest near Goat's Bridge.

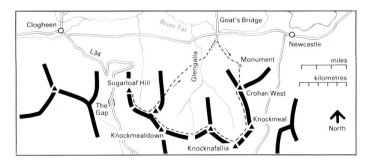

BRANDON MOUNTAIN

Map *OS 1:126,720 Sheet 12* **Start/Finish** *Faha (491125)/Ballybrack (420090)* **Distance/Time** *6 miles/10km, 4 hrs*

> **Grading** *A classic walk over a spectacular mountain giving expansive views over the Atlantic Ocean.*
> **Escape Routes** *None. The described route takes the easiest line. In difficulty simply turn back.*
> **Transport** *Bus service: Dingle/Cloghane/Tralee.*
> **Accommodation** *Hotels in Cloghane and Dingle. B & B locally. Independent hostel at Dingle but no Youth Hostel on the peninsula.*

Down at the tip of the Dingle Peninsula in Co. Kerry rises Brandon Mountain, 3,127ft/953m. Named after St Brendan, a fifth-century saint who meditated at the summit of mountains when he was not away on adventurous voyages, Brandon is the favourite peak of many lovers of our island hills, including the redoubtable Hamish Brown, doyen of hill walkers in Britain and Ireland.

The restless Atlantic pounds the northern slopes of Brandon giving it maximum status. After rain, streams course down the layered tiers of bare sandstone which support narrow ridges running out like tentacles from the summit pyramid. Vegetation, encouraged by the warm, wet climate, grows profusely over the lower, more broken, ground giving an overall impression of lush greenery.

Like Croagh Patrick, Brandon is a pilgrim's mountain and a pilgrimage to St Brendan's Oratory is held annually. Although many feet have established well-trodden paths over Brandon, the mountaineer can still find much of interest and challenge.

The Pilgrim's path starts from Faha, and it is waymarked with posts bearing the advice *Aire Cnoc Gear*, or Beware Dangerous Mountain. As you traverse round the coum the scenery becomes dramatic, steep rock walls descend to a string of tiny paternoster lakes draining into Lough Nalacken and, finally, Lough Cruttia.

At the head of the coum, under the precipitous, but tantalising, east ridge, the path winds tortuously upwards through boulders, slabs and scree to reach the cliff-top just 300ft north of Brandon's summit.

An alternative start to the Pilgrim's path is from the road running into the Owenmore Valley, two miles south of Cloghane. This route enters the great coum near Lough Cruttia and joins the Pilgrim's path from Faha at Lough Nalacken.

If you have time, and the weather is kind, walk north over the subsidiary top of Masatiompan to Brandon Head and gaze over the stupendous cliffs to the western horizon.

An easy descent can be made via the Saint's Road to Ballybrack on the west side of Brandon. The slopes are gentle and the path is well cairned.

Since transport difficulties may be experienced in returning from Ballybrack to Faha, mountaineers might consider a descent of the sharp east ridge of Brandon. This is loose and exposed and the negotiation of several rock steps involves mild rock climbing, but the confident mountaineer will relish the airy positions and absence of pilgrims and waymarks.

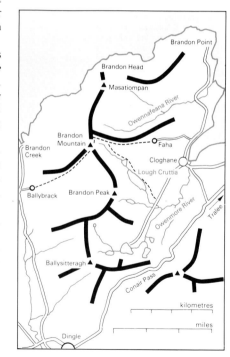

MACGILLICUDDY'S REEKS

Map OS 1:50,000 Sheet 78   **Start/Finish** Kate Kearney's Cottage (870878)/Lough Acoose (758850)
Distance/Time 11 miles/18km, 6-7 hrs

Grading A high mountain walk along a switchback and often rocky ridge.
Escape Routes N down Hag's Glen from the col SE of Carrauntoohill.
Transport Railway station at Killarney. Bus service: Killarney/Killorglin. Alight at Beaufort Bridge for Kate Kearney's Cottage.
Accommodation Hotels and B & B at Killarney and Killorglin. Youth Hostel at Gap of Dunloe.

South-west Ireland thrusts out long spits of mountainous country into the Atlantic Ocean. Thus the fjord-like inlets of Bantry Bay, Kenmare river and Dingle Bay divide the wild hill country of County Kerry into four peninsulas, each containing distinct ranges. With the close proximity of the turbulent sea, rocky ridges and severely weathered coums, many of the mountains resemble those of the Western Highlands of Scotland.

Macgillicuddy's Reeks, or 'The Reeks', are the best known mountains in Kerry; they rise west of Killarney and boast four of the seven separate Munros in Ireland, including Carrauntoohill, 3,414ft/1040m, Ireland's loftiest peak. The main backbone is Old Red Sandstone, running east to west and providing the hill walker with magnificent mountain and coastal views throughout the day.

A car may be left at the Information Centre at Kate Kearney's Cottage in the Gap of Dunloe, and rather tiresome peaty slopes ascended to the rounded ridge of the eastern Reeks. Beyond Cnoc an Bhraco you pass a strange gap in the ridge and then some airy scrambling over razor-sharp rocks and exposed towers provides excitement and brings you to the summit of Lackagarrin. You are now in the midst of wonderfully rugged mountain country and, as you clamber along the crest, you can look down steep coums on the north and south sides to Lough Googh and Lough Coomeenapeasta.

Descending Lackagarrin the true ridge over-hangs the northern precipices in places, and it is wise to contour round the south side to easier ground below Coomeenapeasta.

Beyond Coomeenapeasta the ridge broadens, and you can follow the edge of the north-facing coums over Knockacullion until it falls steeply to the pass linking Hag's Glen with Coomeenduff Glen. The descent of the Devil's Ladder from this col is a useful escape route to Hag's Glen.

Looking west you will be captivated by the great wall of mountains ahead: the mighty pyramid of Carrauntoohill, the unrelenting sweep of Caher and the stupendous east-facing coum of Beenkeragh, holding the tiny Lough Gourach. Carrauntoohill carries a cross and a visitor's book and it provides views right across Kerry to Brandon Mountain.

Leaving Beenkeragh for another day, descend steeply to the col under Caher and traverse its delightfully narrow ridge, which overlooks the depths of Coomloughra Glen. Walk easily down the north-west ridge, passing a minor top, to reach the road at Lough Acoose.

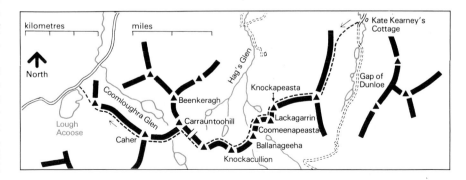

THE MANGERTON HORSESHOE

Map OS 1:50,000 Sheet 78 **Start/Finish** Road bridge near Tooreencormick Battle Field (984848)
Distance/Time 8 miles/13km, 4 hrs

Grading An easy walk over mainly grassy hills.
Escape Routes None. The line of the walk is the easiest way on and off the mountain.
Transport Railway station at Killarney (4 miles from start). Bus service: Dublin/Killarney; Cork/Killarney.
Accommodation Varied accommodation at Killarney. B & B locally. Youth Hostels at Gap of Dunloe and Aghadoe.

Macgillicuddy's Reeks feature prominently in the Irish section of this book. Not only is the traverse of the Reeks ridge (chapter 197) an expedition of the highest quality, but Carrauntoohill overlooks all that is celebrated in Irish mountaineering; the folded and weathered sandstone mountains of the south-west, rising in perfect harmony against a backcloth of wild ocean.

But many lesser mountains under the shadow of the Reeks give worthwhile expeditions in their own right. In this chapter we move a few miles east, to the legendary Mangerton Mountain which rises south of Lough Leane to a height of 2,756ft/840m.

From Killarney take the road towards Owgarriff Bridge, and turn right to the Tooreencormick Battle Field on the northern slopes of Mangerton.

The high pear-shaped corrie of the Devil's Punch Bowl lies ahead, and a broad track through the heather leads to the outflow of the corrie-lake on the west side of the mountain (Bachelor's Well). As you swing south-east, keeping to the lip of the corrie, the ground becomes rockier and the slopes fall away exceptionally steeply, running straight into the dark water like the Wast Water screes.

Leave the edge of the Devil's Punch Bowl at the highest point, and continue climbing for a short distance to reach the cairn on the rather eroded summit of Mangerton Mountain. A narrow ridge drops due north from Mangerton, dividing the Devil's Punch Bowl from a shapely, curved valley on the east side. This is Glenacappul (Horses Glenn), a deeply scoured, glaciated valley holding three beautiful lakes at stepwise intervals: Lough Garagarry at 869ft, Lough Managh at 1,080ft and Lough Erhogh at 1,414ft.

The extraordinary panorama of rugged peaks which unfolds on all sides is interspersed with fields, forests, lakes, islands and the sea at the Kenmare Estuary. A romantic and moving scene reminiscent of the Trossachs.

As you proceeed eastwards along the escarpment overlooking Glenacappul, do not attempt a descent to Lough Erhogh. If you wish to return along the bottom of the valley, via the three lakes, wait until you have reached the col under Stoompa, whence easier slopes run down towards Lough Managh.

Stoompa, 2,281ft/695m, has twin rocky summits and provides stirring views right into the heart of Mangerton, at the head of Glenacappul.

The north-west ridge of Stoompa descends easily to a bridge at the outlet of Lough Garagarry, one mile from your car.

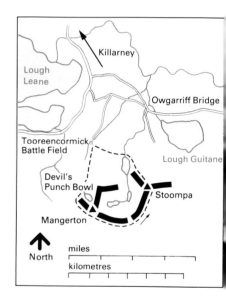

WEST OF THE REEKS: KNOCKNA-GANTEE AND MULLAGHANATTIN

Map OS 1:50,000 Sheet 78   **Start/Finish** Derriana Lough (629739)/Ballaghabeama Pass (752780)
Distance/Time 11 miles/18km, 6-7 hrs

> *Grading* A splendid mountain walk with plenty of rough going and route finding problems, especially if the mist is down.
> *Escape Routes* From Knocknagantee W down the ridge to the start. From the col before Beoun to the Lough Cloon road.
> *Transport* Railway station at Killarney which is also served with bus services to Dublin and Cork. No other public transport nearby. Taxi or car could be hired at Killarney.
> *Accommodation* Varied accommodation in Killarney and Killorglin. B & B locally. Youth Hostels at Gap of Dunloe and Aghadoe.

Many walkers stand on the summit of Carrauntoohill and other giants of Macgillicuddy's Reeks (chapter 197), and gaze west to Slieve Mish and Brandon Mountain or the Dingle peninsula. They may be intrigued, too, by the extremely rocky and rugged hills that rise much nearer, south of the Caragh River, culminating in Mullaghanattin, 2,539ft/773m, the highest peak west of the Reeks.

These mountains form a part of the long backbone of Old Red Sandstone which gives Kerry its unique features: the superbly rocky ridges of the Dingle, Iveragh and Beara peninsulas. There are no tracks on these hills and you must use your own judgment in selecting the most suitable route. Pitfalls abound, from treacherously steep grass and broken crags covered with moss and lichen, to sheer cliffs of exposed rock. In misty weather this wildest of regions should be left to experienced parties only.

Start the walk from the north end of Lough Derriana, at the end of the narrow road running into the hills from Waterville. Walk up Coomavoher, passing a string of five lakes as you climb higher up this magnificent valley, whose cirque-like walls close in with every step.

Scramble up the steep, bouldery slopes at the head of the corrie to reach a plateau, and then turn south to the summit of Knocknagantee which overlooks Eagle's Lough. Keep as far as possible to the highest ground as you continue east to Finnararagh; if you stray too far north you will meet the edge of the great amphitheatre of upper Cloon valley which contains Lough Reagh.

The setting of Lough Reagh is reminiscent of Coruisk for its grand rock scenery surrounding a lonely lake, indeed it was the first place in Kerry to attract the attention of rock climbers.

As you proceed north from Finnararagh the ridge narrows over the minor tops of Coomreagh and Coomnacronia, with umpteen rocky bluffs to be negotiated until the rounded and grassier Beoun, 2,468ft/752m, is reached.

Beoun stands proud above The Pocket, a perfect, rounded, east-facing corrie ringed with cliffs and almost enclosed, save for a narrow exit for the Blackwater River. Set back on the north side of The Pocket rises Mullaghanattin (Summit of the Gorse), which looks north along the entire length of the Reeks and east to Mangerton Mountain.

The north-east ridge can be descended easily to the Ballaghabeama Pass.

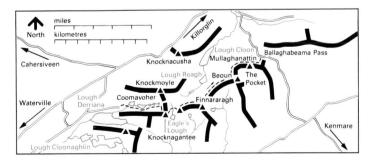

THE BEARA BORDER WALK

Map OS 1:126,720 Sheet 24 and 1:63,360 Sheets 191 and 192   **Start/Finish** Lauragh (775580)/At the tunnels of the Kenmare – Glengarriff road (901610)   **Distance/Time** 20 miles/32km, 8-9 hrs

Grading A long and exhilarating walk over rugged sandstone mountains.
Escape Routes Descend E from the Eskatarriff–Knocknagree col to Glenmore Glen and the Healy Pass.
Transport Bus services: Kenmare/Lauragh/Castletown; Kenmare/Glengarriff passes the finish.
Accommodation Hotels and B & B at Glengarriff, Lauragh and Kenmore. Youth Hostels at Letterdunane and Glanmore Lake.

Five of the Irish walks described in this book have been chosen from the extreme south-west corner, where fingers of mountainous country stretch out into the Atlantic. The Beara Peninsula is defined by Bantry Bay and the Kenmare River and it runs forty miles from Kenmare to Dursey Head. It is one of the thinnest of the south-west peninsulas as well as being the most mountainous thus, from Slieve Miskish and the Caha Mountains, you are never out of sight of the sea. Like the Reeks further north the spine of the hills is of rough, rich, red sandstone although, with the mild, wet climate, it is usually covered in vegetation.

The walk described here traverses the higher Caha Mountains on the east side of the Beara Peninsula keeping, for the most part, to the border between County Kerry and County Cork. In twenty miles of rugged mountain terrain the route is only once crossed by a road – at the halfway point of Healy Pass.

Park the car at Lauragh, tear yourself away from this charming village overlooking Kilmakilloge Bay, and push through dense undergrowth until you emerge onto bare slopes on the north-east ridge of Tooth Mountain. You now skirt round the head of the Drumminaboy River valley above a high coum, holding a tiny lake, known as The Pocket, to Eskatarriff.

After dropping to a low col south of Eskatarriff you round Glanmore Valley and climb steeply to Knocknagree. Another descent follows, but then you can climb to Hungry Hill, the highest point on the Beara Peninsula at 2,251ft/686m, to enjoy views down to Bear Island, over Sheep's Head to the grey Atlantic and away north to the Reeks and Brandon.

From Healy Pass northwards the hills become more barren and desolate. The main ridge twists and turns over Claddaghgarriff, Knock-owen and Cushnaficulla and, with the maps inaccurate, route-finding in mist could be a nightmare. In good visibility, though, it is hugely enjoyable to pick your way across the boulder-strewn summit with wild, crag-fringed coums dropping away beneath you or on all sides, and the sun shimmering on the myriad lakes filling every scoop and hollow.

From Caha take the well-defined north-east ridge over Killane which brings you to the tunnels on the N71 Kenmare to Glen Garriff road.

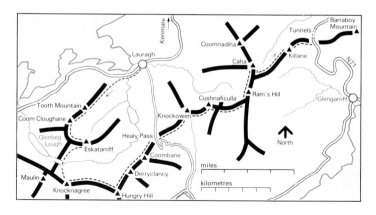

THE GREATEST CHALLENGE:
THE TRAVERSE OF THE CUILLIN RIDGE

Map OS 1:25,000 'The Cuillin and Torridon Hills'; SMT 1:15,000 'The Black Cuillin, Isle of Skye'. *Start/Finish* Glenbrittle House (411213) Sligachan Hotel (480298),
(Greater Traverse) finish at Loch Slapin (561216); *Distance/Time* 16 miles/26km, 17 hrs or 22 miles/35km, 22 hrs for Greater Traverse

Grading *Generally recognised to be the most difficult mountain traverse in Britain. Rock climbing ability to Very Difficult/Severe standard is a prerequisite.*
Escape Routes *It is not easy to escape from the Cuillin Ridge, particularly in mist. Tempting looking scree slopes often end in cliffs. However, easy descents can be found at Bealach a' Garbh-choire, Alasdair Stone Chute, An Stac Screes, Bealach Coire na Banachdich, Bealach na Glaic Moire, Bruach na Frithe N.W. ridge, Bealach nan Lice and the head of Coire a' Bhaster.*
Transport *Daily bus service: Kyleakin/Broadford/ Sligachan/Portree with connections to Fort William and Glasgow; Sligachan/Carbost/Glen Brittle (infrequent).*
Accommodation *Hotels at Broadford, Sligachan and Carbost. Youth Hostels at Broadford and Glen Brittle. Camping/caravan site at Glen Brittle. Climbing Huts: Glen Brittle (B.M.C./M.C. of S); Coruisk (Glasgow J.M.C.S.).*

Any hill walker or mountaineer, who succeeds in completing all the challenging walks described in this book, will have enjoyed 200 of the most magnificently varied routes which Britain and Ireland can offer. I suspect that he or she will rate the Bha Bheinn–Clach Glas traverse in Skye the most technical mountain route, followed closely by the three expeditions that sample sections of the Black Cuillin ridge.

But what about the complete traverse of the Cuillin ridge itself; Gars-bheinn to Sgurr nan

Gillean in a single day? This mountain traverse provides the very best day's mountaineering to be found in these islands, and I am including it as a supplement to *200 Challenging Walks* in the hope that I can encourage certain readers to mount an attempt on the ridge themselves. It was first achieved by McLaren and Shadbolt in 1911.

I am looking to three categories of mountaineer who should be able to tackle the Cuillin traverse.
1. The skilled rock climber, who will have no difficulties with the technical sections, but will be thrilled by the grand mountain and rock scenery of the Cuillin and will, I suspect, be impressed by the expenditure of energy on the switchback ridge.
2. Ordinary walkers/scramblers, who have successfully coped with the Bla Bheinn–Clach Glas, the Aonach Eagach and the great Torridon ridges, and who aspire to complete the toughest challenge of all. These walkers/ scramblers will need to engage the services of a competent rock leader to take charge on the roped sections. They should obtain as much rock climbing and abseiling practice as possible, before venturing on to the ridge.

3. The advanced scrambler/climber who enjoys rock climbing up to about Very Difficult standard, together with the lapsed rock climber who may be wishing to make a comeback to the sport.

For the last two categories I have indicated the easiest alternative to the 'difficult' sections which are still commensurate with a Cuillin ridge traverse.

Whatever the category of mountaineer wishing to attempt the ridge there are two pieces of advice:
1. Make sure you are supremely fit for, although the ridge is only seven miles long, it involves 13,000 feet of ascent.
2. Misty weather is common and route-finding can be problematical, particularly as the rocks are magnetic and the compass can be unreliable. Three sections need a recce before starting the complete traverse: the Sgurr Alasdair – Inaccessible Pinnacle area, the Mhadaidh–Bidein Druim nan Ramh section and the Bhasteir Tooth area.'

The traverse is usually attempted south to north, because this way steep sections on the Thearlaich–Dubh gap, the Sgurr Thearlaich north ridge and Bidein Druim nan Ramh can be abseiled. However, a north-south traverse can provide uplifting views of black rock peaks set against a shimmering sea. The choice is yours.

Gars-bheinn to Sgurr Thearlaich

From Glenbrittle House it is a three hour slog to reach the summit of Gars-bheinn, 2,934ft/895m: first across the boggy, tussocky moor to the base of the mountain and then a rising traverse up execrably steep and loose boulders to the south end of the ridge. Gars-bheinn is littered with coffin-like depressions which have been constructed as bivouac sites by intending traversers.

The quality of this expedition becomes immediately evident as, with a final glance down to the islands of Soay, Eigg and Rhum, you pick your way along the rocky crest above the wild corrie holding Loch Coruisk. Ahead, the bastions of Sgurr nan Eag, Sgurr Dubh na Da Bheinn and Sgurr Alasdair block the view north but, as the ridge bends round to the east, the spire of Sgurr nan Gillean, the final peak, towers into the sky beyond the Druim nan Ramh ridge.

North of Sgurr nan Eag the ridge becomes extremely rough and piles of huge boulders must be negotiated on the descent to Bealach a' Garbh-choire. The rock tower of Caisteal a' Garbh-choire, which now blocks the way ahead, looks rather daunting but is easily traversed on the west side, and loose slopes lead up to the summit of Sgurr Dubh na Da Bheinn.

Purists will now deviate from the main ridge for half-an-hour to ascend the separate Munro, Sgurr Dubh Mor, which lies a short distance

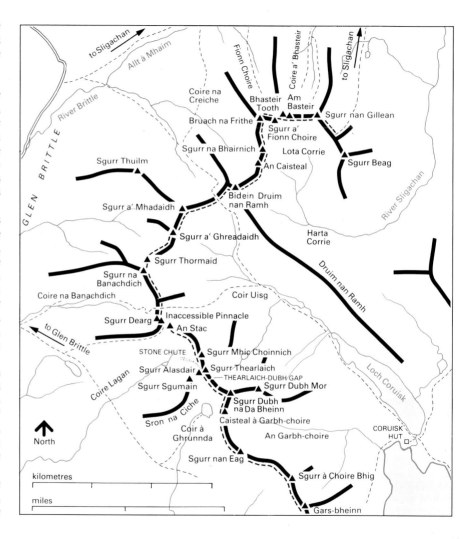

eastwards. Most people, however, prefer to preserve their energy for the imminent obstacle of the Thearlaich–Dubh gap, which is perhaps the most serious proposition on the entire ridge.

As you climb up towards Sgurr Thearlaich, from the rocky bealach north of Sgurr Dubh na Da Bheinn, you surmount an exposed wall on small holds and then arrive at a prominent gap in the ridge. Abseil down into the gap, 30ft, and then make a steep ascent of an awkward 80ft pitch which, for the most part, follows a crack in the polished basalt. The grade is Very Difficult but it is diabolically slippery when wet.

Scramble up to the summit of Sgurr Alasdair, 3,309ft/993m, and then retrace your steps to Sgurr Thearlaich. It is possible to avoid the Thearlaich–Dubh gap by descending into upper Coir' a' Garbh-choire, traversing screes above the loch, and ascending Sgurr Alasdair via Sgurr Sgumain. On this route, Sgurr Alasdair's infamous *mauvais-pas* recently collapsed and the passage is now easier than before involving a scramble up a 60ft crack on the right.

Sgurr Thearlaich to Bruach na Frithe

Descending the north ridge of Sgurr Thearlaich the rock gets progressively steeper and the holds smaller. Most mountaineers arrange a short abseil to bring them safely to the dramatic Bealach Mhic Coinnich.

Sgurr Mhic Coinnich can be climbed direct by the obvious chimney, King's Chimney, which rises ahead (Difficult standard) or traversed on the west side by the easy, but fearfully exposed, Collie's Ledge. This alternative route brings you out onto the ridge just north of the summit of Sgurr Mhic Coinnich, which can be gained by a loose scramble.

Continuing north-west the boulder-strewn ridge overlooks the Coruisk basin and Coire Lagan until the way ahead is effectively blocked by the steep abutment of An Stac. Although the loose rock nose has been climbed (Difficult), most parties make an ascending traverse under the south wall of An Stac and then double-back a short distance to reach its summit.

The colossal rock wedge of the Inaccessible Pinnacle now lies ahead. It is imperative to climb the 'In Pin' for, apart from its historical associations, it is the true summit of Sgurr Dearg. The long east ridge, although exposed, is not difficult and the shorter, steeper, west ridge can be abseiled.

North of Sgurr Dearg a long and beautiful stretch of ridge runs over Sgurr nan Banachdich, Sgurr Thormaid and Sgurr a' Ghreadaidh to Sgurr a' Mhadaidh. It is unrelentingly narrow and exposed but, if taken slowly, plenty of holds can be found. Sgurr a' Mhadaidh has three tops and several rock pitches must be negotiated to overcome them. Many parties use a rope here, either alpine style, moving together, or individually in single pitches.

An easy, broad section now provides some welcome relief, but the ridge soon steepens and a tortuous section follows over Bidein Druim nan Ramh and its satellites. The three tops of Bidein form a triangle and, at the central, highest, top, the ridge turns from south to west. Much time can be wasted here unless a previous recce has established the route, which involves a short abseil over an overhang.

By now most parties are tired, but there is little room to relax on the twisting rock crest of An Caisteal before the only really easy peak on the ridge, Bruach na Frithe, is reached.

Bruach na Frithe to Sgurr nan Gillean

Descend to Bealach na Lice, which divides Fionn Choire from Lota Corrie, and scramble up to the dramatic, sheer south face of the Bhasteir Tooth. It is worth noting that a spring of clear water can be found a short way down the Fionn Choire. Confident rock climbers will enjoy the classic Naismith's route put up in 1898 and traditionally graded Very Difficult. This follows the obvious crack which slants upwards across the face of the Tooth and looks very intimidating.

The less bold mountaineer can descend screes on the Lota Corrie side for 400ft and then scramble up slabs and short chimneys on the side of the Tooth. To gain the summit of Am Basteir (The Executioner) a short but steep chimney (Difficult standard) must be climbed.

A steep, scrambly descent from Am Basteir leads to the west ridge of Sgurr nan Gillean. An imposing pinnacle, the Gendarme, used to guard the bottom of this ridge – a tricky obstacle set above a considerable abyss. One night, in the mid 1980s, quite without warning the Gendarme plunged down to join the screes in Lota Corrie. Luckily no climber was attached at the time. This section has not yet stabilised and it needs care. The sharp summit of Sgurr nan Gillean is a perfect eyrie and you can drink in the expansive view and enjoy immense satisfaction after your traverse.

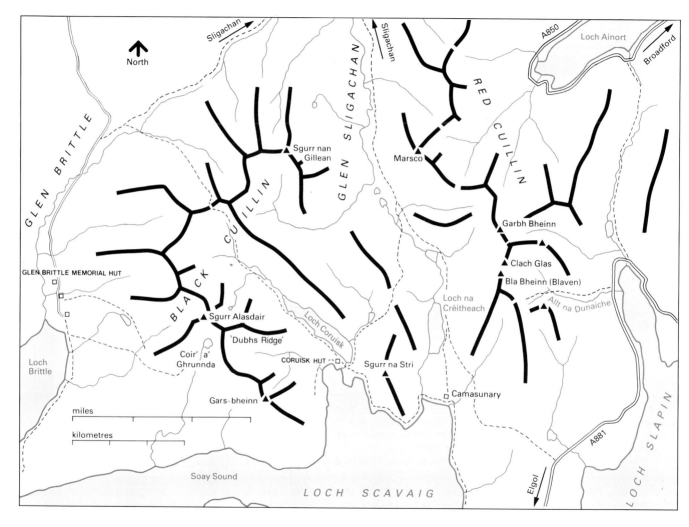

North

Sligachan

Sligachan

GLEN BRITTLE

GLEN SLIGACHAN

RED CUILLIN

A850

Loch Ainort

Broadford

Sgurr nan Gillean

CUILLIN

Marsco

GLEN BRITTLE MEMORIAL HUT

BLACK

CUILLIN

Garbh Bheinn

Clach Glas

Bla Bheinn (Blaven)

Allt na Dunaiche

Loch na Crèitheach

Loch Coruisk

Sgurr Alasdair

'Dubhs Ridge'

Coir' a' Ghrunnda

CORUISK HUT

Sgurr na Stri

Loch Brittle

Camasunary

Gars-bheinn

miles

kilometres

Soay Sound

Elgol

A881

LOCH SCAVAIG

LOCH SLAPIN

Descend the south ridge for a short distance and then follow the well-beaten Tourist Path down rocky corries and then across peaty moors to Sligachan.

The Greater Traverse

The insatiable mountaineer, finding energy to spare on Sgurr nan Gillean, may wish to cross Glen Sligachan and add the Clach Glas – Bla Bheinn traverse to his day's achievement. The extra energy required for this extended expedition is enormous, for a descent almost to sea level must be made before commencing the long slog up from Glen Sligachan to Clach Glas. W. H. Murray, writing in *Mountaineering in Scotland*, describes how he and K. G. Donaldson needed to quaff a pint of 'Mummery's Blood' in Glen Sligachan before finding the resolution to continue.

From Sgurr nan Gillean the natural extension of the Cuillin Ridge should be followed, down the south-east ridge and up to the graceful rock spire of Sgurr na h-Uamha. Returning the short distance to Bealach a'Ghlas-choire a rough descent can be made down the steep corrie to Glen Sligachan. Here the river must be forded to meet the path on the east side which is followed south for a mile to Loch an Athain. Strike up the broad Coire Dubh and make for the bealach between Clach Glas and Sgurr nan Each; this is the same bealach as described in the Bla Bheinn – Clach Glas traverse.

Having completed the traverse of the peaks (see Chapter 9) and arrived at the summit of Bla Bheinn, you will be desperate for a simple, foolproof way off the mountain. This is found on the gentle south-east slopes which run down to Fionna-choire, thence to Coire Uaigneich and the well-beaten track beside the Allt nan Dunaiche which brings you to the road at the head of Loch Slapin.

A full circuit from Glen Brittle

Rather than end the expedition at Loch Slapin, the fanatical Cuillin devotee might opt to descend the South Ridge of Bla Bheinn to Camasunary and thence proceed, by the Bad Step, to Coruisk. From here the coastal path could be taken back to Glen Brittle or, ambitiously, the more direct way using the Dubh's Ridge. Whether such a prolonged itinery could be completed in one push is very debatable, but it would probably be better accomplished with at least one bivouac so that the crossing back over the Cuillin Ridge could be enjoyed to the full.

The Winter Traverse

Although the winter traverse of the Cuillin Ridge will be beyond the powers of most readers of this book, competent exponents of Scottish winter climbing and experienced alpinists should not miss the chance of such an expedition if the opportunity arises.

Crampons, axes, rock and ice pitons, deadmen, plenty of rope and abseil slings, food for three days and bivouac equipment should be carried.

A north-south traverse is usually favoured in winter so as to face into the sun and so that the Bhasteir Tooth and several other difficult passages can be abseiled. The hard short side of the TD Gap is often circumvented by descending the gully and regaining the ridge near Sgurr Dubh.

If you are lucky you may meet crisp snow fashioned by the wind to razor sharp arêtes, with fairy-tale peaks, encrusted in ice, rising into an azure sky. The flavour of such a traverse is evocatively described by Geoff Cohen in *Cold Climbs* and also by Tom Patey in his celebrated account of the first traverse in *One Man's Mountains*.

THE WALKS IN CATEGORIES

A list of 200 walks is rather daunting, particularly when it attempts to satisfy a variety of tastes from rock scrambling and backpacking to moorland marathons and coastal rambles. Thus, in an attempt to help readers find their way round this guidebook, and make the correct choice, I have divided the walks into nine categories.

The routes which appear under the scrambling headings are listed in order of technical difficulty. The long and serious mountain traverses and the expeditions on Munros are arranged to reflect their overall challenge and seriousness, placing particular emphasis on remoteness from escape routes. The other categories are just given their book order.

TOUGH SCRAMBLES

These routes involve some rock climbing and many parties will wish to use a safety rope on the more difficult sections. They are unsuitable for the hill walker with no experience of rock climbing and abseiling.

The Black Cuillin Ridge (follows 200)
9   Bla Bheinn – Clach Glas
7   The Round of Coire Lagan
67   Aonach Eagach Ridge
29   An Teallach

MODERATE SCRAMBLES

Itineraries that have exposed rocky sections that demand the use of hands. A safety rope should be carried as in bad weather the difficulties can become quite serious. Greater weight is given to inescapability and walks marked † have short technical sections that can be avoided. Overall remoteness is also taken into account.

5   Sgurr nan Gillean
13   Arran's Rocky Ridges
37   Liathach
32   Mullach Coire Mhic Fhearchair †
10   The Cuillin of Rhum
21   Suilven
159   The Snowdon Horseshoe
44   Saddle of Glen Shiel
36   Beinn Eighe
156   Tryfan and the Bristly Ridge
6   Across the Cuillin
35   The Flowerdale Forest
23   Stac Pollaidh
80   A Day on the Cobbler †
98   Great Gable †
24   Ben More Coigach
197   Macgillicuddy's Reeks
93   Saddleback by Sharp Edge
95   Helvellyn by Striding Edge

REMOTE AND SERIOUS EXPEDITIONS

Walks that are serious by nature, because of their length, loneliness, the difficulty of the terrain and the distance from help in an emergency. In blizzard conditions they are potentially lethal and several have dangerous river crossings after heavy rain.

44   Loch Mullardoch Circuit
54   Beinn a'Bhuird/Ben Avon
64   A Ben Alder Crossing
42   Glen Affric: Mam Sodhail
65   Ben Nevis/Lochaber Traverse
63   Ben Alder Forest
47   Ladhar Bheinn
33   The Loch Maree Traverse
26   Beinn Dearg Forest
31   The Great Wilderness
57   Cairngorm 4000s
49   Across Knoydart: Ben Aden
48   Sgurr na Ciche
76   The Crianlarich Hills
66   The Mamores
55   Ben Macdui and Glen Luibeg
30   Beinn Dearg Mhor
27   Coast to Coast
56   Lairig Ghru
60   Glen Tilt
59   Minigaig Pass
18   The Stack of Glencoul

169 The Rhinog Ridge, Gwynedd
191 The Glencoaghan Horseshoe
199 Knocknagantee / Mullaghanattin

OTHER EXPEDITIONS ON 3000ft PEAKS

High mountains are serious by nature, particularly when they must be reached by a long approach walk.

100 Lakeland Three Thousanders
158 The Welsh Three Thousanders
193 The Lug Walk Classic
28   The Fannichs
75   Ben Lawers / The Tarmachans
43   The Five Sisters of Kintail
72   Ben Lui Horseshoe
62   Creag Meagaidh
45   The South Kintail Ridge
68   Bidean nam Bian
73   Ben Cruachan
38   Beinn Alligin
69   Buachaille Etive Mor
53   Balmoral Forest: Lochnagar
34   Slioch
196 Brandon Mountain
71   The Black Mount
161 Llanberis to Beddgelert
194 The Galty Ridge
154 The Northern Carneddau
20   Ben More Assynt
78   Ben Vorlich / Stuc a'Chroin
46   Spidean Mialach / Gleouraich
160 Snowdon by the Miners' Track
81   Ben Lomond
155 The Cwm Eigiau Horseshoe

157 The Glyders from Pen-y-Gwryd
11   Ben More of Mull
74   Schiehallion

All the walks in the remaining lists are arranged in their book order.

OTHER MOUNTAIN WALKS – UNDER 3000ft

3   The Clisham Ridge
4   Explorations in Trotternish
8   The Red Cuillin Traverse
12   The Paps of Jura
14   The Pirnmill Hills
16   Ben Loyal
17   Foinaven and Arkle
19   Quinag
22   Cul Mor / Cul Beag
25   Beinn an Eoin
39   Beinn Damh
40   The Applecross Hills
50   The Rois Bheinn Ridge
51   Garbh Bheinn
52   Beinn Resipol
77   The Loch Lubnaig Hills
86   The Merrick
87   Around Loch Enoch
96   Fairfield / Deepdale Horseshoe
97   The Buttermere Circuit
99   The Ennerdale Horseshoe
101 Shap to Ravenglass
102 The Great Langdale Horseshoe
103 The Wast Water Circuit
104 The Coniston Fells
162 Moel Siabod and Moel Meirch
163 Cnicht and the Moelwyns

164 Moel Hebog to Craig Cwm Silyn
168 Arenig Fawr to Rhobell Fawr
170 The Berwyns / The Arans
171 Cadair Idris from the South
178 The Brecon Beacons
179 Carmarthen Fan
184 The Aghla – Errigal Horseshoe
187 The Mourne Wall Walk
188 The Benbulbin Group
190 Mweelrea
192 The Maum Turks
195 Knockmealdown
198 The Mangerton Horseshoe
200 The Beara Border Walk

FELL COUNTRY – ROLLING, GRASSY HILLS

79   The Ochils
82   The Pentlands
83   The Southern Uplands
84   The Ettrick Hills
85   Cairnsmore of Carsphairn
88   The Cheviot Hills
89   Hedgehope Hill
90   Kielder Forest
91   Hadrian's Wall
92   The Back o' Skidda'
94   High Street
105 Harter Fell / Black Combe
106 The Manx Hills
108 Teesdale and Crossfell
110 Wild Boar Fell / The Howgills
111 Ingleborough / Penyghent / Whernside
112 Pen Hill / Buckden Pike
113 Great Whernside / Buckden Pike
117 Wolf Fell / Fiendsdale

152   The Clwydian Hills
172   Across the Dovey Forest
173   Plynlimon (Pumulumon)
175   Radnor Forest to Llandeilo Hill
177   The Black Mountains
185   The Sperrin Skyway
189   The Nephin Ridge Walk

WILD MOORLAND WALKS

58   Fungle / Clash of Wirren
61   Corrieyairack Pass
70   Rannoch Moor
107   Around Weardale
109   Around Swaledale
116   Bowland: Ward's Stone
118   The Lyke Wake Walk
119   Black Hambleton
120   Across the North York Moors
121   High Peak: Marsden to Edale
122   The Derwent Watershed
123   The Eastern Edges
124   Kinder Scout from Edale
125   The Western Peak
129   The Roaches to Axe Edge
130   Long Mynd / Stiperstones
146   Exmoor: The Dunkery Circuit
147   Eastern Dartmoor
148   Dartmoor North to South
149   A Visit to Cranmere Pool
150   The Granite Tors of Bodmin Moor
153   The Denbigh Moors
166   The Migneint and Arenig Fach
167   Eastern Migneint
174   Strata Florida / The Teifi Pools
176   The Abergwesyn Common, Powys

181   The Presely Hills, Dyfed

COASTAL WALKS

1   The Orkney Coastal Walk
2   The Hoy Coastal Walk
15   Cape Wrath
141   The South Downs
142   The Dorset Coast
145   The Exmoor Coast Path
151   Lamorna Cove to Pendeen Watch
165   The Rivals / Mynydd Mawr
180   St David's Head to St Non's Bay
182   Stackpole Quay to Freshwater West
183   The Gower Peninsula
186   Donegal Coast: Slieve League

DOWNLAND AND PASTORAL WALKS

114   Malham Cove / Gordale Scar
115   Wharfedale: the Dales Way
126   Dovedale
127   The White Peak: Eight Dales
128   The Manifold Valley
131   Caer Caradoc
132   Brown Clee Hill
133   High Dyke
134   The Malvern Hills
135   Forest of Dean
136   The Cotswolds
137   The Chilterns
138   The Ridgeway
139   The Wiltshire Downs
140   The North Downs
143   The Mendip Hills
144   The Quantocks

A note about the lists

It may seem surprising that mountain walks have escaped the well-defined grading that is universally accepted for rock climbs. But when you consider the enormous number of variables that should be taken into account when assessing walking routes perhaps it is understandable.

The nineteenth century Scottish mountaineer W. W. Naismith was the first man to quantify mountain walks with his famous formula for the total time to be allowed. In metric form this is one hour for every 5km plus one minute for every 10m of ascent.

D. J. Unwin, writing in *Climber and Hill-walker* in 1985, attempted to grade the routes in *The Big Walks*. He used a combination of distance and ascent per km, producing a list headed by the Lakeland 3,000s with a grade of 4.7. Interestingly this compares with 7.6 for the Bob Graham round of forty-two Lakeland peaks.

But the planning of every day in the hills must include weighing up many other factors. The route might not be possible at all if technical sections involving rock pitches cannot be circumvented, thus these technical grades provide the basis for the short list of Tough Scrambles. Many other routes include moderate rock scrambling sections on remote ridges, far from help and assistance, where the actual difficulties may become far harder than the quoted technical grade because of exposure, weather conditions and fatigue. Such routes include Suilven and The East Ridge of Mullach Coire Mhic Fhearchair.

My third category includes routes where no specific technical difficulties should be encountered in good weather, but which are remote, exposed and long and involve the crossing of particularly wild and rugged terrain. All these factors have been considered in producing the overall order within this category. Thus the Ben Alder Crossing and Ladhar Bheinn come above the Cairngorm 4,000s because the latter route is on smoother terrain, is more popular and is reasonably close to a good emergency shelter and various escape routes. The Great Wilderness is placed above the Crianlarich Hills and The Mamores because of its remoteness and because it has several potentially dangerous river crossings.

I must emphasise again that severe weather can affect the hills of Britain and Ireland at any time of the year, particularly between October and May. To be caught in a blizzard is a frightening experience, for conditions can become impossible in a very short period of time. Accidents occur regularly on our hills and moorlands but we could learn from three notable incidents: the 1951 New Year blizzard which claimed the lives of four well-equipped and experienced walkers just 2½ miles from Corrour Lodge in the Ben Alder Forest; the deaths of six schoolchildren in a blizzard on an exposed slope just under the Cairngorm plateau in November 1971 and the accident in December 1954 when five naval cadets slid to their deaths down steep ice when descending from Ben Nevis to the Carn Mor Dearg arête.

Unexpected difficulties can easily arrive: a friend had a disastrous first day in the Cuillin when he read the guidebook's warning of *mauvais pas* as *pas mauvais*!

In conclusion, I hope the above lists will help walkers choose the routes most appropriate to their experience and aspirations. Although I have indicated my guidelines the lists are still subjective to a high degree.

INDEX

Abergwesyn Common 190
Aden, Ben 63
Affric, Glen 55, 56
Aghla More 198
Alasdair, Sgurr 21, 217
Alder, Ben 77,78
Alligin, Beinn 52
An Teallach 43, 44, 45
Aonach Dubh 82
Aonach Eagach 81
Applecross Hills 54
Arans, The 184
Ardgour 64, 66
Arenig Fach 180
Arenig Fawr 182
Arkle 31
Arran, Isle of 27, 28
Avon, Ben 68
Axe Edge 140, 143

Balmoral Forest 67
Bannau Sir Gaer 193
Barrisdale Bay 61
Beara Border 214
Benbulbin 202
Benvane 91
Berwyns, The 184
Bhuird, Beinn a' 68
Bidean nam Bian 82
Bla Bheinn 23, 219
Black Combe 119
Black Hambleton 133
Black Mount 84
Black Mountains 191
Bleaklow 135,136
Bodmin Moor 164
Border Fells 104
Bowland, Forest of 130, 131
Box Hill 154
Brandon Mountain 210
Brecon Beacons 192
Bristly Ridge 170
Brown Clee Hill 146
Brown Willy 164
Buachaille Etive Mor 83
Buckden Pike 126
Buttermere 111

Cadair Idris 185
Caer Caradoc 145
Cairn Gorm 71
Cairngorms 67, 68, 69, 70, 71

Cairnsmore of Carsphairn 99
Calf, The 124
Cape Wrath 29
Carmarthen Fan 193
Carn Eige 55, 56
Carnedd y Filiast 181
Carneddau 168, 169, 172
Carrauntoohill 211
Cheviot Hills 102, 103
Chilterns, The 151
Ciche, Sgurr na 62, 63
Clach Glas 23
Clash of Wirren 72
Cleuch, Ben 93
Clisham 17
Clwydian Hills 166
Cnicht 34
Cobbler, The 94
Coniston Fells 118
Conival 34
Corfe Castle 156
Cornish Coast 165
Corrieyairack Pass 75
Corse, Glen 96
Coruisk, Loch 20
Cotswolds, The 150
Cranmere Pool 163
Creag Meagaidh 76
Crianlarich Hills 31
Cross Fell 122
Cruachan, Ben 87
Cuillin of Rhum 24
Cuillin of Skye 20, 21, 22, 23, 215
Cul Beag 36
Cul More 36
Cwm Eigiau 169

Damh, Beinn 53
Dart Mountain 199
Dartmoor 161, 162, 163
Dduallt 182
Dearg, Beinn 40, 41
Dearg Mhor, Beinn 44
Deepdale 110
Denbigh Moors 167
Dessarry, Glen 62
Dovedale 140
Dovey Forest 186
Drosgl 182
Drum 168
Drygarn Fawr 190
Dunkery Beacon 160

Edale 135, 136, 138
Eighe, Beinn 50
Ennerdale Horseshoe 113
Enoch, Loch 100, 101
Eoin, Beinn an 39
Errigal 198
Ettrick Hills 98
Exmoor 159, 160

Fairfield 110
Fan Foel 193
Fannichs, The 42
Fiddler, The 38
Fiendsdale 131
Flowerdale Forest 49
Foinaven 31
Forcan Ridge 58
Forest of Dean 149
Fungle, The 72

Galty Mountains 208
Garbh Bheinn 65
Gars-bheinn 216
Ghabhar, Stob 85
Gillean, Sgurr nan 19
Glascwm Hill 189
Glencoaghan Horseshoe 205
Gleouraich 60
Glyders 171, 172
Goat Fell 27
Gordale Scar 128
Gorllwyn 190
Gower Peninsula 197
Goyt Valley 139
Great Calva 106
Great Gable 112, 113
Great Hangman 159
Great Rhos 189
Great Whernside 127
Great Wilderness 45

Hadrian's Wall 105
Hart Fell 97
Harter Fell 119
Haytor Rocks 161
Hedgehope Hill 103
Helvellyn 109, 114
Herefordshire Beacon 148
High Cup Nick 122
High Force 122
High Street 108, 115
Hound Tor 161
Howgills, The 124
Hoy, Island of 2

Ingleborough 125
Irton Fell 117

Jura, Island of 26

Kielder Forest 104
Kinder Scout 135, 136, 138
Kings Seat 102

Kintail, Five Sisters of 57
Knockmealdown 209
Knocknagantee 213
Knockowen 214
Knott 106
Knoydart 61, 62, 63

Ladhar Bheinn 61
Lagan, Coire 21
Lair, Beinn 47
Lairig Ghru 70
Land's End 165
Langdale 116
Lathkill Dale 141
Lawers, Ben 89
Lawley, The 145
Ledi, Ben 91
Liathach 51
Linhope Spout 103
Llandeilo Hill 189
Lleyn Peninsula 179
Lochaber Traverse 79
Lochnagar 67
Lomond, Ben 95
Long Man of Wilmington 155
Long Mynd 144
Loyal, Ben 30
Lubnaig, Loch 91
Lughnaquilla 207
Lui, Ben 86
Luibeg, Glen 69
Lulworth Cove 156
Lyke Wake Walk 132

Macdui, Ben 69, 71
Macgillicuddy's Reeks 211
Malham Cove 128
Malvern Hills 148
Mam Sodhail 55, 56
Mam Tor 136
Mamores 80
Man, Isle of 120
Mangerton 212
Manifold Valley 142
Manx Hills 120
Maree, Loch 47, 48
Maum Turks 206
Mendips, The 157
Merrick, The 100
Migneint 180, 181
Miller's Dale 141
Minigaig Pass 73
Moel Hebog 178
Moel Fammau 166
Moel Meirch 176
Moel Siabod 176
Moelwyns 177
Moidart 64
More Assynt, Ben 34
More Coigach, Ben 38
More, Ben (Crianlarich) 90
More, Ben (Mull) 25
Mourne Wall 201

Mullach Coire Mhic Fhearchair 46
Mullaghanattin 213
Mullardoch, Loch 55
Mullwharchar 100
Mwdwl-eithin 167
Mweelrea 204
Mynydd Du 193
Mynydd Mawr 179

Napes Needle 112
Nephin Ridge 203
Nevis, Ben 79
North Downs 154
North York Moors 132, 133, 134

Ochils, The 93
Offa's Dyke 147
Oir, Beinn an 27
Orkney 15
Oss, Ben 86
Ossoms Hill 142
Oxwich Bay 197

Paps of Jura 26
Peel Fell 104
Pembroke Coast 194, 196
Pen Hill 126
Pen-y-Fan 192
Pennant Ridges 178
Pentland Hills 96
Penyghent 125
Pillar 113
Pirnmill Hills 28
Plynlimon 187
Presely Hills 195
Purbeck Hills 156

Quantocks, The 158
Quinag 33
Quirang 19

Radnor Forest 189
Rannoch Moor 84
Red Cuillin 22
Resipol, Beinn 66
Rhinns of Kells 100
Rhobell Fawr 182
Rhinogs 183
Ridgeway, The 152
Rivals, The 179
Roaches, The 143
Rogan's Seat 123
Rois Bheinn 64
Rosedale Railway 134

Saddle of Glen Shiel 58
Saddleback 107
Schiehallion 88
Scafell 114
Scafell Pike 114
Seven Sisters 155
Sharp Edge 107
Shutlingsloe 139

Silbury Hill 153
Skidda, Back o' 106
Skiddaw 114
Slieve League 200
Slioch 48
Snaefell 120
Snowdon 172-175
South Kintail Ridge 59
Southern Uplands 97-101
Sperrin Skyway 199
Spidean Mialach 60
St David's Head 194
St Non's Bay 194
Stac Pollaidh 37
Stack of Glencoul 32
Stackpole Quay 196
Stanage Edge 136
Stiperstones 144
Stob Binnein 90
Stoompa 212
Storr, The 18
Strata Florida 188
Striding Edge 109
Stuc a' Chroin 92
Suilven 35
Swaledale 123
Swirral Edge 109

Tarmachans 89
Tilt, Glen 74
Torridon 50-53
Tromie, Glen 73
Trotternish 18
Tryfan 170, 172
Twelve Bens (Connemara) 205

Upper Teesdale 122

Vorlich, Ben 92

Wansdyke 153
Ward's Stone 130
Wast Water 117
Waun-oer 186
Waun Fach 191
Wayland's Smithy 152
Weardale 121
Wetherlam 118
Wharfedale 129
Wheeldale 132
Whernside 125
Wicklow Mountains 207
Wild Boar Fell 124
Willstone Hill 145
Wilmington, Long Man of 155
Wiltshire Downs 153
Wolf Fell 131
Wolfscote Dale 140
Worcestershire Beacon 148
Wye Valley 149

Yewbarrow
Yr Aran